YALE PUBLICATIONS IN THE HISTORY OF ART, 17

Sumner McK. Crosby, Editor

The interior of the Pantheon seen from the doorway

THE

ARCHITECTURE OF THE

ROMAN EMPIRE

I AN INTRODUCTORY STUDY

REVISED EDITION

WILLIAM L. MacDONALD

92-007

NEW HAVEN AND LONDON

YALE UNIVERSITY PRESS

Designed by John O. C. McCrillis
and set in Linotype Garamond.
Printed in the United States of America by
Vail-Ballou Press, Binghamton, N.Y.

Library of Congress Cataloging in Publication Data

MacDonald, William Lloyd.
    The architecture of the Roman Empire.

    (Yale publications in the history of art ; 17)
    Bibliography: p. 205
    Includes index.
    1. Architecture—Rome.   I. Title.   II. Series.
NA310.M2   1982   722'.7   81–16513
ISBN 0–300–02818–0   AACR2
ISBN 0–300–02819–9 (pbk.)

10   9   8   7   6   5   4

To the Memory of

ROBERT PIERPONT BLAKE

1886–1950

CONTENTS

PREFACE

In the whole body of architecture in Roman lands, the most striking and fundamental change in stylistic direction took place during the latter half of the first century and the early decades of the second. It was then that the sculptured, linear forms of the classical past were first firmly challenged by the canopied volumes of the future. The vital significance of this shift for the history of architecture has been generally recognized, but the principles and meaning of the new style have not been explored in detail. Major problems remain unsolved and some of the most characteristic and instructive monuments of the period have gone unstudied or are in need of re-examination. The present volume, self-contained within the limits described below, is offered as an introduction to this original architecture of the Roman Empire. Later I hope to enlarge this discussion by analyzing additional buildings and sites in Italy and the provinces, and by attempting to solve stylistic and historical problems other than those considered here.

My objective has been to give direction to a vast quantity of refractory evidence. Any extended attempt to study the nature of the forms, principles, and meaning of imperial architecture is hampered by an embarrassingly large number of existing buildings and fragments (among the handbooks only Crema's suggests the magnitude of this number). Thus I have begun with a manageable and homogeneous division of the evidence, one that may provide a basis for further study. The buildings that have been chosen for analysis are the Esquiline wing of Nero's Domus Aurea (built in 64–68), the palace of Domitian on the Palatine (ca. 87–96), Trajan's Markets beside his Forum (first decade of the second century), and Hadrian's Pantheon (118/119–ca. 126). In addition to these, a structure that was most probably a part of Nero's Domus Transitoria (built sometime between 54 and 64) will be discussed briefly at the outset.

The more purely practical reasons for this selection are as follows. The identities and nearly exact dates of the four principal examples are firmly established. The buildings make a compact group chronologically, for the total span of years does not exceed that of a long lifetime. They are rather more accessible than many other important monuments of the same period, and this may be useful to anyone who wishes to correct and improve this study. They are sufficiently well preserved to be fruitful subjects for analysis, though as yet only the Pantheon has been described in any detail. Relevant passages in ancient texts exist for all but one example (Trajan's Markets). The names of the architects of the Domus Aurea and Domitian's palace are known, as well as something of the career of the man who was probably Trajan's chief architect and master of works. Hadrian's deep personal commitment to architecture is not in doubt. Thus the designs of these buildings can be linked directly or circumstantially to the names of particular men, an unusual occurrence in the study of Roman architecture and one of some consequence.

There are additional reasons why these buildings were chosen. Together they record or foreshadow the chief characteristics of specifically imperial architecture. Conceived in response to direct imperial commissions, they were planned and constructed by thoroughgoing professionals who significantly altered the history of design and construction. They expressed Roman programs and intentions in monumental forms that represented not the past but a new age. They were built in the paramount city of the Empire, and this, together with the relevancy and quality of their design, gave them great prestige. Their shapes, effects upon the senses, and to a certain extent their structural principles, were soon imitated or adapted in the provinces, and the debt owed by the architecture of the capital to that of non-Latin lands was in a sense repaid. The architecture defined by these examples appeared in every imperial city and town, displaying the image of Rome and its claims. This wide extension of influence through the agency of Roman rule is important because these buildings embody concepts crucial to much subsequent architecture. In short, they represent fairly a highly creative and historically significant period of Mediterranean and Western art.

The emphasis throughout is upon the direct testimony of the buildings as they stand today. Almost no attempt is made to solve the perplexing questions of their pre-imperial origins or to define the degree of their incipient medievalism. They are taken, in the main, on their own terms. Because their major spaces are vaulted and their structural solids are chiefly of concrete, the traditional architecture of stone columns and wooden roofs is slighted. Certain links between vaulted and unvaulted design have been cut as a result of limiting the evidence in both quantity and kind. This does not mean that post-and-beam buildings, composed primarily of rectilinear shapes and prismatic volumes, were abandoned during the Empire. On the contrary, they were built in quantity and their stylistic canon was creatively re-interpreted by imperial architects. But traditional designs such as the temple form and the monumental colonnade were not the only sources of imperial imagery, for vaulted architecture came increasingly to express and embody the meaning of the Empire. Its potential in this respect was first recognized and given definition in Rome itself, and it is these dramatic events that are under discussion.

The study of imperial architecture has been advanced in recent years by the late Miss Blake, by Bloch, Boëthius, Brown, Crema, Lugli, von Gerkan, Nash, Tamm, and Ward Perkins, among others. Their books and articles have enlarged the ground covered in older works such as those of Anderson-Spiers-Ashby, Durm, Jordan, Rivoira, and Robertson. My heavy debt to both groups, and to the authors of numerous excavation reports and studies of specific problems, will be recognized by every student of Roman architecture. But it may be proper to emphasize that the present volume is neither a handbook nor a survey of a period, and that most of its substance has been derived from the examination and study of the selected buildings, with exceptions consisting mainly of certain facts taken from authoritative publications cited in the notes.

The reader may question the use of the word "imperial," so often applied pejoratively today. Fully developed Roman architecture of the period from Nero to Hadrian was the product and expression of social and artistic forces best described in this way, as I hope I have shown. And some will be curious about the degree of precision of the drawings. These are not exact archaeological reports, but are either explanatory diagrams or essays in graphic restoration intended to complement the text. Several of the drawings are original, constructed from my own measurements and calculations. Some have been re-drawn or evolved from the work of others. The remainder are composites based upon more than one source; the use of published information is acknowledged in the List of Illustrations. A considerable amount of technical material appears in the text, but it is intended to be the servant of an attempt to analyze architectural effects and meaning. The references in the Index will serve as a glossary of any unfamiliar terms. The dimensions of the major examples, unless they are necessary to the immediate argument in the text, are given in the Appendix. The designation A.D. has been excluded except in a few cases of possible ambiguity.

In the study of architecture there can be no substitute for leaning against one's buildings. Roman architecture is spread from the Tyne to the Euphrates, and I should have seen a much smaller part of the broad context of evidence without financial assistance. Travels in Europe, North Africa, and the Near East were made possible in part by the generosity of the Honorable John Nicholas Brown, by the award of a Prize Fellowship in Classics for 1954–56 by the American Academy in Rome, by a grant toward summer travel expenses in 1959 by the American Philosophical Society, and by assistance from the Provost's Fund of Yale University. To Mr. Brown and these institutions I wish to offer grateful thanks. Laurance P. Roberts and Richard A. Kimball, successive directors of the American Academy in Rome, facilitated my studies by many kindnesses. I am indebted to Helen Chillman, Maria Cozzolino, Kenneth John Conant, Sterling Dow, George M. A. Hanfmann, Leonard Opdyke, and John Dane, Jr., for help both direct and indirect. The book was largely completed, and its sequel begun, with the support of a Morse Fellowship from Yale University during 1962–63.

Three-quarters of the drawings were made by Bernard M. Boyle, M.A., M.Arch., and it is a pleasure to acknowledge the value of the give and take of our discussions. The remainder of the drawings were made by Der Scutt, R. Larason Guthrie, and Duane

Thorbeck, all architects. The William L. Bryant Foundation contributed to the cost of the drawings and photographs. The extent to which I have made use of Ernest Nash's excellent Fototeca in Rome is recorded in the List of Illustrations. The quotations from the Loeb Classical Library are reprinted by permission of the Harvard University Press.

I am much indebted to George A. Kubler, Sumner McK. Crosby, and Spiro K. Kostof for cogent criticisms of manuscript drafts. Frank E. Brown also read these, and I have profited greatly from his detailed suggestions and from his extraordinary knowledge, so freely given, of the Roman world. The staff of the Library of the American Academy in Rome, led by Signora Inez Longobardi, was an unfailing source of help. Many Italian scholars, officials, and custodians were also most courteous and helpful; I would like particularly to thank Professors Giulio Ansaldi, Guglielmo Gatti, and Pietro Romanelli. I also owe a good deal to discussions at various buildings and sites with friends—Marion Blake, Frank Brown, Ferdinando Castagnoli, Henry Millon, Ernest Nash, Norman Neuerburg, and John Ward Perkins. I claim all the errors in the book, as well as an awareness of many problems left unexplored. The secrets of architecture are not easily discovered.

These pages are inscribed to the memory of the late Robert Pierpont Blake, Professor in Harvard University, because of his guidance and encouragement. Few who are committed to late antique and early medieval studies can be more fortunate than those who began their work with him. Finally, my principal debt is to my wife, Dale Ely MacDonald, for her continued help and sustaining patience.

New Haven, Connecticut
November 1964

W. L. M.

PREFACE TO THE REVISED EDITION

For this edition errors have been corrected, the Bibliography modernized, and a chapter added in which some recent studies are mentioned and questions of style considered. I would like to thank the staff of the Yale University Press for their support and patience.

W. L. M.

Northampton, Massachusetts
April 1981

LIST OF ILLUSTRATIONS

Drawings not otherwise credited were made by the draftsmen named in the Preface; photographs not otherwise credited were taken by the author. (F) = Fototeca di Architettura e Topografia dell'Italia Antica, Via Angelo Masina 5, Rome; (Y) = Yale University Art Library, Slide and Photograph Collections. For the other abbreviations used, see the List of Abbreviations on pp. xix–xxi. All subjects are in Rome unless otherwise indicated.

FRONTISPIECE
The interior of the Pantheon seen from the doorway (F)

LIST OF ABBREVIATIONS

used in the Notes, Bibliography, and List of Illustrations

AB	*Art Bulletin*
ActaArch	*Acta archaeologica*
AJA	*American Journal of Archaeology*
ArchClass	*Archeologica classica*
Atti	*Atti del . . . congresso* (sometimes *convegno*) *nazionale di storia dell'architettura* (*Atti, 3* [1938, pub. 1940], is also entitled *Saggi sull'architettura etrusca e romana*)
AttiPontAcc	*Atti della pontificia accademia romana di archeologia*
BC	*Bulletino della commissione archeologica communale di Roma*
BdA	*Bolletino d'arte*
Blake, *1*	M. E. Blake, *Ancient Roman Construction in Italy from the Prehistoric Period to Augustus* (Washington, 1947)
Blake, *2*	M. E. Blake, *Roman Construction in Italy from Tiberius through the Flavians* (Washington, 1959)
Bloch	H. Bloch, *I bolli laterizi e la storia edilizia romana* (Rome, 1947; reprinted from *BC*, 64, 65, and 66 [1936–38])
Boëthius	A. Boëthius, *The Golden House of Nero. Some Aspects of Roman Architecture* (Ann Arbor, 1960)
BollCentro	*Bolletino del centro di studi per la storia dell'architettura*
Bourne	F. C. Bourne, *The Public Works of the Julio-Claudians and Flavians* (Princeton, 1946; privately printed)
CAH	*Cambridge Ancient History*
CIL	*Corpus Inscriptionum Latinarum*
Crema	L. Crema, *L'architettura romana* (Turin, 1959; = *Enciclopedia classica, 3.12.1*)
Durm	J. Durm, *Die Baukunst der Etrusker. Die Baukunst der Römer* (2nd ed., Stuttgart, 1905)
EncIt	*Enciclopedia Italiana*

ESAR   *Economic Survey of Ancient Rome*, ed. T. Frank (6 vols. Baltimore, 1933–40; reprinted, Paterson, N.J., 1959)

FUR   G. Carettoni, A. M. Colini, L. Cozza, and G. Gatti, *La pianta marmorea di Roma antica. Forma urbis Romae* (2 vols. Rome, 1960)

Giovannoni   G. Giovannoni, *La tecnica della costruzione presso i romani* (Rome, 1925)

JDAI   *Jahrbuch des (königlich) deutschen archäologischen Instituts*

JRS   *Journal of Roman Studies*

JSAH   *Journal of the Society of Architectural Historians*

Kähler   H. Kähler, *Hadrian und seine Villa bei Tivoli* (Berlin, 1950)

Lanciani   R. Lanciani, *The Ruins and Excavations of Ancient Rome* (London, 1897; the pagination of the Boston-New York edition of the same date is slightly different)

Lugli, *Roma*   G. Lugli, *Roma antica. Il centro monumentale* (Rome, 1946)

Lugli, *Tecnica* G. Lugli, *La tecnica edilizia romana con particulare riguardo a Roma e Lazio* (2 vols. Rome, 1957)

MAAR   *Memoirs of the American Academy in Rome*

Meiggs   R. Meiggs, *Roman Ostia* (Oxford, 1960)

MemPontAcc   *Atti della pontificia accademia romana di archeologia, Memorie*

Nash   E. Nash, *Pictorial Dictionary of Ancient Rome* (2 vols. London, 1961–62)

NS   *Notizie degli scavi di antichità*

OCD   *Oxford Classical Dictionary* (Oxford, 1949)

OpusArch   *Acta Instituti Romani Regni Sueciae, Opuscula Archaeologica*

Ostia   G. Calza et al., *Scavi di Ostia. I. Topografia generale* (Rome, 1953)

PBSR   *Papers of the British School at Rome*

Platner-Ashby   S. B. Platner and T. Ashby, *A Topographical Dictionary of Ancient Rome* (Oxford, 1929)

Quaderni   *Quaderni dell'istituto di storia dell'architettura*

RE   Pauly's *Realencyclopädie der classischen Altertumswissenschaft*, ed. G. Wissowa et al.

RendPontAcc   *Atti della pontificia accademia romana di archeologia, Rendiconti*

Rivoira   G. T. Rivoira, *Roman Architecture and Its Principles of Construction under the Empire* (Oxford, 1925; translation by G. McN. Rushforth of *Architettura romana. Costruzione e statica nell'età imperiale* [Milan, 1921])

RM   *Mitteilungen des deutschen archäologischen Instituts, Römische Abteilung*

Rostovtzeff   M. I. Rostovtzeff, *Social and Economic History of the Roman Empire* (2nd ed. 2 vols. Oxford, 1957)

SHA   *Scriptores Historiae Augustae*

Tamm   B. Tamm, *Auditorium and Palatium* (Stockholm, 1963; = *Stockholm Studies in Classical Archaeology*, 2)

Zorzi   G. Zorzi, *I disegni delle antichità di Andrea Palladio* (Venice, 1959)

THE ARCHITECTURE OF THE ROMAN EMPIRE

I

AN INTRODUCTORY STUDY

I

BACKGROUND

THE NEW ARCHITECTURE of the Roman Empire first appeared fully characterized in Nero's Domus Aurea. The exceptional importance that can quite properly be attached to the great wing on the Oppian spur of the Esquiline, the major surviving part of the palace, is not the result of accidents of preservation or of the present state of Roman studies. Enough is known of Roman architecture to make it clear that Nero's architect was the first to design a building in which the major principles and effects of the new style appeared.[1] But he and his contemporaries inherited a considerable knowledge of vaulted design and construction that had been accumulating for more than two centuries, and in this sense the Domus Aurea wing was not an entirely spontaneous creation. It is the purpose of this chapter to outline the pertinent events that preceded the design of the Domus Aurea, and to stipulate the chief characteristics of vaulted design, the most obvious common element of the new architecture.

The story of the background of the Neronian architectural revolution is a complicated one, but it can be summarized baldly in a paragraph. The Romans learned of the arch either from the Etruscans or, more probably, from Hellenistic builders who brought it to Italy early in the third century B.C.; they soon made it their own. Their interest in the possibilities of its form and structure, and in those of its natural extension, the barrel vault, was stimulated by new methods of construction made possible in part by increasingly reliable mortars. For some two centuries only the arch and the barrel vault were used, chiefly for utilitarian purposes, but by late republican times the repertory of curved shapes had been expanded to include such forms as the dome, the cloister vault, and the annular vault (see Figure 1, p. 16). Meanwhile architecture was deeply affected by the changes that took place in Roman society. The growth of the state and its resources and the changing direction and increasing complexity of Roman life caused a demand for new building types and encouraged the study and use of vaulted design.

1. For recent evaluations of the wing in these terms, see for example Kähler, pp. 99–101 (full titles are given in the List of Abbreviations, pp. xix–xxi); J. B. Ward Perkins, "Nero's Golden House," *Antiquity*, 30 (1956), 219; id., "Roman Concrete and Roman Palaces," *The Listener*, 56 (1956), 701–03; Boëthius, p. 128.

Tradition was challenged in many ways. Markets, warehouses, baths, elaborate tombs, large substructures and terraces, and a variety of engineering works were among the vaulted structures built before the time of Nero. One exceptionally creative period, the two or three decades before the death of Sulla in 78 B.C., stands out. But the exciting promise of those years was not consummated in republican or Augustan times, for it was obscured first by rounds of civil wars and then by the official sponsorship of trabeated designs derived mainly from indigenous and Hellenistic precedents. The architects of Tiberius and Claudius sometimes broke sharply away from tradition and produced innovative buildings, but the architecture prefigured in Sulla's lifetime came to fulfillment only at the end of the Julio-Claudian period. The imperial system was the catalyst of that fulfillment.

There were two basic early techniques of vaulted construction. The first was that of false vaulting.[2] Structures of this kind were usually corbeled: their stones were laid in horizontal courses, each edged out over the one below and depending upon superposed masses of stone or earth for their stability. Recalling on a modest scale the corbeled round tombs of the Mycenaeans, such buildings were fairly common in ancient Italy; they were descended from a prehistoric tradition of stone piling. The second technique produced true arches and simple vaults from cut stone.[3] Stone voussoir arches appear in the walls of Cosa, a Roman colony of the third century B.C. on the Tuscan coast, northwest of Rome.[4] During the second and first centuries, stone arches were used in a number of utilitarian structures, such as the massive bridges provided for the great consular highways radiating from the capital. Stone barrel vaults and arcades were also built.[5]

The chief importance of these early structures lay in their provision of an initial range of shapes and procedures that were at hand when the Romans began to use concrete. Mortar and wall facings were the vehicles of the evolution of this essential and typical Roman building material. Structural adhesives of lime, sand, and water were well known in parts of the pre-Roman Mediterranean world. In Italy they were in use from at least the time of the First Punic War, and were employed with increasing confidence thereafter.[6] At Cosa and other early sites there are walls made of fitted stone facings that enclose rubble masonry, a random fill of stones and building debris more or

2. Discussed by A. Minto, "Pseudocupole e pseudovolte . . .," *Palladio*, 3 (1939), 1–20; G. Rohlfs, *Primitive Kuppelbauten in Europa* (Munich, 1957; Italian ed., Florence, 1963); J. Fink, *Die Kuppel über dem Viereck* (Freiburg, 1958). See also Crema, Fig. 14; and *AJA*, 65 (1961), 385 and Pls. 121–22. The false arch, a related phenomenon, appeared very early in Italy. There is one at Paestum of the early fourth century B.C.: *Archaeology*, 12 (1959), 33–34.

3. See G. Lugli, "Considerazione sull'origine dell'arco a conci radiali," *Palladio*, 2 (1952), 9–31; and Crema, pp. 6–12.

4. F. E. Brown, "Cosa I. History and Topography," *MAAR*, 20 (1951), 39–40, 106.

5. For bridges, see Blake, *1*, 206–19; for arcades, id., *1*, 220–23; for stone barrel vaults, Lugli, *Tecnica*, *1*, 679–80. See also L. Laurenzi, "L'origine della copertura voltata . . .," *Arte antica e moderna*, 3 (1958), 203–15.

6. Blake, *1*, 308–23, gives the terminology, a description of the materials, and an historical sketch. See also Crema, pp. 12–17.

less surrounded by mortar.[7] During the last centuries of the Republic this technique of construction was gradually improved; the end product was artificial stone of great strength and durability. At some point, perhaps in the early second century B.C., the Romans began adding pozzolana to their mortar, a volcanic substance with the apparent property of combining with lime and sand to fortify and waterproof the mass as it cured. This, the pit-sand of Vitruvius, was a standard ingredient of imperial concrete in central Italy.[8] Meanwhile various kinds of thin wall facings of small stones were evolved from the early facings of rubblework cores; they aided in laying up walls and in protecting the structural concrete. Late in republican times wall facings of kiln-baked brick began to be used. These were derived from the occasional practice of substituting broken or sawn terra-cotta roof tiles for the small facing stones then normally employed.[9] Brickwork soon became the favored facing, and in the last third of the first century A.D. great yards in and near Rome began producing accurately formed bricks and other standardized terra-cotta elements on an industrial scale.[10]

By the time of Nero a sound practical knowledge of beamless structures, made from semiliquid substances and small tectonic units, had been acquired, and the human and economic resources of the imperial system had begun to bear powerfully and effectively upon the supply and use of these materials. The necessary understanding of carpentry had been gained. The new method, its materials mass-produced in part and then assembled in a methodical way, helped to expand the repertory of architectural shapes because of its flexibility. The architects of the Empire were able to compose architectural spaces by casting on a monumental scale. Walls and piers of concrete, encased in sheets of brick precisely laid up, could be made structurally continuous with masses of masonry curving high overhead, and very large unobstructed spaces became possible. But the new architecture was not evolved primarily from a system of construction that was peculiarly suited to vaulted design. Masterpieces such as the Pantheon were above all expressions of immanent cultural forces, and technology, though important, was a secondary factor in their creation. Engineering is rarely architecture, however relevant new materials and methods of construction are to the formation of a style. In the case of imperial architecture, structural techniques were the mechanical servants of a new imagery.

There are certain republican and early imperial buildings in and near Rome that are landmarks of the awakening interest in an architectural expression freed from the past. One of the earliest is the Porticus Aemilia (Plate 1), a vast warehouse built during the first half of the second century B.C. on the east bank of the Tiber just down river from the Pons Sublicius.[11] Composed of some two hundred barrel-vaulted chambers set in

7. Brown (above, n. 4), p. 109; Blake, *1*, 325–27.

8. Vitruvius, 2.6. Cf. the references to pozzolana in Pliny, *Natural History* 16.202, 35.167; and in Seneca, *Inquiries into Nature* 3.20.3.

9. Blake, *1*, 292–98; Crema, pp. 134–38.

10. The partial industrialization of the Roman building industry will be discussed more fully in a later chapter, as will other subjects mentioned in this sketch.

11. The identification and date are based in part upon Livy, 35.10.12. The most detailed discussion is by G. Gatti, " 'Saepta Iulia' e 'Porticus Aemilia' nella 'Forma' severiana," *BC*, 62 (1934),

long, tiered rows, it covered an area 60 by 487 meters. The vaults did not rest upon solid walls but rather upon perforated supports resembling pier arcades, so that each chamber was open laterally as well as axially to its neighbors (Plate 2).[12] The result was a practical, fire-resistant building of ordered clarity, well suited to warehousing and transshipping goods. It was as Roman as the arcades of the great aqueducts, and it depended upon similar arcades, in combination with simple vaults, to make useful spaces. The combination of barrel vaults and arcuated supports on a grid plan, whether or not it first appeared here, was an important step in the evolution of mature vaulted architecture. By reduplicating the basic element of design, visual and spatial as well as functional continuities were established, and the resulting interpenetration of spaces pointed toward a coming interest in the possibilities of complex volumetric compositions. The serial and reciprocal buttressing of the vaults and the effective clearstory lighting derived from the tiered roofs clearly show that particular advantages of vaulted design were already well understood. This logical, straightforward design was carried out in *incertum*, concrete faced with small stones cut to approximately polygonal shape.[13]

The market buildings or bazaars of the early first century B.C. that can be seen at Ferentino (Plate 3) and Tivoli are of somewhat more sophisticated design. Each consists of a central, barrel-vaulted hall flanked by vaulted side chambers that open onto the main hall at right angles to it.[14] The amount of masonry used may seem excessive, and the lighting problems may not have been satisfactorily solved, but these buildings

123–49; for his restoration see Crema, Fig. 59, or F. E. Brown, *Roman Architecture* (New York, 1961), Pl. 30. A later date has been suggested, but it does not seem to be supported by the evidence of the remains and has not been generally accepted; see G. Lugli, *I monumenti antichi di Roma e suburbio*, 3 (Rome, 1938), 595–606; A. Boëthius, "Vitruvius and the Roman Architecture of His Age," ΔΡΑΓΜΑ, *Martino P. Nilsson . . . dedicatum* (Lund, 1939), p. 133, n. 32; Blake, 1, 249, 312–13; *AB*, 33 (1951), 136; *Göttingische gelehrte Anzeigen*, 209 (1955), 261–63; Boëthius, pp. 28–29; Crema, p. 61.

12. The chambers measured approximately 8 by 14 m. in plan, and about 13 m. in maximum height. Variant exterior roofing forms are shown on Pls. 1 and 2, but the presence of barrel vaults is certain because the lowest zone of some of them can still be seen. See also F. Fasolo and G. Gullini, *Il santuario della Fortuna Primagenia a Palestrina*, 1 (Rome, 1953), 332 and Fig. 477 on p. 369; and cf. Durm, Fig. 270. For additional illustrations see Nash, 2, 238–40; *JSAH*, 22 (1963), Fig. 4 on p. 122 (a drawing by Clérisseau). Pl. 2 here is based upon the remains and Gatti's study (note 11, above). The floor plan is shown on a

fragment of the Severan marble plan of Rome (Forma urbis Romae), reproduced here on Pl. 2 (the other large structures are the Horrea Galbae: see Nash, 1, 481–84; *FUR*, 1, 81–82).

13. This term, together with others describing kinds of wall facings, appears in Vitruvius (2.8.1, for example), but there are others in common use today for which there is no ancient authority; see Blake, 1, 2; G. Lugli, "La terminologia dei sistemi costruttivi usati dai romani," *Accademia dei Lincei, Rendiconti*, 5 (1950), 297–306; id., *Tecnica*, 1, 40–49; cf. Meiggs, p. 535, n. 1. For incertum, see Blake, 1, 227–53, and Fasolo and Gullini (above, n. 12), pp. 375–90.

14. See A. Boëthius and N. Carlgren, "Die spätrepublikanischen Warenhäuser in Ferentino und Tivoli," *ActaArch*, 3 (1932), 181–93; A. Bartoli, "L'acropoli di Ferentino," *BdA*, 4 (1949), 293–99; G. Gullini, "I monumenti dell'acropoli di Ferentino," *ArchClass*, 6 (1954), 215–16 and Tav. LVIII.3, LX–LXIII, LXVI, LXVII. At Tivoli only one side of the central hall is flanked by smaller chambers. The historical position of these buildings is discussed by A. Boëthius, "Appunti sul Mercato di Traiano, I," *Roma*, 9 (1931), 447–54, 501–08.

in modest towns record an increasing recognition of the utility of vaulted architecture and its appropriateness to Roman needs. At this time, when knowledge of the new concepts of design and construction had been accumulating for more than a century, Roman architecture was galvanized by commissions for monumental public buildings whose remains are major documents for the study of ancient architecture. Three of them may have been built for Sulla or members of his circle; all were in part of vaulted design. They are the sanctuaries of Hercules at Tibur (Tivoli), of Jupiter at Anxur (Terracina), of Fortuna Primagenia at Praeneste (Palestrina), and the Tabularium at Rome; the last-named was built by the consul Q. Lutatius Catulus in 78 B.C.[15]

At Tivoli the terrace that supported the cult building proper was bordered by long files of vaulted porticoes.[16] Along part of the exterior these were arranged one above the other. The arched openings of the lower file were separated by massive engaged buttresses with stone quoining (Plate 4), and those of the upper file by engaged columns made of the same concrete as the walls and vaults and structurally inseparable from them (Plate 5). Part of the terrace was honeycombed with spaces covered with various kinds of vaults, including approximate cloister or pavilion vaults (see Figure 1, h, p. 17) set over interconnecting chambers of square plan aligned in a row. There was also a long interior gallery about 8.50 meters wide, covered with a barrel vault and lit by a sequence of square skylights let into its crown. A similar interest in vaulted design is evident at Terracina (Plate 6).[17] The forms of the actual temple buildings at these sites were traditional, but the design of their imposing elevated terraces looked to the future.

The majestic sanctuary at Palestrina is the most revealing example of this period of intense architectural creativity. An Olympian composition of ramps, terraces, arcades, and hemicycles, firmly locked to a superb hillside site, it records the extraordinary vision of an unknown master (Plates 7 and 8).[18] A rising frame of ramps and platforms, symmetrically placed on either side of a commanding and unifying axis, suggests the concept that determined the design of Trajan's Markets (compare Plate 75). The tiers of arcaded and vaulted terraces at Palestrina were constructed in much the same fashion as the terraces at Tivoli and Terracina, but they were not subordinated to a great temple

---

15. See Fasolo and Gullini (above, n. 12), where the Tivoli, Terracina, and Rome buildings are discussed on pp. 353–66. For discussions of dating, esp. of Palestrina, see also C. C. Van Essen, *Sulla als Bouwheer* (Groningen, 1940); G. Lugli, "Nota sul santuario della Fortuna Prenestina," *ArchClass*, 6 (1954), 133–47 and references; and H. Kähler, "Das Fortunaheiligtum von Palestrina Praeneste," *Annales Universitatis Saraviensis* (1958), pp. 189–240. There is a vaulted, apsidal room, perhaps of Sullan date, at Hadrian's Villa; Tamm, p. 149, no. 2, and Fig. 54.2.

16. See C. Carducci, *Tibur* (Rome, 1940; = *Italia romana*, 1, part 3), pp. 64–68; and Fasolo

and Gullini (above, n. 12), 1, 353–63, 424–33. I have not seen the sanctuary or the interior of the market at Tivoli.

17. See G. Lugli, *Anxur-Tarracina* (Rome, 1926; = *Forma italiae*, 1, part 1.1); and Fasolo and Gullini (above, n. 12), 1, 415–21.

18. See the citations above, n. 15; R. Delbrueck, *Hellenistische Bauten in Latium*, 1 (Strassburg, 1907), 47–90, and 2, (1912), 118–80; *RE*, supp. 7, cols. 1243–54; Crema, pp. 52–57; Brown (above, n. 11), pp. 20–21. Only the main structure is shown here on Pl. 8; below it were other buildings and vast terraces.

building above. Instead they were parts of a unified whole, guiding the eye and progress of the visitor up to a large theatre-like hemicycle capped by an elegant tholos centered at the highest point of all (not shown on Plate 8).

At several points arches, vaults, columns, and curved plans were skillfully combined in integrated compositions. The two hemicycles located on one of the intermediate terraces show the surprising maturity of the architect's grasp of vaulted design (Plate 9). In their original state these were semicircular in plan, with seven columns set concentrically within an embracing wall of opus incertum. The spaces between the half rings of columns and the curving walls were roofed by coffered annular vaults also traversing 180° in plan (Plate 10). Curving vertical walls rose directly above the columns, terminating in cornices marking the pavement level of the terrace above; behind these walls were the doubly curved volumes defined by the annular vaults. The inner or central half circles of space defined by the columns were unroofed. Though the columns were used as structural members, they were given new spatial and visual functions. They were not *around* anything solid, like those of a circular temple with a cylindrical cella; their purpose was reversed. Their primary function was to form screens seen from places defined or suggested by their embracing forms, yet open to the sky and landscape. Because they were set out along curves these screens implied motion, an implication strengthened by the curving walls behind and the continually changing, concentric travel of the vaults above. The columns could not be lined up by the eye, and each movement of the observer placed them in an altered relationship. The wide intercolumniation increased the implications of motion by narrowing the angles between the column positions, resulting in a less steady and fixed rhythm of vertical accents. Thus the parts of the hemicycles combined to suggest motion and to shape and localize open, unroofed space. Slight though the cross-axes stated by the hemicycles may have been in the context of the whole design, their curving and vaulted forms generated palpable forces.

Several kinds of vaults were used at Palestrina, including ramping and annular forms (see Figure 1, b and f). Almost all of the walls, and all of the vaults, were of concrete. The architect had sufficient confidence in his structural technique to allow the façade of the terrace above the hemicycles to bear directly upon the annular vaults below. This vertical noncongruity of plan and structure gave Roman architects a new freedom of design. A vertical section taken radially (Plate 10) also shows that the hemicycle partially prefigured the vaulting systems of buildings such as S. Costanza and S. Vitale.[19] In these systems inner supports of minimized silhouette (the columns) are assisted in bearing their loads by additional supports placed at a greater distance from the central volume (the concentric walls), and the two are joined radially by masonry that both stabilizes and supports (the annular vaults). A similar relationship among verticals and vaults was used at Palestrina in the large theatre-like hemicycle atop the highest terrace.

19. On this subject see my article, "Some Implications of Later Roman Construction," *JSAH*, 17 (1958), 2–8; cf. Fasolo and Gullini (above, n. 12), 1, 252–55.

The Tabularium, a hall of records, was erected upon the steep southeast slope of the Capitoline facing the Forum. Part of the façade (Plate 11), the gallery behind it, and some rooms and stairs remain.[20] The gallery was composed of reduplicated vaulted bays, a method of composition used in many other pre-imperial vaulted buildings. Here, as at the sanctuary of Hercules at Tivoli, engaged columns were placed between the arched façade openings; at the Tabularium the columns were of stone and the square bays behind the arched openings were roofed with cloister vaults cast in concrete. Though this may have been done in part to support a superstructure, the Tabularium gallery is evidence of the early application of the effects and technology of vaulting to the design of public buildings in the capital, and of the growing interest in transforming traditional building types, such as the ancient wooden-roofed walkway or stoa, into boldly new and emphatically Roman forms.

Few of the generals and magnates who competed in the chaotic struggles for power during the last decades of the Republic were important builders. Their surviving buildings show a relatively small degree of interest in vaulted design; there is nothing to compare with the commitment and sophistication of Palestrina. The supporting structure of Pompey's Theatre in Rome, dating from 55–52 B.C., was built of vaults of concrete rising from walls of *reticulatum* (concrete faced with roughly pyramidal stones or terra cottas, their square bases forming exterior surfaces of quite regular, net-like patterns).[21] There were similar substructures in the Theatre of Marcellus, dedicated about 13 B.C.[22] Permanent theatres such as these, requiring wedge-shaped volumes, many ramps and stairs, and strong sloping supports for rows of seats, invited the study and use of vaulting; the perfected assembly of these elements can best be observed in the Flavian Amphitheatre.[23] At this time the construction of concrete walls became quite common, though they were not necessarily used to support vaults. This development can be traced at Ostia, the port city of Rome, in buildings and fragments of buildings

20. Delbrueck (above, n. 18), *1*, 23–46; Fasolo and Gullini (above, n. 12), *1*, 361–63; Lugli, *Roma*, pp. 42–46; Nash, *2*, 402–08. The stairs were roofed with stepped barrel vaults; cf. the Porticus Aemilia.

21. For the theatre, see Lugli (above, n. 11), *3*, 70–83; for reticulatum, Blake, *1*, 253–75.

22. See A. Calza-Bini, "Il teatro di Marcello," *BollCentro*, 7 (1953), 1–44; he shows, pp. 38–40 and Fig. 61, that the two apsidal halls flanking the structure behind the stage were groin vaulted, basing his reconstruction on a few existing elements of the structure, fragments of the marble plan (cf. *FUR*, *1*, 90, and *2*, Tav. XXIX), and drawings by Baldassare Peruzzi and Battista da Sangallo (Uffizi 626 and 1270, which he reproduces); cf. G. Giovannoni, "La basilica dei Flavi

sul Palatino," *Atti*, 3, 92–93; and M. Bieber, *The History of the Greek and Roman Theater* (2nd ed. Princeton, 1961), pp. 184–85 and Fig. 641. Because of their advanced plan and the complexity of their spatial formations, both noted by Calza-Bini, it is probable that these halls were built considerably later than the theatre itself, perhaps in the restoration by Vespasian mentioned by Suetonius, *Vespasian* 19; cf. the remarks about the earliest appearance of groin vaulting by Blake, *2*, 50–51. If the few remaining structural fragments are Augustan, perhaps they originally supported timber roofs.

23. See P. Colagrossi, *L'Anfiteatro Flavio* (Florence, 1913); G. Cozzo, *Ingegneria romana* (Rome, 1928), pp. 196–251; Lugli, *Roma*, pp 319–48; Nash, *1*, 17–25.

not destroyed when the city was heavily rebuilt in the second century, as well as at Pompeii and Herculaneum.[24]

The architecture of Augustus' reign was in general conservative. Many of the emperor's policies, and the outward public temper molded by them, reflected the hope that the stern and upright principles of ancient republican life could somehow be recovered and rehabilitated. At the same time Augustus made it impossible for this to become reality, for he found it necessary to manipulate the processes of government in such a way as to obviate republicanism and its supposedly inherent advantages. Old Rome was gone forever, but the new was not yet fully revealed. Augustus more than any one person, and probably more than any one historical agent, made the Empire possible, but he himself was not truly of the Empire. The ancient world was suspended between the past and the future from the will of a man of consummate political ability. During this period of enforced stability, official architecture changed very little. The Hellenistic envelope was supreme.

This reaction in favor of conservative principles is reflected in the attitudes of Vitruvius, Augustus' contemporary. In Vitruvius' time vaulted construction was well known, but its more purely visual potential, as the informing characteristic of a distinct style, was not yet recognized. Though in his manual Vitruvius includes information about vaults, and about concrete and brick,[25] he seems to have been immune to their architectural potential. He emphasizes traditional ideas. He is attractively modest and forthright, and one would not wish to underrate our good fortune in possessing his work, but it is important to notice that he does not discuss the nontraditional designs that had appeared before he wrote down the results of his experience and study. From reading him one would never know that the great Sullan buildings existed, yet it is impossible to believe that he did not know of them. He was a conservative—he strongly disapproved of contemporary painting and found it extremely foolish—and it is apparent that the external use of the orders, freestanding or engaged to walls, represented for him and for many others the essence of suitable and acceptable architecture.[26] Thus Vitruvius, though

24. See *Ostia*, pp. 97–114, 181–93; Meiggs, pp. 535–39. For the Campanian towns, A. Maiuri, *L'ultima fase edilizia di Pompei* (Rome, 1942); id., *Ercolano. I nuovi scavi* (1927–1958) (Rome, 1958). See also the remarks by A. Boëthius, "The Neronian *'nova urbs.'* Notes on Tacitus' *Annales* . . .," *Skrifter utgivna av Svenska Institutet i Rom*, 2 (1932), 87–88.

25. 6.8.3–4 (arches); 5.10.3, 7.3.1–3 (false vaults); 2.5, 5.10.3, 5.10.5 (vaults); 2.3–6, 2.8, 7.1.1 (brick, mortar, concrete). The most useful English translation is that of M. H. Morgan (Cambridge, Mass., 1914; reprinted New York, 1960), but a thorough restudy of the text in the light of more recent knowledge of Roman

architecture is very much needed; see for example the problems discussed in *AB*, 33 (1951), 136 and n. 3. For Vitruvius' objectives in writing the *Ten Books on Architecture*, see F. E. Brown, "Vitruvius and the Liberal Art of Architecture," *Bucknell Review*, 11 (1963), 99–107.

26. The passage on painting is 7.5.3–4; cf. 1.4.9. Vitruvius was angered because structures were depicted that could not be built—the Romans took their architecture very seriously; cf. Boëthius, p. 91 and references; and Brown (above, n. 25), p. 106. There is a passage in a letter of Cicero's that seems to imply a dislike of vaulted architecture: *Letters to Quintus* 3.1.

he gives much practical information, is of little help in studying the background of vaulted and curved design in Roman architecture.

The definition of Augustan public architecture as conservative and in general traditional is not qualified by the buildings of Augustan date that belong to the development under review, for these formed a small minority and were usually built for private purposes. At the same time they show that interest in vaulted architecture did not lapse entirely in the Augustan age. The mausoleum of the emperor and his family, erected in Rome in 28 B.C., was in effect a huge artificial tumulus, constructed mainly of concrete and containing vaulted circular corridors and massive supporting walls disposed radially in plan (Plate 12).[27] Because of the private nature of the interior, which was emphasized by the encircling wall, only the monumental exterior was meant to be seen;[28] the vaults were mainly functional. This was quite common usage; there is a remarkable example of about the same date at Gaeta, the tomb of L. Munatius Plancus (Plate 13).[29]

The so-called Temple of Mercury at Baia on the north shore of the bay of Naples, presumably of Augustan and certainly of pre-Neronian date, is an important early imperial document of the vaulted style.[30] Baia was a resort area of villas, baths, and casinos. The architects who worked there, away from the influence of classicizing designers in the capital, were experimentally minded.[31] The Temple of Mercury, part of a thermal bath, is a large domed rotunda with an interior diameter of 21.55 meters (Plate 14b). A major interior axis is established by two large rectangular rooms opening onto the rotunda; the diagonals are marked by four curved niches. The dome rises directly from the cylinder below. It is constructed of irregularly shaped pieces of stone, set in mortar and pointing more or less toward the center of the hemisphere, that are positioned as voussoirs but that function as the robust aggregate of a rough concrete (Plate 14a). This fabric rises to a central oculus where the vault is a mere 0.58 meters thick. There were partial prece-

27. It is mentioned by Suetonius in *Augustus* 100, and again in *Vespasian* 23. See A. M. Colini and G. Q. Giglioli, "Relazione della prima campagna di scavo nel Mausoleo d'Augusto," *BC, 54* (1926), 191–234; Nash, 2, 38.

28. The original appearance of the exterior is problematical; see Lugli (above, n. 11), *3*, 198–99, and Crema, Figs. 263–64. It is 87 m. in diameter.

29. See G. Q. Giglioli, "La tomba di L. Munazio Planco a Gaeta," *Architettura ed arti decorativi, 1* (1921–22), 507–16; S. Aurigemma and A. de Santis, *Gaeta, Formia, Minturno* (Rome, 1957), pp. 7–8. Some interior construction appears to date from the High Empire. There is an article by R. Fellmann in the publication of the Swiss Institute for Pre- and Early History for 1957, which I have not seen.

30. See A. Maiuri, "Il restauro di una sala termale a Baia," *BdA, 10* (1931), 241–52. There is a plan in Crema, Fig. 183.

31. Augustus' Forum in Rome was tentatively experimental. See Tamm, pp. 160, 167, 179, and Fig. 60.10; Brown (above, n. 11), p. 27 and Pl. 37. Excavation at Baia is in progress: A. Maiuri, "Terme di Baia. Scavi, restauri, e lavori di sistemazione," *BdA, 36* (1951), 359–64; id., *I campi flegrèi* (3rd ed. Rome, 1958), pp. 66–91. P. A. Paoli, *Antiquitatum Puteolis, Cumis, Bais existentium reliquiae* (Naples, 1768), is still useful; his work was reproduced by G. d'Ancora, *Guida ragionata per le antichità . . . di Pozzuoli e luoghi circonvicini* (Naples, 1792)—in the latter see pp. 96–107 and Tav. XXXV. For Baia in ancient times, see R. M. Haywood, "Let's Run Down to Baiae," *Archaeology, 11* (1958), 200–05.

dents for this design in baths at Pompeii and in other circular structures in Campania, but in these the curve was not used as the informing principle of a style.[32] In the Temple of Mercury curves were used because of their suitability to bath design, but the architect went beyond this to compose them in a coherent and effective way and produced a work of architecture, a building whose appearance and meaning were derived from the consistent application of a principle. He created a focused, enclosed world, its circumscription punctuated and fixed by axial rooms and niches. It was spectacularly lit, and its centrality powerfully fixed, by the round oculus overhead.[33] The surfaces were seamless, for the structure had no beam system, being confidently shaped in concrete. Among existing pre-Neronian buildings the Temple of Mercury must be ranked with the Porticus Aemilia and the sanctuary at Palestrina as primary evidence of Roman architectural inventiveness.

The importance to the history of architecture of the nature of the Julio-Claudian dynasty and its government needs emphasis. The carefully calculated presentation of the emperor as merely the leading citizen, fostered by Augustus, disappeared during the reign of his successor, Tiberius (14–37), and was replaced by a fairly direct display of autocratic power. The dynasty, its more spectacular failures notwithstanding, produced men of ability. The later Julio-Claudian rulers considered themselves innovators, shapers of a future free from stultifying conservatism. Irrespective of one's opinion of the reality or nature of progress, it is true that these men, reluctant or avid, alone or at the instance of their officials and advisors, were responsible for many significant changes in the ancient world. In addition to more purely political accomplishments they drained miasmatic marshes, built aqueducts, constructed ports and necessary supply facilities, tried to cut the isthmus of Corinth, irrigated otherwise unproductive land, and promulgated sound building regulations.[34] These efforts and a good deal more belong on the credit side of the historical ledger even if a few grand projects failed in the end. Much of this work influenced architecture, especially as the imperial system provided for a relatively effective concentration of resources. The existence of the court and its novel requirements was even more significant. Whatever utilitarian assignments might be given to vaulted design—and such assignments were widespread during the period—the combination of these elements in such a way as to form a style, an architecture, took place at the imperial center. The later Julio-Claudian emperors broke away from Augustus'

---

32. The argument that structures such as a circular corbeled tomb found at Cuma (Crema, Fig. 14) were the inspiration for the great round bath chambers at Baia seems incorrect; they are opposed in program and technology and have in common only circular plans. On this subject see B. Crova, "Le terme romane nella Campania," *Atti, 8,* 271–88; R. Salinas, "Le cupole nell'architettura della Campania," *Atti, 8,* 289–91.

33. There were also four relatively small rectangular windows let into the haunch of the vault.

The building is now partly flooded, and apparently the original height is not known, but it was probably equal to the diameter, a relationship recommended by Vitruvius for round buildings (5.10.5; cf. 4.8.3).

34. Bourne, pp. 31–53, has collected much of the extensive textual and epigraphical evidence for the works of the Julio-Claudians. If the known archaeological materials were added to this useful list the true magnitude of early imperial construction would begin to become apparent.

modest manner of private life in the most pronounced, not to say enthusiastic, fashion.[35] In less than sixty years after Augustus' death they spread their palaces and parks over adjoining portions of four of Rome's fourteen Augustan regions (the second, third, fourth, and tenth), an area of perhaps three hundred thousand square meters. Nearly every fragment that remains of these palaces is part of a vaulted design.

The student of imperial architecture early discovers that not much has been preserved of the Julio-Claudian palaces built before Nero's Domus Aurea. Tiberius began and Caligula extended a sumptuous dwelling upon the northern part of the Palatine, but its superstructure has long since disappeared, and the lower parts lie buried or are encased within works commissioned by Domitian and his successors (Plate 15).[36] A thick encrustation of vaulted substructures, ramps, and passageways girdles the entire hill, whose original contours cannot be determined.[37] The Domus Tiberiana covered a space perhaps 120 by 160 meters atop the hill and apparently was composed around a large peristyle. Caligula (37–41) extended Tiberius' works to the north almost as far as the Temple of Castor and Pollux in the Forum. Of the Domus Tiberiana only cellars and supporting structures can be seen, all of concrete and all vaulted. From Caligula's time a cross-vaulted room with a rectangular skylight, and a two-story cistern, nearly 12 meters high and made up of a group of barrel-vaulted chambers, have been partially preserved.[38] The model of the city as it was in imperial times, built on a scale of 1:250 and installed in the Museo della civiltà romana in Rome, shows vaulted-style buildings above these various substructures, but presumably they are to be read as interpretations of later construction (Plate 16).[39]

Certain monuments of the reign of Claudius (41–54) clearly record a change in architectural tempo, a restless desire to break the bonds of traditional design. Banded and rusticated masonry, very anticlassical in feeling, was applied boldly to both traditional and vaulted buildings. This was done at the Porta Maggiore (Praenestina) in

35. Augustus lived for forty years in a quite simple house on the Palatine: Suetonius, *Augustus* 72–73; cf. Ovid, *Fasti* 6.

36. For the Palatine in the early Julio-Claudian period, see Lugli, *Roma*, pp. 479–86; Blake, *1*, 16, 20–23; Tamm, pp. 64–72; Nash, *1*, 365–74. The great fire of the year 80 must have destroyed much of the early palace; Tacitus, *Histories* 1.2; Pliny, *Natural History* 36.111; Josephus, *Antiquities* 19.1.111; Plutarch, *Poplicola* 15.2; Suetonius, *Caligula* 22, *Titus* 8, *Domitian* 5; Dio Cassius, 66.24.1–3.

37. See the illustrations in Nash, *2*, 167–69.

38. The remains of the Domus Tiberiana were partially excavated in 1728 and during the 1860s; see Platner-Ashby, p. 192, and the modern works cited above, n. 36. The substructures along the southwest side can be made out dimly in an old

photograph, taken before the area was terraced, published by R. Lanciani, *Ancient Rome in the Light of Recent Discoveries* (London, n.d.), opp. p. 108. What little is known of the plan is given by Lugli, *Roma*, Tav. VIII. See also Tamm, pp. 25, 28, 65, 75–76, 186; E. B. Van Deman, "The House of Caligula," *AJA*, 28 (1924), 368–98; cf. *JDAI*, 36 (1921), 28–31. I have not seen the cross-vaulted room or the cistern. The Villa of Tiberius at Capri, where the substructures were also vaulted, is better preserved; see A. Maiuri, *Capri, storia e monumenti* (Rome, 1956), pp. 29–53. For the villa at Sperlonga, which may be Tiberian, see F. Fasolo, "Architettura classiche a Mare," *Quaderni*, 14 (1956), 1–6.

39. For the model, see C. Pietrangeli et al., *Museo della civiltà romana, Catologo* (Rome, 1958), pp. 406–09.

Rome (Plate 17) and at Claudius' constructions at Porto on the northwest side of the mouth of the Tiber (Plate 18).[40] The vast terrace of the Claudianum on the Caelian in Rome was supported in part by two stories of reduplicated vaulted chambers faced with rusticated piers and arches (Plates 19 and 20).[41] But there is no evidence in Rome that Julio-Claudian architects worked in a fully thought-out, mature vaulted style before the year 54, when Nero succeeded Claudius. What these examples of Claudian architecture do show is that a new idiom, expressive of the age, was being sought. They also speak of a strong reaction, even on the part of state architects, against the more or less official canon of the previous hundred years. But the momentum and authority of tradition were not overcome by these forces alone. The climax came in the architecturally liberal atmosphere of Nero's reign.

These buildings, selected from a period of over two centuries, show that the Roman use of curves and vaults cannot be explained simply in terms of structural technology. The designs of several of them were based upon an awareness of the sensory and aesthetic effects of curving surfaces and vaulted spaces. After the middle of the first century these effects were exploited deliberately and with great skill. Although Roman vaulted buildings, and particularly their structure, are given space in all handbooks, discussions of the properties of vaults as elements of design are more rare, and it may be useful to close this introductory sketch with some observations about vaulted design.[42]

40. The Porta Maggiore: A. Petrignani, *Porta Maggiore, il suo ripristino . . .* (Rome, 1938); *Capitolium*, 30 (1955), 318–25. Porto: G. Lugli and G. Filibeck, *Il porto di Roma imperiale e l'agro portuense* (Rome, 1935), building no. 52 on Tav. II; for the recent discoveries at the site of the great Claudian port see V. Scrinari, "Strutture portuali relative al 'porto di Claudio' messo in luce . . .," *Rassegna dei lavori pubblici*, 3 (1960), unpaginated; G. Valci, "Dal primo porto di Roma ai turboreattori di Fiumicino," *Capitolium*, 38 (1963), 182–87; O. Testaguzza, "The Port of Rome," *Archaeology*, 17 (1964), 173–79.

41. A. M. Colini, "Storia e topografia del Celio nell'antichità," *MemPontAcc*, 7. (1944), 137–61; A. Prandi, *Il complesso monumentale della Basilica Celimontana dei SS. Giovanni e Paolo* (Rome, 1953), pp. 373–80. This Temple to the Divine Claudius, begun by Agrippina during the years 54–59, was altered by Nero and completed by Vespasian; Suetonius, *Vespasian 9*. I. A. Richmond suggests, in *JRS*, 59 (1959), 182–83, that Claudian rustication should be explained in economic terms: leaving the stones untrimmed would save the contractor enough to "be worth a handsome bribe to an Imperial freedman."

He cites his *City Wall of Imperial Rome* (Oxford, 1930), p. 206, n. 6, where he gives evidence of the intention on the part of the ancient masons to smooth and decorate all the stones of the Porta Maggiore. But was the rustication of the Porto columns and the Claudianum arcade also the result of bribes? And could not that of the Porta Maggiore have resulted from artistic impulses? On the whole, it seems reasonable to group these mid-century buildings together for stylistic reasons. See Crema, p. 154; Lugli, *Tecnica*, 1, 330–31. For the discussion about whether or not the Porta Nigra at Trier belongs to this Claudian group, see G. Lugli, "La Porta Nigra di Treveri," *Rivista del nazionale istituto d'archeologia e storia dell' arte*, 18 (1960), 97–102; cf. H. Kähler, *Rom und seine Welt* (text vol. Munich, 1960), pp. 377–79.

42. An important book of 1921, Rivoira's *Architettura romana*, is chiefly concerned with vaulted buildings, though the examples cited are made to serve the thesis that imperial as well as much subsequent vaulted architecture was exclusively the creation of native Romans; it is the English edition of 1925 that is cited here as "Rivoira." A detailed descriptive catalogue of

If an architectural space is vaulted, its roofs are formed by curving surfaces of masonry. The word vault is derived from the past participle of the Latin verb *volvere*, to roll, to turn about. Vaulted architecture is one of turnings, particularly of turnings well above the pavement. A vault springs and curves inward from vertical supports, either walls or shaft-like forms, and the junction of these supports and the superposed vault is essentially very gradual (Figure 1). Normally, no angle appears between the vertical side elements that rise from the plan of a vaulted space and the curved surfaces that arch across it. The vertical supports and their vault usually meet, in vertical section, as straight lines are tangent to curves. There are exceptions to this, as in segmental vaults (Figure 1c), but the inherent nature of vaulted design and construction is such that the transition from the verticals below to the curves above begins more or less imperceptibly.

Solid masonry masses define the upper boundaries or surfaces of vaulted spaces. The thickness and weight of masonry outside and beyond these interior surfaces are necessary structural parts, but not necessary visual parts, of the design. This is emphatically different from the visual function of masses in the round, such as columns or piers, which are essential features of ancient post-and-beam architecture. Whatever nonstructural elements such as cornices may be inserted along the springing lines of vaults, and whatever decorative features may embellish a vaulted design, an enframing geometry of curves tends to predominate. These bound the upper spaces with rounded surfaces of single or double curvature (a straight line can be drawn upon a surface of single curvature, such as a barrel vault, but not upon one of double curvature, such as a hemispherical dome; see Figure 1, a and e).

A vault forms a ceiling while partaking of the nature of sides, because of the gradualness of its travel upward and inward from the supporting verticals below. Ideally considered, a vault's undersurface or intrados begins as a wall, passes through an intermediate stage in which it is visually part wall and part ceiling, turns through its maximum height as a ceiling, and then continues back down symmetrically to meet its responding support. Many shapes are possible in vaulted architecture. Care should be taken to distinguish between the draftsman's precise geometry of circles, portions of circles, cylinders, cones, ellipses, and spheres, and the actual shapes produced by pouring con-

---

vault forms, showing actual examples, theoretical geometry, structural solutions, and variant terminology, is needed. One can use F. Derand, *L'architecture des voûtes, ou l'art des traits, et coupe des voûtes* (Paris, 1643), and there is useful information in Lugli, *Tecnica, 1,* 657–93, and J. Fitchen, *The Construction of Gothic Cathedrals* (Oxford, 1961), passim. Comparatively little has been written about the visual and other sensory effects of vaults, as opposed to their construction and statics, but see H. Sedlmayr, "Das erste mittelalter-liche Architektursystem," *Kunstwissenschaftliche Forschungen, 2* (1933), 25–62; id., "Zur Geschichte des justinianischen Architektursystems," *Byzantinische Zeitschrift, 35* (1935), 38–69; M. Berucci, "Esperienze costruttive ed estetiche dell' architettura romana," *BollCentro, 6* (1952), 3–5; id., "Ragioni statiche ed estetiche delle proporzioni degli ambienti coperti a volta," *BollCentro, 12* (1958), 25–34; E. Goethals, *Arcs, voûtes, coupoles* (2 vols. Brussels, 1947).

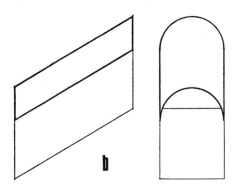

a

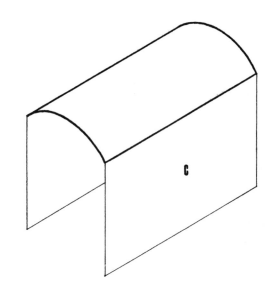

b

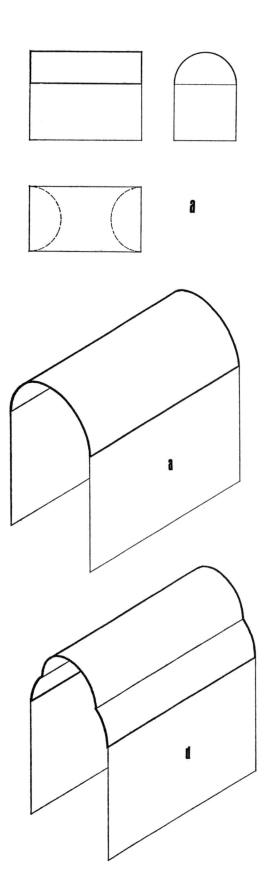

a

c

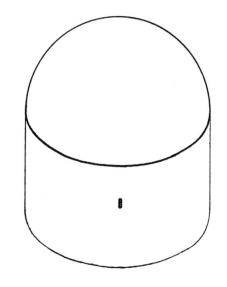

d

e

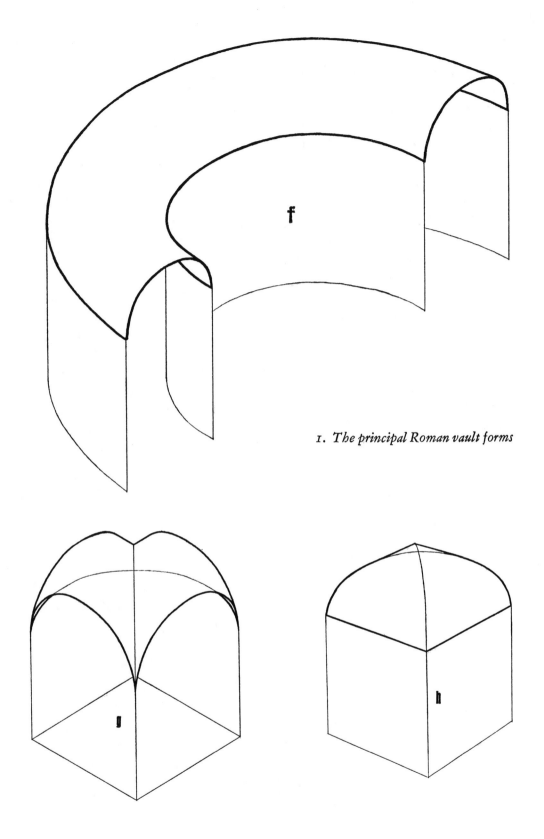

1. *The principal Roman vault forms*

crete against rough forms and by techniques of construction wherein the bases of the curves are located in space or upon temporary platforms.[43]

Having no beam members, and being essentially compression systems, simple masonry vaults in theory work to thrust their lower parts and their vertical supports out and away from the space enclosed. The force of these thrusts is determined by dimensions, materials, and other factors. In some Roman designs the immediate vertical supports were insufficient to assure the stability of the whole, at least during construction, and auxiliary arches and vaults were used as buttresses. Many buildings, especially those of considerable size, were kept in equilibrium by masses of additional masonry added above the springing lines of the vaults. By such means, among others, the Romans solved engineering problems inherent in the design of vast unobstructed interior spaces, and were able to vault great spans with thousands of tons of masonry.

Vaulted buildings are characterized by modulated surfaces and non-prismatic spaces. No vaulted building is polygonal both in plan and in all vertical sections because curved surfaces are always present. Vaulted buildings are also related by their common quality of interiorness. The spaces and visual effects of the interiors of Roman vaulted buildings were almost always emphasized more than the design of their exteriors. Compared to spaces, solids were of secondary importance. The moods and impressions created were derived from concave interior surfaces which were chiefly the consequence of vaulting. The strength of these effects was frequently increased by the presence of curving walls, and by vertical central axes that were often strongly apparent in fully developed vaulted buildings. The word "arcuated" is deficient in its implications as a description of this kind of architecture. Although Roman vaulted architecture did indeed originally evolve partly from the arch, the surfaces, structure, and visual and other sensory effects of vaulted designs were much more complex and subtle than those of that relatively simple device.

These characteristics may be summarized as follows:

Solids were of secondary importance to the spaces they bounded and defined; significant hollows, not visible masses, were the essence of this architecture.

Interior spaces and effects were emphasized.

The boundaries of these spaces were non-prismatic, for surfaces of single or double curvature, or both, were always present.

These spaces were unobstructed by interior supports.

Vertical, centralizing axes were often readily apparent.

43. Figure 1, p. 16, does not include all Roman vault forms. Pyramidal and conical vaults were built, the latter with both horizontal and slanting crown lines. Oval, more or less elliptical, and many mixed and warped forms were also constructed. Trajan's Markets in Rome, the substructures of the Pozzuoli amphitheatre, and the baths at Baia are particularly instructive about the nature and shapes of Roman vaults.

When trabeation was used, its importance to the concept of design was almost always subordinated to that of the spaces and impressions derived from vaulting.

The basic structural fabric, in Rome and its vicinity from Nero's time onward, was composed of brick-faced walls, of arch-forms, and of vaults—all of concrete.

There are other distinctive features of Roman vaulted architecture, but this list will indicate what is meant when the phrase is used here. This summary is offered provisionally, not as a perfected or final statement, though it applies without exception to the buildings to be discussed. It suggests only that a homogeneous architectural group can licitly be separated from the immense and apparently stylistically mixed body of Roman architecture in general. One additional observation would seem useful: in these pages the words "Roman architecture" refer to the architecture of Roman times in lands ruled from Rome, but they do not imply that the designers and builders were all necessarily Romans of the city of Rome.

II

NERO'S PALACES

NERO'S PALACES show how powerfully architectural thinking was affected by the conception and claims of the imperial office, so greatly expanded after Augustus' death. The extent of Nero's direct participation cannot be determined, though it is unlikely that he was inarticulate about the work of his architects and artists. The ancient historians and biographers, understandably hostile to a criminally willful youth who repeatedly violated law and tradition, clearly record his serious if unfocused interest in art.[1] Nero rejected conservative restraints and in retrospect can be seen as embodying many of the forces of a new age irrespective of his personal instability. During his reign (54–68) the course of empire was becoming firmly marked and many barriers to the expression of fresh architectural ideas were rapidly vanishing. The opportunities created by the necessity of rebuilding part of Rome after a catastrophic fire heightened this receptive atmosphere, and architectural innovation flourished.

The glittering and often sordid court life described by Suetonius and others can hardly be taken as the substance of imperial civilization. There are fairer and more useful gauges, such as the sense of purpose that animates the hero of Tacitus' reverent *Agricola* or that makes Frontinus' *Concerning the Aqueducts* so straightforward and practical a treatise. Similarly, the serious content of a host of inscriptions and other documents of public and private life, and the artistic quality and appropriateness of form seen in many surviving monuments, are more relevant records of the nature of the post-Augustan age. Among the monuments, Nero's two palaces in Rome are especially instructive. The earlier one, the Domus Transitoria, was begun before 64 only to be ruined, perhaps before it was finished, in the great fire of that year.[2] A few isolated parts remain, wholly

---

1. There is substantial evidence for Nero's genuine devotion to the arts embedded in Suetonius' biography: *Nero* 10, 16.1, 20–21, 41.2, 52; cf. Tacitus, *Annals* 15.33, 15.42, 16.4. For modern, less caustic opinion, see *OCD*, p. 604 and cf. pp. 899–900; *CAH*, 10, 710, 718–19; M. P. Charlesworth, "Nero: Some Aspects," *JRS*, 40 (1950), 69–76; cf. Tamm, pp. 107–08. The period needs to be carefully restudied in order to ascertain the nature and degree of positive accomplishment recognized by Suetonius (*Nero* 19.3) and even by Tacitus (*Annals* 15.41, 15.43, 15.46).

2. The name is ancient: Suetonius, *Nero* 31.1; cf. Tacitus, *Annals* 15.39.

inadequate for a reconstruction of the plan but sufficiently well preserved to convey some sense of architectural principles. The second palace, the Domus Aurea, was begun immediately after the fire, and at the time of Nero's death was still under construction though presumably nearly finished.[3] Scattered foundations and other fragments of this immense undertaking can still be seen, as well as a major wing of which more than a hundred rooms have been cleared.

THE REMAINS UNDER THE TEMPLE OF VENUS AND ROME

The first palace, the Domus Transitoria, was intended to join the imperial residence on the Palatine (the Domus Tiberiana) with the Gardens of Maecenas on the Esquiline more than a thousand meters to the northeast. The gardens had become imperial property in the time of Augustus, and popular opinion held that it was from a tower there that Nero watched the great fire.[4] A part of the Domus Transitoria exists under Domitian's palace (the Domus Flavia) on the south side of the Palatine (Figure 2). It consists of several chambers, once brilliantly decorated, adjoining a fairly small and very elegant fountain-court.[5] The main feature of the latter was a miniature theatre stage of baroque design, partly composed of colored marbles (Plate 21a). Its vertical backdrop was formed of nine niches separated by projecting spur walls, both screened by columns, in the manner of numerous theatre stage-walls and façades of public buildings of the High Empire.

In 1828, beneath the terrace of Hadrian's Temple of Venus and Rome four hundred meters northeast of the Palatine nymphaeum, Nibby discovered a rotunda intersected by barrel-vaulted corridors set at right angles to each other (Figure 3, a restoration seen from the north). The pavement of this structure is about five meters below the present ground level, and its spaces are cut through by foundation walls of the Domus Aurea (not shown on Figure 3). Since Nibby's time several writers have called attention to the building. It has sometimes been identified as part of a sumptuous late republican house, but there is little doubt that it is a fragment of the Domus Transitoria.[6] Aside from the

3. In *Nero* 31.2, Suetonius says that Nero dedicated the palace when it was finished; but in *Otho* 7.1, that it was still incomplete in the year after Nero's death. The name is ancient, appearing in both Pliny, *Natural History* (33.54, 34.84, 35.120, 36.111, 36.163), and Suetonius, *Nero* (31.1, 38.1), and derives not from the decoration of the vault of room 18 on Pl. 24 here, as Blake, 2, 50, would have it, but rather from the generous application of gilding inside and out, as Pliny (33.54) and Suetonius (*Nero* 31.2), make clear; cf. Boëthius, p. 105 and n. 18.

4. Suetonius, *Nero* 38.2; cf. Dio Cassius, 62.18.1. But Tacitus, by far the most reliable source in spite of his anti-imperial bias, says in

Annals 15.39 (quoted on p. 26 here) that during the fire Nero sang in his private theatre; cf. Platner-Ashby, p. 269, and *CAH*, 10, 723.

5. G. Carettoni, "Costruzioni sotto l'angolo sud-orientale della Domus Flavia," *NS*, 3 (1949), 48–79; Nash, 1, 375–79. Cf. P. Grimal and J. Guey, "À propos des 'Bains de Livie' au Palatin," *Mélanges d'archéologie et d'histoire de l'école française de Rome*, 54 (1937), 142–64; Crema, Fig. 312; Tamm, p. 74.

6. The entrance to these remains is about 15 m. southwest of the location of no. 31 on the upper right-hand corner of the map of the Forum area inserted between pp. 128–29 in *Roma e dintorni* (6th ed. Milan, Touring Club Italiano,

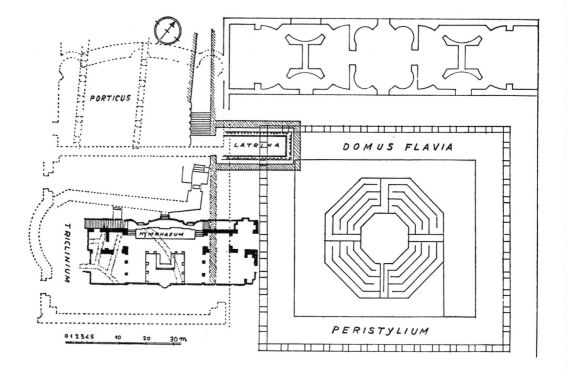

2. *Plan of the nymphaeum court of the Domus Transitoria under the Domus Flavia on the Palatine*

evidence of its architectural style, this identification is based upon location, the character of the design and its decoration, and the direct superimposition of the Domus Aurea walls along precisely the same lines of orientation as those of the barrel-vaulted corridors.

The rotunda is located on the line between the Domus Tiberiana on the Palatine and the area of the Gardens of Maecenas on the Esquiline. The Domus Aurea foundation walls rest directly upon its pavement, and the pavement is unworn; these facts fit the sequence of Nero's building programs exactly. The decoration of the rotunda and corridors followed the same principles of design, using the same materials, as that of the Domus Transitoria remains on the Palatine, where colored marbles and small pieces of glass were combined to give an effect of luxurious intimacy.[7] The orientation of the porticoes and vestibule of the Domus Aurea is the same as that of the barrel-vaulted corridors opening onto the rotunda.[8] This shows that the architect of the Domus Aurea, when he began work here after the fire, followed the alignment of the earlier design. It would have been natural for him to make as much use as possible of the work that had so recently gone into the Domus Transitoria. Since the later construction is laid directly upon the earlier, and the earlier was used only briefly and was decorated in very much the same way as a known part of the Domus Transitoria, the identification of the rotunda and corridors as a fragment of the Domus Transitoria seems certain.

The intersection of the domed rotunda by corridors formed a cross plan. The rotunda was not a closed, continuous shape, for the corridors opened directly onto it, forming four doubly curving arches where the surfaces of the barrel vaults and that of the cylinder met. The result was a central, focal volume defined by the dome and its four broad, concave piers. Presumably the direct light for this space came through an oculus. In

---

1962), or just north of the position of the letter "I" in the word "VELIA" on Tav. IV, opp. p. 112, in Lugli, *Roma*. The literature consists of several brief notices. In the following list the authors' opinions about date or use are indicated: A. Nibby, *Roma nell'anno MDCCCXXXVIII. Parte II. Antica* (Rome, 1839), p. 733 (a private house); Lanciani, p. 200 (a private mansion; but cf. p. 361); E. B. Van Deman, "The Sacra Via of Nero," *MAAR*, 5 (1925), 121–22 (probably the Domus Transitoria); Platner-Ashby, p. 195 (the Domus Transitoria); M. Barosso, "Edificio romano sotto il Tempio di Venere e Roma," *Atti*, *3*, 75 (a sumptuous house of late republican or early Augustan date); Lugli, *Roma*, p. 340 (probably the Domus Transitoria); Kähler, pp. 98–99 (plan, Abb. 12; early imperial); J. B. Ward Perkins, "Nero's Golden House," *Antiquity*, *30* (1956), 213 (the Domus Transitoria); Blake, 2, 36–37 (probably Nero's father's house, embel-

lished by Nero); Crema, p. 270 (plan, Fig. 307; the Domus Transitoria); Boëthius, p. 109 (implies a pre-Neronian date); Nash, *1*, 375 (the Domus Transitoria). Barosso's is the only factual description; Kähler's the only analysis.

7. Carettoni (above, n. 5), p. 52; Barosso (above, n. 6), pp. 75–77. Cf. the paving preserved from Nero's villa at Sublaquea (Subiaco), mentioned by Blake, 2, 41.

8. For the Domus Aurea orientation, see Van Deman (above, n. 6) and her Pl. 62. Her reconstruction of the plan of the Domus Aurea in this area is corroborated by the position and alignment of the Domus Aurea walls (which she did not see) that cut through the rotunda. These walls are structurally identical with those of the Domus Aurea on the Palatine that are also set directly upon remains of the Domus Transitoria; see Carettoni (above, n. 5), pp. 77–78; Kähler, p. 98; Nash, *1*, 377–78; and Pl. 21a here.

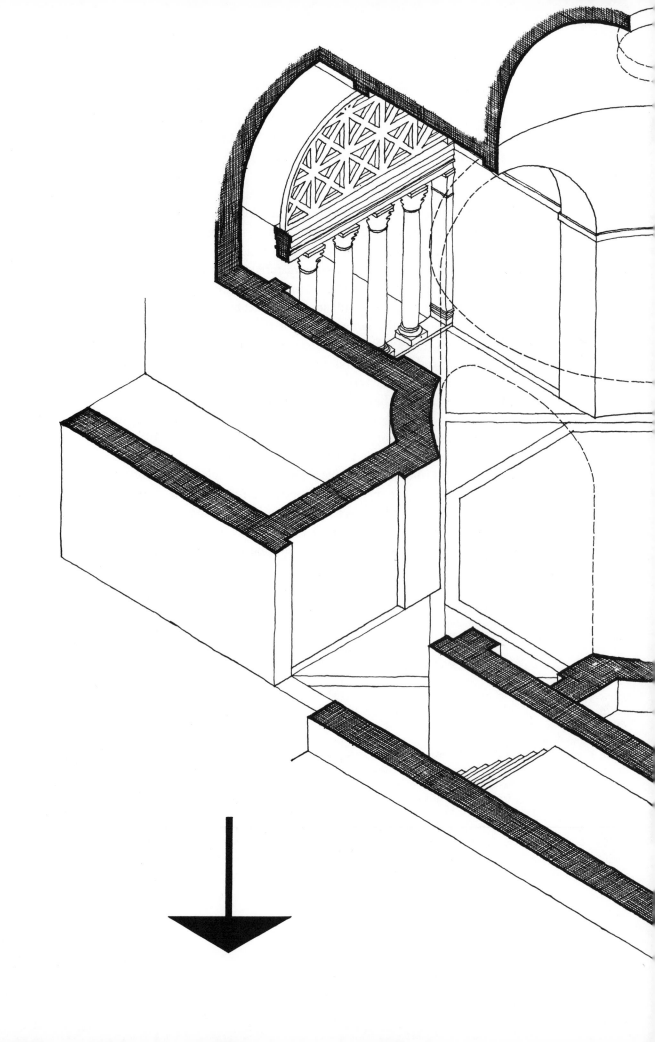

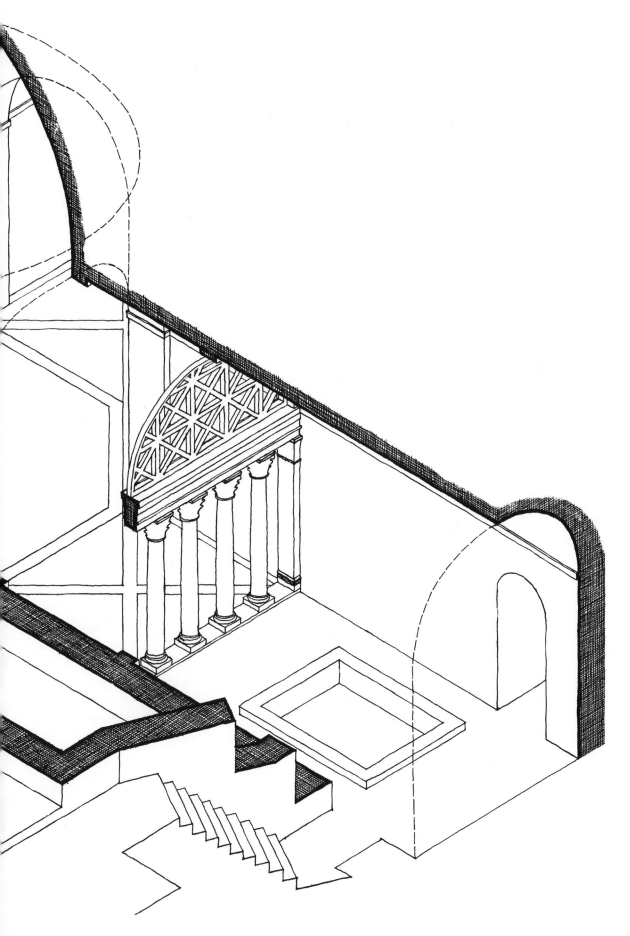

3. *Rotunda and corridors of the Domus Transitoria, restored, seen from the north*

the pavement, an octagonal figure was inscribed within the circular plan. Alternating sides of this figure were extended diagonally under the four arches and out along the paving of the corridors until they met the corridor walls. The junction points of these extended lines with the walls fixed the location of small-scale colonnades, each of four columns, that were set at right angles to the long axes of the corridors. Probably each of these transverse colonnades carried above its entablature a grille of bronze or marble, semicircular in elevation, that reached up to the intrados of the barrel vault overhead. Within the rotunda, and out into the corridors at least as far as the column screens, the pavement was richly wrought of small triangular and diamond-shaped pieces of deep red, dark green, and azure glass, and of ivory-white palombino marble. Several square meters of this magnificent floor are still visible. In the northwest corridor, on the side of the column screen away from the rotunda, there was a shallow rectangular pool lined with white and edged with colored marble; farther to the northwest there are remains of hydraulic installations. The piers were encrusted with marbles, the corridor walls were plastered and painted, and the thresholds and pilaster bases of the column screens were edged with narrow strips of colored marbles.

Domed cylinders expanded volumetrically and visually by niches or other spatial extensions were not new in Nero's time. The so-called Temple of Mercury at Baia, perhaps a half-century earlier than the Domus Transitoria, is a case in point. There are round tombs of pre-Neronian date that have four axial chambers on a cross plan, with one chamber forming the entrance.[9] But at the Domus Transitoria the axial extensions were corridors rather than chambers, and the design was based upon a free flow of space rather than upon its firm enclosure. The corridors, whose continuity was interrupted only tentatively by the column screens, surely extended to parts of the palace now unknown. In function each corridor was a cryptoporticus and the rotunda was a well-lit center of communications; in design these geometric forms were subservient to the principles of the vaulted style.

The assembly of these vaulted volumes was such that their individuality, within the cross of space bounded by the column screens, was surrendered to a dominant continuity of space. Curve met curve, which suggested rather than blocked the sense of flow; the openings into the rotunda were generously scaled; and the extended diagonal lines of the pavement design, reaching out into the corridors, worked toward locking the neighboring volumes together. The perforated column screens helped to define the unity of the central cross shape but did not hide it from the approaching visitor, for they quickened his discovery of it by marking it off with architectural punctuation. Their columns and entablatures functioned purely visually. A shallow pool, on one side of the rotunda at least, forced a deviation from the axial direction of the corridor in the same manner as the pool of the traditional atrium house, generating a sequence of axial and angled views during the approach to the central space. The columns introduced a subtle counterpoint to the

9. For example, Giovannoni, Tav. VII; Crema, Fig. 305.

turning surfaces overhead, and from within the central space they suggested extended distances by creating non-axial, tangential views of the corridor walls beyond. The colonnades were transparent partitions or filters, at once both solid and open, that revealed only a part of what was yet to be seen and marked a moment of passage from one experience of form to another. These closely spaced, comparatively slender verticals, associated in an entirely visual fashion with curved surfaces, created unresolved and indefinite vistas. The effects produced by this kind of combination of columns and vaults were to be much prized in imperial and early medieval architecture.

THE CONSEQUENCES OF THE FIRE OF 64

The great fire that broke out in Rome on the night of July 18th of the year 64 burned for nine days. Of the fourteen city regions, three were all but destroyed: *III* (the Oppian hill, forming the southern spur of the Esquiline), *X* (the Palatine), and *XI* (the Circus Maximus). Only four regions seem to have been spared completely, and the remainder were damaged, especially *VII* (the Via Lata) and *IX* (the Campus Martius). Tacitus, who was about ten years old at the time, later wrote of the catastrophe at some length. The passage contains much valuable information.

> There followed a disaster [Tacitus has just described some Neronian excesses], whether due to chance or to the malice of the sovereign is uncertain—for each version has its sponsors—but graver and more terrible than any other which has befallen this city by the ravages of fire. It took its rise in the parts of the city touching the Palatine and Caelian hills; where, among the shops packed with inflammable goods, the conflagration broke out, gathering strength in the same moment, and, impelled by the wind, swept the full length of the Circus: for there were neither mansions screened by boundary walls, nor temples surrounded by stone enclosures, nor obstacles of any description, to bar its progress. The flames, which in full career overran the level districts first, then shot up to the heights, and sank again to harry the lower parts, kept ahead of all remedial measures, the mischief traveling fast, and the town being an easy prey owing to the narrow, twisting lanes and formless streets typical of old Rome. . . . [The fugitives] combined by their dilatoriness or their haste to impede everything. Often, when they glanced back to the rear, they were attacked on the flanks or in front; or if they had made their escape into a neighboring quarter, that also was involved in the flames, and even districts which they had believed were remote from danger were found to be in the same plight. . . .
>
> Nero, who at that time was staying in Antium [Anzio], did not return to the capital until the fire was nearing the palace by which he had connected the Palatine with the Gardens of Maecenas [the Domus Transitoria]. It proved impossible, however, to stop it from engulfing both the Palatine and the palace and all their surroundings. Still, as a relief to the homeless and fugitive populace, he opened the Campus Martius, the building of Agrippa, even his own Gardens, and threw up a

number of extemporized shelters to accommodate the helpless multitude. The necessities of life were brought up from Ostia and the neighboring municipalities, and the price of grain was lowered to three sesterces. Yet his measures, popular as their character might be, failed of their effect, for the report spread that, at the very moment when Rome was aflame, he had mounted his private stage, and typifying the ills of the present by the calamities of the past, had sung of the destruction of Troy.

Only on the sixth day was the conflagration brought to an end at the foot of the Esquiline, by demolishing buildings over a vast area and opposing to the unabated fury of the flames a clear tract of ground and an open horizon. However . . . the fire resumed its ravages, but in the less congested parts of the city, so that while the toll of human life was not so great, the destruction of temples, and of useful and convenient porticoes, was on a wider scale. The second fire produced the greater scandal of the two, as it had broken out on the Aemilian property of Tigellinus [Nero's Praetorian Prefect; the property was probably in the southern part of the Campus Martius] and appearances suggested that Nero was seeking the glory of founding a new capital and endowing it with his own name. Rome, in fact, is divided into fourteen regions, of which four remained intact, while three were laid level with the ground: in the other seven nothing survived but a few dilapidated and half-burned relics of houses.

It would not be easy to attempt an estimate of the private houses, insulae [tenement blocks, apartment houses], and temples, which were lost; [and] the flames consumed [many venerable shrines]. To these must be added the precious trophies won upon so many fields, the glories of Greek art, and yet again the primitive and uncorrupted memorials of literary genius; so that, despite the striking beauty of the rearisen city, the older generation recollects much that it proved impossible to replace. . . .

However, Nero turned to account the ruins of his fatherland by building a palace, the marvels of which were to consist not so much in gems and gold, materials long familiar and vulgarized by luxury, as in fields and lakes and the air of solitude given by wooded ground alternating with clear tracts and open landscapes. The architect and engineer were Severus and Celer, who had the ingenuity and courage to try the force of art even against the veto of nature and to fritter away the resources of a Caesar. They had undertaken to sink a navigable canal running from Lake Avernus [near Baia] to the mouths of the Tiber along a desolate shore or through intervening hills; for the one district along the route moist enough to yield a supply of water is the Pomptine Marsh; the rest being cliff and sand, which could be cut through, if at all, only by intolerable exertions for which no sufficient motive existed. None the less Nero, with his passion for the incredible, made an effort to tunnel the heights nearest the Avernus, and some evidences of that futile ambition survive.

In the capital, however, the districts spared by the [new] palace [the Domus Aurea] were rebuilt, not, as after the Gallic fire [390 B.C.], indiscriminately and piecemeal, but in measured lines of streets, with broad thoroughfares, buildings of restricted height, and open spaces, while porticoes were added as a protection to the front of the insulae. These porticoes Nero offered to erect at his own expense, and also to hand over the building sites, clear of rubbish, to the owners. He made a further offer of reward, proportioned to the rank and resources of the various claimants, and fixed a term within which houses or insulae must be completed, if the bounty was to be secured. As the receptacle of the refuse he settled upon the Ostian marshes, and gave orders that vessels which carried grain up the Tiber must run downstream laden with debris. The buildings themselves, to an extent definitely specified, were to be solid, untimbered [beamless?] structures of Gabine or Alban stone, that particular stone being proof against fire. Again, there was to be a guard to insure that the water supply—intercepted by private lawlessness—should be available for public purposes in greater quantities and at more points; appliances for checking fire were to be kept by everyone in the open; there were to be no joint partitions between buildings, but each was to be independent, with its own walls. These reforms, welcomed for their utility, were also beneficial to the appearance of the new capital. Still, there were those who held that the old form had been the more salubrious, as the narrow streets and high-built houses were not so easily penetrated by the rays of the sun; while now the broad expanses, with no protecting shadows, glowed under a more oppressive heat.[10]

Suetonius, who wrote about 120, describes the fire briefly,[11] and in another passage observes that Nero

> devised a new form for the buildings of the city and in front of the houses and insulae he erected porticoes, from the flat roofs of which fires could be fought; and these he put up at his own cost. He had also planned to extend the walls [of Rome] as far as Ostia and to bring the sea from there to the city by a canal.[12]

The reliability of Tacitus' evidence is strengthened by his adamant opposition to the monarchy, which he believed had no place in the Roman constitution, and by his deep suspicion of imperial motives. Given these convictions, his willingness to describe without prejudice and to praise more than once the efforts of Nero and his government is most

---

10. *Annals* 15.38–43; the translation above, like most of those given here, is based upon that in the Loeb edition.

11. *Nero* 38.1. There is another version in Dio Cassius, 62.16–18, and the fire is mentioned by Pliny, *Natural History* 17.1.5. See A. Profumo, *Fonti e tempi dell'incendio neroniano* (Rome,

1905); *CAH*, 10, 722–26, 982–83; cf. Nash, *1*, 60–62.

12. *Nero* 16.1. Suetonius refers to other projects in 9, 19.2, 31.3, 41.2; cf. his remarks in 19.3 about praiseworthy works. For the Avernus-Ostia/Rome canal, see also Pliny, *Natural History* 14.61.

telling.[13] He could not resist appending a phrase or two about what the city may have lost in rebuilding, but obviously he was impressed by what was accomplished. Both Tacitus and Suetonius speak unhesitatingly of the creation of an *urbs nova,* and Tacitus refers without equivocation to its striking beauty. He also gives a clear summary of a new official building code, and testifies to the ingenuity and courage of Severus and Celer. Suetonius simply gives the credit to the emperor himself, but he is no less ready than Tacitus to emphasize the distinctive character of Rome's post-fire architecture.

These striking passages show beyond any doubt that this architecture was new and different, and that it made a profound impression. The new quarters were planned in a methodical way and were made safer and more pleasant by the provision of public squares and wide streets bordered by porticoes. The post-fire buildings, the majority of them insulae, were restricted in height and were characterized by a new form. That this Neronian architecture was the model for many urban quarters and buildings of the High Empire, at least in central Italy, is confirmed by the results of excavations at Ostia and Rome and by the testimony of the marble plan of the capital made in Severan times. The significance of these complementary sources has not been neglected by modern scholars,[14] but certain points in the texts, and the role of the fire in the consolidation of the new style, deserve further examination.

The first point concerns the connection between planning and the government. Tacitus makes it clear that the rebuilding was based upon principles thought out in advance, that it was the work of professionals. We are entitled to infer that these men were in the employ of the government, either permanent civil servants or other experts drafted to meet the emergency. It is evident that they took matters in hand quickly and firmly. The debris was rapidly and efficiently removed, the cleared areas surveyed, and the lines of streets and city blocks marked out. The building code and the buildings themselves were creations of men who not only thoroughly understood the practical necessities of architecture but who also had a vision of a new city. The government of Nero did not stand in the way of either the concept or its execution. On the contrary, it approved and encouraged, and at this critical moment in the story of Roman architecture the facilities and resources of the imperial administration were at the disposal of architects who did not feel bound by tradition. Certain of the building regulations, such as the one that limited maximum permissible height, lost their force within a generation or so, and the scheme for a new city marked by broad avenues was as little followed as that of Wren's for London, and for somewhat the same reasons. But in Nero's time the new architecture itself came firmly and irrevocably to the fore, and this could not have happened without the direct support and participation of the government.

The second point raised by the texts concerns the structure and form of the new buildings. Tacitus says that they were required to be of stone and without beams to a degree

---

13. Cf. *OCD,* p. 877.

14. Boëthius, Chap. 4, cites most of the literature; see especially his article on "The Neronian 'nova urbs' . . .," *Skrifter utgivna av Svenska Institutet i Rom,* 2 (1932), 84–97; Blake, 2, 43–46.

that was spelled out in the official version of the code.[15] He uses the words *sine trabibus*, which can be rendered, quite properly, as "untimbered" or "without timbers." If this is his exclusive meaning, the reference is to a desire to reduce the amount of timber framing in floors, roofs, and masonry walls.[16] But without questioning the intent of the regulation, which was to diminish the use of inflammable building materials, a different meaning can be inferred. Tacitus may very well be using *sine trabibus* to indicate vaulted structures, which would be beamless. If so, he is in agreement with the evidence of the Neronian buildings and fragments in Rome, which are of concrete and are vaulted. Also, this interpretation clearly fits with Suetonius' reference to "a new form for the buildings of the city." The specification of Alban and Gabine stone is governed in the text by a verb meaning to make firm, solid, or sound, to strengthen: *aedificiaque ipsa certa sui parte sine trabibus saxo Gabino Albanove solidarentur*. This phrase, which evokes an image of beamless, massy structures, matches the archaeological facts precisely. Tacitus does not mention concrete, but it is reasonable to suppose that he is indicating that the parts not of stone were to be of concrete, and that the buildings were roofed with vaults.[17] This interpretation is offered to show that the evidence of the texts and that of the remaining buildings can be reconciled, and to suggest that there is a tendency to interpret these texts along what might be called Vitruvian or somewhat anachronistic lines. In dealing with ancient references to imperial architecture, the possibility of alternative meanings ought to be kept in mind.

The third point, which concerns the nature of the porticoes mentioned by both Tacitus and Suetonius, is of a similar kind. In the texts, the word used is *porticus*, usually translated as "(covered) colonnade" or "porch." But the alternative meaning of "arcade" is also possible, and though it is not clear from the texts themselves which meaning is intended, there is evidence that arcuated or vaulted structures are implied. Arcades were built before Nero's time, and when his architects refashioned the Sacra Via in the area where the Arch of Titus now stands, they lined it with arcades.[18] The vaulted arcade was

15. On Roman building codes, see J. H. Middleton, *The Remains of Ancient Rome*, *1* (London, 1892), 88–91.

16. Timber framing in masonry walls can be studied for example at Herculaneum; see Boëthius (article cited above, n. 14), p. 87; A. Maiuri, *Ercolano. I nuovi scavi (1927–1958)* (Rome, 1958); Blake, 2, 157; the illustration in H. Kähler, *The Art of Rome and Her Empire* (New York, 1963), p. 141; cf. Vitruvius, 2.8.20.

17. In the event, the specification of Alban and Gabine stone, which was probably for facings and reinforcement, was ineffective; see Blake, 2, 3, 42; cf. Lugli, *Tecnica*, *1*, 329–31. H. Furneaux, *The Annals of Tacitus*, *3*, ed. H. F. Pelham and C. D. Fisher (Oxford, 1907), 372, n. 1, concludes that *sine trabibus* in conjunction with *solidarentur*

means "that the lower stories were to be vaulted in stone."

18. Pre-Neronian arcades: Blake, *1*, 220–23; Boëthius (article cited above, n. 14), p. 96. For the Neronian arcades beside and near the Sacra Via (which may have been two stories high), see Van Deman (above, n. 6), Pls. 62 and 64; id., "The Neronian Sacra Via," *AJA*, 27 (1923), 415–19 and Pl. 3; also Blake, 2, 44–45. For a villa, possibly Neronian and certainly early imperial in date, with an arcaded portico, see A. Schiavo, "La villa romana di Minori," *Palladio*, 3 (1939), 129–33; it is evident from the description in *Campania* (3rd ed. Milan, Touring Club Italiano, 1963), p. 400, that more of the villa has been recovered since Schiavo's article was written; I have not seen it. For the word "porticus,"

known at least as early as Sulla's time (see Plates 6 and 11, for example). Furthermore, it was common to the urban architecture of the High Empire which was itself derived in great part from the Neronian *urbs nova*.[19] The possibility that Tacitus and Suetonius refer to arcades rather than to colonnades ought not to be ignored.

The opportunity provided by the fire was eagerly seized by talented men confident of full government support. For several years Rome was filled with the sights and sounds of building on a grand scale. The amount of reconstruction was vast and the necessity for rapid completion pressing, and concrete construction, requiring only a very small proportion of highly skilled labor, was employed whenever possible. Resistance to fire and structural reliability were both increased, and the use of vaulting in the solution of roofing problems was encouraged. The buildings themselves show that brick-faced concrete, inexpensive and easily prepared, quickly became the major structural material after the fire so brutally exposed the inadequacy of much traditional construction.[20] A corollary of this was the immediate expansion of the manufacture of bricks and other architectural terra cottas. A certain proportion of the bricks were stamped with the name of the master potter or the brickyard, perhaps to simplify inventory and bookkeeping.[21] This methodical habit, so helpful to historians and archaeologists, first became widespread after the fire. It is additional evidence of the rapidity with which attitudes toward architecture and building methods were changing.

Thus the fire was responsible for a sudden alteration in the appearance of the city and for a pronounced shift of emphasis in structural methods. True to their nature, the Romans effected these changes in an orderly way. Tacitus refers to "the measured lines of streets" that replaced the meandering alleys and passageways of the burnt-over districts. The new buildings were constructed of materials whose assembly, preparation, and use could be readily subdivided for convenient processing and application by organized gangs; the rise of the great guilds of suppliers and builders began during this period. Most important, a rich strain of creativity pervaded this rational structure of events. The fire took place at a moment when the accumulated experience of vaulted design was susceptible to inventive and successful recapitulation, and this was of even greater consequence than either the opportunity of rebuilding part of Rome or the confirmation of the advantages of vaulted construction in concrete. The fire suggested to Nero the possibility of a spectacular villa-palace, a luxurious country seat in the heart

---

see A. Maiuri, "Portico e peristilio," *Parola del passato, 1* (1946), 306–22; cf. his "L'origine del portico ad arche girate su colonne," *Palladio, 1* (1937), 121–24.

19. Boëthius, pp. 157–58; cf. G. Gatti, "Caratteristiche edilizie di un quartiere di Roma del II secolo d. Cr.," *Quaderni, 31–48* (1961; = *Fest. V. Fasolo*), 49–66, esp. Figs. 13 and 16.

20. For the rapid increase in the use of concrete, see Boëthius (article cited above, n. 14), p.

88; Lugli, *Tecnica, 1,* 633; Blake, *2,* 10; Meiggs, p. 237.

21. Bloch, p. 336; cf. his articles on "The Roman Brick Industry and Its Relationship to Roman Architecture," *JSAH, 1* (1941), 3–8, and "The Serapeum of Ostia and the Brickstamps of 123 A.D., A New Landmark in the History of Roman Architecture," *AJA, 63* (1959), 225–40. See also *ESAR, 5,* 209.

of Rome that would be even larger and more grand than the Domus Transitoria. It was this project that gave his gifted architect and engineer a major opening for the expression of their ideas. It is above all the design and construction of the new palace, recorded in the surviving wing upon the Esquiline, that show how important the events described by Tacitus were to the history of architecture. The fire gave a mortally egocentric autocrat the chance to demand a unique, monumental expression of what he considered his worth and position to be. The results of this union of Nero's illusions with the opportunity created by the fire would perhaps have appeared in due time, but the fire, in its suddenness and ferocity, called the various elements of the new style into play simultaneously.

THE ESQUILINE WING OF THE DOMUS AUREA

The perimeter of the Domus Aurea was immense. It enclosed the part of the Esquiline known as the Oppian Hill, much of the Caelian, part if not all of the Palatine.[22] In the low ground where the Flavian Amphitheatre now stands, an artificial lake was formed, either by damming a stream flowing down the draw between the Esquiline and the Caelian or by diverting the waters of an aqueduct.[23] Tacitus' brief description of the palace has been quoted above on p. 26. In addition, there is the following important passage in Suetonius' biography of Nero.

> There was nothing however in which [Nero] was more ruinously prodigal than in building. He made a palace extending all the way from the Palatine to the Esquiline, which at first he called the Domus Transitoria, but when it was burned shortly after its completion and rebuilt, the Domus Aurea. Its size and splendor will be sufficiently indicated by the following details. Its vestibule was large enough to contain a colossal statue of the emperor a hundred and twenty feet high; and it was so extensive that it had a triple portico a mile long. There was a pond, too, like a sea, surrounded with buildings to represent cities, besides tracts of country, varied by tilled fields, vineyards, pastures and woods, with great numbers of wild and domestic animals. In the rest of the palace all parts were overlaid with gold and adorned with gems and mother-of-pearl. There were dining rooms with fretted ceilings of ivory, whose panels could turn and shower down flowers and were fitted with pipes for sprinkling the guests with perfumes. The main banquet hall was

22. C. C. Van Essen, "La topographie de la Domus Aurea Neronis," *Mededelingen der Koninglijke Nederlandse Akademie van Wetenschappen, Afd. Letterkunde,* n.s. 17.12 (1954), 371–98, has defined the perimeter; see his map on p. 377. There is a very useful discussion by Ward Perkins, cited above, n. 6. For the Domus Aurea and the Palatine, see Tamm, pp. 72–75; below, n. 31.

23. E. B. Van Deman, *The Building of the Roman Aqueducts* (Washington, 1934), p. 266, says that the branch of the Aqua Claudia that

Nero's engineers brought to the top of the Caelian was "designed in part, it would seem, for the great lake below its distributing reservoir." T. Ashby, *The Aqueducts of Ancient Rome* (Oxford, 1935), pp. 244–45, does not connect this new supply with Nero's lake; cf. Frontinus, 20. The stream may have been the Nodinus: H. Jordan and C. Huelsen, *Topographie der Stadt Rom im Altertum, 1.3* (Berlin, 1907), 112, n. 2; Lanciani, p. 29 and map (Fig. 1, opp. p. 1).

circular and constantly revolved day and night, like the heavens. He had baths supplied with sea water and sulphur water. When the palace was finished in this manner and he dedicated it, he deigned to say nothing more in the way of approval than that he was at last beginning to be housed like a human being.[24]

A quip went round the city: "Rome is being made into a palace—off to Veii, citizens, unless Veii has been taken over, too."[25]

Although the palace was dedicated by Nero, the original grand design was probably never completed. Otho, one of those who quarrelled for the throne during the year following Nero's death, directed that a large sum be used to bring the project to a conclusion. Vitellius and his wife, who lived for a short while in the palace in 69, complained that it was unsatisfactory and lacked elegance.[26] During the seventies the shrewd Vespasian and his son Titus turned most of the buildings and the great park over to the people.[27] Domitian (81–96) preferred the Palatine, where he built an entirely new palace, and there the official residence of the emperors remained. In the years 80 and 104, other fires, less disastrous than the one of 64, destroyed part of what yet remained of Nero's work.[28] Immediately after the fire of 104, Trajan's engineers, in order to secure an elevated terrace for his Baths, began to fill the Esquiline wing, by then perhaps the last existing major part of the fabled Domus Aurea.[29] The vestibule with its colossus, the arcades of the portico, and the baths have all disappeared, but paper restorations of the vestibule plan and the plan and elevation of the arcades alongside the Sacra Via have been made on the basis of surviving fragments.[30] Here and there over a vast area there are other identifiable remains of the palace—foundation walls and a cistern or vivarium (fishpond) on the Palatine, a large nymphaeum, later rebuilt, on the Caelian, and, just

24. Nero 31; he corroborates and extends Tacitus' remarks. There are additional references to the Domus Aurea in Pliny (see above, n. 3); for the mechanical devices cf. Seneca, *Letters* 90.15. Suetonius describes a landscape similar to those seen in Roman paintings; see for example M. Rostowzew, "Pompeianische Landschaften und römische Villen," *JDAI, 19* (1904), Taf. 6.1; cf. id. (but spelled Rostovtzeff), "Die hellenistisch-römische Architekturlandschaft," *RM, 26* (1911); A. Maiuri, *Roman Painting* (Geneva, 1953), p. 122; R. Herbig, *Nugae Pompeianorum* (Tübingen, 1962), Taf. 56. For a restoration sketch of the Domus Aurea, see P. MacKendrick, *The Mute Stones Speak* (New York, 1960), Fig. 7.13. For the vestibule, portico, and colossus, see Pliny, *Natural History* 34.45; Martial, *On the Spectacles* 2.2; *SHA, Hadrian* 19.12–13; the articles by Van Deman cited above, nn. 6, 18; Platner-Ashby, pp. 130–31; A. Boëthius, "Et crescunt media pegmata celsa via," *Eranos, 50* (1952), 129–37; Tamm, pp. 102–08.

25. Suetonius, *Nero* 39.2.

26. Suetonius, *Otho* 7.1; Dio Cassius, 64.4.1–2.

27. Martial, *On the Spectacles* 2.

28. For the fire of 80, see above, Chap. 1, n. 36. For that of 104, Bloch, p. 45 and citations.

29. For the date of Trajan's Baths, see Bloch, p. 49; cf. Van Essen (above, n. 22), p. 373. F. Weege, "Das goldene Haus des Nero," *JDAI, 28* (1913), 127–244, discusses both the history of the exploration of the wing and the decoration visible in his time. See also A. Bartoli, "Il ricordo della 'Domus Aurea' nella topografia medievale di Roma," *Reale Accademia dei Lincei, Rendiconti, 18* (1909), 224–30; Van Essen (above, n. 22), pp. 393–98; id., "La découverte du Laocoon," *Mededelingen* (as in n. 22, above), *18.12* (1955), 291–308; cf. *ArchClass, 10* (1958), 199.

30. Van Deman (above, nn. 6, 18), criticized by Tamm, pp. 102–03; see also *Gnomon, 33* (1961), 666.

north of the Temple of Venus and Rome, an arcaded and vaulted structure (Plate 21b) built to buttress the cutting of the Velia, a ridge that connected the Oppian and the northeast slope of the Palatine.[31]

The Esquiline wing, which is not mentioned specifically in the texts, is the most extensive and significant part of the palace known today. It is a fragment, albeit a sizable one, a chain of scores of rooms whose original extended setting is unknown. Located about two hundred meters northeast of the Flavian Amphitheatre, it is embedded in the cellars of Trajan's Baths. The area is shown on Plates 22–24.[32] The broad Viale della Domus Aurea, seen in Plate 22 running eastward free of traffic along the Oppian shoulder of the Esquiline, indicates in a general way the orientation of the south façade of the wing. The basements of the straight and curving portion of the southwest front of Trajan's Baths appear in both plates. The two circular openings in the terrace atop these basements, visible in Plate 22, define the alignment of the palace wing below. The easternmost opening, seen at the top center of the photograph in the middle of a keyhole-shaped clearing, is the oculus of room 27 on the plan (Plate 24). The wing is oriented exactly east and west, and apparently the hillside was cut into to receive its northern rooms and corridors. From the south façade the ground sloped down to the lake, beyond which the grounds and fountains on the Caelian slopes could be seen. The structural fabric of the wing is of concrete throughout, its piers and walls faced with triangular bricks of fair quality that were made by cutting square tiles diagonally.[33] Most of the rooms shown on the plan retain their Neronian vaulting; the remainder were also vaulted originally. Slight modifications were made in the design by Nero's immediate successors, and a number of openings were blocked in Trajan's time.[34] These alterations do not appear on Plate 24, for only the Neronian design will be considered here. The original purpose of all but a very few of the rooms is conjectural.

31. For these remains see Van Essen (above, n. 22); also Lanciani, pp. 361–62; Carettoni (above, n. 5); Lugli, *Roma*, pp. 234, 498; A. M. Colini, "Storia e topografia del Celio nell'antichità," *MemPontAcc*, 7 (1944), 143–47. There are additional references in Platner-Ashby, pp. 166–72; and Nash, *1*, 339. The ancient sources for the Palatine in Nero's time have been collected by G. Lugli, *Fontes ad topographiam veteris urbis Romae pertinentes*, *VIII.1: Regio X (Mons Palatinus)* (Rome, 1960), pp. 165, 172–74. The reservoir known as Sette Sale, 200 m. northeast of the Esquiline wing, is not Neronian but Trajanic; see F. Castagnoli, "Le 'sette sale' cisterna delle Terme di Traiano," *ArchClass*, 8 (1956), 53–55. The flat and featureless northeast side of the structure shown here on Pl. 21 was unfaced; the high ground that it abutted (the Velia ridge) was removed thirty-odd years ago during the construction

of the Via dei Fori Imperiali: see A. Muñoz, *Via dei Monte e Via del Mare* (2nd ed. Rome, 1932), pp. 15, 30, and Tav. XLVI.

32. Of the two plans, that on Pl. 24 is the more accurate; Pl. 23 is included for purposes of orientation.

33. Not surprisingly, they were hastily made; Blake, 2, 51–52.

34. No comprehensive report or study of the intermittent excavation of the wing exists. Part of it has been accessible at least since Renaissance times; for the sporadic clearing of modern times, see the literature cited by Nash, *1*, 339. For the Flavian and Trajanic modifications, see G. Zander, "La Domus Aurea: nuovi problemi architettonici," *BollCentro*, *12* (1958), 47–64. The Trajanic construction is readily identified by its distinctive brickwork.

It is unlikely that there was a major second story of duplicate plan.[35] In the entire area cleared thus far (about 200 by 60 meters, less the five-sided court) only two flights of stairs have been found (by number 34 on Plate 24). These narrow staircases back in a service area presumably gave access to the upper Esquiline north of the wing. Other such stairs may have existed near numbers 9 and 11. The vaults preclude throughout the supposition that there were once wooden stairs (which in any event were presumably prohibited by the new building code). Although the Romans rarely if ever built monumental interior staircases, the total lack of any suitable access anywhere in the remains argues against a congruent upper story. There may perhaps have been *diaetae* (summer houses) above the ground floor, of the kind seen in certain Pompeian paintings and found at Domitian's palace on the Palatine.[36] If so, they were apparently reached only after walking a considerable distance from the principal rooms. That the existing floor functioned as the piano nobile appears to be borne out by the nature of the décor. The rooms along the south façade and the five-sided court were richly decorated with marble paneling, gilded and painted stucco, and perhaps mosaic as well. They were, as the plan makes clear, the more important rooms. If they were in the mere basement or pianterreno of the palace one would expect them to be decorated in the same manner as the subsidiary rooms and service corridors to the north, where in fact the famous wall paintings of the Domus Aurea, mistakenly identified as the principal decoration of the palace, chiefly appear.[37] Also, a full upper story would have cut down the amount of sun reaching the rooms opening upon the court and, depending upon its design, reduced seriously or eliminated the overhead light needed for the octagonal room and its dependencies (number 27 on Plate 24; cf. Plate 32). But none of this proves that there was originally only one story. There may indeed have once been a monumental stairway. Even if there was not, the narrowness and the apparent inadequacy of the original stair systems might be explained in terms of palatine security.[38]

Quite naturally it has been assumed that Severus, Nero's architect, designed the five-sided court as the middle feature of the wing. But it is possible that the central north-

35. Kähler (above, n. 16), p. 103, states that it had a second story, "brighter and certainly more splendid" than the existing one. Boëthius, p. 116, says that "the façade might have had a height of two or even three stories," but seems to find, on pp. 113–15 and especially in n. 30 on p. 113, the existing floor the major one.

36. See below, Chap. 3, n. 59.

37. Kähler (above, n. 16), p. 104, argues that since the paintings do not correspond to the luxurious décor described by Suetonius, this cannot be the piano nobile. But these paintings are located, as Boëthius, p. 116, points out, in the utilitarian parts of the wing. Relationships between décor and architecture are discussed below, in Chap. 8.

38. An examination of the plan (Pl. 24) may suggest that the architect not only provided easy communication and good ventilation, but also concerned himself with security problems. The disposition of openings and passages is such that a minimum of guards would have been required to seal off visually various groups of rooms. There are several locations where a dozen or more rooms could have been kept under surveillance from the four corners of surrounding rectangles of enfilades and corridors. See Blake, 2, Pl. 19, Fig. 3, for an illustration of one of the enfilades.

south axis of the original plan was the same as that of the octagonal room.[39] There are several indications of this, such as the mirror symmetry of rooms 22–23 and 31–30, and the location and orientation of the oblique wall at 35. The octagonal room may have been a central hall or atrium, and the oblique wall the northwest boundary of a lost five-sided court to the east, a duplicate or near duplicate of number 20. During the clearing of the easternmost rooms of the wing the oblique wall was identified as Neronian; unfortunately it is not accessible today.[40] It is almost parallel to the northwest wall of the existing five-sided court, and this, taken together with the symmetry of 22–23 and 31–30, suggests that originally there may have been two polygonal courts in a wing more than three hundred meters long. It would have been natural for Trajan's architect to order the demolition of the eastern portion of such a wing because of its unsightly projection beyond the southeast perimeter wall of the Baths (see Plates 23 and 73).

The fact that the oblique wall at 35 on Plate 24 is not exactly parallel to the northwest wall of the existing five-sided court is no bar to the possibility that there were once two such courts. The plan of the wing shows a number of deviations from precise symmetry, such as the difference in the lengths of the north-south sides of the existing court and the dissimilar angles that these sides form with their adjacent oblique walls. These particular discrepancies arose in part because room 22 was given the same dimensions as room 31 but not the same as room 16, the logical twin of 22 if the existing court was in fact the axial feature of the original plan. This in turn suggests that the octagonal room and its dependencies were built first and were intended to be the central unit of the composition.

A colonnade presumably extended along the south façade. Only two column bases are visible today (at number 1, the location of the present entrance to the wing, on Plate 24).[41] Whether this colonnade was straight in plan or followed the lines of the five-sided court cannot be determined. Possibly a broad intercolumniation or an arcuated entablature emphasized the central feature of the wing. The five-sided court, which could be described as half of an elongated, slightly irregular octagon, has often been compared to representations of buildings and exedrae of apparently trapezoidal or half-hexagonal plan seen in Pompeian wall paintings. The painting most frequently invoked, repro-

---

39. Boëthius, p. 115, compares the plan of the Roman villa at Minori (near Amalfi), which has a central hall and cascade, with the plan of the Domus Aurea wing, where the cascade is in room 26 on Pl. 24 here. He concludes that in view of this "the asymmetrical position of the [Domus Aurea] octagon and its waterfall is rather surprising"; cf. his remark on p. 114 about the center of the façade. For an incomplete plan of the Minori villa, see Schiavo (above, n. 18), p. 130.

40. This identification appears on the 1:200 excavation plan kept at the site, and on the plan published by Zander (above, n. 34), Fig. 5. Presumably the excavators of the 1950s were able to examine the wall when the roofs in this area were restored; their conclusions are accepted here even though the wall appears to have the same orientation as the row of substructure walls built in Trajan's time (see Pl. 23 here; Boëthius, Fig. 53 on p. 98).

41. The bases are illustrated in Blake, 2, Pl. 19, Fig. 2, and Nash, 1, 340; cf. Zander (above, n. 34), Fig. 5; OCD, p. 297. G. Lugli, "Nuove forme dell'architettura romana nell'età dei Flavi," *Atti*, 3, 97, reproduces a plan showing two columns just south of room 22 on Pl. 24 here and in line with those to the west.

duced on Plate 25, is from the house of M. Lucretius Fronto and probably dates from the second quarter of the first century. But this painting is of a relatively small building with projecting wings, not of a grand courtyard recessed in a façade. Nor does it necessarily depict a structure of polygonal plan. It could be that the projecting wings are shown in an approximation of one-point perspective, and that we are entitled to read them as parallel; certainly the pitched-roof structure above and behind the central feature is drawn in this way. The central feature itself is undoubtedly an exedra, but it is apparently semicircular in plan and contains a tempietto or aedicula; in any event it is ambiguously presented.[42] There do not seem to be any five-sided courts in extant pre-Neronian buildings or paintings of buildings, and the idea, used fairly frequently by architects of the High Empire, may have been Severus' own.

Within the plan as we have it there are four major groups of spaces, each clearly defined by a localized, self-contained symmetry generated from the axis of a primary rectangle or polygon. Three of these groups have north-south axes (through numbers 5, 20, and 27 on Plate 24); the fourth is aligned east and west (through numbers 8 and 12). It is apparent that Severus regarded the groups themselves as much more significant than the way in which they were joined together. He seems either to have designed the groups independently, linking them afterward in a rather indifferent way, or to have divided his outline plan into sections which he then developed more or less autonomously. This emphasis upon focally discrete areas, in combination with the use of polygons and curves, inevitably produced a number of irregularly shaped rooms (such as 15, 19, or 32) which the emperor and his court rarely if ever saw. The existence of these spatial by-products argues for Severus' originality, since in an example of a well-established architectural style one would find a more integrated plan, relatively free of such solecisms.[43] In his enthusiasm for evocative and unhackneyed visual and spatial combinations, Severus concentrated first and above all upon the groups, which he subsequently connected with unembarrassed practicality.

What he accomplished in the design of the groups was the elevation of an ancient principle, the Latin devotion to the straightforward equality of right and left, to a more sophisticated level. In plan, he increased the use of axially located curves and various systems of symmetrically balanced spaces; in elevation, curves appeared in every room. On the center line of each group he placed a barrel-vaulted room or rooms, open wide to the main space. The axes of revolution of these vaults unified the groups both in plan and in three dimensions. In the octagonal group the horizontal axis was subordinated to the vertical center line of the octagon, a special case of the architect's devotion to the

---

42. There is a color reproduction in Kähler (above, n. 16), p. 105. Cf. Rostowzew (above, n. 24), pp. 104–06 and Taf. 5.1; P. W. Lehmann, *Roman Wall Paintings from Boscoreale in the Metropolitan Museum of Art* (Cambridge, Mass., 1953), Fig. 58; Boëthius, Fig. 63.

43. Compare for example Rabirius' work of

some twenty-five years later (Pls. 40, 58 here). For somewhat different views of the significance of the oddly shaped Domus Aurea rooms (which were confidently roofed with complex vaults) see Lugli (above, n. 41), p. 96; Ward Perkins (above, n. 6), p. 217; cf. *BC*, 69 (1941), 200–01.

principle of dynamic axiality. The key to this principle was the centered, focal volume, always vaulted, that functioned simultaneously as a visual climax, as the source of power for the projection of the intangible, central line of the composition, and as a terminal receptacle that gave the axis its necessary end or resolution.

On the ground this principle would have been least apparent in the group centered around room 5. But the design of this group is no less instructive than that of the others, for it too shows how far Severus departed from the norms of traditional design. In this case his point of departure was the file of rooms bordering the colonnaded peristyle of the conventional atrium house, a practice he repeated in the rooms centered upon number 3. In the group around 5 he imaginatively altered the shapes of the principal rooms by making free with both curving and rectangular alcoves, as in rooms 6 and 7 (Plates 26 and 27). Every room was opened both to its neighbors and to a colonnade. By doubling files Severus obtained, in one intercommunicating assembly, orientations suitable for changes of season and weather.[44] In the northern file the sequence of shapes (a b a c a b a) and spans (2 1 3 4 3 1 2) accentuated the individuality of the axial room, an effect reinforced by a window in the center of the alcove and two columns set in the wide northern opening.

In the remaining groups the impact of dominant axes was much more pronounced. Their lines of force were skillfully anchored in terminal volumes. The axis of the interior courtyard (8 on Plate 24) was fixed by rooms 3 and 12, by the directional design of the central fountain basin, and by an elaborate spatial coda of diminishing volumes and transverse chambers (12 and environs; 13 and 14). This axis terminated upon a fountain centered against the east wall of an artificial grotto or nymphaeum (room 13).[45] Similarly, vitality and emphasis were given to the center line of the five-sided court by toeing in its sides. These oblique triads of rooms were themselves designed around dominant central volumes, in harmony with Severus' general method (17 and 21).[46]

44. On this subject, see Vitruvius, 6.4; Pliny the Younger, *Letters* 2.17, 5.6; cf. Boëthius, pp. 113–14 and n. 30. Kähler, pp. 107–08, discusses our room 5 and reproduces a detailed plan of rooms 4–6 (Abb. 19 on p. 108). See also below, n. 46.

45. Zander (above, n. 34), Figs. 6–8, gives a detailed plan of the area of our rooms 12 and 13 and restoration views from which post-Neronian construction has been eliminated. For room 13, in which a vault mosaic was recently found, see also F. Sanguinetti, "Lavori recenti nella Domus Aurea," *Palladio*, 7 (1957), 126–27; id., "Il mosaico del ninfeo ed altre recenti scoperte nella Domus Aurea," *BollCentro*, 12 (1958), 34–35. Cf. Tamm, p. 181 and Fig. 87 (= our room 7), where the unity in the designs of the vault, the niche, and the focal statue base, similar to that of

room 13, is clear. The area immediately to the north of room 13 has not yet been cleared.

46. For other buildings with recessed façades bordered by *sellaria* (sitting rooms open to the light and air), see for example A. Maiuri, "Terme di Baia. Scavi, restauri, e lavori di sistemazione," *BdA*, 36 (1951), Figs. 1, 5, 6; Rostovtzeff, *1*, 234; Pl. 58 here. For the *sellaria*, see Pliny, *Natural History* 34.84, 36.111. The problems of interrelationships among sunlight, orientation, and artificial heating in Roman architecture are discussed by E. D. Thatcher, "The Open Rooms of the Terme del Foro at Ostia," *MAAR*, 24 (1956), 168–264; see esp. pp. 177–78, 182–85. Room 21 on Pl. 24 here is said to have been a library; G. de Gregori, "Biblioteche dell'antichità," *Accademie e biblioteche d'Italia*, 11 (1937), 21–23; C. Callmer, "Antike Bibliotheken," *Opus-*

Again the major axis was marked by the largest volume and widest opening of the composition (room 18). The elaborateness of the design of these groups contrasts strongly with the simple shapes of the service areas, where there are no curves in plan and no attempt was made to compose adjoining spaces in any kind of architectural order. These secondary spaces are barrel vaulted, as are the long northern corridors (10 and 33 on Plate 24). The inner rooms were given no natural light, but the long corridors were lit from above by raking windows set into the haunches of their vaults (Plate 28 shows number 33; the bridge carried water to a cascade that terminated in room 26).[47]

Between the eastern long corridor and the south façade is the octagonal salon or atrium. It is unique, the most important Neronian design known, and deserves a full description (Plates 29–34). The central element is basically a pavilion, its lower story perforated by large, almost square openings, the upper partly roofed by a more or less domical vault.[48] Five of the eight openings give onto radially disposed chambers that rise to the height of the central vault. To the south the central volume presumably once connected directly with the colonnade of the façade. It has been suggested that the design was never completed.[49] This is unlikely, for remains of painted stuccoes, of high quality, can be seen in room 25 and elsewhere. Furthermore, both in the radial chambers and in the central area there is clear evidence, in the form of bedding cement carrying pottery shims and negative impressions of thin rectangular shapes, that the vertical surfaces were originally revetted with marbles. Mosaic may have been applied to the central vault, as it was in room 13.[50] There is no connection whatever with the rooms to the north; the opening in room 26 was not for communication but for the cascade (Plates 29 and 30). All of the rooms are brilliantly lit, not only by the broad oculus or opaion, but also by an ingenious clearstory system inserted between the extrados or exterior surface of the vault and the upper parts of the radial chambers (Plates 31–33).

The unusual shape of the central vault is due not only to its octagonal impost but also to the difference in length between its rise and its radius. It rises from a level above the middle of the vertical center line of the pavilion; the Vitruvian rule for a centralized building, calling for a vault diameter equal to the building's height (see Figure 1, e,

Arch, 3 (1944), 160–61; Blake, 2, 50 (where the room is mislocated). The room seems rather too exposed to be a library and two of the recesses that supposedly held book cabinets (those flanking the axial niche; they are not shown here) are awkwardly placed for this purpose.

47. These windows also may argue against the original existence of a second story. For the bridge and cascade, see A. Terenzio in *BC*, 66 (1938), 244.

48. The octagon is discussed by G. Giovannoni, "La cupola della *Domus Aurea* neroniana in Roma," *Atti*, *1*, 3–6. For a view of the superstruc-

ture before restoration, see C. Montani, "La 'Domus Aurea' di Nerone," *Capitolium*, 9 (1933), 98; for the discovery of the room, see the *Nuova antologia* for June 16, 1914, pp. 655–61.

49. By Platner-Ashby, p. 170; and by Blake, 2, 51.

50. See above, n. 45, and below, Chap. 8, n. 8. Vault mosaics seem to have been in use at least as early as Augustan times (Boëthius, p. 102); see H. Stern, "Origine et débuts de la mosaïque murale," *Etudes d'archéologie classique*, 2 (1959), 101–21.

p. 16), was not followed.[51] Because of this and because of the proportionately wide oculus, the intrados or interior surface of the vault bears scant relationship to a true hemisphere. Rather it is composed of two horizontal zones. The lower consists of eight panels that rise from the straight sides of the octagon and turn inward as they narrow in width. At a level about two thirds of the way up the height of the vault, the converging lines between these panels die out. At that level the radial and horizontal curves become more like functions of circles, and the shape of the upper zone very roughly approximates part of an annular vault (Figure 1, f).[52] The wooden formwork was by no means geometrically exact. The remains of a thick coat of cement indicate that originally the transitions between the eight panels, and between the lower and upper zones, would have been less abrupt than those visible in the bare structural fabric today. It is likely that Severus first conceived of the design in abstract terms, but whatever his method of work, we have the clearest proof of his willingness to break with convention, to experiment with new ideas. Given our present knowledge of Roman architecture, it is correct to regard the octagonal atrium as an original design, a conclusion valid also for its structural system.

The central canopy of concrete is set within the upper part of a vertical octagonal cage or frame (Plate 31). The highest level is that of an octagonal opening, placed around and above the extrados of the vault (Plate 32). This octagon is vertically congruent with that defined by the eight elaborately sectioned angle-piers below. The piers, which rise through the whole structure, have inward extensions that narrow in horizontal section to meet the angles between the sloping flat panels that form the extrados of the central vault. These inward extensions, by loading the vault vertically and buttressing it radially, increase the stability of the structure. They do not, however, rise so high as to load the upper, more stable zone of the vault or interfere with the clearstory lighting. At the top of the structure the piers are connected by the inner, higher ends of raking segmental vaults that admit light directly to the radial spaces (Plates 31, 32, and 33b). The entire fabric is ingeniously locked in a structural unity, made rigid and stable not only by concrete, but also by the multiple bearing relationships among the various parts. This can be seen for example in the design of the raking clearstory vaults. The idea of raking vaults was not new, for they appear in various pre-Neronian buildings. But at the Domus Aurea they spring from horizontal barrel vaults below and abut against the piers above, helping to stabilize the pier system with a continuous and reciprocal sequence of pressures. The compression factor is impressively utilized throughout, as in the ring of bricks laid vertically to form the horizontal arch or compression ring that defines the oculus and helps to stabilize the upper zone, or in the multiplicity of structural functions performed so economically by the piers.

---

51. Vitruvius, 5.10.5; cf. 4.8.3. Equality of height and diameter is common in round buildings of the Empire. Here the rise equals 15 Roman feet, and the radius of the circumscribed circle 25.

52. The intrados of the vault is not tangent to the lower plane of the oculus, but meets the ring while still rising, and this tends to emphasize the proportionately great width of the oculus.

That the spaces on seven sides of the octagon were embedded in the extending fabric of the wing does not detract from the structural subtlety of the octagon proper. Its design shows that Severus understood perfectly well how to combine vaults in complex relationships and that his builders, presumably headed by the engineer Celer, knew how to solve the novel problems presented by the actual erection of the building and were able to insure its stability while the concrete and mortar were curing. Structurally, the chief importance of the octagon lies in the abandonment of the simple engineering of parallel vaulting systems where loads are taken 180° opposed, as for example in rooms 4–7 on Plate 24, and in the extraordinary economy of structural means. Severus and Celer plunged into the intricacies of structure and practical building inherent in a design generated from a vertical center line, intricacies they compounded by multiplying, interconnecting, and lighting adjoining spaces.

The architectural effects of this fourth major group are as original and important as the structure that serves them. The flux of space is extraordinary. Each radial chamber ends in a niche-form, and rooms 25 and 28 have transverse extensions as well.[53] The generously scaled openings between the angle-piers bring the radial spaces into unhindered connection with the central volume. This continuity of space extends around and behind the piers, through the southeast and southwest triangular spaces, out into the façade corridors, and up and down through the oculus. About two dozen openings perforate the ideal figures of the design at ground level. Only the walls of the radial chambers limit vision and motion, though it should be remembered that these were once gilded and colored and lit directly during much of the daytime, and that room 26 was rendered somewhat ambiguous in form by its water-show. The dome appears to rest upon thin verticals, and as a result the visual weight of its mass is much reduced.[54] Even those effects derived from basic architectural shapes cannot be shown properly in photographs, for vaulted buildings, especially those of centralized plan, resist the camera. The principal impression today is that of an aerated container, a space expanded by angled mirrors and dominated by the unfeatured circle of the great roof-window overhead. Because of the clearstory the radial chambers are almost as well lit as the central space, whose expansive openness they echo. On most days the lighting is needless to say dramatic: a large, luminous disc slips slowly across the forms (Plate 34).

In short, Severus conceived of a highly sophisticated design, one with quite original effects. In its conception one may perhaps see dimly the ancient atrium with its doorless extensions or *alae*. What is perhaps most remarkable about the octagon is the thorough-

---

53. The extensions and niches of rooms 25 and 28 are two stories high; both stories are open to the groin-vaulted spaces they face (see Pls. 29, 34). The stories are divided by shelves or balconies of masonry supported on vaults that are quasi-elliptical in elevation. These vaults have been restored in part, but their curves are clearly readable in the original portions.

54. The flat arches of brick that appear between the piers on Pls. 29 and 34 are not primary bearing structures, for the loads are taken above the piers chiefly by the concrete cores behind the bricks. The small triangular spaces behind the piers were roofed at about the height of the spring of the dome with shallow false vaults of wood and stucco.

ness with which its complicated structure was subordinated to spatial and visual objectives. Severus and Celer aimed at assembling architectural volumes in a new way and were able to solve the novel, difficult structural problems this involved. All unnecessary solids were eliminated and the remainder handled with an extremely sure touch. The result was a progressive yet completed architectural statement for which, as far as can be ascertained, there was no prototype. If in addition "it is hardly an exaggeration to say that the whole subsequent history of European architectural thought hangs upon this historic event,"[55] then what survives of Nero's great palace is crucial evidence indeed.

THE ROMAN ARCHITECTURAL REVOLUTION

When Nero dedicated his Golden House he said that at last he was beginning to be housed like a human being.[56] Had a man such as Vespasian said this it would have been intended ironically. But Nero, innocent of irony, referred to what he was convinced was his due and proper frame. His fatuous remark shows that as emperor he thought he deserved a setting, an architectural pomp, that set him well apart from all other men. The Romans, excluding the aristocracy, may have approved of this. For a time Nero was not unpopular, and toward the end of his reign he attempted by many devices to preserve his precarious ascendancy and exalt himself. One of these was to commission an extraordinary palace, and for the history of architecture the results were momentous.

In the broadest terms, the Esquiline wing was the first true successor of the forms and technology found in the great vaulted concrete structures of the second and early first centuries B.C. Experiments with vaulted shapes and centralized buildings did not cease during the intervening period, though these were of secondary importance in an age dominated by more traditional designs. At some point the promise inherent in the earlier work began to be recognized and developed by gifted architects. If a greater part of the palaces built by the earlier Julio-Claudians were available, perhaps the process could be more fully documented. But as the matter now stands the Esquiline wing is the earliest monumental design based upon an artistic and architectural, as opposed to a more purely technological, understanding and use of vaulted spaces.[57] It seems unlikely that a major vaulted building of earlier date will be recovered that will show so clearly the application of a governing body of new stylistic principles.

The probability that the Roman revolution in architecture was in fact first expressed in the Domus Aurea is improved by our knowledge of the conditions under which the palace was conceived and built. By the accident of the great fire, and probably it was an accident, the palaces of Tiberius and Caligula had been rendered uninhabitable and the grand design of the Domus Transitoria wrecked. An unprecedented opportunity arose

---

55. Ward Perkins (above, n. 6), p. 219.

56. See p. 32, above.

57. On this crucial distinction, so little discussed, see the works cited above, Chap. 1, n. 42; Lugli (above, n. 41), p. 96; J. B. Ward Perkins, "Roman Concrete and Roman Palaces," *The Listener, 56* (1956), 701-03; id., "The Italian Element in Late Roman and Early Medieval Architecture," *Proceedings of the British Academy, 33* (1947), 168–69.

that worked upon the imaginations of the emperor and his architects: an expanded, huge site suddenly appeared in the heart of Rome. Nero had the resources to take advantage of this opportunity and, what is more to the point, the desire to build an unusual and impressive palace, a desire he had already demonstrated by sponsoring the Domus Transitoria. Had Nero been a conservative the results surely would have been different, but instead he was an enthusiast, who wanted not only to belong to the world of art but also to surround himself with a visible proclamation of what he considered to be his power and his majesty. This helped to make it possible for the elements of vaulted architecture to be fashioned into a stylistic unity. It was under these unusual conditions, in an atmosphere little hindered by tradition, that Severus worked creatively.

Nero was devoted to novelty. He allied himself with progressive artistic ideas. Unstable and insecure, he craved the life he thought artists lived and the kind of recognition they received, and rejected as stuffy conventions the traditional, dignified attitudes of the past. He wished to appear in an unrivaled setting; both the texts and the Esquiline wing bear this out clearly. In the Domus Aurea a theatre of architecture and color was created for him, a novelty then but a substantial architectural achievement when seen in historical perspective. The ancient rectilinear architecture of verticals and horizontals was too limited, too familiar in its repertory of formal expression to satisfy the requirements of the new Neronian order. Instead his architect made brilliant use of the morphology and sensory impact of vaulted space, creating a unique dwelling for a despot of cosmic pretentions.

Nero's taste for novelty was served by mechanical devices built into the rooms of his palaces. Seneca, referring either to the Domus Transitoria or the Domus Aurea, speaks of a dining room "with a ceiling of movable parts so cleverly constructed that it presents one pattern after another, changing as often as the courses." Suetonius knew of dining halls in the Domus Aurea with ceilings of ivory panels that opened to sprinkle blossoms on the guests below. Both speak of pipes from which perfumes were sprayed upon the guests from above.[58] The mechanism briefly mentioned by Suetonius, that "revolved day and night, like the heavens" (see p. 32), has become involved in a debate about the symbolism of the palace. It could have been, so the argument runs, an element of a deliberate policy that made the Domus Aurea the home of a new Sun God, the divinizing abode of the emperor as a cosmocrator. The evidence for this is somewhat thin, and the idea has not been generally accepted.[59] The importance of these devices for the study of

58. These texts are cited above, n. 24; cf. Pliny, Natural History 36.117. For the mechanical background of these devices, and for the automata so popular with the Romans, see A. G. Drachmann, *The Mechanical Technology of Greek and Roman Antiquity* (Copenhagen, 1963); M. R. Cohen and I. E. Drabkin, *A Source Book in Greek Science* (Cambridge, Mass., 1958), pp. 326–51; cf. *Speculum*, 29 (1954), 478–80.

59. The hypothesis was advanced by H. P. L'Orange in "Domus Aurea: der Sonnenpalast," *Symbolae Osloenses*, 11 (1942), 68–100, in *Apotheosis in Ancient Portraiture* (Oslo, 1947), pp. 57–63, and in *Studies on the Iconography of Cosmic Kingship* (Oslo, 1953), pp. 28–31. It has been criticized by A. Boëthius, "Nero's Golden House," *Eranos*, 44 (1946), 442–59; J. M. C. Toynbee, in *JRS*, 38 (1948), 161; Charlesworth

the architecture is that they show the strength of the desire to surprise and astonish. Like them, the architecture was intended to be unusual and remarkable.

Though in the modern literature the Domus Aurea as a whole is repeatedly and quite rightly called a villa, it is important to point out that the architecture of the Esquiline wing was not simply derived and enlarged from existing villa designs.[60] The huge park, with its lake, pavilions, and factitious rusticity, was of course modeled upon the great villas of the late Republic and early Empire. But at least some of the major buildings within the park were not, as the Esquiline wing and the fragment seen in Plate 21b make clear. It has been suggested that the importance of the wing rests chiefly upon the bold introduction of polygonal shapes, and that this was done in order to avoid the monotony inherent in building so many rooms.[61] It is true that the long history of Roman fascination with combinations of polygonal, curving, and rectangular plans began here, but this was by no means the most revolutionary aspect of the Domus Aurea. The design of the groups and their rooms, according to the principles of dynamic axiality, was of far greater consequence.

The imperial ambition, taste for novelty, and resources; the fire; the ripeness of the new technology; the atmosphere of social change—these were the external forces that gave shape, at the center of the Roman world, to the new style.[62] Its artistic essence lay in novel attitudes toward the construction of interior spaces and toward their multiplication and interpenetration. The plain boxlike rooms that confronted traditional atria and peristyles became modulated, carefully proportioned interiors. From larger spaces these rooms drew off volumes that were localized and focused internally. Roofed by high concave surfaces, these new interiors expressed an architectonic vitality, a kind of kinetic presence, unknown in the static world of flat-roofed rooms of rectangular plan.

Thus what had been unintegrated parts of buildings, bounded by flat planes and spatially quite inert, became participating elements of a style, rooms that demanded the architect's attention. In the Esquiline wing most of these rooms were high and narrow,

---

(above, n. 1), pp. 71–72; and Ward Perkins (above, n. 6), pp. 210–12. See also C. C. Vermeule, in *AJA*, 59 (1955), 258–60; S. Eriksson, "Wochentagsgötter, Mond, und Tierkreis," *Studia graeca et latina gotoburgensia*, 3 (1956), 120–22; and Boëthius, pp. 117–26. Ward Perkins points out (p. 211) that such mechanisms were fairly well known before Nero's time, and remarks that although Varro's famous aviary (*On Farming* 4.5.9) rotated in some such way, "nobody has ever suggested that the birds within it had ideas above their station." Any investigation of the symbolism of the Domus Aurea and its decoration must make use of K. Lehmann, "The Dome of Heaven," *AB*, 27 (1945), 1–27. With respect to the mechanism proper, there is no need to think that only the roof revolved, as do the Loeb trans-

lator of Suetonius (2, 36, n. c) and Ward Perkins, p. 211; cf. Boëthius, p. 117 and p. 118, n. 25; and Eriksson, p. 118, n. 2. The most recent discussion is by P. Mingazzini, "Tentativo recostruzione grafica della 'coenatio rotunda' della Domus Aurea," *Quaderni*, 31–48 (1961; = *Fest. Fasolo*), 21–26.

60. See to the contrary the implications of Boëthius, Chap. 4; Kähler (above, n. 16), p. 104; *JRS*, 52 (1962), 253; *OCD*, p. 780; and numerous other similar statements in the modern literature.

61. Lugli (above, n. 41), p. 96.

62. The career of Severus, and relationships between structure and design, will be discussed in later chapters.

and all were dominated by the curves of vaults and the ambiguous effect, with regard to the relationship of load and support, caused by the tangency of vaults and verticals. A kind of architectural apostrophe resulted. As the parallel supports rose to become turning, concave surfaces above, the standing human form and the space within its reach were implied in heroic outline. It is this outline that was the essence of the Roman architectural revolution. The rise of the body and the stretch of its limbs were projected in a strong, simplified form. Even if the observer did not take this in consciously, he could not be entirely free from its implications, just as he could not be entirely free from response to the human measure inherent in the upwardness of a standing column. In Roman vaulted architecture he was embraced and directed by forms in a manner unknown in rectilinear architecture. He was inside, or required to come inside, the limits of his choice of path and view rigorously preordained by the architect. It is no accident that the vaulted style has been used ever since Nero's time to evoke, deliberately or not, these impressions and effects. Reactions to them partly result from conditioning, but in part they are induced directly by the forms themselves.

The celebrated description of human proportions by Vitruvius, used to illustrate his discussion of symmetrical temple design, is directly relevant here.[63] He describes the circle and square ideally defined by the outstretched limbs of the body, a relationship of shapes very similar to the architectural solution he prescribes for vaulted circular buildings.[64] Vaulted spaces also conform to this order. Pavements can be equated with the base of Vitruvius' square, impost levels of vaults with the maximum horizontal reach of the hands, and vault sections with the arc produced when the arms are swung up overhead (compare Figure 4, Plate 34, and Figure 1, p. 16). In the new Roman architecture, man was shown his path and place by vaults overhead as much as by plans and openings. In a rectilinear architectural space all positions on the pavement are in this sense the same because the vertical distance from pavement to ceiling is constant. In a vaulted space an invisible central line or point is impressed upon the senses. It is Severus' command of this effect and his consistent application of it, in contrast to isolated or unintegrated earlier examples, that makes his design so revolutionary. And in addition to being a highly original designer he was also an extremely competent professional in the technical sense, for a concept such as the octagonal atrium could never have been realized unless every detail of the design had been thought completely through in advance.

Of the other examples from the same period none approaches the Esquiline wing in either complexity or stylistic homogeneity. It is possible that Severus stood in the same relationship to the new architecture of the Roman Empire as Brunelleschi stood to that of the Renaissance. Yet there is evidence from the late Julio-Claudian and early Flavian years of other experiments with radically new assemblies of form that were conceived

63. Vitruvius, 3.1.
64. Vitruvius, 4.8.3, 5.10.5. For the Vitruvian figure and architecture, see also R. Wittkower, *Architectural Principles in the Age of Humanism* (3rd ed. London, 1962), pp. 13–16 and Pls. 2–4; cf. E. Panofsky, *Meaning in the Visual Arts* (New York, 1955), p. 68, n. 19.

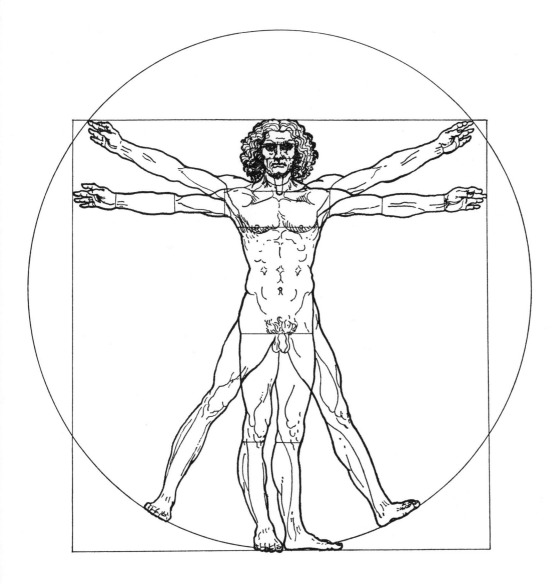

4. Leonardo's Vitruvian figure

in much the same spirit as the Domus Aurea wing. In the Suburban Baths at Herculaneum an example of this fresh architectural vision has recently been recovered (Plates 35 and 36).[65] It is a kind of atrium, more or less square in plan and proportionately quite high. Four columns carry two stories of arches, which in turn carry walls that intersect the roof level to outline a rectangular skylight. The high, narrow spaces between the uppermost zone of arches and the perimeter walls are roofed with barrel vaults and these are cut by raking windows taking light from the central opening. This complex centralized design, a cage and ambulatory composed of columns, arches, and vaults all lit from overhead, records the same kind of enthusiasm for spatial composition that produced the octagonal atrium and the rotunda of the Domus Transitoria.

Extending the search to other baths and building types of Latium and Campania reveals nothing of importance that cannot be seen in the Domus Aurea.[66] Our point of departure, the assumption that the Esquiline wing was the first major structure in the new style, appears to have been a reasonable one. At this distance the matter cannot be settled absolutely. But Severus' buildings, if they did not themselves revolutionize Roman architecture, were in the van of that revolution. The new style, distinguished by its vaulted interiors and their particular effects upon the senses, was quickly adopted at home and in the provinces. Soon it became as much a part of the imagery of the Empire as the eagle or the majestic Corinthian temple front.

65. A. Maiuri, *Ercolano. I nuovi scavi* (*1927–1958*), *I* (Rome, 1958), 154–57 and Figs. 114, 119–21, 2, Tav. XVI; A. W. Van Buren, "Some Campanian Revelations," *Archaeology,* 12 (1959), 240–41. The structure is late Neronian or early Flavian. The construction of its columns, which were built up of masonry and stuccoed over like much late work at Herculaneum and Pompeii, is another sign of changing architectural practices.

66. Items of interest: the villa at Minori (above, n. 18), where there is, among other features, a perspective staircase; the magnificent spacious nymphaeum, with rectangular skylights and mosaic niches, under the Parco di Traiano in Rome, which may have been a part of the Domus Aurea and which, though noticed by A. Muñoz, *Il Parco di Traiano e la sistemazione delle terme imperiale* (Rome, 1936), pp. 13, 21, has not as far as I know ever been published; and the evolution in the first century of the multistoried insula made of concrete, its chief apartments vaulted, for which see Boëthius, pp. 146–63 and citations, and A. R. A. van Aken, *Nieuwe Wegen in de romeinische Woningbouw van Sulla tot Domitians* (Utrecht, 1943).

III

DOMITIAN'S PALACE

THE SHREWD and humane Vespasian (reigned 69–79) avoided the Domus Aurea and the Palatine. He threw Nero's vast park open to the people and together with his sons built the colossal Amphitheatre and the Baths of Titus within its walls. He himself usually lived in a mansion in the Gardens of Sallust on the Pincian Hill, unguarded and accessible to all.[1] Titus (79–81) seems to have lived in the Domus Tiberiana in greater state. In the year 80 a fire swept part or all of the Palatine, but the extent of the damage is not recorded.[2] Domitian (81–96), toward the middle of his reign, began an entirely new palace just south of the Tiberiana, a design as central as any to all Roman imperial architecture. Domitian's palace became the permanent residence of the emperors, for centuries the very center of the far-flung imperial machine. It was still in use when Narses, the conqueror of the Goths, died there in 571, and repairs were made to it a century later by a Byzantine officer, Plato.[3]

The very importance of the palace precluded its preservation. The Palatine, symbol of Rome's greatest age, attracted a long succession of occupants and builders. As a result its rim and slopes are encrusted with vaulted substructures, fallen parts of walls and vaults, and rooms of unknown date and use. Many unstudied pieces of architectural sculpture lie about, and it will be a long time before the complicated architectural history of the hill is properly understood. Yet fortunately some rooms and much of the ground plan of Domitian's palace have survived. One of the most important contributions to the study of these remains is Bloch's. He includes them in his analysis of imperial brick stamps, and shows that the traditionally accepted date is correct: the buildings by the

1. Dio Cassius, 65.10.4. The choice of dwelling and the use of the Domus Aurea (Martial, *On the Spectacles* 2) were part of the Flavian policy of depreciating the name and memory of Nero; cf. Tacitus, *Annals* 15.52.

2. Titus: the meaning of Pliny, *Natural History* 36.37 is unclear; cf. C. C. Van Essen, "La découverte du Laocoon," *Mededelingen der Koninklijke Nederlandse Akademie van Wetenschappen,*

Afd. Letterkunde, n.s. *18.12* (1955), 291–308. For the fire of 80, see above, Chap. 1, n. 36; Blake 2, 100, 115.

3. The texts and inscriptions relating to the imperial period after Domitian can be found in G. Lugli, *Fontes ad topographiam veteris urbis Romae pertinentes. VIII.1: Regio X (Mons Palatinus)* (Rome, 1960), pp. 190–212.

Forum and the public and private sections of the palace on the hill above are all of Domitian's time. The palace proper was completed before the year 92; the Forum-level buildings and the stadium-shaped Hippodromos were built during the last years of his reign, about 93–96.[4]

The palace was never replaced, although it was enlarged by the emperor Septimius Severus (193–211). In subsequent centuries parts of it were occupied by religious groups, and in more recent times various Renaissance and modern families built there, attracted by the prospect of living upon the magnificent site of the Palace of the Caesars.[5] Prior to 1800 the ruins were often exploited by unprincipled owners and profiteering excavators. Marbles were carried off in vast quantities, and exquisite paintings and stuccoes, to judge their quality from eighteenth-century descriptions and drawings, were destroyed or abandoned to the weather. The buildings that were erected sometimes incorporated surviving elements of Domitian's work. This, together with the durability of Roman construction and the increase in official interest during the last century, explains why the palace has not been lost entirely. More or less systematic excavation began about a hundred years ago, and by the mid-1930s the site had been substantially cleared.[6]

4. Bloch, pp. 29, 36, 348; cf. S. Gsell, *Essai sur le règne de l'empereur Domitien* (Paris, 1893), pp. 96–100.

5. The Severan enlargement: Lugli, *Roma*, pp. 517–21; V. Massaccesi, "I restauri di Settimio Severo e Caracalla agli edifici palatini," *BC*, 67 (1939), 130–33. Only the lost Septizodium has been studied; cf. *FUR*, 1, 66–67, 2, Tav. XVII. The post-imperial history of the Palatine: G. Ferrari, *Early Roman Monasteries* (Vatican City, 1957; = *Studi di antichità cristiana*, 23), pp. 88–91; G. Carettoni, "Il Palatino nel medioevo," *Studi romani*, 9 (1961), 508–18; P. Romanelli, "Horti Palatini Farnesiorum," *Studi romani*, 8 (1960), 661–72; C. Huelsen, *The Forum and the Palatine* (New York, 1928), pp. 77–80 and Pls. 63–64. The last post-antique building to be removed from the palace site was the Villa Mills, a Gothic revival structure demolished in the present century; A. Bartoli, "La Villa Mills," *Rassegna contemporanea*, 1 (1908), which I have not seen. A view of the villa appears in *NS* (1929), Fig. 2 on p. 5; cf. H. V. Morton, *A Traveller in Rome* (London, 1957), pp. 417–20. In the area shown here on Pl. 40 only two post-antique buildings remain, the Antiquario and a small galleried tower of the Farnese.

6. Destruction and losses: Lanciani, pp. 157–67; Platner-Ashby, pp. 194–95; T. Ashby, "Drawings of Ancient Paintings in English Collections," *PBSR*, 7 (1914), 1–62; P. Verzone, "La demolizione dei palazzi imperiali di Roma e Ravenna . . . ," *Fest. Friedrich Gerke* (Baden-Baden, 1962), pp. 77–80. Part of the damage was of course due to natural causes; see Suetonius, *Domitian* 15.2; R. Lanciani, "Segni di terremoti negli edifici di Roma antica," *BC*, 45 (1917), 3–28; H. Finsen, *Domus Flavia sur le Palatin: Aula Regia-Basilica* (Copenhagen, 1962; = *Analecta romana instituti danici II supplementum*), p. 8. For the excavations, see F. Bianchini, *De palazzo de' Cesari. Opera postuma* (Verona, 1738); G. A. Guattani, *Monumenti antichi inediti . . . per l'anno MDCCLXXXV* (Rome, 1785), passim (the excavations of Rancoureil); id., *Roma descritta ed illustrata*, 1 (Rome, 1805), 45–56; P. Rosa, "Scavi del Palatino," *Annali dell'Instituto di corrispondenza archeologica*, 37 (1865), 346–67; id., *Relazione . . . sulla scoperta archeologiche della città e provincia di Roma negli anni 1871–72* (Rome, 1873), pp. 75–80; R. Lanciani, "Il 'Palazzo Maggiore' nei secoli XVI–XVIII," *RM*, 9 (1894), 1–36; C. Huelsen, "Untersuchungen zur Topographie des Palatins," *RM*, 10 (1895), 252–76; R. Lanciani, *Storia degli scavi*, 2 (1903), 34–51; G. Boni, "Recent Discoveries on the Palatine Hill, Rome," *JRS*, 3 (1913), 242–52; Huelsen (above, n. 5), pp. 78–80; A. Bartoli, "Scavi del Palatino (Domus Augustana) 1926–28," *NS* (1929), 3–29; id., *Il*

The perimeter of the principal buildings is clear in the main. The setting appears on Plate 37, a view from the east that does not show the precipitousness of the Palatine slopes. At the upper left is the Circus Maximus, and at the bottom center the Arch of Constantine and part of the rim of the Flavian Amphitheatre can be seen. Domitian's palace, flanked on the left by its long sunken court or Hippodromos, lies toward the Circus. At the upper right-hand corner of the Plate, a little to the right of the round church of S. Teodoro, are the high walls of the Domitianic buildings at the level of the Forum. The planted area between them and the palace proper is the site of the Domus Tiberiana (compare Plate 16). Figure 5 outlines schematically the two chief levels and four grand divisions of the new palace, as seen from the south.[7] The divisions are as follows:

A. The Domus Flavia, or official palace.

B. The upper level of the Domus Augustana, or private palace, on the same level as the Domus Flavia.

C. The lower level of the Domus Augustana. Its principal rooms lay beside a sunken court open to the sky. A broad, shallow exedra formed the façade of the Domus Augustana toward the Circus Maximus.

D. The Hippodromos, on the same level as C.

These names are traditional and convenient, though probably the entire palace should be called the Domus Augustana.[8] Exclusive of any additional stories, the four divisions covered about forty thousand square meters.

While this main palace was being built, the Palatine was refaced with numerous rooms and balconies, its approaches were reordered, and the halls at the level of the Forum were erected. The Domus Tiberiana received a new façade on the side overlooking the Forum (see Plate 15). A multistoried ramp was built to connect the Tiberiana with the new halls below (Plate 38).[9] The northeastern approach to the new palace, dignified by the erection of the arches of Titus and Domitian, was improved by paving a broad space (the Area Palatina) at the top of the ascent before the northeast front of the Domus Flavia. A spur was brought from the Claudian aqueduct to the top of the hill (Plate 16, and Plate 37, far left), and reservoirs were provided. Libraries were constructed (Plate 39, and

valore storico delle recenti scoperte al Palatino e al Foro (Pavia, 1932), which I have not seen; id., *Domus Augustana* (Rome, 1938); id., "Tracce di culti orientale sul Palatino imperiale," *Rend-PontAcc*, 29 (1956–57), 17; G. Carettoni, "Excavations and Discoveries in the Forum Romanum and on the Palatine during the Last Fifty Years," *JRS*, 50 (1960), 192–203.

7. For a diagrammatic transverse section showing the relative levels, see Huelsen (above, n. 5), Fig. 27.

8. As in *CIL*, 15.7246, for example. The spelling is sometimes Augustiana, as in *CIL*, 15.1860.

9. This has also been attributed to Hadrian, but more likely it was built by Domitian and restored or added to by Hadrian: Bloch, pp. 32–34; Tamm, p. 79.

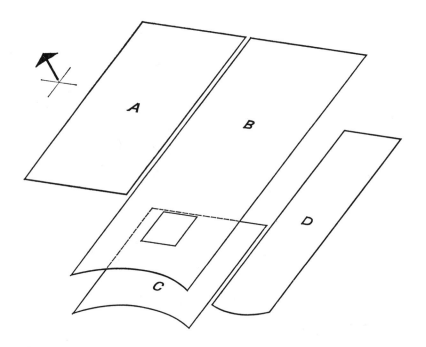

5. *Diagram of the levels and divisions of Domitian's palace*

Plate 40, nos. 15 and 16).[10] Numerous other remains, structurally identical with known Domitianic work, show that the emperor ordered in addition to his new palace the renovation of the rest of the hill.[11]

The palace is mentioned by several ancient writers, though there is nothing as extensive as Tacitus or Suetonius on the Domus Aurea. There is a highly rhetorical but valuable description by Statius of one of the state halls in the Domus Flavia, and Martial gives the name of the architect, Rabirius. The names of a few palace rooms appear in various texts.[12] Fragments or drawings of fragments of the Severan marble plan of Rome exist that record part of the palace.[13] There is a coin of Domitian's that shows one of the façades, and there are the all-important stamps upon a portion of the bricks used to face the structural concrete.[14] These are the sources available to the historian other than the ruins themselves. The remains of the Domus Augustana were cleared only thirty years ago, and the results have not yet been published.[15] The Domus Flavia has been known much longer and has received most of the attention, scant enough in view of its importance, that the site has attracted. Like the imperial baths, the grand suburban villas, and many other major Roman monuments, Domitian's splendid palace remains a challenge to the student of architecture.[16]

10. For the aqueduct and the reservoirs, see T. Ashby, *The Aqueducts of Ancient Rome* (Oxford, 1935), pp. 249–51; and Lanciani, pp. 169, 185–87. For the libraries, which appear on a fragment of the marble plan, see *FUR*, 1, 78, 2, Tav. XXII. See also Suetonius, *Domitian* 20; G. de Gregori, "Biblioteche dell'antichità," *Accademie e biblioteche d'Italia*, 11 (1937), 13–15; C. Callmer, "Antike Bibliotheken," *OpusArch*, 3 (1944), 157–59; Nash, 1, 204–05.

11. See Nash, 1, 369; and Tamm, pp. 76–78. The baths, mentioned by Suetonius, *Domitian* 16, may have been to the southeast of the Hippodromos, where the remains of those built by Septimius Severus now stand; see Blake, 2, 123. No kitchens have been found; Tamm, p. 195, points out that portable ovens were common (see Seneca, *Letters* 78.23). The location of the aula Adonis, mentioned by Philostratus, *Life of Apollonius of Tyana* 7.32, is unknown. The so-called Pedagogium, below the palace to the southwest, was built for Domitian: Bloch, p. 29; Nash, 1, 316, 335–37.

12. The texts are given by Lugli (above, n. 3), pp. 181–90. Statius and Martial are quoted below, pp. 61–62.

13. *FUR*, 1, 44, 77–78, 243 (fragment 20), also Fig. 10 on Tav. C; 2, Tav. III, XXII. G. B. de Rossi, *Piante iconografiche e prospettiche di Roma anteriori al secolo XVI* (Rome, 1879), pp.

123–25, describes an extraordinary map, perhaps of the ninth century, upon which the names of the major divisions of the palace are inscribed; cf. Lanciani, p. 170.

14. For the brick stamps, see above, n. 4. For the coin, see the discussion and citations below on pp. 55–56, and Pl. 51.

15. Bartoli, the excavator, published short notices (see above, n. 6). He died in 1957, but since then his *Curia Senatus* (Rome, 1963) has appeared; perhaps his work at the palace will also be published. The lack of reports and studies explains the brevity of the standard descriptions: Huelsen (above, n. 5), pp. 66–76; Platner-Ashby, pp. 158–66; Lugli, *Roma*, pp. 486–92, 509–16 (the only one that includes the area uncovered by Bartoli). Blake, 2, 115–24, describes the structure and materials of the remains. Bartoli's masons necessarily refaced some of the walls (see Pls. 64, 65) and strengthened other parts of the Domus Augustana. On the need for preservation, and the difficulties preservation and restoration can cause, see Meiggs, pp. 5–6.

16. Recent publications show that the vital architectural problems connected with the palace have not been abandoned: restoration drawings by Löwe in E. Lundberg, *Arkitekturens Formspråk*, 2 (Stockholm, 1951), 177–79; E. Nash, "Der Wohnpalast der Cäsaren auf dem Palatin," *Antike Kunst*, 1 (1958), 24–29; id., "Suggerimenti in-

THE DOMUS FLAVIA

Rabirius began by making nearly half of the Palatine summit into the vast platforms of Figure 5. Earlier buildings were leveled or filled in; where necessary the living rock was cut to required shapes; and the natural contours of the hill, already partly obliterated, disappeared. The plan and air view of Plates 40 and 41 show what is known today of the Domus Flavia and the upper level of the Domus Augustana. The north colonnades (1–2–3 on the plan) and those inside room 4 are conjectural, and the buttresses along the northwest flank have been eliminated from the plan.[17] The Domus Flavia was connected with the older palace to the north by a cryptoporticus entered from a staircase southwest of the apse of 4. The more official approach seems to have been from the Sacra Via by the Arch of Titus, up the Palatine slope along the Clivus Palatinus and under the Arch of Domitian, then across the open Area Palatina to the entrance of the Domus Flavia.[18] It is reasonable to assume that a branch of the Clivus Palatinus brought the emperor directly to the entrance to the Domus Augustana (numbers 17 and 18 on Plate 40; the details in this section are unknown).

In plan the Domus Flavia was oblong and tripartite. Its major axes were those of a huge peristyle (Plate 40, number 10, and Plate 42, a view from the west). The first of the three major divisions consisted of a basilica, a vast reception hall or aula regia, and a relatively small side chamber (Plate 40, numbers 4, 5, and 6).[19] The second was composed of a series of curvilinear and rectangular chambers, the peristyle itself, and rooms leading to the duplicate peristyle of the Domus Augustana upper level (7 through 11). The final division was centered upon a huge triclinium flanked by elaborate nymphaea (12, 13, and 14). The major axis of the Domus Flavia, broken visually only by the apse of the aula regia, marks a progression from public to relatively more private spaces, an ancient tradition in house-planning. There are modifications here for imperial use, but the derivation of the general scheme is apparent.[20] The oblique position of the two libraries

torno ed alcuni problemi topografici del Foro e del Palatino," *ArchClass*, *11* (1959), 227–36; M. Petrignani, "La Domus Flavia," *BollCentro*, *16* (1960), 57–75; Finsen (above, n. 6); and Tamm, esp. pp. 206–16. During 1963, in the area southwest of no. 12 on Pl. 40, excavation was begun again.

17. The buttresses can be seen in Pl. 41. For the colonnades, see Rosa's article of 1865 (above, n. 6), p. 352; Lanciani, p. 161; Platner-Ashby, p. 604; Tamm, pp. 208, 214. For the relatively few alterations made by later emperors, see above, n. 5; Bartoli's article of 1929 (above, n. 6); Bloch, pp. 210–18; G. Carettoni, "Costruzioni sotto l'angolo sud-orientale della Domus Flavia," *NS*, *3* (1949), 48–79; and the plan in G. Giovannoni, "La Basilica dei Flavi sul Palatino," *Atti, 3,* 87.

18. For the approaches to the Palatine and the Area Palatina, see Aulus Gellius, 20.1.1; Platner-Ashby, pp. 50, 124, 126; Nash, *1*, 252, 257; Tamm, pp. 207–08.

19. Bianchini (above, n. 6), seems to have been the first to apply these names to specific rooms. The names are taken from such texts as Martial, *Epigrams* 8.36 (the aula), and Plutarch, *Poplicola* 15.5 (the basilica). Bianchini called room 6 the imperial lararium, but it may just as well have been a vestibule or robing room.

20. For discussions of this point, see A. Boëthius, "The Reception Halls of the Roman Emperors," *Annual of the British School at Athens, 46* (1951), 25–31; Petrignani (above, n. 16), pp. 57–60.

(15 and 16), like that of the wall northwest of 12, probably reflects an adjustment to the orientation of earlier buildings nearby.

The basilica has attracted more attention than any other part of the palace, partly because it seems to prefigure the forms of the Early Christian basilica (Plate 43, a view from the southwest, and Figure 6, B, p. 58).[21] A difficulty is that the square column footings and the marble transenna are dubious modern restorations. The column seen in Plate 43 is apparently original, but it is out of scale in its present position.[22] It is reasonable to suppose that the building did originally have internal colonnades, but the restorations usually offered, of the kind shown in Plate 44, can be accepted only in a general way. The design was derived both from the traditional public basilica and the apsidal cult building found near the Porta Maggiore in Rome.[23] The long architectural life of this kind of building as a proper setting for a supposedly all-powerful figure or the image of a godhead was guaranteed by its presence here at the center of the Roman world. In this sense as well as in more purely architectural terms the basilica of the Domus Flavia was related to the basic form of the Early Christian basilica. In both, the visual principle was the same: a longitudinal axis, reinforced by colonnades, was caught and focused by the apse and its half-dome. At the Domus Flavia this effect may have been emphasized by two columns set just inside the ends of the apse (see Plates 40 and 45).

In the aula regia also the emperor was displayed in an apse fixed upon the main axis. Embassies and audiences saluted him amid unsurpassed splendor in a place calculated to dramatize Rome's claim to majesty and unity. To the effects of the apse and vault Rabirius added those of the richly articulated walls with which he wrapped the great space below the vault. Their surfaces were sheathed, like the pavement, with colored and patterned marbles, and their substance was treated as sculptured architecture. Aediculae or temple-front forms stood in recesses that alternated with low spur walls carrying columns. The columns were ornamental rather than structural, for they carried only ressauts (lengths of entablature) projecting transversely into the central space. Plate 45, a restoration made in 1900 and frequently reproduced, conveys some sense of the appearance of this great hall.[24] In plan the wall recesses were alternately curved and

21. The involvement of the Palatine design in the question of the origins of the Christian basilica can be traced in Rivoira (who championed specifically Roman origins for Early Christian architecture), pp. 106–07; in Boëthius (above, n. 20); and in J. B. Ward Perkins, "Constantine and the Origins of the Christian Basilica," *PBSR*, 22 (1954), 68–89. For the building proper, see Giovannoni (above, n. 17); and Petrignani (above, n. 16), pp. 62–65. There is a building of basilican form, with aisles and an alcove-niche, at Hadrian's villa; Giovannoni, Tav. XI; S. Aurigemma, *Villa Adriana* (Rome, 1961), Fig. 175;

Tamm, p. 168 and Fig. 79.

22. See above, n. 17.

23. See the discussion by Boëthius (above, n. 20). Rabirius may also have drawn upon oriental sources, as Boëthius implies.

24. This drawing should of course be used with great caution. In the light of what has been learned about Roman architecture since 1900 the palace appears drab, and the triclinium and its dependencies have a rather stale neo-imperial flavor. Yet as far as I know it is the only attempt at a perspective restoration of the Flavia. Compare the restorations cited below, n. 34.

rectangular. There was no prospect of large flat planes, and the division into scenic units, each as large as a modest temple façade, emphasized the vastness of the whole. Stylistically the aula walls were much enlarged versions of the baroque nymphaeum of Nero's Domus Transitoria (Figure 2, p. 22, and Plate 21a). The basic idea was apparently Hellenistic, but Rabirius and the other designers for whom his name must stand gave it Roman scale and richness.[25] The temple front, the monumental colonnade, the vault, and the modulated wall screened by columns, entablatures, and pediments were the four primary elements of Roman imperial architecture.

The peristyle that separated the aula regia from the triclinium was apparently called Sicilia (Plate 42).[26] Its columns and pavement were of colored marbles, and the walls may have been faced with the highly polished Cappadocian stone that Suetonius mentions when he says that Domitian took exercise in such a place so that he could see the reflection of whatever was taking place behind his back.[27] Inside the rectangle formed by the colonnade there was a second rectangular feature, a low wall scalloped and rabbeted along its inside surface. Within that rectangle an octagonal labyrinth with channels for some kind of water show was constructed.[28]

The walls of the rooms northwest of the peristyle have been preserved up to a height of two or three meters (Plate 46, a view from the southwest). There Rabirius let his compasses swing freely.[29] The central feature was an octagonal room whose diagonal sides were expanded by semicircular niches. Surely it was covered with a paneled dome rising to an oculus, though the model fails to show this (Plate 16). The four openings on the major axes indicate that the room was a vestibule. Two of the openings led to symmetrical groups of elegantly curving volumes that show how enthusiastically Rabirius had taken up the new style. From the octagonal vestibule the distant, unroofed fountains could be seen through the windows in the intermediate walls (Plate 40, numbers 7 and 9, and Plate 46). But in order to reach them one was forced away from these axial lines of sight through small intermediate spaces, another example of the Roman interest in creating inviting vistas that could not be experienced on foot.[30] Outside the vestibule two white marble voussoirs with curving soffits and concentrically curving moldings on their exterior vertical surfaces can be seen. They appear to be Domitianic,

25. The very difficult but important problem of the relationships between Hellenistic and Roman imperial design goes beyond the limits of this chapter. There is a discussion of the aula interior by P. H. von Blanckenhagen, *Flavische Architektur und Ihre Dekoration* (Berlin, 1940), pp. 64–76; cf. his "Elemente der römischen Kunst am Beispiel des flavischen Stils," *Das neue Bild der Antike*, 2 (Leipzig, 1942), 310–41. For the aula marbles, see Bianchini (above, n. 6), Chap. 5; Guattani's book of 1805 (above, n. 6), p. 55; Lanciani, pp. 159–63.

26. *SHA, Pertinax* 11.6; cf. Lugli, *Roma*, pp. 490–91.

27. Suetonius, *Domitian* 14.4; for the stone, Pliny, *Natural History* 36.193.

28. There is a detailed measured plan in Petrignani (above, n. 16), Fig. 5. The restoration was questioned by Platner-Ashby, p. 160, n. 1.

29. Kähler's discussion (pp. 103–04) of this group of rooms is excellent.

30. Compare the approaches to the Domus Transitoria rotunda, Fig. 3, p. 22.

and may have belonged to an arcuated entablature that marked this entrance to the palace.

Just to the south, a step higher than the paving level of the peristyle portico, lay the state triclinium, probably called the cenatio Iovis (Plate 40, number 13).[31] It was separated from the peristyle only by a colonnade, and its axis, precisely aligned with that of the aula regia, terminated in a shallow but wide apse. The thick side walls were pierced by doors and by generously scaled windows through which the flanking fountains could be seen and the freshened air circulated (Plate 47, seen from the east, and Plate 48, from the west). In effect each side of the hall was composed of six powerful piers.[32] The interior was animated by a geometric paving of colored marbles that echoed the compass-work plans of the rooms to the north, and by the sight and sound of the fountains. Columns centered in front of the piers obviated any dominant impression of prismatic shapes. Again the position of the emperor was emphasized and given a distinctive frame by an apse centered under the unifying vault (Plate 49, seen from the southeast). The forms and colors of the recesses and aediculae in the aula regia were replaced here by views into the fountain rooms on either side.[33] The western nymphaeum has been partially restored (Plates 48 and 50). On the side away from the triclinium it was bounded by a curving wall recessed with deep and shallow niches. The fountain itself was in the form of a tiered island of elliptical shape rising from a pool. The periphery of the pool was niched and indented, and the highest tier of the island was scalloped with vertical grooves and cylindrical indentations. Presumably these fountain-rooms were unroofed.

In addition to the model and the drawing, seen in Plates 16 and 45, several other restorations of the Domus Flavia have been suggested.[34] The evidence on the site is insufficient for more than broadly generalized results. However, a coin of 95 or 96, a sestertius struck during Domitian's seventeenth consulate, may show the great northeast façade (Plate 51). It has been suggested that it shows a temple, or the huge hall at

31. The name appears in *SHA, Pertinax* 11.6.

32. Each of the eight central piers originally measured exactly 6 by 10 Roman feet, exclusive of the thickness of facing materials.

33. Symmetrically balanced vistas terminating in fountains seen through column screens or windows appear also in rooms 7–9 on Pl. 40, in rooms 11–13 on Pl. 58, and in the building of trefoil plan at Hadrian's Villa; Kähler, Taf. 9–10; and J. H. Chillman, "The Casino of the Semicircular Arcades at Hadrian's Villa," *MAAR*, 4 (1924), 103–20. Beside the south wall of room 12 on Pl. 40, an open shaft was found that reaches down to or close to the level of the Circus Maximus, some 35 m. below. This was once thought to be a Neronian or Domitianic cutting, perhaps made to aid in the hoisting of building materials; Boni

(above, n. 6), p. 251; cf. Platner-Ashby, p. 195. I am told by the present superintendent that the shaft was cut for the Farnese.

34. See for example K. Lange, *Haus und Halle, Studien zur Geschichte des antiken Wohnhauses und der Basilika* (Leipzig, 1885), pp. 374–75; J. Bühlmann, "Der Palast der Flavier auf dem Palatin in Rom," *Zeitschrift für Geschichte der Architektur*, 1 (1907–08), 113–34; Huelsen (above, n. 5), Figs. 29–30 and Pls. 48 and 58; W. J. Anderson et al., *The Architecture of Ancient Rome* (2nd ed. London, 1927), p. 136 and Pl. LXXV; B. Fletcher and R. A. Cordingly, *A History of Architecture on the Comparative Method* (17th ed. London, 1961), pp. 232, 232B; F. E. Brown, *Roman Architecture* (New York, 1961), Pls. 82, 83.

Forum level (Plate 52 and Figure 6, A, p. 58).[35] But Roman temples did not take this elaborate, staged form, and the Forum hall did not have three doors nor even an axial door.[36] No building of Domitian's but the palace seems to fit. Coins were struck showing the new Amphitheatre and the Stadium in the Campus Martius, and it is reasonable to suppose that the end of Rabirius' labors was celebrated in the same way. The date in this respect is exactly right. The lack of a column screen around the lowest story is not crucial. The colonnade shown on Plate 40 is traditionally supposed to have existed. Alternatively, the designer of the coin could have suppressed the colonnade in order to emphasize the entrances to the state halls. It may be that the broad projection of the main palace platform that exists in front of the aula regia (see Plates 40 and 41) carried the massive arched feature seen on the coin. The awesome height of the palace is mentioned more than once in the texts,[37] and the representation appears to be more or less in scale. The use of perspective hints at the architect's touch. High in the *fastigium* or gable there appears to be a figure with outstretched arms, perhaps Jupiter *tonans*, the thunderer, with whom Domitian so arrogantly identified himself.

THE ROOFING OF THE STATE HALLS

In the modern literature no consensus has been reached about the nature of the roofs of the four great halls. It has been suggested that the larger one at the level of the Forum, which for convenience will be called the vestibule, was either left unfinished or roofed with a barrel vault (Plate 52).[38] The basilica has usually been given a barrel vault, as in Plate 44, though a wooden roof has also been proposed.[39] The aula regia has been variously restored as an open court lined with porticoes and as a hall covered either with a groin vault or a barrel vault (Plate 45).[40] For the triclinium both wooden and vaulted roofs have been proposed.[41] Aside from their technological interest, these questions are fundamental to the study and definition of imperial style, and it is neces-

35. A temple: H. Mattingly and E. A. Sydenham, *Roman Imperial Coinage*, 2 (London, 1926), 205. The vestibule: Nash, *1*, 371, and his articles cited above, n. 16.

36. Cf. Tamm, pp. 79–82, 214.

37. See the passages quoted below, pp. 61–62.

38. R. Delbrueck, "Der Südostbau am Forum Romanum," *JDAI*, 36 (1921), 8–33; cf. G. Lugli, "Aedes Caesarum in Palatino e Templum Novum Divi Augusti," *BC*, 69 (1941), 29–36; id., *Roma*, pp. 187–91. This may be the building referred to by Aulus Gellius, 4.1.1, 19.13.1.

39. A. Boëthius, "Roman Architecture from Its Classicistic to Its Late Imperial Phase," *Göteborgs Högskolas Årsskrift*, 47.8 (1941), 13, n. 2,

thinks wooden roofs are the only possible solution for the palace halls; he is followed by Finsen (above, n. 6), p. 25. But cf. Bloch, p. 218; G. Rodenwaldt in *CAH*, *11*, 280; Petrignani (above, n. 16), p. 63.

40. See the various restorations cited above, n. 34. For the porticoed open court, see Giovannoni (above, n. 17), drawing on p. 91; Blake, 2, 119. When Crema, Fig. 364, reproduced Giovannoni's drawing, the portion showing the aula porticoes was omitted. For the barrel vault see also G. Lugli, "Nuove forme dell'architettura romana nell'età dei Flavi," *Atti*, 3, 96.

41. Above, n. 34; cf. Blake, 2, 120; Tamm, p. 192.

sary to give them attention. The point of view taken here is that all four halls were barrel vaulted in concrete. Vaulting in cut stone at this time and place can be eliminated, and false vaults hung from timber framing, described by Vitruvius and used in the porch of the Pantheon, could be employed only over comparatively minor spans.[42]

None of the existing walls shows any sign of the spring of a vault, and all are faced with even courses of ancient brickwork. Because Roman facings always end where vaults begin in order to avoid discontinuity in the structural concrete, the maximum wall heights given in the table below represent the minimum visual springing heights for the vaults. No pieces of vaulting remain on the ground, but this is not in any way conclusive. The concrete used by Rabirius in his vaults was lightweight and friable in contrast to that used for foundations and walls, and once broken into smallish pieces it crumbles with astonishing rapidity.[43] The lack of positive physical evidence is countered by the report of Bianchini, who early in the eighteenth century saw pieces of fallen vaulting on the pavement of the aula regia. His testimony in general has been called into question because he so enthusiastically looted the Domus Flavia for his employer, the Duke of Parma, who then owned the site, but it is not necessary to doubt his accuracy because of his cupidity.[44] By then the fallen vault, except for a few large pieces, had either decomposed or had been broken up and carted off for fertilizer or rubblework.

Figure 6 gives the plans of the four halls to a common scale. Their major interior dimensions are as follows:

| | Width | Length | Maximum height of remaining faced walls |
	METERS/ROMAN FEET	METERS/ROMAN FEET	METERS
Vestibule	32.50/110	23.50/ 80	ca. 27.50
Basilica	20.19/ 68	30.30/103	16.25
Aula regia	31.44/107	32.10/109	8.90
Triclinium	29.05/ 99	31.64/107	ca. 3.50

These figures by no means set all the terms of the problem. The widths are not the true spans, which were in fact considerably smaller. In this kind of construction the lower rise of the vault is actually part of the wall fabric.[45] Large Roman vaulted buildings were stabilized in part by masses of masonry added to the structure above the visual springing level of the vaults (see for example Plates 93 and 105), and this was a major factor in bringing the thrusts of the vaults into equilibrium. The end walls of the build-

42. Vitruvius, 7.3.1–3. The Pantheon porch is described below, pp. 97–98.

43. During the winter and spring of 1963 the mortar of concrete chunks newly fallen from the vault of room 5 on Pl. 58 disintegrated into granules and powder (visible in Pl. 59) in the space of two or three months.

44. Bianchini (above, n. 6), pp. 48–50. To-gether with his editors (his book appeared post-humously), Bianchini is bitterly castigated by Guattani and Lanciani; see Lanciani, pp. 162–63; cf. Huelsen (above, n. 5), p. 79.

45. See F. E. Kidder and H. Parker, *Architects' and Builders' Handbook* (18th ed. New York, 1956), p. 1549.

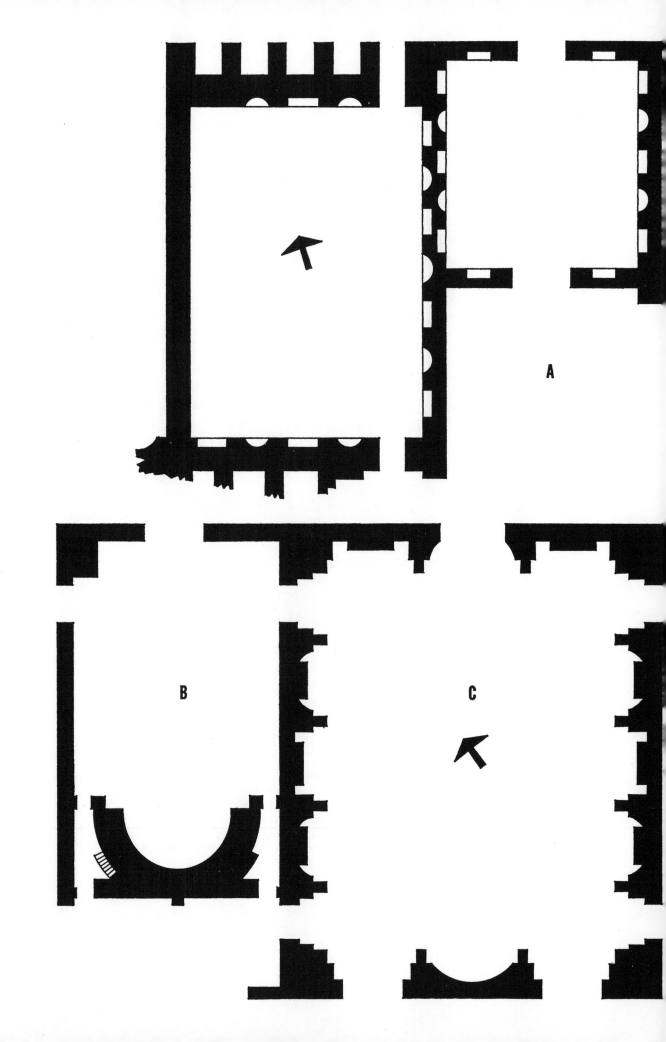

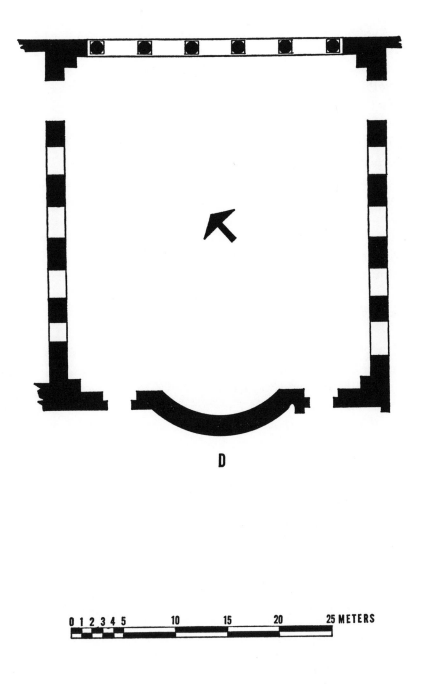

D

0 1 2 3 4 5   10   15   20   25 METERS

6. *Plans of the state halls of Domitian's palace, to a common scale.*
A. Forum-level vestibule. B. Basilica. C. Aula Regia. D. Triclinium.

ings may have acted as ties, and the long horizontal zones of the side walls as beams; both could have assisted in the resolution of the forces inherent in vaulting.[46]

There are other points to be considered. The vestibule, whose vault curved across the long dimension, has immense spur buttresses, each some sixty square Roman feet in horizontal section, spaced along its shorter sides (Plate 52). The aula regia and the triclinium both are flanked by structures bearing against them. Above numbers 4, 6, 12, and 14 on Plate 40 there could have been additional structural supports—arches or spur walls—for the central vaults. The basilica, with its shorter span, was originally built without buttresses on its northwest side. They were added soon afterward, and it is difficult to explain them as supports needed for a timber roof. The extremely robust foundations of all these buildings are made of a marvelously dense concrete containing only the heaviest aggregate. These foundations are wider than the walls but structurally continuous with them, and because of this it is possible that the theoretical lines of thrust resolution passed somewhat outside the actual external wall surfaces. In other words the broad foundations, structurally inseparable from the walls, could have given the buildings a wider reach for statical resolution than that defined by the side walls themselves. It is evident that the interior widths of the buildings and the sizes of their walls and piers are by no means the only important factors.

In every case, as Figure 6 shows, the corners of these buildings were massively reinforced or were buttressed by adjoining constructions, or both. This technique is seen in Plate 53, which shows the inner side of the north pier of the aula regia, and in Plate 54, a detail of the northwest face of the same pier seen from inside the basilica. There is hardly a major barrel-vaulted hall in extant Roman architecture that lacks this corner reinforcement, but it is missing in the great timber-roofed structures whose plans can be recovered. Plate 54 also shows that the aula was constructed before the basilica, for the basilica wall abuts upon the brick facing of the aula. To the right of the plate a down-slot for roof drainage pipes appears, its filling partly lost. If the aula had been an open court, this slot would have been unnecessary. Figure 6, B, shows the reinforcement

46. It is possible to propose hypothetical structural solutions for a range of building heights and vault profiles and then to test their stability by applying an analytical system such as the force polygon. The weights and bearing strengths of Roman concretes are sufficiently well known; see A. Terenzio, "La restauration du Panthéon de Rome," *Mouseion*, 6 (1932), 52–57. But because of our ignorance of other variables that might have influenced the matter decisively one way or the other the results are inconclusive. For examples of structural analyses of ancient buildings, see G. B. Milani, *L'ossatura murale: studio statico-costruttive ed estetico-proporzionale degli organismo architettonici*, 1 (Turin, 1920); and Giovannoni, passim. Giovannoni, who like Rivoira

did so much to stimulate the modern study of imperial architecture, devoted himself chiefly to the structural aspects of the subject; see also his "La tecnica costruttiva e l'impero di Roma," *L'Ingegnere*, 12 (1938), 299–307, and his chapter entitled "Building and Engineering" in *The Legacy of Ancient Rome*, ed. C. Bailey (Oxford, 1951), pp. 429–74. The conjectural restoration of vaults over ancient and early medieval buildings in cases where there is no positive archaeological evidence for vaults has recently been discussed by G. Forsyth, "Architectural Notes on a Trip through Cilicia," *Dumbarton Oaks Papers*, 11 (1957), 225, 230–31; by F. Rakob in *Gnomon*, 33 (1961), 243–50; and by Finsen (above, n. 6), pp. 24–25.

added to the north corner of the basilica, probably at the same time as the buttresses mentioned above. The angle piers of the triclinium can be seen in Plates 48 and 49. These
corner reinforcements indicate that the extremities of the vaults were thickened in order
to obtain greater strength and stability, and the later additions to the basilica probably
record the consequences of Rabirius' daring and audacity.

There are at least four texts that bear upon the matter. Rivoira suggested that an isolated sentence in a spare fourth-century chronicle, about a temple built in Domitian's
time without wood, refers to the vestibule.[47] When Rivoira wrote, the vestibule was
thought to be the Temple of Augustus, but even so his suggestion is relevant. The sentence is unambiguous about materials—*Domitianus templum sine lignorum admixtione
construxit*—and the building in question must have been vaulted. By the fourth century
the word "templum" was rather loosely used and could mean not only a sacred place for
religious ceremony, but also the cult building (properly the *aedes*) beside it. On occasion it was also used to mean a monumental structure with no specific religious associations.[48] The building in the chronicle cannot be identified positively, but since Roman
temples were traditionally wooden roofed it may have been one of the palace halls.
It is worth recalling in this connection that Nerva, Domitian's successor, thought that
the palace was a suitable temple to the whole commonwealth.[49] With its intimation of
spectacular innovation, the chronicler's sentence fits Rabirius' work well.

The second text is a poem written about 93 or 94 by Statius. He had attended an imperial banquet in the palace and in expressing his thanks to Domitian described one of
the state halls:

> I think I recline with Jupiter in mid-heaven. . . . An edifice august, huge; mag-
> nificent not with a hundred columns but rather enough to support heaven and the
> gods were Atlas eased of his burden. The neighboring house of the Thunderer [the
> temple of Jupiter on the Capitoline] views it with awe, and the powers rejoice
> that you have a like abode . . . the vast expanse of the building, and the reach of
> the far-flung hall, more unhampered than a plain, embracing beneath its shelter
> a vast expanse of air, and only lesser than its lord; he fills the house, and gladdens
> it with his mighty spirit. Libyan mountain and gleaming Illian stone are rivals
> there, and much Syenite and Chian and the marble that vies with the gray-green
> sea; and Luna also, but only for the columns' weight. The view travels far upward,
> the tired vision scarcely reaches the summit, and you would think that it was the
> golden ceiling of the sky. Here . . . Caesar has bidden the Roman elders, and the
> ranks of equites recline together at a thousand tables . . .[50]

The building has usually been identified as the triclinium, but the emphasis upon the

47. Rivoira, p. 110. The sentence is found in
Hieronymus' version of Eusebius' *Chronicle*, ed.
J. K. Fotheringham (London, 1922), p. 272, ll.
11–12.

48. These variant meanings appear quite early.

See for example Cicero, *On the Laws* 2.8.21;
Virgil, *Aeneid* 4.457; Livy, 1.30, 23.10.5, 26.31.-
11.

49. Pliny the Younger, *Panegyric* 47.4.

50. *Silvae* 4.2.

great number of columns may mean that Statius is speaking of the aula regia.[51] The word vault does not appear; instead poetical equivalents such as heaven and the ceiling of the sky are used. The space of the hall is said to be embraced beneath its roof, and one's view travels far upward (*longa supra species*) to the golden ceiling. Surely Statius' words and phrases are meant to invoke an image of a curving roof, an imitation of the arc of the sky.

The third passage is in an epigram by Martial, Statius' contemporary. In it he advises Domitian to laugh at the wonders of the pyramids, for

> now barbaric Memphis speaks not of her Eastern work. How small a part of the aula on the Palatine would Egypt's toil achieve! Nothing so grand sees the light of day in all the world. You would believe the seven hills rose up all together; Ossa with Thessalian Pelion atop was not so high. It pierces heaven, and hidden amid the lustrous stars its peak echoes sunlit to the thunder in the cloud below . . . And yet, Augustus, this palace that with its pinnacle touches the stars, though level with heaven, is less than its lord.[52]

Thus the aula was roofed, for Martial speaks of its peak (*apex*), which he equates with the highest point or pinnacle (*vertex*) of the palace.

The fourth text is another epigram by Martial, who seems to have been an acquaintance or friend of Rabirius. It was written about 92 or 93 and is relevant because of the words Martial uses to describe Rabirius' gifts.

> Heaven with its stars you, Rabirius, have conceived in your pious soul, who by wondrous art build the mansion of the Palatine. If Pisa [Olympia] shall be set to give Phidian Jove a temple worthy of him, she will beg of our Thunderer these hands of yours.[53]

Again the metaphor is celestial (*astra polumque*); again the Thunderer appears, but this time ambiguously, for the Roman Jupiter is not mentioned. Statius and Martial think of the palace in the same way. Though they flatter Domitian by addressing him as semidivine and thus have to describe his surroundings in inflated phrases, their real feelings show through. To them the new palace was a towering, awe-inspiring building, unique and truly marvelous, where Rabirius had wrought an image of heaven's vault.

The alternatives to vaulting that have been proposed are not convincing. If any or all of these buildings were open to the air, why were such high and massive walls constructed? A timber span for the basilica could have been built, as the wooden roof set

---

51. So Tamm, p. 213. Rivoira, p. 102, takes it for granted that Statius is speaking of a vaulted roof; E. B. Smith, *Architectural Symbolism of Imperial Rome and the Middle Ages* (Princeton, 1956), p. 148, thinks it was domical.

52. *Epigrams* 8.36.

53. *Epigrams* 7.56; cf. Rivoira, p. 89, n. 2. For the other references to the palace in Martial and Statius, see Bourne, p. 65, item 11. For the dates of these passages, see *OCD*, pp. 542, 858; Lugli (above, n. 3), pp. 181–83.

over the somewhat wider nave of the Basilica Ulpia about twenty years later shows. Timber roof frames for the three other halls would have been difficult to manage, though perhaps not beyond the capacities of Roman engineers.[54] The nature of the ground plans, the testimony of Bianchini, and the sense of the texts, when taken all together, suggest strongly that the great halls were vaulted, though they do not prove it conclusively. What is perhaps more telling is that open courts or flat wooden roofs are contrary to all stylistic probabilities. They would have seriously depreciated or canceled entirely the visual and other sensory effects that the plans indicate so obviously. Spaces in Roman imperial architecture that are known to have been roofed and that have curves in plan were usually vaulted. If these four grand rooms had wooden roofs or were open to the sky the probabilities that can be deduced from a study of imperial style clearly would have been violated. Almost certainly Rabirius, "by wondrous art," raised great vaults over the palace halls of state.

THE DOMUS AUGUSTANA

The area covered by the two levels of the Domus Augustana was about twice that of the platform of the Domus Flavia. There were three peristyles instead of one, and comparatively small rooms were arranged around them in groups. With the exception of a few parts the upper level is poorly preserved and must be studied chiefly in plan, but the lower level is nearly complete. The importance of the Domus Augustana lies both in the design of the rooms themselves and the unique ways in which they were grouped, for here Rabirius repeatedly departed from anything seen in the Esquiline wing of the Domus Aurea or known from previous Roman buildings. The Augustana is as important as the Flavia to the history of imperial architecture, and more important than a number of better-known buildings. It was the mysterious and unseen inner center of the monarchy, the private dwelling place of a man who expected to be addressed as *dominus et deus*.[55]

At number 17 on Plate 40 there was a huge propylon carried on immense columns. The large peristyle (18) seems to have been subdivided originally by additional colonnades; together these features formed a reception area for the emperor and his im-

---

54. The timber spans of the Ulpia, the Constantinian basilica at Trier, and Old S. Peter's were of the order of 24–26 m. Pliny had seen a wooden beam 120 Roman feet long (40.67 m.) and 2 feet thick; *Natural History* 16.200.

55. He seems to have insisted on it: Martial, *Epigrams* 5.8, 10.73; Suetonius, *Domitian* 13.2; Dio Cassius, 67.4.7; Hieronymus' Eusebius (see above, n. 47), p. 272, ll. 13–14; Aurelius Victor, *Lives of the Emperors* 11; cf. Tacitus, *Histories* 3.74; and F. Sauter, *Der römische Kaiserkult bei Martial und Statius* (Stuttgart-Berlin, 1934), pp.

40–54. The narrow doorways and the enfilades of openings again suggest security precautions; see Pl. 58, nos. 9 and 10, and Pl. 64, for example. Dr. Richard Frank informs me that Nero's barbarian bodyguard (the *custodes corporis*), dispersed in 68, was apparently revived by Domitian, who entrusted his safety to his freedmen; their captain, Parthenius, wore a general's arms. Pliny the Younger, *Panegyric* 49, refers to Domitian's love of solitude and speaks of the palace as a fortified citadel.

mediate suite. The next peristyle (19), its shafts of colored marble, was a replica of the one in the Domus Flavia.[56] Within it was a low, scalloped wall, elliptically shaped on the northeast side, surrounding the sunken pavement of a pool (Plate 55, a view from the northeast). The peristyle was joined to the Domus Flavia by room 11 and its dependencies. On the side toward the Hippodromos (number 28 on Plate 40) there was a double-apsed chamber flanked by niched cubicles reminiscent of certain Domus Aurea rooms (27). To the southeast this apartment gave onto the upper level of the arcaded or colonnaded portico that once encircled the Hippodromos (compare Plate 72).

To the south and west there was an extraordinary mosaic of chambers of rectilinear and curving plan arranged symmetrically around the long axis of the palace (numbers 20–26 on Plate 40). The entrance was marked by a curved vestibule with columns in antis (number 20 and Plate 55). Enough of the walls has been preserved to show that these rooms were quite high in proportion to their width (Plate 56, seen from the west). They were not carried up to an even level but were given various heights in order to light their interiors.[57] Here Rabirius utterly abandoned the vocabulary of the past. He led the visitor through bewildering chains of spaces that now expanded, then contracted. He played with his vaulted containers in an almost frivolous way as if he wished to show what new kinds of spatial and visual sensations were possible. Successive changes of direction were required even along the main axis of rooms 20–22, where the effects would have been rather similar to those of rooms 7–9 in the Domus Flavia. By coming from varying heights and directions, the light emphasized the various shapes of the rooms. Few walls were allowed the ancient dignity of plain, unmodulated wall surfaces (Plate 57, where the northwest walls of room 24 and its neighbor appear in the upper half of the photograph, which was taken from the south). This extraordinary three-dimensional

56. For this area of the upper level, of which so little remains, see Bartoli's publications (above, n. 6); Lugli, *Roma*, pp. 512–14; Blake, 2, 121. The plans of the Domus Augustana reproduced here on Pls. 40 and 58 were based upon the remains and upon unpublished drawings presumably made by Bartoli or his staff and generously released to me by Professors Pietro Romanelli and Frank E. Brown. The few previous plans will be found in Palladio (Zorzi, p. 99 and Figs. 242–43); G. B. Piranesi, *Le antichità romane*, 2 (two plans); Guattani's book of 1805 (above, n. 6), Pls. 8–9; Bartoli's article of 1929 (above, n. 6), pp. 12–13; and Lundberg (above, n. 16), p. 178. Panvinius also knew something of the plan; see Bianchini (above, n. 6), Tav. I. Rooms shown without doors on Pls. 40 and 58 here are either unexcavated or inaccessible for other reasons.

57. See Löwe's pioneering elevations and sections in Lundberg (above, n. 16), pp. 177–79. In this area, white marble roof slabs in the shape of great tiles, and white marble antefixes with reliefs of eagles, are still preserved. It is just possible that some of these rooms were given over to the Household administration. The rectangular wall niches might have contained the compartmented wooden frames commonly used for the storage of scrolls and records; see Pl. 57, showing the room just northeast of room 24, and Pl. 72, where room 26 can be seen. For a sense of the size and complexity of the civil and palatine staffs, see O. Hirschfeld, *Die kaiserlichen Verwaltungsbeamten von Augustus bis auf Diocletian* (2nd ed. Berlin, 1905), pp. 137–39; and A. H. M. Jones, "The Roman Civil Service (Clerical and Sub-Clerical Grades)," *JRS*, 39 (1949), 38–55; cf. Lugli (above, n. 3), pp. 212–21; and Suetonius, *Domitian* 13.3. Where did this army of subordinates live and work? On the other hand these rooms may have been where Domitian whiled away the hours, catching flies; Suetonius, *Domitian* 3.1; Pliny, *Panegyric* 49.

play, this box of novelties, included two small and very elegant octagonal nymphaea, their sides expanded by alternating semicircular and rectangular niches almost as wide as the sides of the octagons and arranged in two stories (the rooms beside 24 and 25 on Plate 40).[58] In designs such as these, architectural form cannot be read as structure. Sheathed in marble and perhaps encrusted above with mosaic, their spaces would have seemed to be hollowed out of the masonry and their supports conjured away.

Beyond this point the remains of the upper-level rooms are largely inaccessible. Just behind the broad exedra that faces the Circus Maximus there are remains of identical *diaetae* or summer houses (29 and 30). Their plans were preserved on a fragment of the marble plan of Rome now lost but known through a Renaissance drawing.[59] Formed in semicircles, with radially extended pavilions or chambers, they faced in toward the palace. In the triangular spaces between them and the exedra there were sellariae that faced the Aventine from high above the Circus, as the marble plan showed (32 and 33). To the east, between the open court of the lower level and the Hippodromos, there were rooms of curvilinear plan, as Plates 40 and 41 show. It may be that here there was an intermediate floor, between the upper and lower levels shown on Figure 5 (p. 50).

The principal rooms of the lower level are ranged on two sides of a sunken court that is rather smaller than the peristyles of the upper level (Plate 58).[60] At the present time the two levels are connected by a single staircase (number 23 on Plate 40, number 1 on Plate 58), but originally there was another toward the Hippodromos where there is a corridor today (number 6 on Plate 58).[61] The lower level was also connected with the exedra and its sellariae and colonnade (15–18). Probably the existing stair (restored) at the north corner of the block was the chief original entrance to the lower level. It is

58. The western of the two octagons may be that discussed by Guattani in his book of 1805 (above, n. 6), pp. 53–55 and Pl. 14; cf. Blake, 2, 122; and Crema, Fig. 359.

59. For the marble plan, see above, n. 13. For diaetae, see Pliny the Younger, *Letters* 2.17.16; Suetonius, *Claudius* 10; and Statius, *Silvae* 2.2.83, where one is described as being "higher than all the rest" of the rooms. It is likely that certain Roman wall paintings record the appearance of such pavilions; see the illustrations in M. I. Rostovtzeff, "Die hellenistisch-römische Architekturlandschaft," *RM*, 26 (1911), 1–186; L. Curtius, *Die Wandmalerei Pompejis* (Leipzig, 1929), Abb. 98; P. W. Lehmann, *Roman Wall Paintings from Boscoreale in the Metropolitan Museum of Art* (Cambridge, Mass., 1953), pp. 106–08, Fig. 58, and Pls. XVII and XXX. For their use in a provincial Roman villa, see Rostovtzeff, *1*, 234. Cf. also the nymphaea and Temple of Venus at Hadrian's Villa, similar in design to the diaetae and exedra of the Domus Augustana;

R. Vighi, *Villa Hadriana* (Rome, 1959), plan on p. 95; and Aurigemma (above, n. 21), Fig. 21 on p. 44.

60. The idea of a sunken peristyle may have been suggested to Domitian and Rabirius not only by the contours of the hill but also perhaps by the sunken nymphaeum-court of the Domus Transitoria; Crema, p. 319; cf. pp. 21–23, above. The perimeter walls of the Augustana peristyle were decorated with paintings; see Pl. 63 here. Either piers or columns may have been used for the porticoes; see *BC*, 68 (1940), 232; Lugli, *Roma*, p. 510. Löwe's restored section (see Lundberg [above, n. 16], p. 179) shows piers supporting barrel vaults.

61. Fragments of the elaborate marble wall revetment belonging to this stairway can still be seen in situ. The design is the same as that remaining in the stairway near the northeast corner of the Hippodromos (= Lugli, *Roma*, Tav. VIII, F); cf. Blake, 2, 123.

narrow, like most of the openings and corridors in the palace, but opens on the south to a handsome apsidal nymphaeum whose pools were lined with brilliantly colored mosaics (2). This nymphaeum, unroofed, was flanked by very high hairpin arcades reaching up to the vaults supporting the upper level, and through these arcades the visitor descending the stairs saw the water show below. Under the stair there is a latrine. Beyond the stairs to the southwest, service corridors on two levels run toward the Circus Maximus façade (14), while to the southeast the main passage leads to the central court (7).

The rooms beside this lower court, all of which were vaulted except the nymphaea at 2, 11, and 13 on Plate 58, are of special interest. There seem to have been no precise precedents for their individual designs and no precedent at all for the way they were combined with each other. On the northeast side of the court identical octagonal rooms are arranged symmetrically on either side of a square chamber (3–5). These octagons exist in actual shape only at the springing level of their vaults, so numerous are the openings and niches that eat away the structural solids, but it is convenient to describe them in familiar terms. The vaults of 4 and 5 have largely fallen, but that of 3 is well preserved. The concrete appears to have been molded at will, pierced and niched and modeled in a variety of shapes (Plate 59, the west niche of number 5, from above, and Plate 60, the north niche of the same room). Bricks with their inner faces molded to the required radii were manufactured (Plate 61, a detail of Plate 60). There are niches within niches, windows in niches, and passageways intersecting niches tangentially. The octagons were roofed with paneled vaults, for eight flat-sided sections are clearly visible in room 3. The lower halves of these rooms are not surrounded by masses of concrete, as certain published drawings indicate.[62] Nor is the area around the vaults filled in with masonry, as Plate 56 makes clear.

The vault that once covered room 4 is the only feature of the Domus Augustana that has received attention. The portions that remain have been read as the cores of pendentives (Plates 56 and 57). In the enthusiastic search for evidence in Italy of fully developed pendentives of early date the Augustana was pressed into service, for the defenders of the creativity and originality of Roman architects sought to show that the device was a purely Roman invention, in existence before the known Eastern examples and therefore the true inspiration for one of the basic visual and structural mechanisms of Byzantine architecture.[63] A dome on pendentives here would have risen well up into the

62. Kähler, Abb. 16–17, repeated by Crema, Figs. 360–61. Cf. the somewhat similar impression given by Durm, Figs. 309 and 318, and Rivoira, Fig. 119. The octagons are not built against the hillside, as Huelsen (above, n. 5), p. 73, quite understandably thought.

63. See Rivoira, p. 108; G. De Angelis d'Ossat, "La forma e la costruzione delle cupole nell'-architettura romana," *Atti, 3,* 227; K. A. C. Creswell, *Early Muslim Architecture, 1* (Oxford, 1932), 311 and Fig. 376; S. Bettini, *L'architettura*

di San Marco (Padua, 1946), p. 357 and Tav. XXXa; Blake, 2, 121; Boëthius, p. 107; but cf. Crema, p. 320. There is a pendentive dome over an oblong room in the villa of early imperial date at Minori; see A. Schiavo, "La villa romana di Minori," *Palladio, 3* (1939), pp. 129, 130 and n. 4, and illustrations on p. 132. The somewhat misdirected search for early pendentives ought to have been halted by the sensible remarks of J. B. Ward Perkins, "The Italian Element in Late Roman and Early Medieval Architecture," *Proceed-*

room numbered 22 on Plate 40; a pendentive dome (a continuous spherical surface), being much lower, could have been used, but at this date a groin vault is much more likely.[64]

The suite of rooms on the northwest side of the court was designed for the emperor's personal use (numbers 8–13 on Plate 58). The projecting salon or pavilion (8), the inner cubiculum flanked by large fountain rooms (11–13), and the isolation both of the whole complex and its inner core by corridors and enfilades (such as 9, 10, and 14) bear this out. Room 8 projected into the portico and was open to the court (Plate 62, seen from the southeast). Its side walls were pierced by arched openings set on the long axis of the adjoining portico (Plate 63, showing the spring of the northeast arch, seen from the south). The inner space was roofed with a groin vault, the longitudinal barrel of which may have continued out over the portico. The whole was traversed internally by an enfilade of openings (number 9, seen from the southwest in Plate 64) and flanked by narrow corridors, one of which, number 10, is seen from the southeast in Plate 65. On axis with the pavilion is the cubiculum (12), sunk deep in the building and flanked first by antechambers and beyond them by the unroofed fountain rooms (11 and 13; the pool of the latter is seen from the southeast in Plate 66).[65] The fountain rooms were given large windows that opened to all of the neighboring rooms of the suite, and number 13 was open to the entrance corridor and stairs beyond. The suite was separated from the perimeter wall by the narrow service corridor, number 14 (Plate 67).

The result is a palace within a palace. The design is clear and rational, better thought out though more complex than the comparable group in the Esquiline wing of the Domus Aurea (see Plate 24, numbers 4–7). By using proportionally very large windows and by conceiving of walls as planes rather than as containing surfaces, Rabirius broke down the spatial individuality of the rooms and gave the suite volumetric unity. Four of the five rooms of the inner core have no doors, for one end of each of these four is open. The side walls were simply planes, attached to space-defining walls only at one corner. Thus the several parts of the design are at the service of the spatial fluidity of the whole. The suite is one of the most ingenious yet calmly ordered designs in all Roman architecture.

In the inner rectangle of the open court there is a low platform, inscribed with semicircular niches and channels, rising from a pool (number 7 on Plate 58, and Plate 68). This display of geometry recalls the plan of the rooms beside the peristyle of the Domus Flavia and looks forward to the design of the structures erected upon the island of the

---

ings of the British Academy, 33 (1947), 163–72. Cf. Forsyth (above, n. 46), p. 225: "Domes seem to have an irresistible attraction for some architectural historians."

64. The so-called House of the Fish at Bulla Regia has a semidome whose extrados, covered with mosaic, rises above the paving level of the next story. The Bulla Regia sunken peristyle houses may be directly related to the design of the Domus Augustana.

65. Number 13 was seen by Guattani, who characterized it in his book of 1785 (see above, n. 6), p. XXIX, as being of mixtilinear and trite design, somewhat in the manner of Borromini.

so-called Maritime Theatre at Hadrian's Villa.[66] Presumably there were once fountains and planting within the Domus Augustana court. If the concrete foundations that are spaced between the niches and channels originally carried columns and a superstructure, the effect could have been similar to the airy, scenic compositions of fountains and delicate architecture seen in late Pompeian painting.

The southeast wall of the court is unbroken except for the entrance to the stair at 6 on Plate 58.[67] Nor are there any openings along the southwest wall, other than that leading to the large vestibule (number 15), once vaulted, that connects with the exedra (16). The latter was bordered by triads of sellariae set out radially (17 and 18 on Plate 58, and Plate 69). In front of the curving foundation for the exedra colonnade (visible in Plate 70) there is a large piece of fallen vault, and it is probable that the curving walkway between the colonnade and the sellariae was roofed with an annular vault.[68]

The lofty façade of the Hippodromos that faces the Circus Maximus is seen in Plate 70 (from the southeast) and Plate 71 (from the southwest; the *spina* or center wall of the Circus appears in the foreground). It was formed of two stories of vaulted chambers. The central space of the lower story was a nymphaeum, and from the loge above, the emperor watched the games. The Hippodromos proper lies to the northeast (Plate 72, view from the south; compare Plate 41). It was restored and strengthened by Septimius Severus, and again by Theodoric.[69] The word hippodromos was sometimes used by Latin writers to describe a garden or park laid out more or less upon the lines of a circus, such as the one at Pliny's Tuscan villa. This connection between a palace or a villa and a circus shape was common in later antiquity and was revived or continued by Renaissance architects.[70] The Palatine Hippodromos is frequently called a stadium because of its

66. Kähler, Taf. 6; Aurigemma (above, n. 21), illustrations on pp. 68–74.

67. See above, n. 61.

68. The great changes wrought in the appearance of the Palatine in the first century are shown by Bartoli's discovery in this area of the remains of a house of the Republican period; Lugli, *Roma*, p. 512.

69. F. Marx, "Das sogenannte Stadium auf dem Palatin," *JDAI*, 10 (1895), 129–43; C. Huelsen, "Untersuchungen zur Topographie des Palatins," *RM*, 10 (1895), 276–83; Massaccesi (above, n. 5), pp. 121–30; and cf. Platner-Ashby, p. 164. A thorough study of the Hippodromos was once begun (so Lugli, *Roma*, p. 514) but apparently never finished.

70. See Pliny the Younger, *Letters* 5.6.14–16; cf. *RE*, 8 (1913), col. 1745. The reasons for the association of circuses or stadiums (or architectural or pictorial simulacra of them) with important buildings that were secular or religious shrines need study. The combination appeared in

several suburban villas, such as Domitian's at Albano (see below, n. 76), and Hadrian's villa had a "stadium," used as a garden and nymphaeum (recently excavated); Kähler, Taf. I, building L-L; Aurigemma (above, n. 21), pp. 79–81. Many if not all late imperial palaces and villas adjoined or contained circus-shaped buildings, for example the Palace of Maxentius on the Via Appia just outside Rome, the villa near Piazza Armerina (where there is a pavement mosaic of a circus in a circus-shaped room), and the palaces at Thessaloniki and Constantinople; G. V. Gentili, *La villa imperiale di Piazza Armerina* (3rd ed. Rome, 1956), plan and pp. 19–20; C. Makaronas, "The Octagon of Salonika," *Praktika* (1950), p. 319 and Fig. 16; A. Vogt, *Le livre des cérémonies. Commentaire*, 1 (Paris, 1935), plan; cf. Crema, Fig. 321. Several early Christian basilicas had circus-shaped plans and were located beside important tombs or martyria; see the examples in F. W. Deichmann and A. Tschira, "Das Mausoleum der Kaiserin Helena und die Basilika

length and shape. It is much too small (50 by 184 meters) for a circus, for Roman racetracks measure, on the average, 80 by 400 meters, and it lacks the track surface, spina, and chariot stalls necessary for a practice track. In all likelihood it was intended to be a secluded garden, an allée, for the private use of the imperial family and their guests.

This remarkable construction was lined by an arcaded and vaulted portico (a restored portion can be seen toward the right of Plate 72). A large altar stood at the approximate center of the open space. At each end, in more or less the positions that would be occupied by the *metae* or goals of an actual circus, there were two elaborate fountains of semicircular plan; the remains of one can be seen on Plate 41. To the northeast, at the upper level of the Domus Augustana and not quite on axis with the Hippodromos, are the remains of an elaborate nymphaeum. Its central feature, a large semicircular niche open to the southwest and originally covered with a semidome, was flanked by groups of rectangular chambers, the whole forming a composition of a type seen fairly often in imperial architecture.[71]

THE SIGNIFICANCE OF DOMITIAN'S PALACE

The violence and anarchy that broke out after the death of Nero left the Empire "adrift and in danger."[72] Political life was soon stabilized by the competent Vespasian, the first of a century-long sequence of rulers whose policies, broadly considered, nourished the peace and unity of the ancient Mediterranean world. He and his sons were great builders. Domitian's semi-orientalized, quixotic despotism was fed by such a vast proliferation of construction that he was said to have a building disease.

> Should anyone who wonders at the costliness of the Capitol visit any one gallery in Domitian's palace, or hall, or bath, or the apartments of his concubines, he would think that Epicharmus' remark about the prodigal applied to this emperor: "It is not beneficence, but truth to say, a mere disease of giving things away." It is neither piety, he would say, nor magnificence, but indeed a mere disease of building, and a desire, like Midas had, of turning everything to gold or stone.[73]

der heiligen Marcellinus und Petrus . . .," *JDAI*, 72 (1957), 44–110 and esp. Abb. 25–28. There are a number of Renaissance villas with gardens laid out in circus shapes, and Bramante's design for the Cortile del Belvedere was also derived in part from this tradition; see J. S. Ackerman, *The Cortile del Belvedere* (Vatican City, 1954), pp. 130–38. Perhaps the whole tradition has its roots in the relationship of Domitian's would-be holy palace (*sacrum palatium*) to the quasi-sacred place where Romulus and Remus raced (the site of the Circus Maximus), and in the replica of this circus-palace confrontation that Rabirius built within the palace proper.

71. Cf., in addition to the buildings referred to above, n. 59, the Serapeum in Rome, *FUR, 1*, 97–102, 2, Tav. XXXI; and that at Hadrian's Villa, discussed by C. Tiberi, "L'Esedra di Erode Attico a Olympia e il Canopo della Villa Adriana presso Tivoli," *Quaderni*, 31–48 (1961; = *Fest. V. Fasolo*), 35–48. Lugli, *Roma*, p. 514, finds the Palatine example bizarre.

72. Suetonius, *Vespasian* 1.1.

73. Plutarch, *Poplicola* 15.5; cf. Pliny the Younger, *Panegyric* 51.

At least thirty major buildings in Rome alone can be attributed to him and his government, and these, taken with the Baths and Arch of Titus and the stupendous Amphitheatre, give the scale of the Flavian commitment to architecture.[74]

In all this activity the creative ferment, by no means limited to the Palatine, was at least as great as in Nero's time.[75] Its effect is apparent in Domitian's other new dwelling, an elaborate palace-villa built between what are now Castel Gandolfo and Albano. The fragmentary remains, scattered over an area a kilometer and a half long, give the strong impression that the design was as unrelated to received canon as that of the Palatine. Not surprisingly, Rabirius' name has been proposed.[76] The slope up to the ridge bordering Lake Albano was reshaped into three immense terraces buttressed by masses of concrete so vast that they call to mind modern methods of production and pouring. There were aqueducts, reservoirs, baths, a long street bordered by a half-dozen large nymphaea, a theatre, a circus, and a cryptoporticus originally over 300 meters long (a 120-meter stretch can still be seen). The palace proper was composed in several stories, probably three, and seems to have had the same tripartite division in plan as the Domus Flavia. There were domed circular nymphaea, with niches on their diagonal axes and diameters ranging from three to fifteen meters. But there really is not enough left for stylistic analysis, and the palace in Rome remains the major subject for the study of the new imperial style in Flavian times.

Rabirius' creativity has not gone unnoticed. Rivoira found that he "spoke a new word," and more recent writers have characterized the design of the palace as sensational and highly original.[77] The core of the great southwest façade of the Domus Augustana (Plate 71), shorn of its superstructure and décor, still records his understanding and successful use of the magnificent site Domitian chose. From the terrace in front of

74. For Flavian construction known from inscriptions and texts, see Bourne, pp. 54–69; for the remains of buildings in Rome and Italy, Blake, 2, 87–157. The Baths of Titus, erected hurriedly (Martial, *On the Spectacles* 2.7, and Suetonius, *Titus* 7.3) in the area just west of wall number 2 on the plan of the Domus Aurea wing (Pl. 24 here), are known chiefly from drawings made by Palladio: Zorzi, pp. 65–66 and Figs. 89–95; cf. R. Lanciani, "Gli scavi del Colosseo e le terme di Tito," *BC*, 23 (1895), 110–15, and D. Krencker et al., *Die Trierer Kaiserthermen* (Augsburg, 1929), pp. 265–66. Palladio's drawings indicate that the architect of the Baths was instrumental in developing one of the most characteristic building types of imperial architecture, the grand social center symmetrically planned around a lofty groin-vaulted hall. For the Amphitheatre, see P. Colagrossi, *L'Anfiteatro Flavio* . . . (Florence-Rome, 1913), and Lugli, *Roma*, pp. 319–46. For the

financing of Domitian's vast building program, see R. Syme, "The Imperial Finances under Domitian, Nerva, and Trajan," *JRS*, 20 (1930), 55–70; C. H. V. Sutherland, "The State of the Imperial Treasury at the Death of Domitian," *JRS*, 25 (1935), 150–62; and D. M. Robothan, "Domitian's Midas Touch," *Transactions of the American Philological Association*, 73 (1942), 130–44.

75. See the remarks by Rivoira, pp. 91–96, and the article by Lugli cited above, n. 40.

76. By G. Lugli, "La villa di Domiziano sui colli Albani, I," *BC*, 45 (1917), 41; his description of the villa continues in *BC* through 1920; cf. Blake, 2, 134–38. The relevant ancient texts are cited by Bourne, p. 66, item 28.

77. Rivoira, p. 111; Boëthius (above, n. 20), p. 28; J. B. Ward Perkins, "Roman Concrete and Roman Palaces," *The Listener*, 56 (1956), 701–03; Crema, p. 320.

S. Pietro in Montorio on the Gianicolo one can see how tellingly the palace was related to the hill and to the city. It was banked high along the steep rim of the Palatine for a distance of over two hundred meters, an architectural incarnation of majesty. The interiors were designed to the same purpose, for Rabirius' directive, expressed or implied, called for a house suitable for a *dominus et deus*. He was asked to create a tangible rhetoric of power, a panegyric in architecture of the emperor's claim to omniscience.

Domitian imposed absolutist tendencies upon society and the state to a degree previously unknown.[78] The rather pragmatic fabric of Roman life had been increasingly infused with an ideology of Near Eastern flavor that implied the quasi-divine nature of the ruler, a process he deliberately accelerated. After his death a powerful reaction set in, and his extremely unpopular administration was as unsuitable a model for his successors as Nero's had been for Vespasian. But his policies, though despotic, had a far-reaching influence upon architecture. The imperator, once an honored general, was now the possessor of ultimate authority, using the ancient title as a praenomen. His rank and presumably sacrosanct person required an architecture that broadcast impressions of the majesty he wished to impose upon the world. Splendor, great size, and luxury, though important, were insufficient. Novelty alone would not do. It was necessary that the imperial architecture lead, as the imperator presumably led, that it allow him to be seen and thought of in dwellings both unique and pertinent. This was the challenge that Rabirius met.

A building is a palace not only because a ruler resides in it but also because of its location and symbolic connotations. The word palace designates an official residence while conveying strong implications of stateliness and splendor. The word itself, as well as its meanings, is derived from the buildings under discussion. The hill upon which the palace of Domitian stood is properly called the Palatium, not the Palatinus, which is a later form;[79] the name of the hill was soon transferred to the buildings themselves. These familiar facts help to define the special quality and importance of Rabirius' buildings by showing first that he had to concern himself with special problems of design, and second that his solutions made lasting impressions.[80]

The new palace, unlike the Domus Aurea, was a continuous, enclosed structure without external grounds or gardens for the emperor's use. Rabirius naturally provided it with peristyles, and because these are so obvious in plan the design is always called a peristyle palace. This is technically correct but misleading. It implies that the design of the palace was derived from or directly related to Hellenistic buildings whose dominating peristyles

78. See *OCD*, pp. 295–96.

79. See *RE, 18.3* (1949), col. 5; S. Viarre, "Palatium 'palais'," *Revue de Philologie*, 35 (1961), 241–48.

80. Tamm, p. 206, referring to Smith (above, n. 51), pp. 53–56 and 147, says that the palace was in all probability the model for later imperial residences. I think this is likely, but not enough is known of post-Domitianic palaces around the Empire to make it certain. A very useful study in this connection would be that of the so-called imperial palace at Ostia; see L. Paschetto, *Ostia colonia romana* (Rome, 1913), pp. 407–21 and plan on Fig. 122; *Ostia*, pp. 147, 225–26, where the date is given as ca. 145–50; and Meiggs, pp. 107, 451–52.

were surrounded by flat-roofed chambers of comparatively low silhouette.[81] Actually there are very few discernible connections between the palace and this earlier architecture other than the peristyles themselves. What distinguishes Domitian's palace from other palaces and great mansions are its rooms, groups of rooms, and great halls—Rabirius' interiors. It is their visual and spatial effects, unrecorded by plans, that define a style unknown in Hellenistic times.

It is clear that Rabirius based his general plan upon the identical peristyles of the upper level, from which the basic dispositions of the major groups of spaces roundabout were projected. He subdivided those groups symmetrically around the extensions of the peristyle axes in obedience to the traditional equality of left and right. But this is not where his originality lies. He first made this grand bow to convention and then, supremely conscious of the radical difference between plans and spaces, worked entirely within the principles of the new architecture. Axial sequences of light and shade, known so long in Roman architecture, were composed from vaulted volumes. The rooms between the peristyles and between the peristyles and the perimeter walls of the palace were given novel shapes. In the Domus Augustana the roofs of the lower level formed a firm terrace, an artificial ground level, for a vertically noncongruent plan above (compare Plate 10b). The potential of this freedom from exact duplication at different levels is an important feature of the vaulted style.[82] With it Rabirius was able to differentiate between the functions and effects of the two levels and to give to each its own individual forms.

The palace shows a greater degree of stylistic maturity than the remaining work of Severus, though the basic principles underlying the design of some of the barrel-vaulted rooms are much the same. The internal elements of Domitian's palace were more logically and comprehensibly arranged than those of the Domus Aurea wing. Polygonal

81. For the derivation of the palace from Hellenistic prototypes, see A. Boëthius, "Three Roman Contributions to World Architecture," *Fest. J. Arvid Hedvall* (Göteborg, 1948), p. 66; K. M. Swoboda, "Palazzi antichi e medioevali," *BollCentro*, 11 (1957), 6; Petrignani (above, n. 16), pp. 57–59. Cf. the remarks of G. Tosi, "Il palazzo principesco dall'arcaismo greco alla Domus Flavia," *Arte antica e moderna*, 7 (1959), 241–60, and of Tamm, p. 24. Tamm's detailed analysis on pp. 147–79 of the Italian evolution of apsed rooms is extremely useful; she is able to show that technologically the Domus Flavia basilica was evolved from Italian precedents. For examples of peristyle houses and palaces, see *RE*, Supp. 7 (1950), cols. 263–75; G. Pesce, *Il "Palazzo delle colonne" in Tolemaide di Cirenaica* (Rome, 1950); J. B. Pritchard, *The Excavations at Herodian Jericho* (New Haven, 1958; = *Annual*

of the American Schools of Oriental Research, 32–33); C. H. Kraeling, *Ptolemais, City of the Libyan Pentapolis* (Chicago, 1962), 83–89, 119–39, and Plan XII; P. Petsas, "Ten Years at Pella," *Archaeology*, 17 (1964), 74–84. The so-called palace at Palatizia in Macedonia, published by L. Heuzey and H. Daumet, *Mission archéologique de Macédoine*, 1 (Paris, 1876), 184–86, 2, Pls. 7 and 14, which seems at first to be such a promising subject for comparison with Domitian's palace, was probably a bath; see K. A. Rhomaios, "The Palace at Palatizia," *Archaiologike Ephemeris*, 1 (1953–54; = *Fest. Oikonomos*), 141–50 and Fig. 2; cf. W. B. Dinsmoor, *The Architecture of Ancient Greece* (London, 1950), pp. 325–26 and Fig. 119; A. W. Lawrence, *Greek Architecture* (Harmondsworth, 1957), p. 306, n. 3.

82. Cf. Vitruvius, 6.8.1, who insists on vertical congruity even if vaulted substructures are used.

and curving shapes were set within the large rectangles and alongside the peristyles in an economical way, and very few odd volumes were left over. Yet as at the Domus Aurea the more intricately shaped structures were not clear of rectilinear enclosures or freed from contact with adjoining rooms; the clear exposure of the exteriors of complex vaulted shapes was to be the work of Rabirius' successors. Yet he did prepare the way for this by thinning down the verticals of his vaulted polygonal rooms, implying thereby that they did not have to be embedded within a building, and by freeing their super-structures from superfluous loads of masonry.

For the exterior nothing was overlooked that by association would evoke feelings of reverence for the palace and imply a numinous presence there. If our interpretation of the sestertius of 95/96 is correct, the temple form was adapted at both large and small scale (Plate 51). The columns used to screen the Circus façade of the Domus Augustana are the first positive evidence of the application of a colonnade of municipal scale to the wall of a dwelling.[83] Severus may have provided a colonnade for the Domus Aurea wing, and the Domus Flavia may also have had one, but both of these are conjectural. While the Augustana was being built Domitian's architects were erecting files of columns in front of the long, high walls of the new Forum Transitorium, columns that carried transverse ressauts like those of the aula regia.[84] The implication of the palace colonnade was that the Commonwealth and the emperor were one, that the Augustus in his palace was the incarnation of the ancient genius of Rome that suffused the fora. The point was driven home by the looming form of the great vestibule that encroached upon the original Forum, an inescapable reminder of the emperor's claims (Plate 52).[85]

Within the palace the visual instruments of the new style served those claims. Curving surfaces were the key to the matter. The vaulted imitations of the heavenly arc invited the celestial analogies of the poets. By placing the emperor at the center of an apse the unbroken continuity of imperial authority was implied, for the embracing surface, free from angles and curving around his person at a constant distance, suggested his surveillance of the realm from its center.[86] Apses also firmly directed attention to the seat of power, an effect quickened by the iterated meter of the columns and spur walls that lined the sides of the great halls of state and closed toward the presence framed beneath an

83. See A. M. Colini in *BC*, 69 (1941), 200–01.

84. See von Blanckenhagen's book of 1940 (above, n. 25), pp. 9–47, 147–68; Nash, *1*, 433–38.

85. That the exterior façades of the palace may have been rather more baroque and less sober in appearance than the restorations seen here on Pls. 16 and 45 is suggested by the elevated diaetae, the forms seen on the coin (Plate 51), the design of the Forum Transitorium and the aula regia inter-ior, and the façades seen in certain more or less contemporary paintings; for the latter see for example V. Fasolo, "Rappresentazioni architet-toniche nella pittura romana," *Atti*, 3, 207–13 and Tav. 2. The baroque aedicular architecture so often represented in paintings and mosaics seems often to be more closely related to Palatine than to theatre architecture. Cf. for example the diaetae of the Domus Augustana upper level, nos. 29 and 30 on Pl. 40 here, with the architecture seen in the mosaics of S. George in Thessaloniki; W. F. Vol-bach, *Frühchristliche Kunst* (Munich, 1958), Pls. 122, 124–27; H. Torp, *Mosaikkene i St. Georg-Rotunden i Thessaloniki* (Oslo, 1963), p. 62.

86. See Tamm, pp. 215–16.

arch in the distance. An apsidal vault over the imperial figure completed this geometry of sovereignty.

An imagery of presumptive boundlessness was also skillfully infused into the design of the Domus Augustana. In the web of upper-level rooms there was no evident visual conclusion to the serial experience of spaces. Vaulted volumes, their intercommunicating openings so located as to require frequent changes of direction, proliferated on every side.[87] The domed octagonal chambers of the lower level, each generated in radial symmetry from a vertical center line, implied seamless perfection. Each was dominated by an overarching vault that absorbed the force of any horizontal directives created by openings at human level. These enclosing shapes described completed worlds. It was as if apses and semidomes had been built facing each other in order to fix the emperor in the oneness of his place. Purely rectangular volumes, bounded by planes meeting at sharp angles, would not have evoked these associations. Fixed and inelastic, devoid of any suggestion of unlimited circumference, such forms could not intimate the ecumenical pretensions of the emperor. In the secular world prismatic shapes belonged to municipal buildings, houses, and other familiar structures. Domitian could not associate himself with these forms while insisting upon his uniqueness, nor could he dwell in the cellas of the gods. Yet he claimed the rounded whole of the earth, and it was this that Rabirius' creation was intended to declare.

87. Something of the interior appearance of these rooms when their décor was intact and their fittings were in place is perhaps conveyed by certain paintings; see for example Curtius (above, n. 59), Abb. 106; cf. *CAH, 11, 765.* The effects of the motion and sound of water, of light upon the fountains and pools, should not be forgotten. There was water on every side, playing against or contained by colored marbles and mosaics.

IV

TRAJAN'S MARKETS

DURING Trajan's reign (98–117) Roman enthusiasm for building never slackened. Social and utilitarian architecture predominated, and a paternalistic but comparatively moderate government sponsored or authorized new construction in hundreds of prosperous provincial cities and towns. New temples, administrative buildings, baths, public nymphaea, triumphal arches, aqueducts, roads, bridges, flood control works, and ports were built.[1] The vaulted style in particular answered many contemporary architectural needs. By the time of Trajan's death it was visible in every corner of the Empire, its aesthetic and technological principles firmly established. The experience of these years was the cardinal inheritance of the men who designed the superb buildings of Hadrian (117–38).

As always, Rome was richly rewarded. The spacious Baths of Trajan, built over the Esquiline wing of the Domus Aurea, were typical of the grand architectural scale sponsored by the new administration (Plate 73). The comparatively modest Baths of Titus that stood nearby were probably the model for this definitive vaulted design that governed the architecture of municipal bath buildings for over two centuries.[2] With great audacity Trajan's engineers excavated beside the mouth of the Tiber a spacious artificial harbor, a hexagonal basin 715 meters across, giving the imperial capital an adequate

---

1. For building activity during Trajan's reign, see Pliny the Younger, *Panegyric* 51.2–5; R. Paribeni, *Optimus princeps*, 2 (Messina, 1927), 23–149; *CAH*, 11, 205–12, 545, 619; G. Rodenwaldt, "Römische Staatsarchitektur," *Das neue Bild der Antike*, 2 (Leipzig, 1942), 357; F. J. de Waele, *Marcus Ulpius Traianus* (Nijmegen, 1956), pp. 48–60. For urbanization, see Rostovtzeff, 1, 134–35, 2, 592–602.

2. For the Baths of Titus, see above, Chap. 3, n. 74. For Trajan's Baths, see Zorzi, pp. 67–68 and Figs. 106–09; D. Krencker et al., *Die Trierer Kaiserthermen* (Augsburg, 1929), 266–69;

Bloch, pp. 36–49; id., "Aqua Traiana," *AJA, 48* (1944), 337–41; Lugli, *Roma*, pp. 355–58, 369–74; F. Castagnoli, "Le 'sette sale' cisterna delle Terme Traiano," *ArchClass, 8* (1956), 53–55; Nash, 2, 472–77. The symmetrical bath building centered around a large groin-vaulted hall probably first appeared in the Baths of Titus. Trajan's architect expanded from this model and surrounded the main building on three sides with a large open space girdled by libraries and other buildings of a social and cultural nature, and this was the basic scheme followed in the great baths of later emperors.

port at last.[3] Connected with both the river and the sea by artificial channels, the basin was surrounded by a small city of marine facilities and warehouses. Only a few fragments of the Baths are visible today (see Plate 22), and the remains of the buildings by the great port are rarely made accessible for study.[4] Of all the Trajanic examples of the vaulted style the well-preserved Markets beside Trajan's Forum are the most instructive. Though not entirely neglected by architectural historians the Markets have not received the attention their quality and importance merit, and the evidence they give for the nature and meaning of Roman architecture has remained largely uncapitalized.

Superlatives have rained upon the marble-laden Forum and Basilica Ulpia in modern times as in ancient, and understandably so (Plate 74).[5] The paved open space measured some 89 by 118 meters and the total length of the Basilica (approximately 169 meters) was half again that of the Parthenon. In the Forum area proper apparently only the libraries were built of brick (Plate 74, E–E), perhaps in the hope of absorbing any excessive humidity. All the rest of the vast composition was of stone except the roofs of wood and tiles.[6] But at the Markets this system of trabeation with its chromatic envelope of marbles was exchanged for arches and vaults of concrete and facings of brick (Plate 75). Lacking columns, the bold shapes of the Market buildings are unscreened, and the effect of their plain wall surfaces is comparatively austere. The traditional design of fora and basilicas, as well as the difference in program, partly account for this contrast, but fundamentally it is explained by the pervasive success of the new style.

Bloch has shown that the Markets were built during the first decade of the second century.[7] Apparently there is no direct reference to the Markets in ancient literature,

3. G. Lugli and G. Filibeck, *Il porto di Roma imperiale e l'agro portuense* (Rome, 1935); Meiggs, pp. 58–62, 149–71, 568–69; cf. *ESAR*, 5, 222; Zorzi, Fig. 255. A port was also built by Trajan to the northwest at Centumcellae; S. Bastianelli, *Centumcellae (Civitavecchia) Castrum Novum (Torre Chiaruccia)* (Rome, 1954), pp. 15–18, 38–42; cf. Pliny the Younger, *Letters* 6.31.15–17.

4. For the difficulties involved, see Meiggs, p. vii; I was able to examine the site for a day in 1959 through the courtesy of Professor Herbert Bloch. The remains of the warehouses and other buildings are almost entirely of vaulted construction in concrete.

5. Pausanias, 5.12.6, 10.5.11; Dio Cassius, 68.16.3; Ammianus Marcellinus, 16.10.15–16; Cassiodorus, *Variae* 7.6. The Forum is mentioned as late as ca. 590 by Venantius Fortunatus, *Poems* 3.23. For modern opinions, see for example Stendhal, *Promenades dans Rome*, 2nd ser. (Paris, 1873), pp. 59–62 (= June 28, 1828); Lugli, *Roma*, p. 282; Crema, pp. 358, 370.

6. For the libraries, see Bloch, pp. 57–61; Lugli, *Roma*, pp. 284–85; Nash, 1, 455. For the amount of marble used, see *ESAR*, 5, 67–68, 222.

7. Bloch, pp. 49–57 and 348; the Markets were finished before the Forum was dedicated in 112. Texts of the fourth and sixth centuries assign Trajan's Baths and Forum to Domitian: *Monumentae Germaniae Historica*, 9 (Berlin, 1892), 146, 11 (1894), 140 (the Baths and the Forum); Aurelius Victor, *Lives of the Emperors* 13.5 (the Forum). Because of this it has been suggested that Rabirius designed both. It is just possible that the Markets were planned in Domitian's time, but since the Baths and Markets are entirely Trajanic, as Bloch has shown, and since it would have been quite out of keeping for Trajan's administration, as we know it, to have adopted projects of Domitian's, it appears likely that chroniclers and annalists of later centuries confused the Baths of Titus with those of Trajan, and the Forum of Nerva (the Forum Transitorium, built by Domitian but dedicated by Nerva) with Trajan's Forum. For these points see Platner-

unless a passage in a fourth-century biography of the emperor Commodus (reigned 180–93) that mentions a Basilica of Trajan refers to the large vaulted hall or aula marked H on Plate 74.[8] From the early medieval period onward the Markets were occupied and built upon by various parishes and religious organizations.[9] Some Renaissance *vedute* show elements of the original buildings, chiefly the upper half of the great hemicycle (Plate 74, between G and J, and Plate 75), and there is a sketch plan and section of Renaissance date of the hall at H.[10] When the Via dei Fori Imperiali was driven from the Piazza Venezia to the Flavian Amphitheatre in the fascist era, the Markets were cleared by Ricci and much unstudied Trajanic fabric was revealed intact. Necessary tie rods and preservative masonry were added, and some of the upper walls were built up to even levels to support new roofs.[11]

The original extent of the Markets is unknown.[12] Today one hundred and seventy

---

Ashby, p. 241; R. Paribeni, "Apollodoro di Damasco," *Atti della reale Accademia d'Italia, Rendiconti*, 7.4 (1943), 125–28; Bourne, p. 67; Lugli, *Roma*, pp. 53, 280; id., *Tecnica*, 2, captions to Tav. CLXVIII.3 and CCI.1; Blake, 2, 105. For Apollodoros, whose name is often coupled with the Markets in the modern literature, see below, Chap. 6.

8. *SHA, Commodus* 2.1; for a discussion of this point see A. Boëthius, "Appunti sul Mercato di Traiano, I," *Roma*, 9 (1931), 447–54, who suggests that the text refers to the aula and that one of the Constantinian reliefs of the Arch of Constantine shows the emperor sitting in the aula.

9. The church and monastery of S. Catherine of Siena, Lanciani, p. 316; the church and monastery of SS. Abbaciro (= SS. Ciro Abbate e Giovanni), M. Armellini, *Le chiese di Roma* (3rd ed. Rome, 1942), pp. 226–28; a church of S. Pacera, perhaps the same as SS. Abbaciro, according to F. Clementi, "I mercati Traianei e la Via Biberatica," *Roma*, 8 (1930), 512; the monastery of S. Basilii in Scala Mortuorum, G. Ferrari, *Early Roman Monasteries* (Vatican City, 1957; = *Studi di antichità cristiana*, 23), pp. 62–64; and various palaces, among them those of the Ceva-Roccagiovane, Tiberi, and Caetani. There is information on the history of the Markets before their excavation in H. Jordan, *Topographie der Stadt Rom im Altertum*, 1.2 (Berlin, 1885), 457–58; Platner-Ashby, pp. 240, 245; R. Paribeni, "Inscrizioni dei Mercati Traiano," *NS* (1933), pp. 503–23; G. Incisa della Rochetta, "D'un cartone di Giulio Romano e dell'aula coperta dei mercati Traianei," *Miscellanea Bibliothecae Herzianae* (Munich, 1961), pp. 204–06.

10. For drawings and paintings of the hall, see Giovannoni, Fig. 15; Incisa della Rochetta (above, n. 9), Figs. 136–37. For *vedute*, early drawings, and pre-excavation photographs of the Markets, see A. Desgodetz, *Les édifices antiques de Rome* (2nd ed. Paris, 1779), pp. 138–40; C. Ricci, "Per l'isolamento e la redenzione dei resti dei Fori imperiali," *BdA*, 5 (1911), Figs. 3, 4; Rivoira, Fig. 128; A. Boëthius, "Från Trajanus' och Augustus' romerska prakttorg," *Ord och Bild*, 38 (1929), 241–56; Platner-Ashby, Pl. 30 and p. 605; Clementi (above, n. 9), Pl. LIII; A. Pernier, "Rilievi e note sulla costruzione dei Mercati di Traiano in Roma," *Atti*, 3, Fig. 5; Lugli, *Roma*, Fig. 79; G. Fiorini, *La casa dei cavalieri di Rodi* (Rome, 1951), Figs. 5–7; M. R. Scherer, *Marvels of Ancient Rome* (New York, 1955), Pls. 167–68 and p. 409; and *Capitolium*, 31 (1956), p. 101. For a good air view, see *Capitolium*, 38 (1963), 8. For the site during excavation and restoration, see G. Lugli, "I mercati Traianei," *Dedalo*, 10 (1929–30), 527–51.

11. As in the case of Domitian's palace, no excavation report has appeared, and the results of this immense undertaking have been published only in summary form: C. Ricci, *Il mercato di Traiano* (Rome, 1929); C. Ricci, A. M. Colini, and V. Mariani, *Via dell'Impero* (Rome, 1933), pp. 115–21. See also *BC*, 61 (1933), 253–57; Pernier (above, n. 10); and the description in Lugli, *Roma*, pp. 299–309. The modern wood and tile roofs of the highest ranges of rooms (see Pl. 75 here) replace the original barrel vaults, long since lost. Restoration and consolidation were carried out in 1929–30, and the vault of the aula (Pl. 74, H), which had been cut through at some

rooms are either accessible or visible in the curving, radiating, and tangential blocks arranged in tiers up the steep south slope of the Quirinal hill. The buildings rise to a height about 35 meters above the pavement level of the Forum (equivalent to the height of Trajan's Column), and occupy a space about 110 by 150 meters. At several interior points the rock of the hillside is visible, but it is not possible to determine the extent to which Trajan's engineers cut and shaped the hill. It has been said that the general scheme was adapted to the natural form of the hill,[13] but it is more likely that the outline of the Forum was determined first and the lower parts of the Markets were planned accordingly (similarities to the site and design of the Sanctuary of Fortune at Palestrina, Plates 10–12, should not be overlooked). Lanciani thought that the Markets were balanced on the far side of the Forum by a series of rooms arranged around the pendant southwest hemicycle. He published a conjectural plan showing this, but the subsequent excavation of the perimeter wall of Caesar's Forum invalidated his assumption (Plate 74, M).[14] Apparently there was originally a concentric colonnade that extended around the southwest hemicycle as far as Caesar's wall, but the Markets were not balanced by symmetrical constructions between the colonnade and the Clivus Argentarius on the slope of the Capitoline.[15]

The Markets were conceived in part as a replacement for the many *tabernae* (shops) and facilities that were destroyed to make room for the Forum and Basilica. Possibly the rooms at the level of the Forum were occupied by the *arcarii caesariani,* the cashiers of the imperial treasury; the upper-level shops would have been used for the distribution of the state dole or leased to private vendors.[16] The derivation of the name Biberatica,

---

time unknown to make openings rather like oculi, was repaired; see Incisa della Rochetta (above, n. 9), Fig. 136; the drawing in Boëthius (above, n. 10), p. 248; *Architettura ed arti decorativi,* 9 (1929), 283. For an idea of the principles of restoration followed in Ricci's time, see G. Calza, "Assetto e restauro delle rovine di Ostia antica," *Atti,* 3, 343–48.

12. Durm, p. 616, suggests additional shops just north of the aula (Pl. 74, H, here), but as far as I know there is no evidence for this. There were shops just north of the Basilica Ulpia, as Pl. 74 here indicates, known from the marble plan; *FUR,* 1, 72, 89, 2, Tav. XXVIII. The most useful plans of the Markets are to be found in Pernier (above, n. 10). On most general plans several levels of the Markets are shown; this is true of Pl. 74 here, where for example the hemicycle shops and corridor are on the second level above the Forum pavement but the aula at H is shown at its gallery level some 14 m. higher.

13. By Paribeni (above, n. 7), p. 127; cf. Pernier (above, n. 10), p. 108. For the cutting of the hill, see G. de Angelis d'Ossat, "Il sottosuolo dei Mercati Traianei e del Foro d'Augusto," *Atti-*

PontAcc, 84 (1931), 227–33; cf. *BC,* 61 (1933), 255–56.

14. Lanciani, Fig. 119 and pp. 315–16. Trajan extended Caesar's Forum toward the west with a vaulted hall (probably the Basilica Argentaria), as well as with a number of shops; Lugli, *Roma,* Tav. V and pp. 53, 256–57; Nash, 1, 431.

15. The colonnade is reported on Tav. Agg. A, opp. p. 256, in *BC,* 61 (1933), and indicated on Pl. 74 here; cf. Crema, pp. 155–58.

16. The Markets were given their name by Ricci in his pamphlet of 1929 (above, n. 11). That the majority of rooms are shops is not in doubt because of the analogical evidence at Ostia and on the marble plan. Specific uses can be suggested in only a few cases, as where there are drains for fish- or wineshops. For discussions of the general purpose of the Markets and the uses of the various parts, see Platner-Ashby, p. 240; G. Lugli, "I mercati Traianei," *Dedalo,* 10 (1929–30), 537–46; F. Clementi, "I mercati Traianei e la Via Biberatica," *Roma,* 8 (1930), 505–20; *ESAR,* 5, 232–33; Lugli, *Roma,* pp. 306–08. Cf. Rostovtzeff, 2, 568, n. 36; and see below, n. 35.

given to the principal street of the Markets (Plate 74, J–J), has been variously explained.[17]

These streets, offices, and shops were planned as integral parts of an urban redevelopment program. The renovation or creation of city quarters was common in the early second century; compare for example the extensive works at Ostia, Porto (the new harbor-town by the Tiber mouth), Timgad, or Antioch.[18] The careful planning that preceded the building of the Markets is evident in the relationships between the streets and shops, the functional locations of the stair systems and ramps, and the pains taken to bring adequate lighting and ventilation to nearly every roofed space (Plates 75 and 76). A number of terraces commanded fine views across the new Forum to the west and south.

Between the Forum hemicycle and the curved façade of the Markets there was a thick fire wall of tufa blocks and a paved street with travertine sidewalks (Plate 77). The wall was faced with marble pilasters and paneling on its concave or Forum side, and its curve was broken at the center by a rectangular apsidal shape flanked by columns.[19] The Forum hemicycle was the point of departure for the design of the lower levels of the Markets. The hemicycle, of brick-faced concrete like all the rest of the Markets, was set on the same axis as the Forum hemicycle but its curve was struck from a different center. The semicircle thus produced was repeated up through the first three levels, but above and beyond the Via Biberatica the design became less symmetrical. The Via Biberatica, in plan a spread-out W (Figure 7), was connected with the fora below and the city quarter above by stair systems, ramps, corridors, and adjoining streets.

The Markets were the creation of a brilliant and audacious designer, a master of architectonic form and the new structural technology. The scale of his design is generous. The rise is steep, the levels numerous, and the plan complex. There are six major levels, though the pavements of a few corridors and rooms are located between them. As at the Domus Augustana, the plan of a superposed level is not necessarily vertically congruent with that below. To facilitate description and discussion the Markets can be divided into six major divisions, three on each side of the Via Biberatica (Figure 7).

A1   lies between the hemicycle and the apse of the Basilica Ulpia.
A2   is the hemicycle block.

17. For example by Clementi (above, n. 16), pp. 511–20; and by Lugli, *Roma*, p. 299 (following Ricci).

18. *Ostia*, pp. 123–39 and Figs. 51–52. Porto: see above, n. 3. Timgad: E. Boeswillwald et al., *Timgad, une cité africaine sous l'empire romain* (Paris, 1905); C. Courtois, *Timgad, antique Thamugadi* (Algiers, 1951). Antioch: G. Downey, *A History of Antioch in Syria* (Princeton, 1961), pp. 213–18. For the buildings that were replaced by Trajan's vast project in Rome, see G. Lugli, "Le mura di Servio Tullio e le cosi-

dette mura serviane," *Historia*, 7 (1933), 22 and Fig. 6; *ESAR*, 5, 232; and Rostovtzeff, 2, 694, n. 3. For redevelopment and reconstruction in Rome, see F. Castagnoli et al., *Topografia e urbanistica di Roma* (Bologna, 1958), pp. 35–38; Boëthius, Chap. 4.

19. Rectangular features frequently appear at the center of semicircular forms in imperial architecture. See for example the design of the so-called Serapeum at Pozzuoli; A. Maiuri, *I campi flegrèi* (3rd ed. Rome, 1958), pp. 24–27 and plan on p. 29; and above, Chap. 3, n. 71.

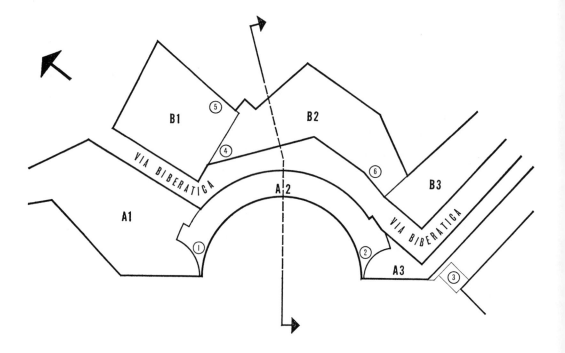

7. *Diagram of the main divisions and stair systems of Trajan's Markets*

A3   lies between the hemicycle and the Forum of Augustus.

B1   consists of the large hall, or aula Traiana, and its dependencies (Plate 74, H).[20]

B2   is the central upper section.

B3   is the upper section beside the eastern turn of the Via Biberatica.

The major existing stairs and stair systems have been numbered as follows:

1   connects the hemicycle street at Forum level with the upper levels of A1 and A2, and with the Via Biberatica.

2   connects the hemicycle street with the upper levels of A2, part of those of A3, and the Via Biberatica.

3   rises from the southeast extension of the hemicycle street; originally it connected the Forum with the city region to the east.

4   connects the Via Biberatica with the floor level of the aula of B1.

5   connects the main hall of the aula with its galleries and the adjacent upper rooms of B1 and B2.

6   connects the Via Biberatica with the upper parts of B2 and B3.

The highest point of the Via Biberatica is approximately at the point where A3 and B3 meet (Plate 75; cf. Plate 84). To the east the street falls steadily to meet the lower portion of the present Salita del Grillo. Going the other way it falls slowly as it curves toward stairway 4, and then more rapidly, becoming level at its lowest existing portion (Plate 75). This last is a straight stretch that divides A1 from B1 and is cut abruptly today at its northern end by the high retaining wall of the Via Quattro Novembre. At a right angle to this level portion and directly in front of the north façade of the aula of B1 a further stretch of the Via Biberatica, or a street that it intersected, is preserved at the basement level of the aula. The original paving is preserved in all but the easternmost part of the street. The maximum change in level is about seven meters.

In spite of this rise and fall of the Via Biberatica the architect imposed upon his design a horizontal layering which, though not asserted with drawing-board accuracy, was carried quite clearly through the whole scheme. The major exception is B1, where the various pavement levels are staggered between the controlling levels listed below. The general plan on Plate 74 shows a selection of levels rising to that of the aula gallery; the list that follows refers to Plate 76.

I.   The hemicycle street and its extensions.

II.   The pavement of the annular-vaulted semicircular corridor of A2 and the rooms that radiate from it. The straight north portion of the Via Biberatica and the pavements of the shops flanking it are on this level.

III.   The terrace atop A2, over the annular-vaulted corridor of level II. The floor

20. The name aula Traiana is modern; cf. above, n. 8.

of the main hall of the aula and the connecting rooms of B2 are very slightly above this level.

IV.   The floors of the aula galleries of B1 and the connecting rooms of B2. The roof line, now lost, of the range of seven shops atop A2 between the semicircular terrace and the Via Biberatica was presumably also at this level.

V.   The paving level of the row of rooms above the east gallery of the aula of B1 and the connecting rooms of B2.

(VI.   There was, originally, another row of rooms above the east gallery of the aula.)

Thus the Markets are methodically staged at vertical intervals of about seven meters. The room entrances and paving levels beside the Via Biberatica are accommodated to the changing elevation of the street. There are a few basement rooms in B2, below level III, that are entered by going down short flights of steps from the street. The floor levels of the seven shops atop A2 drop in sequence along the curving decline of the street toward the northwest (Plate 75; and cf. Plate 84); it is probable that their roof lines all reached the same height (level IV). These step-like gradations correspondingly affected the heights of the rooms set out radially from the annular-vaulted corridor of A2 on level II below, for there the vaults become lower as the hemicycle sweeps around toward the west. To the north and east of B2 there are fragmentary remains of construction at various levels, and a part of another paved street runs north and south along the east flank of B2. This uppermost street, whose original termini are unknown, rises slightly toward the north. Between the Torre delle Milizie (see Plate 91) and the Via Quattro Novembre a few wall fragments are preserved that probably belong to the Markets. At levels I, II, and III in A1 the corridors and rooms extend into a modern building but entrance to them is barred. There is some medieval and later construction atop the southern half of B2.

WEST OF THE VIA BIBERATICA

Division A1. Here the major features echo the design of the Forum hemicycle. Three curved walls of cylindrical shape rise in tiers up through level IV (see Plate 75). The half-cylinder facing the Forum-level street is encased in surrounding construction and is roofed by a large semidome that springs from level II (Plate 78, a view from the northeast). Just to the north there is another half-cylinder of smaller diameter covered by a semidome springing from a height between levels I and II. Around and behind this smaller semidome, with windows looking out on its extrados, are two annular-vaulted corridors, one above the other, leading to rooms to the north that are now inaccessible (Plate 75). The third concave feature is concentric with the second but more shallow. Stair system number 1, a vertical stack of flights, landings, and access corridors, connects the division with the three levels of A2 and with the Via Biberatica. The complex shapes that result from conjunctions of annular, barrel, and ramping vaults in this stair system record the confidence and technical competence of the builders. At one level, over a landing stage common to four stairs and corridors, there is a complex, multigroined vault of exceptional design formed of six different curving surfaces.

The two blind windows at the end of the main hemicycle, like those seen in Plate 87, mask the extrados of the bigger semidome from below. The Forum-level room itself is entered through the opening directly under the first blind window (see Plate 75). The relatively small size of this opening emphasizes by contrast the very ample dimensions of the semicircular room and its eight large, crisply outlined windows (Plate 78). The windows are composed in two rows, three over five, placed in the upper two thirds of the façade because of the neighboring perimeter wall of the Forum (not shown in Plate 75). Below the three central vertical rows of windows are tall niches, and at the far end of the room is a passageway, now blocked, that once led to more rooms to the north. On the façade the three uppermost windows are framed by thin cornices of terra cotta (Plate 79). Only these relieve the stark plane of the façade, for the architect did not wish to diminish the effect either of his bold shapes or of the contrast between the handsome windows and the surface through which they appear to have been cut.

The upper half of the extrados of the domical vault is visible from the annular corridors and the terraces behind it (Plate 80; the column is the only one that can be seen today in the entire Markets). The crown of the vault is approximately even with level III, and its curving haunch was loaded with stabilizing masonry. Its theoretical extrados meets the chord-wall of the lesser semidome (Plates 74 and 81). The space outlined by this tangent wall and the rising surface of the bigger dome was leveled as a terrace. The exterior surface of the lower, smaller semidome carries the impressions of the bipedales (tiles two Roman feet square) that once protected the structural concrete from the weather and may have helped to prevent the viscous concrete from slumping after the pour.[21] A half-oculus lights the chamber below. The level of the lower annular-vaulted corridor is that of the spring of the semidome; above rises the second, similar corridor.

Division A2. The lower façades of A1 and A3 lie along extensions of the diameter-chord of A2. The great hemicycle itself extends upward through three levels: I, with eleven rooms, two stairway entrances, and the entrance to A1, all opening onto the street; II, a curving vaulted corridor lit by twenty-five windows in the hemicycle wall and opening behind onto nine radiating rooms; and III, the terrace and shops atop the curving corridor and radiating chambers (Plates 82–84). At the ends of the hemicycle the several levels are connected by stair systems 1 and 2. The shops at level III faced inward, opening onto a terraced sidewalk of the Via Biberatica (Plate 84, a view from the northeast), but compositionally they belonged to A2. The whole division is admirably preserved except for the level III shops, of which only part of the pavements and lower walls remains.[22] At level III, about a third of the radial width of the division is

21. The Roman foot equals 0.295 m., but because of kiln shrinkage these great tiles average 0.56–0.58 m. on a side.

22. Part of the westernmost level III shop is preserved up to level IV. Lugli, *Roma*, p. 299, speaks of the Markets hemicycle (A2) as being

taken up by the terrace toward the Forum. At level II, the corridor wall pierced by twenty-five windows is somewhat thicker than the largely modern terrace parapet above.

The annular vault over the corridor of level II is unusual (Plate 85). Above the longer or hillside wall slightly concave tympana are set in the vault above the radial tabernae. This does not occur on the outer or window side, where the vault rises smoothly from its curving impost. The contrast between the shapes of the two sides of the vault emphasizes the presence and individuality of the radiating chambers, and the tympana add to the play of varied, modeled surfaces that sweep rhythmically around the corridor.

The shallow rooms of level I are approximate rectangles in plan. Their doorways projected from the hemicycle wall and were originally framed in travertine in the manner of almost all of the shops and offices of the Markets. Above these frames there were rectangular attics with small windows; one of these individual façades was restored by Ricci (Plate 86). The center line of the hemicycle passed between two of them. The proportion between the heights of the two levels as defined by the major cornices is approximately 4:3. The lack of concentricity of the Forum and Markets hemicycles has been pointed out. It causes the street between them to expand in width from about seven to about twelve meters, but at the center it is narrowed by the rectangular apse of the Forum wall.

Decoration on the brick façade is confined to the zone between levels II and III. The alternate openings (including the four blind niches at the extremities of the hemicycle) are enframed by shallow, simplified aediculae made of bricks with moldings of terra cotta. The pilaster bases and capitals are of travertine (Plate 87, the four southernmost openings). All these features project so slightly that they would have been barely distinguishable were it not for their variety of triangular, curving, and raking pediments (see Plates 76 and 83).[23] The distribution of these is not symmetrical around the hemicycle center line. There is no aedicula around the window on the center line, for the central, segmental, pediment is over the window just to the right, the sixteenth of the twenty-nine windows and blank niches, reading from the left. The play of the various pediment forms extends from this point in regular sequence in both directions only to end, of necessity, with unlike forms over the second and twenty-eighth features. The aediculae enframe fourteen of the twenty-nine windows and blanks; below these fourteen

---

symmetrical and regular in all its parts, but the level I openings and the system of pediments between levels II and III are not evenly balanced around the center line. The semidomed rooms of A1 and A3 are of different size and design. For drawings of stair system 2, see Desgodetz (above, n. 10), p. 139; G. Boni, "Esplorazione del Forum Ulpium," *NS* (1907), Figs. 48–49.

23. For a measured drawing of one bay of A2, see G. C. Mars, ed., *Brickwork in Italy* (Chicago,

1925), frontispiece; cf. Crema, Fig. 416. For examples of the use before the year 100 of alternating pediments in Roman architecture, see R. Naumann, *Der Quellbezirk von Nîmes* (Berlin, 1937), Taf. 17, 29; A. Maiuri, *L'ultima fase edilizia di Pompei* (Rome, 1942), Tav. IX–X; Boëthius, Fig. 42a; Pl. 51 here. Cf. Crema, Figs. 255, 330, 536, 543–45, 564; *AJA*, 67 (1963), 218.

windows, with one exception, are the shops and stairway entrances of level I. This asymmetry of the façade decoration may not have been particularly apparent in ancient times, but it is an enlivening note today because one's attention is quickly caught by these ancient forms executed in terra cotta. This is the only extant part of the Markets where a wall surface was treated with any detail other than simple horizontal string courses or segmental moldings (such as those of A1). Where the hemicycle meets the façades of A1 and A3 its level II decoration is terminated by pilasters of the same dimensions as those of the aediculae (Plate 88).

The most striking visual feature of the hemicycle today is the color of the brick, a rich red-brown weathered and stained in places to a deep gray. The necessary consolidation and restoration undertaken by Ricci's masons was done with sensitivity and discretion and can almost always be quickly identified (see for example the unworn brickwork visible in Plate 87). It has been popular in restoring Roman imperial brick-faced buildings on paper to clothe them with veneers of marble or stucco, but this probably should not be done for buildings designed after the time of Domitian without positive archaeological evidence. In the Markets the crispness of the brickwork, the tooling of the exposed edges of the bricks, and the lively texture and color of the surfaces may mean that the brickwork was left bare.[24]

Division A3. Here there is another semidomed chamber, balancing that of A1 (see Plate 75). It is smaller than its pendant and is entered through the street façade rather than through an opening in the hemicycle wall. There are only three façade windows, which are composed triangularly, the highest being on axis with the entrance. The extrados of the vault is covered by a terrace at level III. A file of shops flanks the stair and ramp system numbered 3, and a second file directly above opens onto the Via Biberatica as it descends toward the east. Parallel with this file and on the other side of stairway 3 there are the remains of another street of shops that extended as far as the north corner of the Forum of Augustus (Plate 74, between K and L). At the end of this last row of shops (toward Trajan's Forum) there is construction of the time of Domitian, and there are rooms of the same date behind the high loggia of the Knights of Rhodes (Plate 76, far right).[25] A wide passageway, supported by arches that span the Via Biberatica, leads from B3 to a high terrace at level IV (Plate 84).

24. The apparent lack of preservation of any original stucco is not by itself conclusive, but the care taken in making the various moldings of terra cotta might indicate that they were left bare; cf. J. H. Middleton, *The Remains of Ancient Rome*, 2 (London, 1892), 33–34; E. B. Van Deman, "Methods of Determining the Date of Roman Concrete Monuments, *AJA*, 16 (1912), 415; Crema, p. 363. There are second-century pediments and designs in terra cotta at Ostia and Isola Sacra, some if not all of which were left bare; see for example G. Calza, *La necropoli del porto di Roma nell'Isola Sacra* (Rome, 1940), Figs. 26, 34, 37; *Ostia*, Tav. XI.2; R. Calza and E. Nash, *Ostia* (Florence, 1959), Tav. 31, 146. There do not seem to be any cramp-holes at the Markets for fastening marble sheathing, nor are there any signs of nails used to secure stucco or cement to the brickwork, as at Domitian's palace.

25. See above, n. 7; also Ricci et al. (above, n. 11), pp. 113–15; Bloch, p. 54; Lugli, *Roma*, pp. 276–78.

The Aula Traiana and Its Dependencies

Division B1. From the high terrace of A3 the upper part of the aula Traiana south façade can be seen some seventy meters to the north (Plates 75 and 82; the lower portion of the aula is obscured by the intervening structure of B2). In plan, division B1 is a trapezium, narrowing toward both the south and west (Plate 89, a plan at gallery level, level IV). Within the great hall the visitor is not conscious of this asymmetry. In transverse section the four extant stories, on levels II–V, are stepped up the hillside from west to east.[26] The bottom story, a row of tabernae, faces the low, straight north-south stretch of the Via Biberatica, and across the street is another row of shops belonging to A1 (Plate 90, seen from the north). Though somewhat restored, this is one of the best preserved of all multistoried street fronts in the new imperial architecture. Here at level III there were balconies, carried on travertine corbels, that were perhaps simply elements of design, though they might have been used as emergency passageways leading to walkways and ladders now gone. Or just possibly they were first-story platforms for fighting fires, of the kind called for by Nero's building code after the disaster of 64. Similar balconies existed on the façades of B2 (Plate 84), many Ostian buildings of the second century, and the great southwest curve of Trajan's Baths.

Thirty-five out of the forty-five rooms that were originally part of this division are intact. The main hall, part of a religious establishment for many centuries, is in remarkably good condition (Plate 91). Stairs 4 and 5 were rebuilt in this century, and the great central vault and its supports, eaten away here and there but almost entirely original, has been strengthened with metal tie rods and cinctures.

The main hall, rising to level V from its paving at level III, is lined with rooms barrel-vaulted at right angles to the longitudinal major axis (Plates 92 and 93; in the latter the perspective has been deliberately forced). Upon these flanking vaults lie the open galleries and shallower rooms of level IV. The party walls of the flanking rooms of both levels III and IV are aligned vertically, but not transversely. These and the piers carrying the central vault are staggered in plan, perhaps the result of hurriedly or roughly dividing the unequal flank-lengths of two sides of the trapezium (Plate 89). There is a terrace at the south end of level IV that connects the galleries with the neighboring spaces of B2 (see Plate 75). The nature of the original entrance at the opposite, northern end that led over or from the street to the pavement of the great hall is unknown. Near the northeast corner there are a corridor and a stair that connected the gallery level with the area toward the Torre delle Milizie, and the now lost room at the top of the northwest corner once contained a staircase leading to the terrace at level V atop the gallery rooms (Plate 91, right).

The basic disposition of the level III spaces is the same as that of the market at Feren-

---

26. There are useful analytical drawings of B1 which include the basement rooms, in B. Fletcher and R. A. Cordingly, *A History of Architecture* on the *Comparative Method* (17th ed. London, 1961), p. 186 (where the plans are not entirely correct); see also *Arkitekten*, 5 (1963), 20.

tino (Plate 3). At Rome, however, the design becomes far more complex at the upper levels. The central vault springs from a relatively higher position, and bays are formed by crossing the main longitudinal barrel vault with six transverse barrel vaults somewhat warped in shape by the necessity of accommodating them to the staggered plan of the piers below. The result is a long canopy of concrete, resting upon fourteen short but fairly deep piers and opened at the sides by a dozen generously scaled clearstory openings (Plate 94).[27] The piers, which rise from the party walls of the tabernae below, were made necessary in part by the difference between the span of the longitudinal vault and the spans of the transverse vaults. The longitudinal vault sprang not from the wall-planes below but from large stone corbels placed well above level IV. The transverse vaults spring from the piers at a still higher level because of their lesser spans. In this way the central space was made higher, the main span decreased (by the corbels), the crowns of all the vault shapes brought to a uniform level, and the clearstory openings enlarged.[28] This is an extremely well thought out and ingenious design, the product in one sense at least of trying to solve a major problem faced by western architects a thousand years later: how to obtain continuous and level crown lines over consecutive cross-vaulted bays substantially wider than they are long.

The galleries at level IV that flank the upper half of the central nave are broken into unroofed bays by transverse brick arches that bridge the distance from the vault to the shallow tabernae behind. These arches are filletted and coved to the walls of the shop-fronts and are centered behind the largest masonry masses of the main vault (Plate 93). It is tempting to read them as buttresses in the high medieval sense, but their position and the structural nature of the building preclude calling them flying buttresses. The near-monolithic quality of the vault is such that once the concrete had cured the arches would be brought into play very little and probably not at all. Like most of the so-called relieving arches and vaults of buildings in the vaulted style these features were chiefly of use during the construction and earliest days of the building, and they stand ready to give a certain lateral support should the building move. They also load the main vault somewhat toward its main longitudinal center line. This load is difficult to measure accurately, but it exists, and it helps to give stability to the whole. The aula is composed

27. Incisa della Rochetta (above, n. 9), p. 203, says that the bays of the vault were separated by (transverse) arches of brick as shown in a painting by Giulio Romano illustrated in his Fig. 136. But this is not the case. Only the ends of the aula had brick ribs fitted under the semicircular arc of the vault (see Pl. 82 here); at the northern end the rib rose from spur walls that narrowed the entrance (see Pls. 89 and 91 here). The five divisions between bays are marked by the piers, which are sheathed in brick up to the level from which the transverse vaults spring (Pl. 94). The consoles that projected from these piers, and the

concrete masses that rose directly from the consoles, have all been lost.

28. G. Giovannoni, "La tecnica costruttiva e l'impero di Roma," *L'Ingegnere, 12* (1938), 307, shows the longitudinal vault springing from too high a level and describing, in transverse section, less than its actual 180°; his drawing is reproduced by Crema, Fig. 419. Giovannoni's plan of the aula (p. 306) is, however, the best available (= Crema, Fig. 418). The word "vaults" is used here to distinguish between the different shapes that make up the aula roof, but the roof is all one concrete mass.

of stable and quite rigid concrete members sufficiently loaded from above to keep the lines of theoretical thrust resolution quite close to vertical and well within the bounding planes of the structural solids.[29]

There is no indication of the origins of this design among remaining Roman buildings other than the simplified relationship between longitudinal and transverse elements found in buildings such as the markets of Ferentino and Tivoli.[30] In comparison to these the Trajanic aula is so advanced that it may be reasonable to assume an intermediate link. Such a design may have been used for the central hall of the Baths of Titus, but the restoration of that building depends upon Renaissance drawings that are inadequate for comparative analysis. The alternative to the existence of an intermediate step is that the aula was an original creation, but this cannot be stated as a certainty. It has been suggested that the design may have been derived from covered market streets in the east.[31] If this is correct the idea appeared in the Hellenistic world before the Tivoli and Ferentino structures. As yet no eastern examples have been reported.

EAST OF THE BIBERATICA

Division B2. The plain façades of B2 have been partly restored (Plates 75, 82, and 83). The northern part of the division extends vertically from the basement rooms beside the Via Biberatica up through levels III, IV, and V. There are horizontal communications with B1 at levels III and IV, but connections with B3 are uncertain. There is an opening on the north side of B2 that connects with the fragmentary upper street and structures beyond. Toward the Via Biberatica the upper part of the B2 façade was cut back in order to increase the light in the aula (see Plate 75). Just to the southeast of this

29. Crema, p. 364, says "Cosí le sollecitazioni non solo si trovano concentrate in punti nodali ma sono ivi accolte da elementi isolati di sostegno cui solo assicura la stabilità l'agile contrasto degli archi, con ardita anticipazione sulle concezioni strutturali del gotico." This concept is expressed or implied by other writers, for example Fletcher-Cordingly (above, n. 26), p. 185 E and F; and Incisa della Rochetta (above, n. 9), p. 206. It is very doubtful that a vault of poured concrete acts and is sustained in such a fashion once the structural mass has dried and cured. Presumably the transverse gallery arches of the aula helped to insure the equilibrium of the structure during the drying-out period, and stand ready to give a certain lateral support should the building move.

30. To the best of my knowledge there is no evidence of a comparable building in Roman architecture. The nearest equivalents to the aula nave were seen in the main halls of the imperial baths, where narrower transverse vaults usually rose from a higher level than the main longitudinal vaults. It may be that the aula was the intentional result of combining the central bath hall, as found in the imperial baths, with files of barrel-vaulted tabernae. In order to make full use of the site, and to concentrate the Markets' facilities, the files of tabernae were reduplicated vertically and the gallery system was devised to solve the resulting problems of lighting and communications. When the huge markets or *horrea* are excavated that occupy Is. XX, Reg. I, at Ostia, certain affinities with the Trajanic Markets may be revealed. The Ostian building, however, was roofed with a barrel vault over its central nave and had cross vaults over some if not all of the adjoining rooms. It dates from Hadrian's time: *Ostia*, p. 138 and Plan 1; cf. Meiggs, p. 138.

31. By R. M. Riefstahl, "Appunti sul Mercato di Traiano, III. Mercati e fondachi coperti nell' oriente islamico," *Roma*, *10* (1932), 168. Cf. below, n. 34.

is a plain and unadorned wall, perforated by a sensitively unbalanced window grouping, which from a distance is one of the most prominent features of the Markets. The uppermost part of the walls and the tiled roofs are modern but the effect is authentically Trajanic.

In plan this façade is only about thirty meters from the rectangular apse of the Forum hemicycle, but it rises somewhat more than that distance above the Forum level. From this the steepness, scale, and some of the visual effects of the Markets can be inferred. Midway in B2 the façade breaks cleanly at an angle of about 130°. Beyond this break, toward the south, the original structure is preserved only up to about level IV. At this level there were once balconies carried on narrow segmental barrel vaults sprung from stone corbels. Below the balconies are four shops with large mezzanine windows; above them the fabric is medieval (Plate 84).

At level III the rooms northwest of the vertical break-line can be entered from the floor of the aula. They consist first of a large semicircular chamber, seen in section on Plate 76, flanked by rooms of very irregular shape that take up the slack of the plan in a manner reminiscent of the plan of the Domus Aurea wing. The semicircular room was vaulted with a depressed semidome having a longitudinal section approximating a quarter of an ellipse. The adjoining irregularly shaped rooms are barrel-vaulted along their longest axes, the vaults having been ingeniously warped and fitted over the asymmetrical plans.

Above the semicircular room and its environs, at level IV, there is a suite of rooms of different plan. They can be entered either from the gallery level of the aula or from the north side of B2 through the opening mentioned above. Again the plan is partly fragmented. The chief features are two large rooms, one of them with a shallow apse (Plate 76, level IV, and Plate 89, upper right). Several writers have thought that these rooms were offices, perhaps those of the official in charge of the Markets, because of the wall-niches that presumably would have contained shelving or cabinets for storing records (Plate 95).[32] In the remainder of the division there are passageways, stairs, and many more vaulted rooms, some at intermediate levels.

Division B3. This has been partly destroyed. The remains consist of a high, shallow arcade that faces the Via Biberatica and masks part of stair number 6 (Plate 84). It is at the southern end of this arcade that the bridge crosses the street and connects B3 with the level IV terrace of A3. Along the side of the east-west portion of the Via Biberatica there are the remains of a few typical tabernae. This leg of the Via Biberatica descends to the present-day Salita del Grillo, where there is a profusion of terraced ruins that once were probably continuous with B3. They are bordered on the east by shops and a stepped ramp or cordonata that is parallel to the Salita.[33]

---

32. Lugli, *Roma*, pp. 305–06.

33. For illustrations of this area of the Markets, see A. von Gerkan, *Von antiker Architektur und Topographie* (Stuttgart, 1959), Taf. 14.1–2; Nash, 2, 58.

THE MARKETS AS URBAN SOCIAL ARCHITECTURE

The consanguinity of the Markets' block-like units with the functional *horrea* (warehouses) and insulae of Ostia, which reflected contemporary practice in Rome, is self-evident. Yet the general composition, with its picturesque grouping of rising, sweeping curves below tall prismatic masses joined at different angles, was highly original (Plate 75).[34] Roman architects had been fascinated by hillside sites for a long time but their earlier designs were based upon axial balance and symmetry. At the Markets the center line of the hemicycle was not used to control the overall plan and no balanced rectilinear silhouette was attempted. There were no peristyles or courts because the Markets existed for the life of shops and streets.[35] The result both functionally and visually was an urban unit, a city quarter with an irregular skyline, curving and turning streets, changing vistas, and an elaborate internal communications system. The place is so large and its plan so complex that it could not have been comprehended at once; it invited exploration and disclosed itself only part by part.

An ascent from the street at Forum level reveals the directional flexibility implied by the curving sweep of the hemicycle façade. All straight axes are relatively short, brought either to turns or intersected by other axes that branch away at various angles. Beside and opening onto these axes are clearly defined volumes, *places* that punctuate the potential of motion that permeates the entire design. In this way also the Markets resemble a city. The sense of motion is increased by the laconic treatment of the vertical surfaces, and the sequence of visual events works smoothly. The divisions are connected not only

34. Paribeni (above, n. 7), pp. 127–28, finds the Markets essentially military in conception and execution. This interpretation might be strengthened by a study of the similarities between the façade of A2 and fortified Roman gates; see Zorzi, p. 63 and Fig. 83; Crema, Figs. 223, 227, 232, 234–35. J. B. Ward Perkins, "The Art of the Severan Age in the Light of Tripolitanian Discoveries," *Proceedings of the British Academy*, 37 (1951), 297, n. 21, finds the Markets dynamically modern and strictly Italian in derivation and treatment; in his "Severan Art and Architecture at Lepcis Magna," *JRS*, 38 (1948), 62, he rejects a military origin for the design of Trajan's Forum. R. Martin, "Apollodorus of Damascus," *Encyclopedia of World Art*, 1 (1959), 512–13, considers the Markets completely functional in design, the result of engineering influences. Boëthius, pp. 77–80, says that the idea behind the aula of the Markets and the Hadrianic building at Ostia mentioned above, n. 30, was derived from covered streets in the east, and that when this idea reached Rome it was developed, through the medium of concrete, in a new monumental way. He implies

(p. 79) that the warehouses and market types of the imperial age were derived from earlier, Eastern sources, and cites as an example of these sources the Seleucid Agora at Dura-Europos, published by F. E. Brown in *The Excavations at Dura-Europos, Preliminary Report of the Ninth Season* (New Haven, 1944), where pp. 7–15 and Fig. 11 are pertinent. But this building was related to the markets and horrea of imperial Rome and Ostia only in function, and differed from them in plan, elevation, and structure, for it was the product of entirely different architectural attitudes. Any links that may have existed between East and West are as yet unknown; cf. Riefstahl (above, n. 31), p. 168. On balance it would seem that Ward Perkins' conclusion is correct.

35. For illustrations of the tabernae, see Ricci's pamphlet of 1929 (above, n. 11), p. 19; Lugli (above, n. 16), pp. 544, 547; and cf. Boëthius, Chap. 4. For a recent study of tabernae, see G. Girri, *La taberna nel quadro urbanistica e sociale di Ostia* (Rome, 1956). Some of the barrel vaults over the tabernae of the Markets are segmental, with arcs of about 135–140°.

physically but also by the uniform color and texture of the brickwork, the rhythmic shadows of the openings, and the visual and kinetic directives set up by the well-planned communications system. Between the groups of tabernae are less static elements such as stair systems or semicircular and apsidal rooms that function as spatial vestibules to the next serial experience of places.

The aula Traiana displays all of these characteristics. Spaciousness, simplicity, and clarity are its primary attributes. The oblong bays avoid the static quality of square units, and because the vaults spring from well up in the second story and not from the pavement level of the gallery, the central space seems to gain in height. This effect is emphasized by the stilting of the flanking or clearstory arches, which spring from short piers that rise to the impost level of the vault forms and are perhaps unique in Western architecture (Plate 94). The design of the superstructure is such that ample light, circulation of air, and upper-level communications are provided by one coherent solution. The planar continuity of the lower wall surfaces and the perspectives they frame is uninterrupted, for no free-standing verticals obstruct the central space. The inner surfaces of the squat piers are continuous with those of the wall below, and the semicircular ends of the transverse barrel vaults and the clearstory arches they form are not visually detached from the rest of the space. This in turn emphasizes the unity and size of the interior volume. The vault piers were reduced to minimum size (Plate 92). No cornice was used to mark the inner edge of the gallery floor at level IV, and nowhere were there columns or decorative forms taken from the traditional orders. Nothing breaks the sweep of space. It is unfair to the architect to describe the aula as merely utilitarian architecture. It was indeed utilitarian, and probably very successfully so, but it is also a work of art.

The forms of the aula were familiar ones but were used imaginatively in new juxtapositions. An exciting space and massing resulted, all the more eloquent because of the familiarity of the basic, simple shapes that were used. The aula is a coherent whole, an entity in itself, and thus characteristically Roman. The discipline behind the design is extremely strong. It pulses from the central space of the building through to the outside, where it becomes a single line of axial force, attracting and directing attention. Once inside the hall the crosscurrents set up by the side openings and the transverse elements of the vault give the visitor a powerful sense of place. The architect wished to accentuate the difference between the sensation or knowledge of being in *a* place and the transient experience of passing from one location to another. This Roman sense of place is almost overwhelming. Inside there is ideal human order undisturbed by any suggestion of movement between places.

The vault of the aula is higher than any of the others in the Markets and covers the largest unobstructed area. The visitor is placed in a volume that is neither too great nor too small and is not interrupted by structure. Impressions of surface are heightened at the expense of mass. The reciprocal relationships among structural solids, lighting, and proportions create a harmonious whole, strong and permanent. The design is not static or abstract, for the curving surfaces and groins convey a sense of action. Nor does it crush or overwhelm, for the gallery openings between the thin piers make the vault read as a canopy. With its unencumbered, noble space the aula Traiana belongs with the Pantheon in the very first rank of imperial architecture.

The application of the same principles to the other divisions was less spectacular but no less consistent. The entire Market is an inside-outside place planned for the Italian climate and way of life. Everywhere large openings release the interior spaces from any sensation of being encased by overbearing weights. Light and air are plentiful. In the interior corridors tangential views through the windows appear in regular rhythms. Each interior, unimpeded by transverse horizontal forms, is lifted upward by the rounded surface of a vault. The entire design is permeated with the visual energy of the new style. A continuous flow of surface and form was created by curving walls, the use of piers in place of columns, and the exclusion of rectilinear relationships between supports and superstructure. The architect made maximum use of his structural system as an essential part of the design, to the point where structure and architectural effects very nearly became a unity.

The interior spaces are housed in bold and simple forms whose curved surfaces and planar expanses were massed contrapuntally in a masterful way. These effects were enhanced by brickwork of which any master mason would be proud. The courses are exactly horizontal, the walls geometrically true, and the lines and angles of junction precise and neat. The builders were experienced professionals of the first rank who knew exactly what they wanted to do and how to do it. The most obvious result of the architect's attitudes toward relationships between design and structure is the most striking: there are no columns, and there are few moldings. His is not an architecture of façades, of overcoating with polite architectural phrases. Where traditional decorative forms were used they were not of stone but of terra cotta, of simplified form and in such low relief as to be almost as flat and shadowless as the wall surfaces themselves. The strength of tradition and the history of Roman style before Trajan's time make this all the more impressive and emphasize by contrast the significance of the Markets for the history of architecture. To build early in the second century more than two hundred rooms, some of them quite large, without requiring the use of a single structural column was a revolutionary act. More than that, it occurred not at a barracks or port but at the center of the Roman world beside the marble-laden and gilded Forum and Basilica Ulpia. The latter were essentially axial compositions obeying overriding rules of symmetry (Plate 74). Their curves, in contrast to those of the Markets, were the servants of an underlying rectangularity, conceived not as independent and expressive rounded forms but rather as variants of straight walls. Beyond and above this fixed and circumscribed splendor the forms and volumes of the Markets proliferated in time and space. There the new style filled the architect's vision, and the tyranny of the straight entablature was overthrown.

As important as the quality and originality of their design is the evidence the Markets give of acceptance of the new style as proper for major social programs. In this respect they belong in the same category as the imperial baths, though it is only at the Markets that the superbly successful interrelation of design, structure, and function that characterizes Roman vaulted social architecture at its best can be seen and experienced. Here this finely gauged reciprocity among the essentials of architecture, free of decorative embellishment derived from a past and alien style, has been preserved in its every nuance. This is not to discount the great importance of Ostia in this respect, but most of the stylistically coherent Ostian buildings were built later than the Markets. It was in Rome that the new architecture was carried to the peak of expression, and it was the Markets that ushered in the great age of vaulted-style social architecture of the first half of the second century. Many features of their design and construction can be traced to previous experiments and developments, but the overriding significance of the Markets lies in the confident and successful use of the new principles in the service of a vast urban social program.

The new style was exactly suited to the kind of city life encouraged by the imperial system. Its design and effects had few if any pre-imperial associations. With his Markets the architect challenged the ascendancy in public architecture of the ancient basilica form and the hallowed imagery of the colonnaded temple. In doing this he reflected the growing secularization of much ancient life, and he embodied and described in his design the nature of the increasingly unified metropolitan civilization of the High Empire.

V

THE PANTHEON

HADRIAN, of all the Roman emperors, had the deepest personal interest in architecture. He was a poet, amateur architect, painter, administrator, and soldier, a universal man in the Renaissance sense, turning his attention and talent to every public and private interest.[1] The lands of the empire are strewn with buildings of his reign (117–38); his effect upon architecture was profound. In Rome he built among other structures the Temple of the Divine Trajan, the Temple of Venus and Rome, his mausoleum (Castel Sant'Angelo), and the Pantheon. He continued and expanded Trajan's redevelopment of Ostia and erected a truly vast villa for himself near Tivoli. He embellished Athens, where he served as archon, with many new buildings and finished the Temple of Zeus Olympios. He founded several Hadrianopoleis, refounded and refurbished a number of older towns, and was hailed not without some justification as "father" and "founder" in settlements from Spain to Syria. A fourth-century biographer said that "he built public buildings without number but he placed his own name on none of them except the temple of his father Trajan."[2]

Hadrian was by no means an ideal, clement prince, and in his later years he became disillusioned and dissatisfied with life, but his sense of public responsibility, like that of Vespasian and Trajan, was acute. Autocratic and paternalistic, he put great sums of money and the machinery of the imperial bureaucracy at the service of architecture. He and his architects favored vaulted buildings, and during his reign trabeated and vaulted

1. He claimed to know everything of "peace and war, of public and private life," according to Dio Cassius, 69.3.2. Cf. *SHA, Hadrian* 14.8.11, where his many talents are listed, and he is said to have been "in the same person austere and genial, dignified and playful, dilatory and quick to act, niggardly and generous, deceitful and straightforward, cruel and merciful, and always in all things changeable." This fourth-century biography is by no means always reliable (see *OCD*, pp. 431–32), but the quotation conveys

something of the many-sidedness of Hadrian's personality, which baffled his contemporaries; cf. Dio Cassius, 69.5.1.

2. *SHA, Hadrian* 19.9, 20.4; he "built something in almost every city" (id., 19.2); cf. Suetonius, *Domitian* 5. Fronto said that one might "see memorials of his journeys in most of the cities of Europe and Asia," Loeb edition, 2, 206–07; cf. Dio Cassius, 69.5.3. For architecture in Hadrian's time, see Rivoira, pp. 118–59; Kähler; Crema, pp. 335–506.

systems were synthesized with great success. In the Near East the tradition of cut-stone construction continued, but in general Hadrianic architecture is characterized by a continued and highly imaginative development of the vaulted style. The concepts of the architects of Nero, the Flavians, and Trajan were brought to maturity between the time when Hadrian began his reign by burning in the Forum of Trajan the records of debts to the imperial treasury, and when he died at Baia, "hated by all."[3] Of his buildings the Pantheon is the most significant. Indeed, it is one of the most important buildings for the history of architecture ever erected.

The image of the Pantheon is so well known and the building itself so readily accessible that it might seem superfluous to describe and discuss it at some length. But its unique effects, enigmatic meaning, and intriguing structure have apparently not yet been explored in any one place.[4] No claim is made here to completeness of detail or of understanding, but the pages that follow may serve as an introduction to this mighty building.

DESCRIPTION

The Pantheon is located in the Campus Martius, the ninth Augustan region, and faces almost exactly due north (Plate 96). Its Greek name means "all gods"; the question of whether or not ἱερόν (a holy place or *templum*) should be understood will be reserved for the moment. The Pantheon is composed of three primary geometric elements: a pedimented octastyle porch, an immense domed cylinder, and a rectangular feature as wide as the porch and as high as the cylinder, inserted between the two. Care-

3. *SHA, Hadrian* 25.7; cf. Dio Cassius, 69.23.2. For the remission of debts, see *SHA, Hadrian* 7.6; *CIL*, 6.967; N. Lewis and M. Reinhold, *Roman Civilization*, 2 (New York, 1955), 149–50. There is a contemporary relief that shows the records being brought to the fire; see E. Strong, *La scultura romana*, 2 (Florence, 1926), Fig. 125; Nash, 2, 176.

4. Misapprehensions linger in the modern literature. They chiefly concern the date and homogeneity of the building, the design and function of the structure within the rotunda walls, and the nature of the dome fabric. The first two points have generated a considerable polemical literature; otherwise there are fewer publications than might be expected for so famous and influential a building. There is a good basic bibliography in Nash, 2, 170–71; the fundamental works are as follows: A. Desgodetz, *Les édifices antiques de Rome* (2nd ed. Paris, 1779), pp. 1–26 and Pls. I–XXIII (the best study of the Pantheon, dating from 1676–77; it includes criticisms of the studies of Desgodetz' famous Italian predecessors, and original measured drawings; cf. *AB*, 40 [1958], 23–24 and citations; Desgodetz' foot = 0.325 m.); L. Beltrami, *Il Pantheon* (Milan, 1898); Durm, pp. 548–74; A. M. Colini and I. Gismondi, "Contributi allo studio del Pantheon. La parete frontale dell'avancorpo e la data del portico," *BC*, 54 (1926), 67–92; G. Cozzo, *Ingegneria romana* (Rome, 1928), pp. 255–97; L. Beltrami, *Il Pantheon rivendicato ad Adriano, 117–138 d.C.* (Milan, 1929); Platner-Ashby, pp. 382–86; A. von Gerkan, "Das Pantheon in Rom," *Gnomon*, 5 (1929), 273–77; J. Guey, "Devrait-on-dire: Le Panthéon de Septime Sévère? À propos des estampilles sur briques . . . ," *Mélanges d'archéologie et d'histoire de l'école française de Rome*, 53 (1936), 198–249; G. Lugli, *I monumenti antichi di Roma e suburbio*, 3 (Rome, 1938), 123–50; Bloch, pp. 14–19, 102–17; R. Vighi, *Il Pantheon* (Rome, 1955 and subsequent printings; Eng. trans. by J. B. Ward Perkins [Rome, 1957], cited here). There is a guidebook by V. Bartoccetti, *Santa Maria ad Martyres (Pantheon)* (Rome, n.d., but ca. 1958).

ful modern studies of the fabric and the brick stamps have shown conclusively that the entire building dates from Hadrian's reign. It was begun sometime between July of 118 and the end of the following year and finished between 125 and 128.[5] Of all the pertinent brick stamps studied by Bloch and others the largest number from any one year are of 123, the year of the consulship of Paetinus and Apronianus.[6] The famous inscription across the entablature of the porch, which has caused so much confusion, refers to an earlier building; the metal letters are modern.[7] The Pantheon has been repaired many times, but almost all of its Hadrianic structural fabric and much of its original marble work remain intact.[8] It was consecrated as a church, S. Maria ad Martyres, early in the seventh century by Boniface IV, and was last repaired and restored thirty-odd years ago.[9] From time to time various towers appeared upon the porch and the intermediate

5. Bloch, pp. 102–17; his conclusions in the matter are worth quoting (pp. 116–17): "Dall'esame dei bolli del Pantheon risultò l'assoluta omogeneità del materiale adoperato per la costruzione delle diverse parti del monumento, e una strettissima affinità di questo materiale con quello usato per l'innalzamento di alcuni altri edifici, che si possono tutti indipendentemente datare al principio del governo di Adriano. Il Pantheon, gravamente danneggiato intorno all metà del periodo traianeo, fu ricostruito da Adriano immediatemente dopo il suo primo arrivo a Roma; nella seconda metà del 118 o nel 119 si iniziarono i lavori, che quanto all'ossatura furono terminati entro pochi anni. È assai probabile che la dedicazione del tempio abbia avuto luogo durante il soggiorno dell'imperatore a Roma tra il primo e il secondo viaggo, cioè 125–128"; cf. his "The Serapeum of Ostia and the Brickstamps of 123 A.D. . . .," *AJA*, 63 (1959), 225–40. Hadrian was in or near Rome during the years 125–28 after an absence of four years, and it is known that he dedicated his Temple of Venus and Rome on April 21, 128; see J. Dürr, *Die Reisen des Kaisers Hadrian* (Vienna, 1881), pp. 69–70; A. Garzetti, *L'impero da Tiberio agli Antonini* (Bologna, 1960; = *Storia di Roma*, 6), 678–80; W. Weber, *Untersuchungen zur Geschichte des Kaisers Hadrianus* (Leipzig, 1907), pp. 277–78; cf. *CAH*, 11, 318–19. It is most probable that the Pantheon was dedicated during this period. It has been known since the late eighteenth century that all parts of the structure belong to one building period; see Colini and Gismondi (above, n. 4), pp. 69–70. The more recent argument about the date and homogeneity of the building, chiefly concerned with the interpretation of brick stamps, can be traced through their article; through

Bloch, pp. 14–19; and Crema, pp. 377, 380. For the earlier literature on this, see R. Lanciani, "Il Pantheon e le terme di Agrippa. Prima relazione," *NS* (1881), pp. 255–94; id., "Seconda relazione," *NS* (1882), pp. 340–59.

6. Chedanne discovered that these and other Hadrianic stamps existed throughout the building and were not just evidence of restoration; see *Comptes rendus de l'Académie des inscriptions et belles-lettres* (1892), pp. 122–25, 171, 408–09; cf. Lanciani, p. 480; id., "La controversia sul Pantheon," *BC*, 20 (1892), 150–59; and *Journal of the Royal Institute of British Architects*, 2 (1895), 175–82.

7. Vighi (above, n. 4), p. 9. The Augustan date, given by this inscription (see Pl. 96), persists; see for example J. Gloag, *Guide to Western Architecture* (New York, 1958), p. 78. The name of the empress Julia Sabina, Hadrian's wife and Trajan's grandniece, is said to have been visible at one time upon some part of the marble décor of the apse. Apparently it is not there today, and it is not clear where it was located; see Lanciani, p. 481; H. Jordan and C. Huelsen, *Topographie der Stadt Rom im Altertum*, 1.3 (Berlin, 1907), 585, n. 74. On the architrave of the porch façade there is an inscription recording restorations carried out for Septimius Severus (193–211) and Caracalla (211–17). These were of minor importance unless one assumes, as does Vighi, p. 38, that they may have included the redecoration of the interior attic (the zone just below the spring of the dome); see also Lugli (above, n. 4), pp. 141–42; and below, n. 51.

8. For some of the marbles, see F. Corsi, *Delle pietre antiche* (Rome, 1845), pp. 356–57.

9. For an introduction to the history of the building and the repairs that have been made to

block. The last and most famous of these were the two open lanterns added by Bernini for Urban VIII (1623–44), which were removed late in the nineteenth century.[10]

Today the paving to the north of the building is considerably higher than in ancient times (Plate 97). Originally a flight of five steps, as wide as the porch, led from a paved court in front of the building up to the floor level of the porch (Figure 8). The colonnaded court was approximately as wide as the rotunda and extended at least as far north as the present church of the Maddalena. Presumably this court was entered on the north through some kind of propylon, and it is very probable that a free-standing triumphal arch stood within the open space; the details of Figure 8 are conjectural.[11]

The monolithic shafts of the porch façade are of gray Egyptian granite.[12] Behind the

---

it over the centuries, see Lanciani, pp. 483–88; id., *Storia degli scavi*, 2 (Rome, 1903), 236–40; F. Cerasoli, "I restauri del Pantheon dal secolo XV al XVIII," *BC*, 37 (1909), 280–89; C. Montani, "Il Pantheon e i suoi recenti restauri," *Capitolium*, 8 (1932), 417–26; A. Terenzio, "La restauration du Panthéon de Rome," *Mouseion*, 6 (1932), 52–57; id., "Pantheon," *EncIt*, 26 (1935), 212–14; P. Tomei, "Le vicende del rivestimento della cupola del Pantheon," *BdA*, 32 (1938), 31–39; Vighi (above, n. 4), pp. 12–18; and Bartoccetti (above, n. 4), pp. 15–25. Terenzio, "Restauration," p. 52, said that he hoped to publish a detailed account of the results of his work, but this has not appeared. His repairs to the brick facing are easily identified by the irregular surfaces of the modern bricks; see the upper courses visible on Pl. 120b here. A selection of the numerous vedute of the building will be found with Terenzio's encyclopaedia article, in Vighi's pamphlet, and in H. Egger, *Römische Veduten*, 2 (Vienna, 1931), Taf. 92–96.

10. These, the famous "orecchie d'asino," have been criticized as frivolous and unsuitable, but they were quite sober in design; see Vighi (above, n. 4), p. 17. Cf. Bernini's far more dramatic towers for S. Peter's; R. Wittkower, *Art and Architecture in Italy, 1600 to 1750* (Harmondsworth, 1956), pp. 118, 126, and Pl. 63b. Bernini's additions to the Pantheon had a profound effect upon the designers of post-seventeenth-century domed and porticoed rotundas; see for example the material in C. L. V. Meeks, "Pantheon Paradigm," *JSAH*, 19 (1960), 135–44.

11. For the court and arch, see Lanciani, "Seconda relazione" (above, n. 5), pp. 346–47 and Tav. XXI; Platner-Ashby, p. 42; Lugli (above, n. 4), Tav. IV; Crema, p. 380; *FUR*, 1, Fig. on

p. 232; cf. R. Lanciani, *Ancient Rome in the Light of Recent Discoveries* (London, n.d.), pp. 3–4. A detail of the model of Rome, showing these features, can be seen in Vighi (above, n. 4), p. 8; and in F. E. Brown, *Roman Architecture* (New York, 1961), Pl. 65. The dates of these constructions are not certain (the arch would seem to antedate Hadrian's Pantheon), but a Hadrianic date for the colonnaded court is indicated because it was a necessary if not an inseparable part of the Pantheon's exterior design; see p. 111, below. On Lanciani's Tav. XXI the columns of the eastern portico of the court are reported as having been set upon a line both parallel to the main axis of the Pantheon, and, by extension, tangent to the exterior wall of the rotunda; these relationships would seem at least to eliminate a pre-Hadrianic date for the court. For the area today, see the well-illustrated article by B. Blomé, "Piazza della Rotunda al Pantheon," *Opuscula romana*, 4 (1962), 1–28.

12. C. H. O. Scaife, "The Origins of Some Pantheon Columns," *JRS*, 43 (1953), 37, has shown that they were very likely quarried at Gebel Fitery between the Nile and the Gulf of Suez; he notes that there is a fragment of the same kind of stone beside the Column of Trajan that probably belonged to Hadrian's Temple of the Divine Trajan. For a sense of the scale of the Pantheon columns, see *MAAR*, 4 (1924), Pl. LVII.1. Recent work on the porch is reported by F. Sanguinetti, "Sul consolidamento della trabeazione del pronoa del Pantheon," *Palladio*, 6 (1956), 78–79; see also below, n. 59. Details of the porch measurements will be found in Desgodetz (above, n. 4), Pls. V, VIII–X, XII–XIII; and in L. Beltrami's book of 1929 (above, n. 4), p. 68.

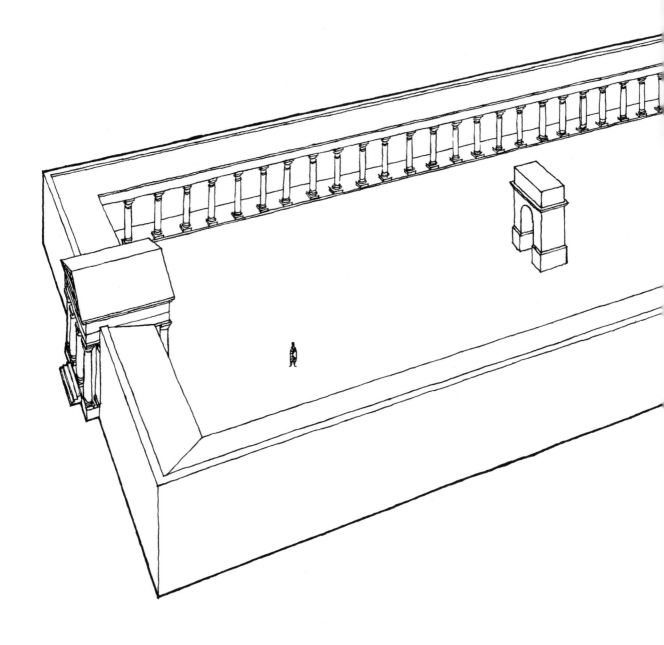

8. *Perspective sketch of the Pantheon with its forecourt restored conjecturally*

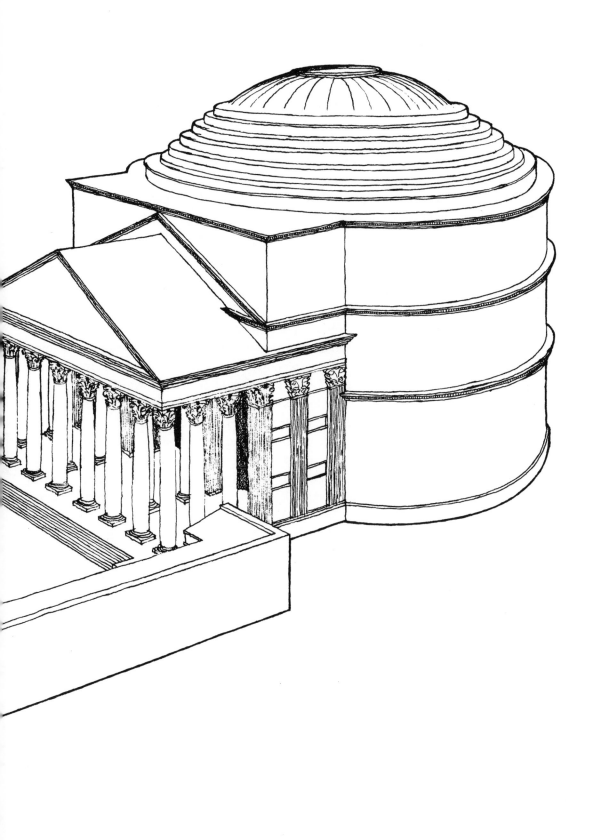

first, third, sixth, and eighth façade columns there are two additional columns in file to the south (Plates 98 and 99). The flank columns were also originally all of gray Egyptian granite, but the three on the east, including the corner one, fell at some time unknown together with their entablature. One was re-erected in 1625 for Urban VIII, and the other two and the entablature were added shortly afterward for Alexander VII (1655–67). These replacements, of reddish granite, were apparently taken from the ruins of the Baths of Alexander Severus nearby (see Plate 119). The four inner columns are of reddish Egyptian granite, and all the original capitals and bases are of Pentelic marble. The pavement of the porch is of blocks of marble and granite arranged in a pattern of circles and rectangles.

The four inner columns of the porch carry marble entablatures. Upon these, above the four columns and the responding pilaster piers of the intermediate block, there are piers of roughly squared stones (Plate 100). These are connected by files of arches running north and south that together with the stone piers and the exterior entablatures support the timber work of the roof. The woodwork and tile covering of the roof are not original. Urban VIII removed an enormous weight of ancient bronze from the porch superstructure, and it has frequently been said that this was in the form of trusses, for Renaissance drawings of beam-like metal forms have been preserved. But it is not certain that ancient bronze, which surely had very little compression strength, would have been strong enough in beam form to support a roof with an area of nearly six hundred square meters. Perhaps the original roof was framed in timber much as the present one is, but with the beams encased in metal.[13] Hung vaults, of the kind described by Vitruvius, closed off the view into the superstructure.[14]

The four north-south files of columns lead to the intermediate block, which is of brick-faced concrete. It rises to a height of about three and a half meters above the ridge line of the porch roof and is finished with a slightly sloping terrace continuous with the one that encircles the exterior of the dome (Figure 8 and Plates 101 and 102). Within the intermediate block, on either side of the main entrance to the rotunda, are

13. For the drawings, see Lanciani, pp. 485–86, Fig. 188, and the sketch on p. 486; Crema, Fig. 450. Cf. Rivoira, p. 122; and Platner-Ashby, p. 384. A. Choisy, *L'art de bâtir chez les romains* (Paris, 1873), Fig. 91, published a composite drawing of the structure based upon the earlier graphic records; cf. C. Fea, *L'integrità del Pantheon, rivendicata a Marco Agrippa* (Rome, 1820), Tav. IV. Encased beams would explain both the nails mentioned by Lanciani (p. 486) and the raking cuttings, still visible in the stonework above the entablatures (Pl. 100 here), into which transverse, angled beams could have been socketed. The present timberwork appears to be largely of the nineteenth century.

14. Vitruvius, 7.3.1–3. There were three of these, semicylindrical in shape, running north-south and springing from the entablatures above the files of columns. At the south, upon the face of the intermediate block, the semicircular forms against which these false vaults ended can still be read; at the north, on the back side of the stone pediment, the same form can be seen for the west aisle. Choisy's drawing (above, n. 13), outlines the vaults in transverse section; see also the analytical drawing of the Pantheon published by C. Heimsath, "Curvilinear Forms in Architecture. The Pantheon and the Olympic Sports Palace," *Concrete in Architecture*, 63 (1960), 4. Cf. *Hommages à A. Grenier*, 1 (1962), 457–61.

two chambers of approximately triangular plan that extend all the way to the top of the block and contain stair systems. In ancient times these chambers were entered by doors through the eastern and western sides of the block. This is still true in the case of the western chamber, but there the stairs now extend only about two thirds of the way to the terrace.[15] The stairs in the eastern chamber, which continue all the way to the terrace, are reached through a door cut at some time unknown in the great east niche of the block (see Plate 98). A system of landings and openings gives access to neighboring spaces within the rotunda walls and, in the case of the east staircase, to large rooms located over the great niches and the barrel-vaulted main entrance to the rotunda (Plate 103). Through the centuries some of the openings have been blocked up, but it is still possible to visit several of the spaces that honeycomb the huge cylindrical structure and to reach the upper, more or less level surfaces of the two interior ring cornices (access openings are visible, just above the cornices, in Plate 104).

The north-south files of porch columns respond to a triple vertical division of the intermediate block. The huge niches may have once contained statues of Augustus and Agrippa, though this is not certain.[16] Between them is the barrel-vaulted entranceway to the rotunda, its elevation in harmony with the design of the niches. The entranceway is framed by pilasters of white marble, finished like the capitals of the porch with exquisite workmanship (see Plate 100). The soffit of the barrel vault above the entrance is coffered and the undersides of the entablature blocks of the porch have recessed panels. Above the doors proper, which are in the plane of tangency of the intermediate block and the exterior of the rotunda, there is a rectangular opening in which a metal grille is fitted; above this and under the barrel vault there is a tympanum wall (Plate 104). The threshold is a huge block of portasanta marble, and the valves of the door are hung from bronze pilasters. The huge doors, restored in the time of Pius IV (1559–1565), are made of sheets of bronze attached to timber frames with bronze nails.[17] Beyond the doors one passes under a barrel vault into the vast unencumbered space of the domed rotunda, a volume of about seventy thousand cubic meters (see the Frontispiece).[18]

15. At some unknown date, this stairwell was roofed over at the level of the second interior ring cornice, forming a room connecting with those above the barrel-vaulted entranceway to the building that are now reached by the opposite, eastern stair system (see Pl. 103). All of these interconnecting rooms are now occupied by the Pontificia Accademia dei Virtuosi al Pantheon; cf. Bartoccetti (above, n. 4), pp. 30–31. Both stair systems are supported on powerful ramping arches; cf. Durm, Fig. 394.

16. Dio Cassius, 53.27.3, quoted below on p. 119.

17. Lanciani, p. 486, says that according to documents he discovered, the doors "were practically cast over" for Pius IV. There are drawings of the doors in Desgodetz (above, n. 4), Pl. XIII; L. Canina, *Gli edifizi di Roma antica*, 2 (Rome, 1848), Tav. LXIX; and in the *Oxford History of Technology*, 2 (Oxford, 1956), Fig. 383D.

18. Professor William Jordy tells me that the rotunda of the Guggenheim Museum in New York encloses 35,000 m.[*] The stilted barrel vault of the Pantheon entrance is wide enough for the warped quality of the line (made by the intersection with the rotunda cylinder) to be perceived instantly (see Pl. 104); a similar line occurs over the

The present interior paving dates largely from 1873 but follows the pattern and contains some of the stone of the ancient paving. It is composed of alternating circles and squares of colored marbles and granites arranged in both longitudinal and transverse files (see Plate 98). There are no rooms below the paving, only a system of drainage channels.[19] In addition to the central entrance just described there is only one other passage through the rotunda. Corridors cut through the pier walls west of the apse lead by way of an intermediate chamber to a file of rooms, south of the Pantheon, placed at right angles to the main axis of the building. These passages are not antique, and above them, in the dome, very large fissures were found and closed about thirty-five years ago.[20] The rooms that lie just to the south of the rotunda were originally part of the Basilica of Neptune, a large Hadrianic structure.[21] They have been restored in modern times and now house a chapel, a vestry, and storage areas.

The Pantheon is a complicated building with an advanced and ingenious structural system. To describe it in further detail coördinates are needed. It will be helpful to divide the building first into horizontal levels and then into vertical positions separated radially. There are five major levels (Figure 9 and Plate 105):

I.   The paving of the porch and rotunda. The rotunda paving appears to be very slightly crowned.

II. The first interior ring cornice, separating the great niches from the attic zone that now contains blind pedimented windows alternating with rectangular panels (Plate 104). There is a cornice on the exterior of the rotunda that is slightly below this level, but for convenience both of these cornices will be considered to be at level II.

III. The second interior ring cornice, from which the hemispherical dome appears to spring. There is an exterior cornice at almost exactly this level.

(wider) apse at the south. The interruption at these two positions of the horizontal interior cornice by arched moldings prefigures an association of forms common in later antiquity; see for example Crema, Figs. 714, 716, 809, 811. The Pantheon was not the first building where this appeared, but its use there lent stature to a fundamentally anti-classical element of design. The warped line could have been a source for the exploitation by Maderno and later architects of the design possibilities inherent in such intersections. See N. Pevsner, "The Three-Dimensional Arch from the Sixteenth to the Eighteenth Century," *JSAH*, 17 (1958), 22–24; some of the forms he discusses and illustrates were in use in Roman times.

19. These are shown in the drawing published by Heimsath (above, n. 14); a number of graves were found when the paving was renovated in the nineteenth century. Tav. LVI, in *EncIt*, 26 (1935), is labeled as showing underground rooms, but what is seen is construction to the south of the Pantheon, level with the rotunda pavement; cf. Montani (above, n. 9), pp. 420–21.

20. Terenzio, "Restauration" (above, n. 9), pp. 54–55 and Pl. XI (opp. p. 80); *EncIt*, 26 (1935), ill. on p. 214. The openings to the apse and to the aedicula, shown on Pl. 98 here, are now blocked. There is still a major fissure, ranging up to 10 cm. in width, visible in the attic chamber above the apse.

21. G. Gatti, "Il portico degli Argonauti e la basilica di Nettuno," *Atti*, 3, 61–73; cf. *FUR*, 1, 98; and above, n. 19. For other structures near or attached to the rotunda, see G. Gatti, "'Saepta Iulia' e 'Porticus Aemilia' nella 'Forma' Severiana," *BC*, 62 (1934), 123–49; *FUR*, 1, 18; cf. Brown (above, n. 11), Pl. 65.

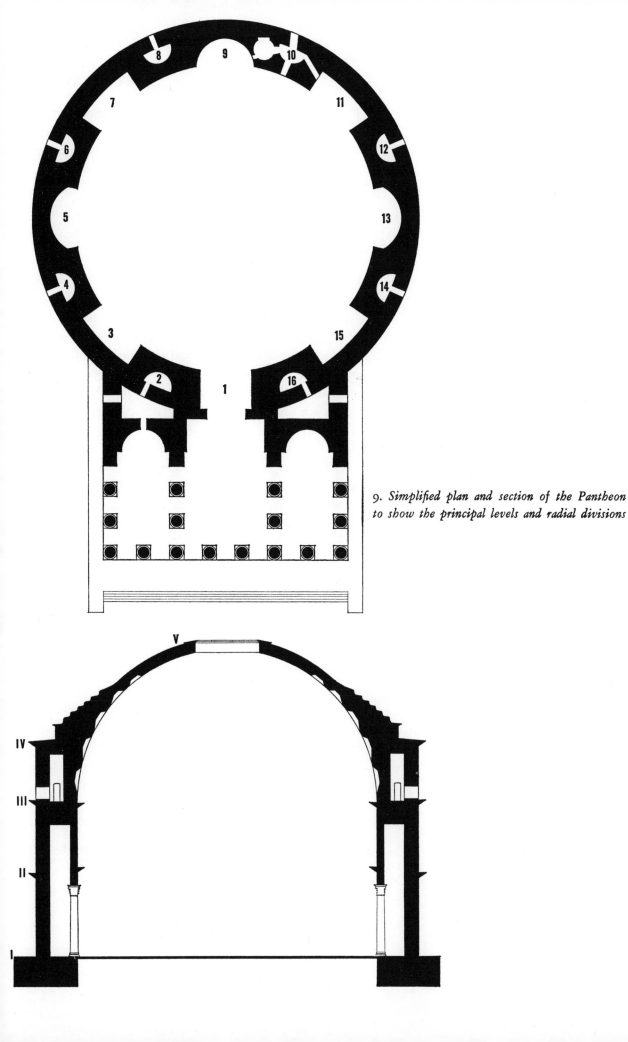

9. *Simplified plan and section of the Pantheon to show the principal levels and radial divisions*

IV. The third exterior ring cornice. This is at the same height as the top of the intermediate block, and at about the level of the center of the second range of interior coffers. It extends inward, sloping slightly upward, to form the terrace that circles the exterior base of the dome.

V. The plane defined by the upper opening of the oculus.

The rotunda cylinder can conveniently be divided vertically into sixteen positions according to the niches and chambers that are set within the circular walls (Figure 9 and Plate 103):

1. At levels I and II this is the barrel-vaulted entranceway to the rotunda. At III there are two L-shaped rooms.[22]

2. Three semicircular, semidomed chambers of key-shaped plan rising from each of the first three levels; for convenience they will be called key-chambers. All three connect with the stair shaft in the intermediate block. At level III all of the key-chambers (even-numbered positions) are cut through by centered radial walls pierced with arched openings. At this and all even-numbered positions there are aediculae at level I that project slightly into the rotunda space (Plate 104).

3. The position of the first of the six great interior niches screened by columns between levels I and II. The side walls of the position 3 niche are in planes that pass through the vertical center line of the cylinder and dome, and the back wall is concentric with the exterior wall of the cylinder. Just below level II a floor was inserted in post-antique times, and a glazed window has been set into the inner cylinder wall. The chamber thus formed, reached by way of the stairs and the position 2 key-chamber, is divided into three compartments by two radial arches carrying superincumbent walls (Plate 106). Between levels III and IV there is a space somewhat similarly divided, once accessible from the level III exterior cornice (Plates 103 and 105). The niche and chamber are both roofed by massive vaults.

4. Similar to position 2 except that the level I and level III key-chambers open respectively to the outside ground level and the level III exterior cornice.

5. The position of the second interior niche. The curve of the back wall, having a shorter radius, is more pronounced than that of the niche at position 3. There is no floor here at level II so the niche space rises to within three meters of level III, to a point just above the open interior attic window between II and III. Though a massive vault limits the rise of this space in the same way that the level II chamber is limited at position 3, an additional vault, rather like part of a semidome in shape, rises from the curve of the back wall. Between levels III and IV there is a chamber exactly like that at position 3.

22. See above, n. 15. The spaces in front of the apsidal recesses of the L-shaped rooms were originally square, but in each case one corner was later strengthened by a block of masonry; both of these spaces are groin vaulted.

6. The same as position 4.

7. The same as position 3, including the intermediate floor at level II but excluding the attic window between levels II and III (see Plate 105).

8. The same as position 4 except that the key-chamber at level I is entered from the adjacent rooms to the south.

9. At levels I and II this is the apse, similar in height to the entranceway at position 1 but somewhat greater in span, shaped by a semidome instead of a barrel vault (Plate 107). Between levels III and IV there is a chamber like that at position 3.

10. The same as position 8 except that the level I key-chamber now communicates with the interior of the rotunda as well.

11. The same as position 7. In this area the interior attic zone (between levels II and III) was restored about thirty years ago to its ancient forms (Plate 108).[23]

12. The same as position 4.

13. The same as position 5 except for a floor just below level II. The plan of the partispherical vault between levels II and III appears on Plate 103, right.

14. The same as position 4.

15. The same as position 3, including the intermediate floor, attic window, and intercommunication with the neighboring key-chamber by the stairs (position 16) at level II.

16. The same as position 2, except that the uppermost key-chamber, that at level III, can no longer be reached from the west staircase.

Thus each of the even-numbered positions represents a vertical stack of three key-chambers whose floors are at the first three levels. On the interior of the rotunda these positions are marked by the aediculae. The four aediculae that are closest to the transverse axis through positions 5 and 13 carry segmental pediments, the rest have triangular ones. The odd-numbered positions represent the six great interior niches plus the entranceway and apse. The niches are screened by columns, and flanked by pilasters, of yellow-orange marble veined with darker colors. The entranceway is also flanked by pilasters, but the apse is marked by two free-standing columns which with their ressauts or projecting entablature blocks are set out into the rotunda space (Plate 107).[24]

Level III divides the interior height in half. Thus the interior volume, construed ideally as being defined by a cylinder and a hemisphere, would fit exactly into a cube.[25] The height and diameter of the interior each equal 147 Roman feet (almost exactly 142

23. Because of the floor at level II, the grille no longer admits light from above into the niche. Today this happens only at position 5; cf. H. Kähler, *The Art of Rome and Her Empire* (New York, 1963), pp. 154, 156.

24. For the aediculae, see the measured drawing in Desgodetz (above, n. 4), Pl. XX. One of the apse ressauts is illustrated in Vighi (above, n. 4), p. 35.

25. As Vitruvius, 5.10.5 prescribed; cf. 4.8.3. K. A. C. Creswell, *Early Muslim Architecture*, I (Oxford, 1932), 320, thinks the dome is not quite a full hemisphere.

English feet), showing that the architect used a controlling measurement of 150 Roman feet in laying out his plan; the bricks, shims, mortar, and marble of the interior cylinder wall somewhat decreased this round figure. The distance between levels I and II is not the same as that between II and III. The upper is a little less than three quarters of the lower (8.95 : 12.70 meters, the Vitruvian ratio of $1 : \sqrt{2}$).[26] This difference is accentuated by the necessity of reading the great level II interior ring cornice at an angle from the paving, which reduces the amount of visible wall surface of the attic zone between levels II and III. The ancient decoration of the attic was placed above a high band or quadra of smooth marble facing in order to allow for this effect (Plate 108). For the same reason the first horizontal range of dome coffers was begun at a height above the level III cornice greater than the uniform distances between the successive horizontal ranges of coffers (Plate 105).

The coffers are fundamental sources of the interior effects of the Pantheon. There are one hundred and forty in five horizontal rows of twenty-eight coffers each (Plates 103 and 109). Those of the first four horizontal rows are composed of four recesses of consecutively diminishing size; those of the highest row, of three. Their maximum chords (taken along theoretical lines of intersection determined by radial planes passing through the vertical center line of the building) decrease gradually from 3.90 meters in the lowest row to 2.30 meters in the highest. The description that follows is an ideal one, but the coffers approximate it quite closely. All sides that recede from the viewer standing at the center of the floor are flat planes, but the other surfaces, the larger, recessed trapezoidal surfaces facing the viewer, are parts of spheres, and the lines formed by the intersections of these receding and facing surfaces are curved (Plate 110). The receding sides at the top and bottom of each coffer are so placed that if their planes were extended they would meet, theoretically, along a common line (Plate 105, second horizontal row; compare Plate 10b).[27] The receding sides at the left and right of each coffer lie more or less in radial planes passing through the vertical center line of the building. The horizontal surfaces or bands between the ranges of coffers are of uniform height, but the vertical bands, radial on plan, diminish in width as they rise.

STRUCTURE

Few masonry buildings are more structurally ingenious than the Pantheon. Solving the engineering problems inherent in its basic design carried Hadrian's architect and engineers well beyond anything previous examples and experience could teach them.

26. Vitruvius, 6.3.3., the third solution; cf. M. C. Ghyka, *Le nombre d'or* (8th ed. Paris, 1931), Pls. XLI, XLIII.

27. So Beltrami (above, n. 12), p. 38. For the scale of these enormous recesses, see *EncIt*, ill. on p. 214. It has been said, by Platner-Ashby, p. 384, that the uncoffered zone between the oculus and the highest ring of coffers was gilded. Chedanne found bronze bolts in the vault, and these are thought to have anchored gilded rosettes to the centers of the coffers; W. J. Anderson et al., *The Architecture of Ancient Rome* (2nd ed. London, 1927), p. 81.

The construction of earlier domed rotundas such as those at Albano or Baia (see Plate 14) was almost child's play by comparison. The problems inherent in stabilizing a vaulted building of radial or centralized plan were raised to a level of the most demanding complexity by the great width of the Pantheon cylinder and the height and weight of its dome. The fabric itself as well as the speed with which it went up show that every detail of construction was planned in advance with the greatest care. The result, like Hagia Sophia, was a structurally unique building.

Other than the trabeated porch and the column screens of the interior niches the building is of brick-faced concrete, though the intrados of the dome lacks brick facing and stone blocks appear at certain bearing points within the cylinder. The technique of the brick-faced wall construction is the same as that employed at the Markets and Baths of Trajan.[28] Above level IV the dome contains no brick arches or vaults. Drawings and engravings that show a complicated skeleton of brick ribs within the fabric of the great vault above level IV are based upon one of Piranesi's plates. Apparently he examined part of the vaults and arches within the cylinder and dome up to level IV and then assumed that some such system continued up to the oculus; his assumptions have been repeated for nearly two centuries.[29] Plates 105 and 106 show the maximum height actually reached by the internal vaults, arches, and radial walls (in Plate 105 the sections through the vaults are shaded).

The building rests upon a very deep (4.50 meters) foundation ring of concrete that contains layers of large travertine fragments. Either in Hadrian's time or shortly thereafter an additional ring was added outside the original foundation.[30] The stability of the building was perhaps slightly increased by constructions built against the rotunda on the east and south. The outside of the rotunda reads as a continuous cylindrical surface through its 282° traverse from one flank of the intermediate block around to the other (Plate 111). Because of the many hollows at positions 1 to 16 the fabric is modulated to a sinuous or corrugated horizontal section except in the vicinity of level III and level IV,

---

28. Bloch, p. 117, n. 100, final paragraph.

29. G. B. Piranesi, published by F. Piranesi, *Raccolta di tempj antichi*, Part II (Rome, 1790), Tav. XXVII. This rib system was taken as fact by many, including Viollet-le-Duc, and Choisy (above, n. 13), pp. 85–88; cf. Canina (above, n. 17), Tav. LXXIII. Because of this endorsement the understanding of the dome's structure has been obscured, though it was effectively clarified by Beltrami in his book of 1898 (above, n. 4), pp. 21–32; Terenzio's brief reports (above, n. 9) and clear drawings have settled the matter. For various interpretations of the dome's structure, written both before and after Terenzio's publications, see A. D. F. Hamlin, "The Paradox of the Pantheon. A Study of Ancient Roman Vault Construction," *School of Mines Quarterly*, 20 (1899),

365–71, 21 (1900), 170–82, 261–66; Rivoira, p. 126; Giovannoni, Tav. VIII; G. Bagnani, *The Pantheon* (New York, 1929), p. XVII; H. Braun, *Historical Architecture* (London, 1953), p. 90; J. K. Finch, *The Story of Engineering* (New York, 1960), p. 73. Durm, Fig. 643, thought there were brick ribs between the coffers, but these rib-like shapes were cast in concrete as an integral part of the concrete dome.

30. For the foundations, which rest upon a stratum of clay, see Terenzio, "Restauration" (above, n. 9), pp. 52–53 (on p. 55 he gives the result of his calculations of the pressures bearing on the foundations); and Vighi (above, n. 4), pp. 50–51, 58. Until the relatively recent canalization and control of the Tiber, the Pantheon was often flooded; see Lanciani, Fig. 186.

where thick horizontal rings of masonry are continuous and uninterrupted. A solid wall makes its way around the key-chambers that lie within eight huge pier-shapes (Plate 98). Each of these shapes is formed like a thick letter U opening outward and covers an area, including its key-chamber, of about 58 square meters. This system of radial piers, spoke-like in plan, had been used in a number of pre-Hadrianic circular tombs. The piers are not entirely independent structural elements but are physically one with the relatively thin exterior rotunda wall and the thick, continuous horizontal layers of masonry just below levels III and IV. The outer rotunda wall is not married to the masonry of the intermediate block, for at many points on the eastern stair system light can be seen through slits between the unbonded surfaces of the two masses.

Excluding the entranceway and the apse there are four basic shapes between the exterior and interior surfaces of the great cylinder: the two types of interior recesses or niches, the tripartite rooms at level III (Plate 103), and the key-chambers. Within each category the design of individual units is the same. All of the key-chambers that can now be examined are vaulted with semidomes whose crowns reach to within about three meters of the next level above, and each chamber contains all or part of a simple original cornice of terra cotta at the impost level of its vault (compare Plate 78, right center). With the exception of the passageways between positions 2 and 3 and between 16 and 15 the key-chambers at level II are entirely enclosed, as Plate 103, right, shows. There were no openings to them footing on the level II exterior cornice, for there is no evidence of any later blocking up of openings and no trace of the embedded arches that unfailingly appear above windows and entrances in vaulted-style construction during the second century (see for example the small arches over the level III openings visible on Plate 112a). Some of the isolated level II spaces have been examined during works of repair and restoration, and the others can be deduced from the Roman habit of symmetry, so suitable to the design of centralized vaulted buildings. There is no reason to suppose that the twenty-four key-chambers are dissimilar in any significant respect, and the same is true of the odd-numbered rooms at level III.

The radial width through the cylinder (up to level III) is 6.05 meters, twenty Roman feet plus the thickness of the interior finish materials. Between levels II and III there is a brick vault over the entranceway and each of the great niches (the odd-numbered positions); presumably there is also one just above the semidome of the apse. Each of these vaults begins directly behind the decoration of the interior attic and passes all the way through the fabric to the outer surface of the rotunda where it appears to be a huge arch embedded in the curving wall (Plates 111 and 112). These powerful arcs, which help to deflect the superposed weight over and down to the piers, are composed of three concentric rings of tiles and are about 1.60 meters thick (Figure 10).[31] The one over the entranceway is probably a normal cylindrical barrel vault, its intrados visible

31. Two rings of bipedales and a third ring, the outermost, of smaller tiles (see Pl. 112 here). The shape, position, and function of these vaults has been heavily debated; see for example the works of Beltrami, Cozzo, and von Gerkan, cited above, n. 4. Cozzo's argument is summarized by Bagnani (above, n. 29), pp. XIII–XIV. The texts of Terenzio's articles are curiously silent on

from the pavement (Plate 104). If there is also one over the apse semidome, as seems likely, it is radial in plan and conical in shape, judging from the interior form of the chamber above (Plate 103), the evidence of the vaults over the great niches, and the radial setting-out of the columns and their ressauts. But the shape of the remaining six is not in doubt: they are all defined by portions of oblique circular cones. This results from the fact that in each case the span of the vault widens from about 8.90 meters on the interior to about 11.60 meters on the exterior while the crown line and impost plane both remain horizontal. Thus the interior elevations are semicircular, and the external segmental, describing arcs of approximately 150°.[32] Between levels III and IV the odd-numbered positions are vaulted much as they are between II and III except that the vaults are of two rings of brick and are stepped down 1.20 meters under the level IV cornice (Plates 105 and 113). Position 1, where the apsidal spaces are part of the rooms in the highest part of the intermediate block, is probably an exception to this (Plate 103, left). Again the function of these vaults is to help load the piers with the weight of the superstructure.

Under each of the vaults between levels II and III at positions 3, 7, 11, and 15 there are eight arches. Six of these, segmental and spanning in three groups of two the inter-columniations below (Plate 106), run minor loads from above onto the columns and give lateral stability as well. The other two arches, composed of double rings of bipe-dales, are radial in plan and span the distance from the groups of segmental arches to the inner surface of the outside wall of the rotunda (Plate 105) and carry diaphragm walls that reach up to the lower surfaces of the overarching conical vaults (Plate 106). Thus each niche column is born upon from three directions by five arches. Between levels III and IV there is a somewhat similar arrangement (Plate 114) except that the six segmental arches are replaced by three short barrel vaults.[33]

---

the subject. The present description is based upon the visible evidence of the exterior of the build-ing, measurements taken in room II/15, the work of Beltrami, Pl. 114 here, and the drawings pub-lished by Terenzio and repeated by Vighi (above, n. 4), pp. 50, 52; see also below, n. 34.

32. Segmental on a theoretical flat plane; again the lines are warped. The cone in question is ideally one whose altitude is perpendicular to the base circle at a point on its circumference. A length of this altitude would be the horizontal crown line of the vault upon whose extension through the vertical center line of the building the apex of the cone would lie. If the rotunda walls were flat and not cylindrical, the interior semicircular elevation of the vault would be half of a circular section of the cone, and the exterior segmental elevation would be determined by the horizontal impost plane and the widening span of the vault. Durm, Fig. 634, thought the imposts sloped out and

down, and thus drew them as rays of the cones; actually only the theoretical axes slope this way. The theoretical solid produced between two such conic surfaces and placed between the inner and outer rotunda surfaces would be of very compli-cated shape, and needless to say Hadrian's builders in practice made this geometry more manageable; cf. Fig. 10 here, where warped imposts (theo-retically hyperbolic paraboloids) are deliberately shown; cf. Choisy (above, n. 13), Pl. XIII; and Beltrami's 1898 volume (above, n. 4), Tav. V. F. Piranesi drew these vaults accurately, and on his engraving of 1790 entitled "Iconografia dello stato antico del Pantheon" speaks of the "archi formati da tre ordine di tegoloni che si vedono nel estero del Tempio, e che proseguono ancoro nella parte interna."

33. The assumption is made here that between levels II and III, positions 13 and 5 are the same; 3 and 15, which are accessible, are identical.

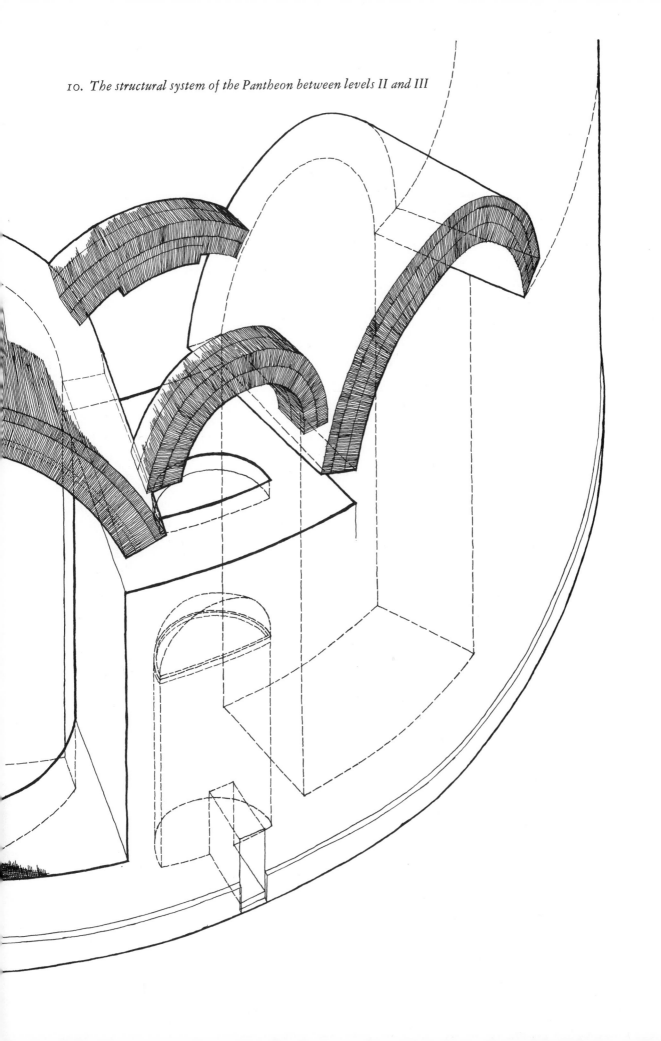

10. *The structural system of the Pantheon between levels II and III*

Semicircular arches, each of two rings of brick spanning about five meters, appear on the exterior of the building between the ends of both horizontal ranges of the great conical vaults (Plate 111, and Plate 112b, left). On the interior there are segmental arches behind the attic decoration at the even-numbered positions between levels II and III but none in the zone above between III and IV (Plate 106). All these arches are probably simply embedded in the walls one or two bricks deep (see Figure 10). If this is correct they are of a kind usually called relieving arches. There are almost certainly no cylindrical or conical vaults passing out through the cylinder over the key-chambers. It has been said that the interior and exterior arches between levels II and III mark the ends of such vaults, but neither the geometry nor the engineering of the building will support this idea.[34] Between levels III and IV each key-chamber is traversed by a centered, radial wall cut by an arched opening, and these walls account for the eccentricity of every other opening onto the level III exterior cornice (Plate 103, left, and Plate 113).

Once the height and diameter of the dome had been determined, the nature of the structure within the vertical fabric was chiefly dictated by the great niches. Probably the architect thought first of niches and then of piers, rather than the reverse, judging from the Roman habit of expanding centralized spaces with cardinal and diagonal recesses.[35] This decision produced the eight-piered and radially vaulted frame of brick and concrete that carries the dome. There is a certain similarity between the structure of the aula of the Markets of Trajan and that of the Pantheon in spite of the basic difference

34. Cozzo (above, n. 4), pp. 269–80 and Figs. 195–96 and 198–204, argues that vaults pass through the entire cylinder width over all the key chambers between levels II and III and between levels III and IV, and that the superposed weight was thus in effect transmitted to 16 rather than 8 piers. If this were the case only about half of the bearing area of the huge U-shaped piers would be directly utilized (as Cozzo, Fig. 199, himself points out), and since the smaller vaults would have to rest in part upon the conical vaults (Pl. 106, here), the latter would tend to shear under the enormous weight angled onto them from above. Also, Cozzo shows the inner and outer faces of his presumed vaults as having the same radius, which they do not (Fig. 10, here). On his Figs. 196 and 203 he assumes that there are interior arches (and therefore ends of vaults) at the even-numbered positions between levels III and IV, but these are not shown by Beltrami in his book of 1898 (above, n. 4), Tav. III–IV; by Durm, Fig. 367; or by Vighi (above, n. 4), p. 52 (a drawing showing the results of Terenzio's investigation of the structure). The only other indication that I have seen of the idea that vaults pass through the rotunda over the key chambers appears on a plate of J. von Egle, *Praktische Baustil- und Bauformlehre auf geschichtlicher Grundlage, 1* (Stuttgart, 1916) Taf. 35, reproduced by Giovannoni, Tav. VIII. Von Egle's unreliability can be inferred from the fact that he shows the dome as semi-elliptical in section. He published on the same plate a section through positions 5 and 13, based on Canina (above, n. 17), Tav. LXX, and Desgodetz (above, n. 4), Pl. VII. The analytical drawings in Beltrami, Cozzo, Terenzio (above, n. 9), and Heimsath (above, n. 14), all either avoid the question of the nature of the structure between the vertically tiered key-chambers or are ambiguous in this respect; but surely the eight great piers are loaded from level IV downward without any structural discontinuity. There is an example of an arrangement of exterior large and small arches similar to that of the Pantheon at Hadrian's villa; Lugli, *Tecnica, 2,* Tav. CCII.2.

35. See for example the publications of G. B. Montano, but note G. Zander, "Le invenzioni architettoniche di Giovanni Battista Montano Milanese (1534–1621)," *Quaderni,* 30 (1958), 1–21, 49–50 (1962), 1–31. See also G. de Angelis d'Ossat, "La forma e la costruzione delle cupole nell'architettura romana," *Atti, 3,* 223–50; A. de Franciscis and R. Pane, *Mausolei romani in Campania* (Naples, 1957).

in plan (compare Plate 93 with Figure 10). The abutting tabernae barrel vaults and the gallery arches of the aula appear at the Pantheon in a more complex arrangement, disposed around a central vertical axis.

From the interior the entire hemisphere appears to be a vault, but structurally this is not the case. Plates 105 and 106 show that the true span of the dome is that at level IV, not at III, for up as far as IV the structure is, however complex, essentially a circular wall and not part of the domical vault.[36] The aggregate of the concrete decreases in weight as the height of the building increases, beginning with travertine in the foundation ring and ending, in the upper zone of the dome, with tufa and pumice. The pozzolana mortar is of very fine quality throughout.[37] The exterior of the rotunda is slightly stepped in at two places, just above level II and again at level III (Plate 105). The theoretical hemispherical shell of the dome is about 1.50 meters thick, but only a third of this shape can be seen on the exterior (Plates 115 and 116). There are seven stepping-ring features that project from the ideal extrados of the dome, loading it with additional masonry through 43° of its rise (approximately two thirds of its vertical height). Above level III there are something like five thousand metric tons of masonry, arching majestically over an unobstructed area of some fifteen hundred square meters, and it is this that the structure below supports and poises in balance.[38]

By way of the east stair system the observer is brought to the roof of the intermediate block at level IV (Plate 116). This level continues around the cylinder as a slightly sloping terrace 3.80 meters wide, and leads past three masonry masses that bulge out from the cylindrical wall of the lowest step-ring at positions 3, 7, and 11 into the terrace area (one can be seen on Plate 116 just to the left of the junction of the drainpipes).[39] The high cylindrical wall of the first step-ring forms the interior boundary of the level IV circular terrace. Toward the south, at positions 7 and 11, there are stairs that lead up to the oculus. Only the one at position 11 is accessible today from the

36. See above, Chap. 3, n. 45. A debate about the true impost of the dome has accompanied that about the nature of the rotunda vaults; see above, nn. 31, 34. For a statical analysis, see G. B. Milani, *L'ossatura murale: studio statico-costruttivo ed estetico-propozionale . . .*, I (Turin, 1920), 44–45 and Tav. 21; the plate is reproduced by Giovannoni, Fig. 9, and Vighi (above, n. 4), p. 56. Apparently Terenzio girdled the base of the dome with chains, "Restauration" (above, n. 9), p. 54; cf. Montani (above, n. 9), p. 425.

37. For materials, see G. de Angelis d'Ossat, "Roccie adoperate nella cupola del Pantheon," *Atti della pontificia accademia delle scienze nuovi Lincei*, 83 (1930), 211–15; G. Rossi, "Pantheon — indagini sulle strutture della cupola," *BC*, 59 (1931), 227–29; Terenzio, "Restauration" (above, n. 9), pp. 53–54; cf. E. B. Van Deman, "Methods of Determining the Date of Roman Concrete Monuments," *AJA*, 16 (1912), 417–21.

38. This estimate of weight does not include the metal covering, ancient or modern. Cf. the dome of Hagia Sophia, which has an average diameter of approximately 31.50 m. (Pantheon = 43.30 m.), traverses in section an arc of 162°, and weighs perhaps 1,800 metric tons.

39. That at position 3 at least is Hadrianic, for its structure is continuous with that of the dome. Those at positions 7 and 11 have been restored; there is none today at 15. Presumably there were originally four, constructed as access platforms for four exterior stairs cut into the extrados of the vault and leading to the oculus; cf. Canina (above, n. 17), Tav. LXVIII. The drainpipes visible in Pl. 116 are modern. Large pipes, said to be antique, project high from the east and west faces of the intermediate block; they are about 0.20 m. in diameter and apparently of bronze (see also Pl. 102).

level IV terrace (Plate 115). It consists of steps, straight and radial in plan, cut into the step-rings and the spherical extrados of the dome.

The dome was originally covered with gilded tiles, probably of bronze, but these were removed in the summer of 663 by the emperor Constans II.[40] The present covering is of lead sheets of various dates arranged in widening radial rows down the sloping surface and over the tops and sides of the step-rings as far as the top of the lowest ring wall (Plates 116 and 117). Near the southwest staircase, sheets bearing the arms and titles of Nicholas V (1447–55) and Clement VIII (1592–1605) can be seen. Under the lead, the dome and step-rings are covered with a layer of pozzolana cement about 0.15 meters thick, laid over a skin of bricks set in the concrete of the vault.[41]

There are seven step-rings (Plate 105). Today their sections are rather irregular, but the middle five are of approximately equal dimensions. They were built in order to add to the load over the critical or haunch portion of the great vault and function as buttresses, helping to bring the structure into stability through compression. In order to provide a substantial mass of masonry at this critical position, where the downward slope of the dome becomes more pronounced, it was practical to build in this fashion.[42] Either circular retaining walls of wood or ring walls of brick (as in the case of the lowest wall) were built in concentric tiers to facilitate construction. The stability of the building required a heavy load of superposed masonry, while the use of the step-rings for this precluded the necessity of first constructing the lower two thirds of a spherical extrados, which would have raised considerable practical difficulties.

The dome was built by pouring successive rings of concrete against a hemispherical dome of wood upon which the huge wooden forms for the coffers were first positioned. As the concrete was poured a grid of ribs was gradually built up between the coffer forms, strengthening the dome by virtue of their thickness. With its supports rising twenty meters from the pavement below, this temporary forest of beams, struts, and domical carpentry is an awesome thing to envision. But it must have been built.[43] The picturesque medieval legend that tells of a mountain of earth heaped up within the cylinder to provide support for the erection of the dome has been told of several great vaulted buildings, but one dismisses it reluctantly, especially as Hadrian is supposed to have seeded the earth liberally with gold pieces in order to insure its speedy removal after the vault was finished.

The final and most spectacular feature of the Pantheon is the central oculus (Plate 118). Its ring encircles an area of 62.80 square meters, about four per cent of the sur-

40. Not in 665 as Vighi (above, n. 4), p. 14, and others state; see F. G. Moore, "The Gilt-Bronze Tiles of the Pantheon," *AJA*, 3 (1899), 40–43; G. Ostrogorsky, *History of the Byzantine State*, trans. J. Hussey (Oxford, 1956), p. 109. Cf. Tomei (above, n. 9).

41. Terenzio, "Restauration" (above, n. 9), p. 54; Vighi (above, n. 4), p. 51.

42. Cf. similar Trajanic techniques: Rivoira, Fig. 131; Zorzi, Figs. 108–09; and Pl. 80 here.

43. See *EncIt*, 26 (1935), 213. The magnitude of the ancient timberwork is suggested by a photograph of Terenzio's scaffolding (which reached to the oculus) published by Montani (above, n. 9), p. 419. Terenzio first used a ladder 40 m. long in order to examine the intrados.

face of the paving below. Surrounding it is the original wide bronze flashing, which slopes gently away from the opening. The vertical ring wall of the oculus, which originally carried a bronze cornice of elaborate design, is made of bricks laid vertically and radially.[44] It is theoretically a compression ring, resisting and helping to balance those forces created by the weight and position of the vault that are directed toward the void below. Being circular, it counterpoises them across an infinite number of diameters in a reciprocating system. Because of this it was essential to the early life of the building, and because of the size and weight of the dome it may still perform this function (the statics of large buildings vaulted in concrete are not easy to understand). There is no railing around either the oculus or the flashing. To lie upon the flashing and look down through the oculus to the paving forty-five meters below is an experience not readily forgotten.

ARCHITECTURAL PRINCIPLES

Through the agency of Hadrian's sophisticated, cool intelligence the Pantheon captured and described the underlying cultural texture of the High Empire. It is as extraordinary a document in this sense as it is a masterpiece of Roman engineering, but its more immanent qualities are harder to pin down. If it is addressed first as a work of architecture the problem of its meaning may be found less refractory.

The combination of a domed cylinder lacking a peristyle with a monumental temple front was so striking an innovation that even now, with the Hadrianic date for both established beyond doubt, it is difficult to believe that the great portico is not a relic of Agrippa's time to which a century and a half later the rotunda was added by an amateur architect. Whether the idea of combining the porch and rotunda was Hadrian's own or that of his architect, it solved the problem of providing a suitable entrance to a round interior. When the volume of a building is described by a continuous and essentially unbroken surface it is difficult to provide a satisfactory expression of the way in, for no axial invitation is extended from the building to the observer on the ground (Plate 111). Roman centralized spaces had previously either been encircled by peristyles, forming purely exterior architecture around compact, non-public cellas, or else they were not free-standing, as in the case of the octagons of the palaces. The Pantheon on the other hand was conceived as an independent presence most emphatically intended to be entered. The combination of a portico with an unscreened rotunda was so successful that it was soon repeated, as at Pergamon about thirty-five years later, and it has been in use ever since.[45] We tend to take it for granted.

The building was given an exterior longitudinal emphasis by both the portico and

---

44. For a section of the oculus, see de Angelis d'Ossat (above, n. 35), Fig. 3, and cf. Figs. 4 and 8; his Fig. 3 is reproduced by Lugli, *Tecnica*, *I*, Fig. 141. For the cornice, see Desgodetz (above, n. 4), Pl. XIX.

45. O. Deubner, *Das Asklepieion von Pergamon* (Berlin, 1938), pp. 54–57, Fig. 1 and Taf. I; cf. Meeks (above, n. 10).

the court to the north (see Figure 8 on p. 96). These powerfully emphasized traditional axial and rectilinear relationships in order that the seemingly incommensurable rounded interior, once gained, would by contrast be even more astonishing. The portico, which today seems to be rather awkwardly attached to the rotunda, is the effective visual servant of a radically new idea, an interior monument composed solely of space, light, and color. In ancient times the antithesis between exterior and interior was more pronounced than it is now, for only a small part of the distant upper sides of the cylinder wall would have been visible while one walked south through the enclosed court. Photographs taken from the considerably higher modern paving north of the building inevitably show much more of that pneumatic shape than would have been seen in ancient times (Plate 96). And the upper part of the glittering dome, its silhouette eroded by light, could be seen only from the northern part of the court, so there was little by which to judge what lay beyond the spreading, familiar forms of the façade. The Pantheon is the finest example of the Roman talent for planning buildings whose full visual impact is withheld until just the right moment.

The portico also serves as a transitional element between the open air and the interior. Porches usually do this, but here the relative scale is particularly important. If the portico were too small or too shallow it would fail to screen the main structure and would look somewhat ridiculous in front of the great bulk of the rotunda—more than one derivative of the Pantheon suffers from a portico of erroneous scale. Had the Pantheon portico been wider or taller the effect of the interior would be somewhat depreciated. In the event, the size and proportions chosen were carefully related both to the forecourt and the rotunda. The façade columns are in the light, but the depth of the portico and the orientation of the building keep the inner ones mostly in shade. The files of powerful shafts describe a familiar architecture, half open and half closed. The observer knows there is some kind of space behind the doors, but even if he has visited the building many times he can hardly fail to react to the extraordinary difference between the forms of the trabeated, shady portico and the breathtaking expanse of airy, illuminated volume beyond.

The portico was also an ancient image, and that may be one of the reasons the architect chose to use it, though it is difficult to understand why it would have been thought necessary to imply that the building was of traditional form. Even if such assurance was given by the portico it would have been dissipated immediately upon reaching the rotunda. It is much more probable that the portico was chosen for the contrast it makes with the effect of the interior space behind it. Pedimented temple fronts had been used before on structures that were not temples and the use of one here does not necessarily mean that the Pantheon was a traditional temple or that one was intended to think that it was for a moment before entering. The Pantheon and its forecourt suggested in architectural language the broad bases of high imperial culture—the Mediterranean city (the porticoed court), ancient religious discipline (the pedimental porch), and the realities of Roman dominion and its concomitant cosmology (the domed rotunda).

The intermediate block has been criticized as clumsy and amateurish both as a unit of the design and from the point of view of its relationships to the porch and the rotunda. Hadrian must have been the architect, some modern writers have said, because the block is so unsuitable and because not all of the cornices of the block and the rotunda meet (Plates 101 and 119).[46] This is a strange argument, for it implies that the emperor was sufficiently accomplished to design the building yet too inexperienced to fit the rotunda and the portico together in a way satisfactory to those who would make him the architect. The question of who actually designed the building probably cannot be resolved, but the question of the suitability of the intermediate block is easier to deal with. Seen from the paving of the forecourt, it was interposed between the observer and the structure behind. As the long flanks of the court helped to disguise the rotunda, so the intermediate block prevented any clear view of the connection between the gilded dome and the majestic portico. Today the dome cannot be seen until one reaches a point about sixty-five meters north of the façade, and in ancient times the distance would have been considerably greater. The closer one came to the portico the more effective this interposition of the block became. By its rectangular shape it heightens the contrast to come. Triangles, rectangles, prisms, and vertical shafts, all powerfully stable forms, pile up and screen the seamless volume that can be found and known only by passing through and under them. The raking cornices on the north face of the block echo and reemphasize the stable stone frame of the façade pediment. Since they join at a more obtuse angle than that of the pediment proper (Plates 102 and 116), they introduce from a distance a false perspective, emphasize the depth of the porch, and make the dome seem even farther away. Finally, the block is important for technical reasons, for stair shafts could not safely or conveniently be placed within the structure of the rotunda.

At the vertical junctures of the intermediate block with the rotunda wall, the level II exterior cornice dies out when it meets the block, as do the prolongations of the portico entablature when they meet the rotunda (Plates 101 and 119). The marble facings of the flanks of the block below the entablature also seem to have come to abrupt stops. These apparent solecisms may be the result of a change of thought about the exterior of the building during construction, but it seems more likely that no one was exercised about an area that was of little importance to the principal effects of the design. These unresolved features of the Pantheon point toward the increasing simplification of exterior design in later Roman imperial architecture.

The marble sheathing on the flanks of the intermediate block (Plate 119) does not

46. For example, G. Rodenwaldt in *CAH*, 11, 796; Vighi (above, n. 4), p. 12 and n. 1; S. Perowne, *Hadrian* (London, 1960), p. 111. Rivoira, pp. 118–22, enthusiastically proposed the emperor as the architect; see below, Chap. 6, n. 46. Lanciani, p. 481, thought Hadrian was an architect but excluded the Pantheon from his list of the emperor's works. For samples of criticism of the design of the porch and intermediate block, see Lanciani, pp. 476–78; Bagnani (above, n. 29), pp. XVII–XVIII ("the porch looks as though it had just been added on haphazard, which is indeed the case. It has absolutely no connection with the great rotunda behind . . . The exterior is certainly a dismal failure"); Crema, p. 380.

necessarily mean that the rotunda exterior was revetted in the same way. The pervasive influence of what in modern times has been held to be "classic" design (actually more romantic or neoclassic than properly antique) has made it difficult to conceive of the cylinder wall as bare or unfeatured. Thus it is usually said to have been sheathed in marble or coated with stucco falsely drafted to look like courses of marble, and it has always been restored this way in drawings and models.[47] There is no certainty about the original appearance of the exterior. Fragments of stone base moldings remain at level I (Plate 120), and apparently the brickwork of the lowest zone was faced in some fashion. The nature of the original surface of the upper zones is more problematical. There are no putlog holes for horizontal scaffolding beams, and judging from ample second-century evidence these ought to have been left open if the entire brick surface was to have been revetted or stuccoed. If marble sheathing was used the holes for the necessary cramps ought to be visible, presumably in some regular pattern, but they are not (for these points see Plates 111–13 and 116). This evidence is not obviated by the damage and restorations the exterior surface has sustained because a great deal of the original brickwork remains intact (the character of the most recent and thorough consolidation can be seen in Plate 120b, where the upper courses of bricks are modern). Also, the general principles of the design should be taken into account. To call attention to the exterior of the rotunda would seem to be at variance with the architectural and sensory effects the building was intended to create. Probably plain stucco was applied, at least in the upper zones. This would have been in keeping with the other devices used by the architect to minimize the attention drawn to the external negative of the immense interior volume.

The model of the Pantheon that used to be displayed in the Metropolitan Museum of Art in New York is an example of attitudes toward imperial architecture that understandably resulted from the study of plates by Canina and other nineteenth-century archaeologists and architects who saw Roman buildings through the glass of romantic classicism (Plate 121, where the high viewpoint is instructive, indicating by contrast how little of the rotunda and dome would have been seen in ancient times from the pavement of the forecourt).[48] To try to make the Pantheon into a drumlike late Greek building is to misappreciate the vaulted style. The errors in the model were compounded by a rather sentimental view of the nature of Greek architecture, and the result is nineteenth-century Hellenistic, a torpid style that did justice neither to Greek nor to Roman architecture partly because of the assumption that they were somehow similar. In actuality the design of the Pantheon, like that of Trajan's Markets, is strong, bold, and

47. Jordan-Huelsen (above, n. 7), p. 585, confidently state that between levels I and II the rotunda was covered with marble, and the upper zones (they speak of three of these) with stucco, but their references do not lead to any conclusive evidence; cf. OCD, p. 643. Desgodetz (above, n. 4), Pl. IV, shows no stucco or revetment. See also above, Chap. 4, n. 24.

48. See for example Canina (above, n. 17), 2, Tav. LXIII, LXVIII, LXXIVA; cf. H.-R. Hitchcock, *Architecture: Nineteenth and Twentieth Centuries* (Harmondsworth, 1958), Pls. 26(A), 109(A).

simple. The horizontal cornice of the pediment is too shallow to have carried statuary, though there is a base, which may not be antique, for a feature of some sort at the apex of the pediment. The modelmaker, by trying too hard to give his Pantheon an acceptably impressive exterior, destroyed the building's grand simplicity and scale. The architect on the other hand did everything he could to avoid implying the real nature and meaning of his design. He gave it outside architecture, but purposefully limited this to the north façade. The Pantheon is inside.

The high, thick columns of the portico, rising from the pavement roundabout, function primarily as foils to the uninterrupted expanse of the rotunda. When the doors are gained and the majestic unity of the interior discovered, the architectural sensations of the immediate past are forgotten (see the Frontispiece). The observer's perceptions, having been subtly misdirected by his experience of the graded heights of the exterior verticals, are abruptly pre-empted by a revelation of an image of the firmament itself. Scale changes instantaneously. His experience of passing through the entranceway, which is sufficiently high and broad to allow him to be exposed to the whole interior at once, passes unnoticed. At first the interior distances are unreckonable, and only gradually, by reference to the aediculae, to the niche columns, and perhaps to other humans, is any partial sense of size established (Plates 122 and 123). Even that is valid only for the level of the pavement. The oculus, the circling coffers, the iterated attic motives, and the girdling cornices are in another zone of experience. As the eye follows the curving wall and vault and it becomes apparent that this vast space is without corners, the spell of the design begins to work. There is really no place to *go*. One may walk about and see the tombs and paintings and observe the building from various points of view, but the Pantheon does not encourage this. About all there is left to do is stand upon the pavement and look, and fairly soon the average visitor is drawn back out through the doors.

This happens because the scale of the building cannot be affected or interpreted by incidental human motion (for scale see the figure on Plate 105). It is too large to become a usable object, except perhaps as a container for ceremonies, too large to be readily digested by mental and sensory processes. There is no place to stand and become related to the surroundings, for in its general revelation the building is seamless. No straight lines, axial vistas, flat walls, or angles can be used to connect the observer with a primary focal point. The oculus is too far away to be useful in this respect. Spreading out one's arms is futile, for the Pantheon swallows up human gestures.

The building is so designed that its dimensions and volume, from any point except the center of the floor, appear to be greater than they actually are.[49] The coffers, with their circular rows and perspective design, appear to be fixed and static only from the center. Viewed from there the vault appears to hover and even to draw down toward the observer, but from all other points it seems to expand. This is because all surfaces of all coffers are visible from the middle of the building. At the center, one's lines of vision

49. See Brown (above, n. 11), p. 35, who   diminish.
speaks of the Pantheon's capacity to magnify and

are locked to the lines of the coffers' radial and perspective construction, creating an optical intimacy, a direct and uninterrupted visual connection, with all of the vault. When the vault is seen at angles oblique to this centralizing geometry of the coffers and the viewer is no longer at its nadir, parts of the hollows become obscured and the penetration of the substance of the dome by the recessed panels becomes more pronounced (Plates 109 and 110). From an angle no coffer appears quite like another. Varying shadows and coulisses are produced that intimate unseen depths and distances beyond the hemisphere, and the vault appears to enlarge. Coming from above, the light picks out both directly and by diffusion the pitched-up lower surfaces of the coffers and charges the dome with a lively, changing pattern. These activated relationships among the dome curves, the trapezoidal and curving perspective recesses of the coffers, and the light source conjure any expression of weight away from the vault. The zone above the last row of coffers reads like a thin shell, eaten through by the central disc of light and poised above an illuminated net whose openings seem to catch light from behind (Plate 109).

The decorative forms that surround the visitor were finished with a truly classic reverence for materials, and the orders of the niches are elegantly proportioned. Some of the marble wall revetment has disappeared and has been replaced by painted imitations, but more than half of the orginal colored marble sheets are still in place.[50] From the level III interior cornice downward the Pantheon was originally encased in a sheath of color, a subdued yellow-orange predominating. There are friezes and panels of dark red porphyry, rectangles of green-black marble, and accents of gilding (the undersides of the level II and III cornices and the oculus cornice were gilded; traces of gilding are still visible on the remains of the latter). The vertical forms and the paving form a well of color. The present bland and tasteless painted stucco decoration between levels II and III dates from 1747 but the restored section over position 11 shows how much more lively the design of that zone once was (Plate 108; compare Plate 114). Metal grilles were fitted in the rectangular openings of all but two of the sixteen positions. Between the openings there were shallow pilasters of reddish marble alternating with marble paneling in three horizontal registers. Gilding was used freely and the design was elevated on a continuous high quadra of white marble veined with blue. Thus the attic was once as brightly colored as the orders and revetment below. This design would have made the physical substance of the attic wall much less apparent to the senses than it is today, for the plasticity and crude rhythm of the eighteenth-century décor works strongly against the intentions of the Roman architect. There are in existence several drawings

50. See above, n. 8. The altar is said to have been cut from a block of marble that originally served as the threshold of the aula regia in Domitian's palace; Lanciani, pp. 159–60. The colors of the marbles would have been more brilliant in ancient times; see the remark of H. W. Pullen, *Handbook of Ancient Roman Marbles* (London, 1894), p. 17, about the dulling effect of dirt and exposure upon giallo antico, the yellow-orange stone that predominates between levels I and II. The vividness of the original colors, when the various marbles, porphyries, and granites were clean and polished, is suggested by the pavement just after it has rained—the difference between the wet and dry stones is that between sunlight and dusk.

and paintings that show the ancient attic system (Plates 123 and 124, the latter a drawing by Raphael).[51]

Perhaps because of rational knowledge of its cubical proportions the Pantheon has been seen as a static design.[52] Within the building this concept is hard to confirm. Any fixed quality that the niches, aediculae, or apse may imply is vitiated by the turning surfaces to which these features are so powerfully subordinated. The axis from the entranceway to the apse is lost in the billowing expanse and overwhelming presence of the intermediate volume, and the apse reads as only another member of the chorus of niches. The two deep belt cornices, their shadows curving eccentrically according to the position of the sun, imply continuous motion. The twenty-eight radial rows of coffers do not line up with the sixteen positions of the cylinder and fail to continue the upward lines of verticals into the dome. This lack of vertical synchronization, which was emphasized by the ancient attic decoration more than by the existing forms, implies a quality of action. The double curvature of the dome, which prevents the coffers from appearing as rational geometric figures except from the center of the pavement, does the same (Plate 109). The forms of the building are not in repose.

Upon stepping through the doors the change in light is as pronounced as the change in scale. In a building composed of remarkable features the use of light is the architect's supreme creation. The camera, which cannot capture the interior of the building at all, can only hint at this effect (Plates 123 and 125). The Pantheon has an atmosphere, a visual climate, of its own. This is the product of its size, the contrast between the unglazed oculus and the solid surrounding it, and the play of light down through the void. In addition to the huge circle of light that moves slowly across the northern intrados and marble decoration there is a general and even daytime illumination of surprisingly high intensity. The darkish niches behind their colored, polished columns increase this by contrast. The niches, the coffers, and the oculus, together with the light that washes the marbles of the cylinder and the paving, tend to desubstantiate the physical reality of the building. They obliterate the massive structure and create an illusion of surface support for the dome. If there were once gilded bronze rosettes in the coffers, catching the light and by contrast darkening and deepening the perspective recesses, the effects of incommensurable scale and denigration of substance would have been even stronger than they are today, and in the net of light there would have been a vision of the stars.[53]

51. See also Zorzi, Fig. 168; Desgodetz (above, n. 4), Pl. XVIII; H. von Geymüller, "Trois dessins d'architecture inédits," *Gazette des beaux-arts*, 3 (1870), 79–81; Platner-Ashby, p. 384, n. 1, p. 386; cf. Anderson et al. (above, n. 27), p. 81. The great circular wall has many of the baroque characteristics of the imperial *scaenae frons*, and of the aula regia of the Domus Flavia.

52. On this point, see A. Riegl, *Die spätrömische Kunstindustrie*, 1 (Vienna, 1901), pp. 24–29; Crema, p. 381; P. A. Michelis, *Esthétique de l'art byzantin* (Paris, 1959), pp. 110–11;

Brown (above, n. 11), pp. 35–37.

53. For the evidence for rosettes, see above, n. 27; for the symbolism of painted stars and rosettes in domes see E. B. Smith, *The Dome* (Princeton, 1950), p. 91 and the citations in n. 139. At the summer solstice the maximum southern reach of the edge of the disc of light on the pavement is the third east-west row of squares south of the entranceway. Earlier in the day the disc plays on the wall and dome as far south as the area between positions 4 and 5, and later in the day between 13 and 14.

The Pantheon was made for light. It captures light and even conquers it, and natural light is not a static thing. It was the prize for which all this concrete was poured. The architect shaped his building to form and manipulate a great shaft of illumination, a visible, almost tangible rod of solar effusion. The thick bulk of the structure, so evident today from the exterior, is subtracted from one's vision and consciousness by this heliophany. Everything in the building is subordinated to it. As the earth rotates, Hadrian's sun-show spins on (Plate 125).

THE MEANING OF THE PANTHEON

During the year after Trajan's death in Cilicia, Hadrian traveled in the eastern and Balkan provinces, arriving in Rome for the first time as emperor in July of 118. Shortly thereafter he entered upon a consulship, which he celebrated by remitting debts to the state and by giving spectacular games and entertainments.[54] Meanwhile the planning for the Pantheon was begun, for construction commenced either late in 118 or during the following year. When after further travels he returned again to the capital in 125 the work was either finished or nearly so.[55] Sometime during the years 125–28 the building was dedicated, and he began to use it as an imperial audience hall.

> [Hadrian] transacted with the aid of the Senate all the important and urgent business and held court with the assistance of the foremost men, in the Forum or the Pantheon or various other places, always seated on a tribunal, so that whatever was done was made public.[56]

Like his games and remission of debts the Pantheon was part of Hadrian's plan to mark the beginning and proclaim the nature of the age that was to be his. There was little point in rebuilding the Palatine or adding to the imperial fora, but Agrippa's Pantheon—damaged and restored more than once and probably in need of attention again—set his mind upon the problem of a temple to the Roman universe. The solution is probably the most significant legacy of his extraordinary personality. His restless, inquiring nature led him to abjure, at least unofficially, the old cults. He wished like all the emperors to leave in Rome a permanent memorial of his reign and he was truly and deeply interested in architectural form and expression.[57] He was a Roman, and must try to conquer and order the unknown. At the same time he embodied in his own person a distillation of the long-lived ways of Greece and Rome, an inheritance that was gathered into one celestial design. The Pantheon gives the measure of his thought and his ambition while expressing the unity of the ancient world at the very moment when the Roman dominion ceased to expand.

But the Pantheon was also a *templum deorum omnium*, a ἱερὸν πάντων θεῶν, contain-

---

54. For the remission of debts, see above, n. 3; for the games, *CAH*, *11*, 303–04.

55. See above, n. 5, for these dates.

56. Dio Cassius, 69.7.1.

57. See Kähler, Part 4, for an analysis of Hadrian's personality and motivations.

ing statues of the gods. Dio Cassius, writing in the third century, apparently did not realize that the building he knew was built for Hadrian. He says that Agrippa

> completed the building called the Pantheon. Perhaps it has this name because it received among the images which decorated it the statues of many gods, including Mars and Venus; but my own opinion of the name is that because of its dome the Pantheon resembles the heavens. Agrippa, for his part, wished to place a statue of Augustus there also and to bestow upon him the honor of having the structure named after him; but when the emperor would not accept either honor, he placed in the temple itself a statue of the former Caesar [Julius] and in the pronaos [re-erected by Hadrian in the niches of the intermediate block?] statues of Augustus and himself. This was done not out of any rivalry or ambition on Agrippa's part to make himself equal to Augustus, but from his hearty loyalty to him and his constant zeal for the public good; hence Augustus, so far from censuring him for it, honored him the more.[58]

Thus in Agrippa's time it was established that the Pantheon was both a religious building and a secular imperial monument. In its Hadrianic reincarnation both meanings were preserved, and the great domed rotunda with its statues expressed them equally and indivisibly. Tradition was acknowledged in a setting implying that Roman dominion mirrored that of the heavens.

A temple and a grand symbol of empire could be made one because by Hadrian's time the ancient cults had been sufficiently depreciated or altered for him to feel, irrespective of his station, that he could combine them with secular forms without risk. The aging, increasingly diluted forces of traditional religion, symbolized by Jupiter and his college, were reduced to mere equality with a declaration on an unanswerable scale of the claims of Rome.[59] In a building celebrating the pantheistic, sophisticated, acquisi-

58. 63.27.2–4; cf. the excellent article "Pantheion" by K. Ziegler in *RE*, *18.3* (1949), cols. 697–747 (cols. 729–41 for the Pantheon in Rome). In *CAH*, 11, 797, it is said that Agrippa's Pantheon of 27 B.C., "in the essentials of shape and construction . . . will have resembled the present building"; for the trabeated, flat-roofed Agrippan building see Vitruvius, 9.8.1, and von Gerkan (above, n. 4). F. Granger, "Greek Origins of the Pantheon," *Journal of the Royal Institute of British Architects*, 40 (1933), 57–61, argues that Hadrian's Pantheon was essentially a horologe, its design derived from the works of a certain Scopinas of Syracuse, a contemporary of Archimedes; see Pl. L in the second volume of Granger's Loeb edition of Vitruvius. On this subject see also Platner-Ashby, pp. 382–83, and P. Mingazzini, "Il Pantheon ed i cosidetti ninfei: l'origine del

nome Museum," *ArchClass*, 9 (1957), 108–09.

59. The arrangement of the forecourt and the building proper preserved the ancient distinction between a *templum*, or open, holy place, and its *aedes*, or cult structure; for this distinction see *RE*, *1.1* (1894), cols. 444–45, and *9A* (1934), cols. 480–85; cf. Brown (above, n. 11), Chap. 1. But the implications of this traditional arrangement were muted by the sculpture in the huge pediment, which formed an imperial fastigium, and by the accessible vaulted "cella." In the shallow pediment there were no statues of divinities such as are shown here on Pl. 121, but rather a relief of a Roman eagle in a wreath with ribbons and fruit, of the kind seen at a much smaller scale in the example from Trajan's Forum now in the porch of the SS. Apostoli (I have the kind permission of Dott. Lucos Cozza, inspector in the Roman

tive mood of the High Empire the gods had no pre-eminent place. Something astrological or quasi-scientific appeared.[60] The all-divine of the heavens were given an architecture which in its rounded forms was familiar from the past but which lately also had been elaborated for the emperors. At the same time this architecture was involved in a pseudo-cosmology that gradually, for educated and ignorant alike, was replacing or infecting many ancient beliefs and practices. The Pantheon sought to make room for all of these tendencies in a temple of Rome, or of Romanism, for although the state gods were served as before, the bond of strict contract between the server and the served was no longer supremely efficacious in men's minds. The mysteries of the celestial mechanism and planetary forces, long identified with the gods, were expressed in a design suggesting that all of these ideas and forces were allied and were inseparable from the persisting mission of the Roman state.

As Dio said, the key to the matter is the symbolism of the heavens, which were both the abode of the gods and the canopy of Empire. The seamless circles around and above the great interior described both the cosmos and Roman rule.[61] The role of giving the

archaeological service, to make this statement about the results of his study of the pediment stones and cramp-holes). For the question of vaulting the cella of an aedes, see Kähler, p. 91 and citations. The cella of the Temple of Venus Genetrix in Caesar's Forum may have been vaulted over during a restoration of Domitian's or Trajan's time; see Lugli, *Roma*, p. 252. The Hadrianeum, presumably erected in the time of Antoninus Pius (138–61), was vaulted; V. Passarelli, "Rilievo e studio di restituzione dell'Hadrianeum," *Atti*, 3, 123–30. See also G. Rodenwaldt, "Die letzte Blütezeit der römischen Architektur," *Forschungen und Fortschritte*, 15 (1939), 245, who speaks of the audacity of the architects who vaulted the cellas of the Temple of Venus and Rome during its restoration early in the fourth century (the version of this article that appears in *CAH*, 11, 567–70, omits this observation).

60. See F. Cumont, "La théologie solaire du paganisme romain," *Mémoirs de l'Académie des inscriptions et belles-lettres*, 12 (1909), 447–51; id., *Les religions orientales dans le paganisme romain* (4th ed. Paris, 1929), pp. 123, 151–58, 191; M. P. Nilsson, "The Rise of Astrology in the Hellenistic Age," offprint from *Meddelande från Lunds Astronomiska Observatorium*, 3 (1943), 1–9, esp. p. 9; K. Lehmann, "The Dome of Heaven," *AB*, 27 (1945), 22–23; Garzetti (above, n. 5), pp. 687–88; and S. Sambursky, *The Physical World of Late Antiquity* (London, 1962), pp. 151, 157. H. Nissen, *Orientation.*

Studien zur Geschichte der Religionen, 3 (Berlin, 1910), 340, points out that the sun rises upon the east-west axis of the Pantheon on Venus' day (April 1st), and on pp. 341–43 attempts to locate the gods' statues in the building. For a false oculus, painted blue, of the fourth century B.C., see A. Vassiliev, *Das antike Grabmal bei Kasanlak* (Sofia, 1959), Taf. 44.

61. On the Pantheon's circles see L. Hautecoeur, *Mystique et architecture. Symbolisme du cercle et de la coupole* (Paris, 1944), p. 167; cf. H. Herter, "Die Rundform in Platons *Atlantis* und Ihre Nachwirkung in der Villa Adriana," *Rheinisches Museum für Philologie*, 96 (1953), 1–20 (the so-called Maritime Theatre at the Villa has the same diameter as the Pantheon). The Senate did homage to Hadrian as the man who had "restored and enriched the circle of the earth" (quoted in *CAH*, 11, 304). C. C. Van Essen, *Précis d'histoire de l'art antique en Italie* (Brussels, 1960; = *Collection Latomus*, 42), p. 96, finds the Pantheon derived solely from Italian precedents of circular design through a "development" from subterranean tombs; this has been questioned by E. Sjöqvist in *Gnomon*, 33 (1961), 205–08. See also G. von Kaschnitz-Weinberg, *Die Mittelmeerischen Grundlagen der antiken Kunst* (Frankfurt-am-Main, 1944), esp. pp. 7–8 and 63–66, who finds rounded Italic and Roman interiors the product of an inherent Mediterranean will to form dating from prehistoric times; cf. his "Vergleichende Studien zur italisch-römischen Struktur. I.

Pantheon life was assigned to the sun, the master planet, and in this sense the building marks the line between the Temple of Apollo at Bassae, with its door cut in the side wall of the cella to illuminate the cult statue, and Hagia Sophia, where multiple, probing rays of light became visible evidence of God's presence and glory. Because of its forms the Pantheon is an activated, light-drenched place, expanding and revolving, visibly connected with the heavens through its cyclopic eye. It has preserved intact the essence of one of the great creative moments of Western and Mediterranean art. Like the Parthenon, Hagia Sophia, Chartres, S. Lorenzo, or S. Ivo it lies at the heart of an age of architecture and embodies and expresses the accumulated experience of a way of life.

Ammianus Marcellinus, an experienced and widely traveled man, thought upon seeing the Pantheon in the fourth century that it was vaulted in lofty beauty, rounded over like a city district. For him Rome was the temple of the whole world.[62] This is the meaning of the Pantheon. Stendhal, saying that he had never met a being absolutely devoid of emotion at the sight of it, asked if that is not what we mean by the sublime.[63] Emotions cannot be eliminated, for art is the communication of feeling. The ambition and daring of the Pantheon design are utterly Roman, but in its planetary rotundity the building is also suffused with a quality of seeking for the comprehension of things beyond knowledge, a quality that records Roman sensitivity to human limits. The Pantheon exists because of a particular man, but the stirring and eloquent message preserved in the universality of its forms belongs to everyone. This is why it is the temple of the whole world.

Baukunst," *RM*, 59 (1944, pub. 1948), 89–128. In the Pantheon the desire for security and enclosure (whose influence upon architecture is so brilliantly exposed by Kaschnitz) was satisfied not only by the forms themselves but also by an implication of imperial concern for all lands and peoples.

62. 16.10.14, 17.4.13. Ammianus, a Greek who wrote his splendid history in Latin at Rome, commented more than once upon works of art; see E. A. Thompson, *The Historical Work of Ammianus Marcellinus* (Cambridge, 1947), p. 12; cf. *AB*, 46 (1964), 435–55.

63. *Promenades dans Rome*, 1st ser. (Paris, 1873), pp. 253–54; see also pp. 255–64.

VI

ARCHITECTS

GREAT BUILDINGS are the work of great architects. The study of the men under discussion must rest chiefly upon the evidence of their buildings, but there are other sources that add details about their lives and broaden our knowledge of their profession and its practice. Texts identify certain men with specific buildings. There are passages in the works of ancient professional writers that mention techniques of architectural drawing, including perspective. A few paintings and mosaics show buildings under construction. Quite a few Roman architectural plans incised on marble have been preserved, and there is at least one plan executed in mosaic. There are instruments from the field and the drafting room. And in spite of Vitruvius' preoccupation with traditional architecture, his work contains instructive passages about professional training and about methods of work common to most Roman architecture. Such sources as these, combined with the evidence of the buildings, make it possible to attempt a brief sketch of the profession and some of its leading men during the years when the direction of ancient architecture was radically shifted.

The modern literature of the subject consists mainly of lists of architects derived from the texts and inscriptions, and of a group of articles which though often valuable are less concerned with architects and their profession than with the question of whether Greek or native personalities and influences were predominant in Roman art.[1] Partly

1. On the nature of this fundamental problem, which pervades much of the modern literature of Roman art, see G. von Kaschnitz Weinberg in *Gnomon, 5* (1929), 195–213 (I owe this reference to the courtesy of Professor P. H. von Blanckenhagen); O. Brendel, "Prolegomena to a Book on Roman Art," *MAAR, 21* (1953), 17–21, 43–47; R. Bianchi Bandinelli, "Römische Kunst, zwei Generationen nach Wickhoff," *Klio, 38* (1960), 267–83. The dilemma resulting from the conviction that Greek artists and influences determined the forms of Roman art is apparent for example in J. M. C. Toynbee, *Some Notes on Artists in the Roman World* (Brussels, 1951; =

Collection Latomus, 6), pp. 14–15; cf. A. Boëthius, *JRS, 43* (1953), 188–90. Vitruvius is often cited as a source supporting the theory that the influence of Greek architects was preponderant in Rome, but his objectives in enumerating Greek names (7.10–14, for example) were to show his hard-won learning, his agreement with the evident taste of Augustus and his circle for certain aspects of Greek art, and his concern about the lack of Roman architectural writings. He takes care to refer to native abilities and reputations (7.14, 17, and esp. 19). For a different interpretation of these passages, see R. MacMullen, "Roman Imperial Building in the Provinces," *Harvard Studies*

because the study of Latin architectural and related terminologies has not yet been carried very far, the lists often do not distinguish among builders, engineers, and surveyors.[2]
In the articles dealing with specific architects the number of attributed buildings is not
infrequently expanded beyond the narrow limits set by the written records.[3] The exceptions to these limitations are few in number.[4] This state of affairs is not surprising in view
of the lack of certain attributions from the period of architectural ferment bounded by
the careers of Vitruvius and Anthemios of Tralles. From the crucial first phase of this
period only a half-dozen major names have survived in texts that describe or mention
their work—four architects (Severus, Rabirius, Apollodoros, and Decrianus), a master
builder or engineer (Celer), and, depending upon one's interpretation of the evidence,
an emperor-architect or imperial dilettante (Hadrian). Almost nothing is known of
Decrianus, who was one of Hadrian's architects,[5] but the other five are known either
to have worked upon particular buildings or to have been closely connected with their
design.

Before discussing the careers of these men it may be useful to summarize in a general
way their possible chronological relationships. In the table that follows the assumption
is made for the first four men that the buildings they designed or were connected with
were begun when they were between thirty-five and sixty years old, and that they did
not live beyond the latter age. The capital letters EB, etc., indicate the earliest and latest
possible dates of birth and death accordingly. The juxtaposition of the names of Apollodoros and Hadrian with the Markets and the Pantheon is purely chronological, for no
one knows for certain who actually designed these buildings.

---

in Classical Philology, 64 (1959), n. 40. For a
classical statement of the pro-Roman view, see
Rivoira, pp. 83–87, and id., *Lombardic Architecture, Its Origin, Development, and Derivatives*, 2
(London, 1910), 108; cf. K. Lehmann, "Piranesi
as Interpreter of Roman Architecture," *Piranesi*
(Northampton, Mass., 1961), pp. 88–89, 97.

2. Lists: C. Promis, "Gli architetti e l'architettura presso i romani," *Reale accademia delle scienze di Torino, Memorie*, 27 (1873), 1–187, a
pioneer work that because of its uncritical phil-
hellenism must be used with some care; E. de
Ruggiero, *Dizionario epigrafico di antichità romane*, 1 (1895), 643–47; Toynbee (above, n.
1), pp. 9–15. Terminology: C. Promis, "Vocaboli latini di architettura posteriori a Vitruvio
oppure a lui sconosciuti," *Accademia . . . di
Torino, Memorie*, 28 (1876), 207–450; W.
Liebenam, *Städteverwaltung im römischen Kai-
serreiche* (Leipzig, 1900), p. 384; E. de Ruggiero, *Lo stato e le opere pubbliche in Roma
antica* (Turin, 1925), pp. 253–73; cf. G. Dow-

ney, "On Some Post-Classical Architectural Terms,"
*Transactions of the American Philological Associ-
ation*, 77 (1946), 22–34. For examples of inscriptions in which the word *architectus* appears,
see *CIL* 1.1216; 3.6178, 6588; 5.3464; 6.2725,
3182, 5738, 8725–26, 9151–52; 8.2850; 10.630,
841, 1446, 1614, 1757, 4587, 6339, 8093;
11.20; 12.186 (the volumes are arranged geo-
graphically).

3. See for example R. Martin, "Apollodorus
of Damascus," *Encyclopedia of World Art*, 1
(1959), cols. 511–14.

4. A. L. Frothingham, "The Architect in History. II. Roman Architects," *The Architectural
Record*, 25 (1909), 179–92, 281–303; R. Paribeni, "Apollodoro di Damasco," *Atti della reale
accademia d'Italia, Rendiconti*, 7.4 (1943), 124–
30. Cf. C. Daremberg and E. Saglio, *Dictionnaire
des antiquités grecques et romaines*, 1 (1877),
374–82; M. S. Briggs, *The Architect in History*
(Oxford, 1927), pp. 28–52.

5. See the quotation given on p. 130, below.

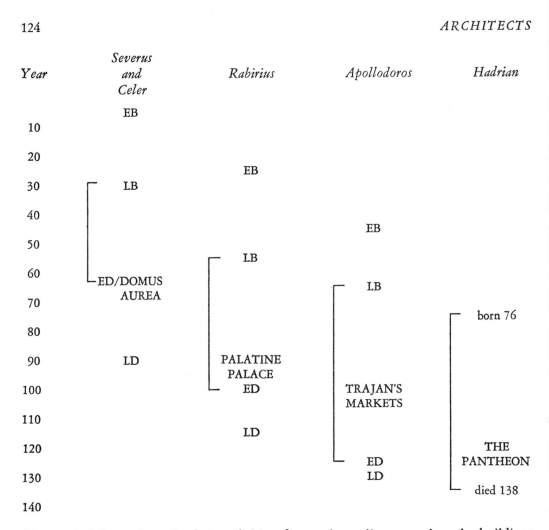

Year	Severus and Celer	Rabirius	Apollodoros	Hadrian
	EB			
10				
20		EB		
30	┌ LB			
40	│			
50	│		EB	
60	│	┌ LB		
70	└ED/DOMUS AUREA	│	┌ LB	
80	│	│	│	┌ born 76
90	LD	PALATINE PALACE	│	│
100	│ └ ED	TRAJAN'S MARKETS	│	
110	│		│	
120	│ LD	│	THE PANTHEON
130		└ ED LD	└ died 138
140				

The vertical lines, given the figure of thirty-five as the earliest age when the buildings were designed, extend through minimum life-spans. In the cases of Rabirius and Apollodoros the approximate ED dates are given in the texts. Martial, writing about 95 or 96, speaks of Rabirius as still alive.[6] Dio Cassius says that Hadrian sent the plans for the Temple of Venus and Rome to Apollodoros, and since the temple was dedicated in 128 this must have happened sometime in the mid-120s.[7]

The table shows that each man after Severus could have worked upon or been concerned with the design of the previous monument. In this sense the case of Rabirius is the most important. It has been suggested that in addition to Domitian's palace he may have designed buildings from Nero's time to Trajan's, and from a strictly chronological standpoint this is possible. He *could* have worked under Severus on the Domus Aurea, and in view of the underlying stylistic affinity of the two palaces it is very possible that he actually did. If he was born about 40 he could have worked with Severus in his twenties, designed Domitian's palace in his late forties, and capped his career by giving

6. *Epigrams* 10.71.   7. See above, Chap. 5, n. 5.

form to Trajan's great urban programs. Apollodoros was probably born no later than the erection of the Domus Aurea and, if he was in Rome during the nineties, as he almost certainly was right after the turn of the century, he would have known Rabirius' great buildings as they rose above the Forum and the Palatine.[8] In addition to the matter of the plans for the Temple of Venus and Rome, Dio Cassius describes a meeting of Trajan with Apollodoros that was attended by Hadrian, so it is quite certain that Trajan's master architect and Hadrian had more than incidental personal contact. In spite of the arbitrary assumptions made in constructing the table it can be said that there is no known obstacle to a series of professional relationships extending for sixty years after the great fire of 64. Apollorodos might appear to be the weakest link because the statement by Dio Cassius that he designed Trajan's Forum does not necessarily mean that he also designed the Markets. But Dio adds that Apollodoros was responsible for Trajan's Baths, and they were clearly in the new style.[9] In any event Hadrian—well educated, observant, aware of art—was in Rome from time to time in the nineties, and he also would have seen and considered Domitian's extraordinary new buildings. Nothing has been proven, but given the evidence available the way is open to the thought that the stylistic and technical evolution evident in the buildings themselves was shaped by the close consecutive association of these men.

SEVERUS

The only known reference to Severus appears in Tacitus' description of the great fire and its consequences, quoted in translation on pp. 25–27 above. The relevant sentences are as follows:

> Ceterum Nero usus est patriae ruinis exstruxitque domum, in qua haud perinde gemmae et aurum miraculo essent, solita pridem et luxu vulgata, quam arva et stagna et in modum solitudinum hinc silvae, inde aperta spatia et prospectus, magistris et machinatoribus Severo et Celere, quibus ingenium et audacia erat etiam, quae natura denegavisset, per artem temptare et viribus principis inludere. Namque ab lacu Averno navigabilem fossam usque ad ostia Tiberina depressuros promiserant, squalenti litore aut per montis adversos. Neque enim aliud umidum gignendis aquis occurrit quam Pomptinae paludes: cetera abrupta aut arentia, ac si perrumpi possent, intolerandus labor nec satis causae. Nero tamen, ut erat incredibilium cupitor, effodere proxima Averno iuga conisus est, manentque vestigia inritae spei.[10]

Concise and vivid as always, Tacitus brilliantly exposes the essentials of Severus' career. Since he will almost never write of crafts or tools, of things he thinks beneath his majestic

8. For Apollodoros in Rome, see the discussion on pp. 131–32, below.

9. Dio's text is quoted and discussed below on pp. 130–31. For the Baths, see also above, Chap. 4, n. 2.

10. *Annals* 15.42.

theme, these sentences are all the more revealing.[11] If what Severus did caught Tacitus' attention and received his praise there is little doubt that Severus was regarded as the foremost architect of his day. Tacitus' aversion to the imperial system has already been mentioned, but it should be said again that this passage is embedded in a catalogue of Nero's vices and inhuman acts. And it was the newness, the freshness and unusualness of Severus' ideas as much as the fire, his immediate subject, that caused Tacitus to speak at surprising length about men outside the political and military centers of society.

There is a lot of information here. First, Tacitus says unequivocally that Severus designed the Domus Aurea, *magister* being used to mean architect in chief or master of the works. This meaning is emphasized by the separate description accorded to Celer, *machinator* or engineer (Tacitus' construction does not mean that each man was both an architect and an engineer). Second, since Severus and Celer designed and built the entire palace, the former was not only an architect but in modern terms a landscape architect as well, and the latter was responsible for the engineering of the 120-foot Colossus in addition to the hydraulic surprises and huge mechanical toys placed in the palace for Caesar's amusement.[12] Third, it is evident that both men were executives as well as practical professionals, for as one begins to fit Tacitus' passage to what is known of the extent of Nero's palace and grounds their substantial administrative responsibilities become apparent. Fourth, as Nero truly did have a passion for the incredible, and had chosen Severus and Celer for the most important commission in his gift, the Avernus-Tiber canal would have been only one of the projects they worked on, selected by Tacitus with his usual fitting economy as both an accurate description of their professional confidence and a telling addition to his portrait of Nero. It follows, fifth, that since no professionals are named in connection with the rebuilding of Rome after the fire (so clearly and fully described by Tacitus) it is possible that Severus was Nero's minister of works, the chief designer of the *urbs nova* and the author of the new city building code. Finally, the references to wastefulness and intolerable labor are shafts aimed at Nero's grotesque arrogance, not at Severus and Celer, who emerge unscathed.

Nero's enthusiasm for novelty, Tacitus' words, and the evidence of the Esquiline wing of the Domus Aurea all point to the same conclusions: Severus was an extremely competent professional, a directing architect as well as a designer, and a vigorously modern artist, eager and able to press beyond accepted and trite solutions. He is the first clear

---

11. For his aversion to mentioning mundane things, see the examples cited in *OCD*, p. 877, par. 12.

12. See above, Chap. 2, n. 24. On the upper surface of the abacus of a capital preserved in the gardens of S. Agnese fuori le mura the inscription CELERI NERONIS AVGVSTIL can be read. Promis, "Gli architetti" (above, n. 2), pp. 137–39, and R. Lanciani, *Wanderings Through Ancient Roman Churches* (London, 1925), p. 258, thought it part of the epitaph of Tacitus' Celer;

the rather generous restoration CELERI NERONIS AVGVSTI L[iberto architecto] has been proposed. Contra: *RE*, 3 (1899), col. 1870; cf. *CIL* 6.14647. The capital appears to be ancient, but the letters are probably considerably more recent; an inscription on an abacus is suspiciously reminiscent of engraved frontispieces in many architectural books of the seventeenth and eighteenth centuries, where piled-up orders carry or enframe titles and descriptions. Promis, p. 138, thinks both Severus and Celer were Florentines.

example we have since Phidias' day of a man atop the pyramid of arts and crafts required in making a great building, and he is proof that Vitruvius' famous prescription for professional education and training, so often thought hopelessly idealistic, did indeed represent a realistic foundation for the careers of the best Roman professionals.[13]

RABIRIUS

Martial's epigram containing the information that Rabirius designed Domitian's palace has also been quoted above, on p. 62. Later Martial referred to him again, this time in connection with the death of Rabirius' parents.[14] Neither of these texts yields anything more about his career. In the earlier epigram his piety is stressed, and in the later his filial devotion. Whether Martial did this because he and Rabirius were friends or because he wished to flatter Domitian by praising his architect is uncertain. No other references to Rabirius are known, though the various texts already discussed in Chapter III are relevant. Rabirius was an old Roman name, but its appearance in the late first century is no surety for Latin origins. Perhaps he was a descendant of one of the men of this name prominent in politics or literature during the first century B.C.[15]

Lack of direct evidence has not discouraged speculation about the possible attribution to Rabirius of buildings spread over a fifty-year period. In the modern literature Rabirius, not Severus, has been assigned the leading role in post-Neronian architecture. It has also been suggested that Rabirius designed the octagonal atrium of the Domus Aurea wing, a suggestion which implies that the interests and capacities of Severus may not have extended beyond making barrel-vaulted spaces.[16] To assign various Flavian buildings to Rabirius seems more natural. He has been given the Baths of Titus, the Albano villa, and the renovation of the Temple of Jupiter on the Capitoline and the Temple of Venus Genetrix in the Forum of Caesar, both of which had been destroyed or badly damaged by fire in Titus' time.[17] Curiously, any link between Rabirius and the Flavian Amphitheatre has been denied.[18] Because Trajanic vaulted architecture was evolved from principles firmly established in Flavian times, the career of Rabirius has been extended into the second century. The way to this has been smoothed by the suspicion if not the proof that certain of Trajan's major buildings were begun by Domitian, and the

13. The Vitruvian passage is quoted and discussed below on pp. 137–39.

14. See above, n. 6.

15. See *RE*, *1A* (1920), cols. 23–29; *OCD*, p. 755.

16. M. Petrignani, "La Domus Flavia," *Boll-Centro*, *16* (1960), 59; Crema, p. 313.

17. For the elements common to Flavian monuments, see G. Lugli, "Nuove forme dall'architettura romana nell'età dei Flavi," *Atti*, *3*, 95–102;

cf. Blake, 2, 162. For the other suggested attributions, see Martial, *Epigrams* 7.56; Statius, *Silvae* 4.3.16; Lugli, *Roma*, pp. 321, 427; id., "La Villa di Domiziano sui colli Albani, I," *BC*, 45 (1917), 41; Blake, 2, 102, 134. Rivoira, p. 97, suggested that Rabirius designed the palace in the Gardens of Sallust in Rome, now known to be Hadrianic (Bloch, pp. 184–85, 349).

18. Lugli, *Roma*, p. 321.

great Baths atop the Domus Aurea and the Markets have both evoked the name of Rabirius.[19]

All of this is only interesting conjecture unless one accepts the theory that a unique feature of the design of a number of Domitianic entablatures indicates Rabirius' hand. In these entablatures two small stone rings, rather like tracery eyeglasses in appearance, were left standing vertically between the dentil blocks. These double circles can be seen on fragments preserved at the palace, on the Capitoline, beside the Temple of Venus Genetrix, and at the Albano villa.[20] Taken by themselves their presence on the site of the Domus Flavia proves only that they were used by Rabirius' craftsmen; that they were necessarily a kind of architect's signature is only an inference, however attractive. The same is true of the two temples, where the circles suggest but do not prove that Rabirius was the architect in charge of the restorations.[21] The case is rather stronger for the Albano villa because both the design and structural technique of the remains, when compared with those of the palace in Rome, suggest Rabirius' style and methods. A thorough architectural study of the villa and its relationships to the palace might settle both the question of attribution to Rabirius and the validity of the double-circle theory.

Rabirius' name, though not yet freed from the polemical literature alluded to at the beginning of the chapter, has begun to be recognized. In 1919 Rivoira wrote of his daring and originality, referring to him as an architect-engineer.[22] Opinion ranges from Lugli's enthusiasm for the "fervido ingegno dell'architetto Rabirio" to MacMullen's more restrained reference to "a certain Rabirius, presumably no narrow specialist."[23] Crema's opinions deserve quotation:

> Nell'ala orientale [of the Esquiline wing of the Domus Aurea] si trova . . . una nuova architettura, che rivela l'intervento di un piú geniale progettista, forse Rabirio, che avrebbe iniziato qui la sua attività, poi largamente esplicatasi nei palazzi flavi. L'ipotesi è attraente e farebbe riconoscere decisamente in questi l'innovatore che avrebbe avviato l'architettura romana al pieno sfruttamento della facile e pieghevole struttura cementizia, nel libero movimento dei muri e delle volte e nella varietà di effetti luministici che davano vita agli spazi interni. Certo, dopo le

19. Inauguration of Trajanic buildings by Domitian and possible Rabirian attributions: *Monumentae Germaniae Historica*, 9 (Berlin, 1892), 146, 11 (Berlin, 1894), 140; Platner-Ashby, p. 241; Blake, 2, 99, 102, 105; Paribeni (above, n. 4), pp. 125–28; Bourne, p. 67, item 31; Lugli, *Roma*, pp. 53, 280, 355; id., *Tecnica*, 2, captions to Tav. CLXVIII.3 and CCI.1.

20. See F. Bianchini, *Del palazzo de'Cesari. Opera postuma* (Verona, 1738), Tav. II, IV; Lugli, *Roma*, p. 252; Crema, p. 272; Blake, 2, 106 (n. 101), 136, 139; Toynbee (above, n. 1),

p. 12, n. 4; Lugli ("La Villa," above, n. 17), p. 35, n. 1.

21. Blake, 2, 102, n. 46.

22. P. 113. Promis, "Gli architetti" (above, n. 2), pp. 119–20, tried hard to make Rabirius a Greek, and gave him only a few lines.

23. Lugli, *Roma*, p. 511; MacMullen (above, n. 1), p. 212 (he feels that the profession "had and kept its roots in the Greek world"). For Rabirius, see also *RE*, 1A (1920), cols. 23–24; U. Thieme and F. Becker, *Allgemeines Lexikon der bildenden Künstler*, 27 (1933), 540.

ultime manifestazioni repubblicane, l'architettura romana riprende di qui il suo slancio che avrà un suo culmine nell'età adrianea e nell'ultima vigorosa ripresa dell'età tetrarchica tramanderà il suo impulso vivificatore al medioevo.[24]

So little is known of Roman architects that it is difficult to resist the temptation to make Rabirius the central figure of the entire Roman architectural revolution. But it is unnecessary either to enlarge his *œuvre* or slight Severus, for his masterpiece upon the Palatine insures his high rank in the history of architecture. He gave a new concept of the palace to Mediterranean and Western society. His design was so appropriate, so evocative of majesty, that it survived for centuries within the variations worked upon it, and it contained answers to needs he could never have known.

APOLLODOROS AND HADRIAN

Possibly more has been written about Apollodoros than about any architect between Vitruvius and Brunelleschi. The texts that mention him name three important buildings he built in Rome for Trajan and refer to a great bridge over the Danube he erected for the same emperor. From these texts and the remains of two of the buildings an impressive career has been inferred which seems for the most part quite probable. He was a man of considerable consequence, a writer and a cosmopolitan citizen of the Empire. He was close to Trajan and was almost certainly his chief *praefectus fabrum* or minister of works. Apollodoros also knew and worked with Hadrian, though Hadrian may have disliked and envied him. The buildings attributed to him in modern studies number at least fifteen, but these attributions have been based more upon Trajanic date and great size than upon archaeological or stylistic grounds.[25] His obvious importance and Syrian origins have inevitably drawn Apollodoros into the discussion about Greek influences in Roman art, where his name has been used freely.[26]

The texts show that Apollodoros and Hadrian knew each other for at least two decades (Hadrian was probably the younger by ten or fifteen years). Because of this and the vital importance of both men to the history of imperial architecture they will be considered together. Excluding the shadowy figure of Decrianus they are the only men who give a sense of personality to the culminating phase of the movement that began in Nero's time. There are more texts for them than for Severus and Rabirius, for Hadrian's

24. Crema, p. 313.

25. See below, n. 40. It has been suggested that he was the master sculptor of Trajan's Column and the great Trajanic frieze now on the Arch of Constantine: R. Bianchi Bandinelli, "Una problema di arte romana: Il 'maestro delle imprese di Trajano'," *Le arti, 1* (1938–39), 325–34, amplified in his *Storicità dell'arte classica* (2nd ed. Florence, 1950), pp. 211–18.

26. Apollodoros as a Hellenistic artist instrumental in forming the taste and style of the capital: Promis, "Gli architetti" (above, n. 2), p. 179; *CAH, 11,* 781–82; *OCD,* p. 780; G. Becatti, *Arte e gusto negli scrittori latini* (Florence, 1951), p. 249; Toynbee (above, n. 1), pp. 14–15. Questioned or disputed by, among others: G. Cultrera, "Apollodoro di Damasco," *EncIt, 3,* 680–81; Paribeni (above, n. 4), p. 129; J. B. Ward Perkins, "Severan Art and Architecture at Lepcis Magna," *JRS, 38* (1948), 62; Bianchi Bandinelli (above, n. 25).

unceasing building activity, archaeologically so evident, was noted by ancient writers. Aelius Spartianus, his fourth-century biographer, says that in almost every city of the Empire, Hadrian

> built some building and gave public games . . . He built public buildings in all places and without number, but he inscribed his own name on none of them except the Temple of his father Trajan [next to the Basilica Ulpia; Plate 74, F]. At Rome he restored the Pantheon, the Saepta [a voting-precinct], the Basilica of Neptune, very many temples, the Forum of Augustus, and the Baths of Agrippa, and dedicated all of them in the names of their original builders. Also he constructed the bridge named after himself, a tomb on the bank of the Tiber, and the Temple of the Bona Dea. With the aid of the architect Decrianus he raised the Colossus and, keeping it in an upright position, moved it away from the place in which the Temple [of Venus and Rome] is now, though its weight was so vast that he had to furnish as many as twenty-four elephants for the work. This statue he then consecrated to the Sun, after removing the features of Nero, to whom it had previously been dedicated, and he also planned, with the aid of the architect Apollodoros, to make a similar one for the Moon.[27]

Procopius of Caesarea, the historian of Justinian's reign, after remarking that Trajan resented the fact that the Danube determined the boundary of the Empire, says that

> he was eager to span it with a bridge so he might be able to cross it and that there might be no obstacle to his going against the barbarians beyond it. How he built this bridge I shall not be at pains to relate, but shall let Apollodoros of Damascus, who was the master builder [ἀρχιτέκτων] of the whole work, describe the operation.[28]

The bridge itself is described by Dio Cassius.

> Trajan constructed over the Ister [the Danube] a stone bridge for which I cannot sufficiently admire him. Brilliant indeed as are his other achievements, this surpasses them. For it has twenty piers of squared stone one hundred and fifty feet in height above the foundations and sixty in width, and these, standing at a distance of one hundred and seventy feet from one another, are connected by arches . . . Yet the very fact that the river in its descent is here contracted from a great flood to such a narrow channel, after which it again expands into a greater flood, makes it all the more violent and deep, and this feature must be considered in estimating the difficulty of constructing the bridge. This too, then, is one of the achievements that show the magnitude of Trajan's designs, though the bridge is of no use to us;

27. *SHA, Hadrian* 19.2–13.   28. *On the Buildings* 4.6.12–13.

for . . . Hadrian . . . was afraid that it might make it easy for the barbarians . . . to cross into Moesia, and so he removed the superstructure.[29]

There is another, more important paragraph about Apollodoros in Dio Cassius. Dio wrote his *Roman History* in Greek about the year 230, but only eighteen of his original eighty books have survived intact. About half of the remainder are preserved in an epitome prepared by a Byzantine monk, Ioannes Xiphilinos, for the emperor Michael VII Dukas (1071–78).[30] Books 68 and 69, which deal with Trajan and Hadrian, are among those that have survived in epitomized form. In Book 69, Dio speaks of Hadrian's jealousy of any who excelled at the many activities for which he thought himself especially well suited and trained.[31] Dio relates some stories about Hadrian, who though vexed with certain philosophers could find no pretext to destroy them. The text of the abridgment continues thus:

> But [Hadrian] first banished and later put to death Apollodoros, the architect [ἀρχιτέκτων], who had built the various creations of Trajan in Rome—the Forum [ἀγορά], the concert hall [ᾠδεῖον], and the baths [γυμνάσιον]. The reason assigned was that he had been guilty of some misdemeanor; but the true reason was that once when Trajan was consulting him on some point about the buildings he had said to Hadrian, who had interrupted with some remark: "Be off, and draw your pumpkins [κολοκύντας]. You don't understand any of these matters"—it chanced that Hadrian at the time was pluming himself upon some such drawing. When he became emperor, therefore, he remembered this slight and would not endure the man's freedom of speech. He sent him the design [διάγραμμα] of the Temple of Venus and Rome by way of showing him that a great work could be accomplished without his aid, and asked Apollodoros whether the proposed structure was satisfactory. The architect in his reply stated first, in regard to the temple, that it ought to have been built on high ground and that the earth should have been excavated beside it, so that it might have stood out more conspicuously on the Sacred Way from a higher position, and might also have accommodated the machines in its basement, so that they could be put together unobserved and brought into the theatre [i.e., the Flavian Amphitheatre] without anyone being aware of them beforehand. Secondly, in regard to the statues, he said that they had been made too tall for the height of the cella. "For now," he said, "if the goddesses wish to get up and go out, they will be unable to do so." When he wrote this so bluntly to Hadrian, the emperor was both vexed and exceedingly grieved because he had fallen into a mistake that could not be righted, and he restrained

29. 68.13.
30. K. Krumbacher, *Geschichte der byzantinischen Litteratur* (2nd ed. Munich, 1897), pp. 369–70; *RE*, *3* (1899), cols. 1720–21; *OCD*, p. 282.
31. Cf. above, Chap. 5, n. 1.

neither his anger nor his grief, but slew the man. Indeed, his nature was such that he was jealous not only of the living, but also of the dead . . .[32]

The texts that mention Apollodoros all refer to him as an *architectus* or ἀρχιτέκτων. Only Procopius says that he was from Damascus, but there is no reason to believe that we are dealing with more than one Apollodoros. Had Procopius not mentioned Damascus, a portion of the modern literature of high imperial art would have a rather different content. Because he did, and because of the marble trabeation of Trajan's Forum and the Basilica Ulpia, Apollodoros has been given a leading role in bringing Hellenistic style and forms to Rome.[33] Actually this process had begun long before, as the monuments and Vitruvius show, and its effects were fully apparent by the time of Apollodoros' birth.[34] As Paribeni remarks: "Non è improbabile, che se Apollodoro fosse nato a Tibur o a Tusculum invece a Damasco, nessuno si sarebbe tanto scalmanato per lui."[35] It is his actual architecture and his position as an advisor and even a colleague of emperors who "built public buildings in all places and without number" that makes him important, not his place of birth.[36]

Trajan's discussion with Apollodoros took place in Rome and was concerned with Apollodoros' buildings there, for Dio's statement that the emperor was "consulting him on some point" follows almost immediately after the enumeration of the buildings and clearly refers back to them. The meeting can be dated approximately. The years when both the Baths and the Forum were under construction were 104–09 (the concert hall has not been identified; Dio may refer to one begun by Domitian). Since Trajan and Hadrian were in Dacia from the early summer of 105 until about the end of 106, the meeting took place either in 104–05 or during 107–09. Hadrian was governor of

32. 69.4.

33. For the expansion of attributions, see Thieme-Becker (above, n. 23), 2 (1908), 29–31; Cultrera (above, n. 26); Paribeni (above, n. 4); R. Bianchi Bandinelli, "Apollodoros di Damasco," *Enciclopedia dell'arte antica*, 1, 477–80. For Apollodoros as a sculptor, see Bianchi Bandinelli (above, n. 25). A bust in Munich, inscribed with the name Apollodoros, has been said to be a portrait of Trajan's architect (it is illustrated in Cultrera, p. 680): P. Arndt and F. Bruckmann, *Griechische und römische Porträts* (Munich, 1897), 46–47; A. Furtwängler and P. Wolters, *Beschreibung der Glyptothek König Ludwigs I. zu München* (Munich, 1910), p. 352. C. Cichorius, *Die Reliefs der Traianssäule*, 3 (Berlin, 1900), sees Apollodoros in the scene on the Column that shows the great Danube bridge (in abbreviated form) in the background; cf. Bianchi Bandinelli, "Apollodoros," p. 477.

34. See pp. 10–11, above.

35. Paribeni (above, n. 4), p. 124; cf. p. 129, where he says that if Apollodoros built Trajan's Forum and Baths, "pochi architetti sono stati più romani di lui"; id., *Optimus Princeps*, 2 (Messina, 1927), 246–47. Cultrera (above, n. 26), p. 680, follows Paribeni: "nessun architetto e più romano di lui."

36. Briggs (above, n. 4), p. 39, remarks that Apollodoros belongs to "that large class of architectural 'ghosts' whose work has never received proper recognition." Our Apollodoros is sometimes confused with the author of a work on siege warfare (which may date from the Hellenistic rather than the imperial period); see C. Wescher, *La poliorcétique des Grecs* (Paris, 1867), 137–38; *Revue des études grecques*, 3 (1890), 230–81, 8 (1895), 198–202; W. Sakur, *Vitruv und die Poliorketiker* (Berlin, 1925), esp. pp. 10–11; *RE*, 21 (1952), cols. 1388–89; cf. Vitruvius, 10.13.

Lower Pannonia during part of the latter period, when in any event the buildings would have been well along and consultation less necessary, so it is probable that the meeting took place about 104. Dio's source for this passage is unknown (he may have used Apollodoros' own treatise for his description of the Danube bridge). Since the story proceeds smoothly and the style is distinctly Dio's it was probably copied directly by Xiphilinos from the original with the thought that it was the kind of anecdote that would please his imperial master.

One further point about this passage should be made before considering its more purely architectural content. The paragraph appears in a section of Book 69 where Dio's theme is that Hadrian's "jealousy of all who excelled in any respect was most terrible and caused the downfall of many, besides utterly destroying several."[37] Paribeni has argued persuasively that Dio set out deliberately to reduce Hadrian's reputation by claiming that he murdered prominent persons out of motives of intellectual and artistic jealousy.[38] First Dio alludes in a vague way to numbers of actual or intended victims. Then the story of Apollodoros appears, which concludes with the statement that Hadrian was envious even of the dead. Hadrian's supposedly base character is cleverly emphasized by inflating the reputations of those whom the emperor is supposed to have destroyed. For example, Apollodoros the architect is presented as a man unafraid either to speak his mind directly and brusquely to the imperial favorite in Trajan's presence or to the same man when he had become the dread autocrat. But the arts of painting and modeling, when pursued by Hadrian, are dismissed as "most trivial."[39] Dio's reasons are usually said to have sprung from his feeling that Hadrian had treated the Senate badly, and as a senator himself he would be bound to dislike such an emperor. This seems a little thin, as Dio served Commodus and the Severans with some enthusiasm and twice attained the consulship. But Paribeni's basic point is surely right, and the reasons given for Apollodoros' murder should be dismissed as well as the act itself. The question of the truthfulness of the rest of the passage remains. Its very circumstantiality argues for its reliability. It is hard to believe that Dio invented the remark about drawing pumpkins just to suggest that Hadrian's interests were inconsequential and silly; it has the ring of truth. Besides, there is another and more sensible explanation for it which will be discussed in a moment. Apollodoros' sarcastic criticism of the relatively low ceiling height of the Temple of Venus and Rome seems genuine and uncontrived. In short, Dio placed authentic incidents in a broader frame calculated to show Hadrian in a bad light.

The first major architectural question raised by the text is whether the reference to the Forum includes the Markets. What is known of the Forum (Plate 74) and the Basilica Ulpia (Plate 126) cannot be used to argue that Apollodoros was not the architect of the Markets. The command and use of both traditional and modern styles by one man was common; witness Rabirius' great Hellenistic peristyles or the porch of the Pantheon.

---

37. 69.3.3.   39. 69.3.2.
38. Paribeni (above, n. 4); cf. Kähler, p. 157.

Dio specifically states that Apollodoros designed Trajan's Baths (Plate 73), which proves that he worked in both styles. Furthermore, the kind of engineering proficiency and organizational competence required by the erection of Trajan's Column and the roofing of the Ulpia (and the Danube bridge as well) was needed to prepare the Quirinal slope and order the complex economy of the Markets' construction. Again a negative conclusion can be reached: there is nothing in the evidence that disqualifies Apollodoros. The Markets were built at the same time as Apollodoros' Forum and were planned with it as part of one huge urban complex, and since he was Trajan's chief designer it seems unlikely that the Markets were designed by another man.

The modern list of buildings attributed to Apollodoros has sprung from Dio's phrase about "the various creations of Trajan in Rome" and the grandeur of the Forum concept. Everything big has been put under his name—the Markets, the vast works at Porto, the port at Civitavecchia, the impressive road cuttings at Terracina, the Trajanic redevelopment of part of Ostia, and so on.[40] It is entirely possible that he supervised all of these. His career as an architect-engineer, with its military overtones, his access to Trajan, and his evident abilities suggest that he was in charge of government construction. He was also an extremely sensitive designer, as the fragments of the Forum and the Basilica Ulpia show, and his boldness can be seen in his plans of the Forum and the Baths. Syrian or not, he was a Roman civil servant or officer, prepared by long training and experience to handle all commissions and responsibilities, the very epitome of Vitruvius' ideal architect. Perhaps when Trajan was a military tribune in the east and his father was governor of Syria he and Apollodoros met.[41] By the time Apollodoros stood beside the emperor he was a truly imperial, Greco-Roman figure, equally at home in east and west.

His career, like that of Rabirius, has been coaxed past the dates of his known buildings. His exchanges with Hadrian have been thought to indicate that he was one of Hadrian's architects and the designer of the Pantheon.[42] But the information actually given by Dio is different and very valuable. An unusual scene, extremely rare in its intimation of working relationships between an artist and his emperor, is briefly disclosed.[43] Trajan is consulting with his master architect, who takes quite a lofty tone with Hadrian, a kinsman and protégé of Trajan though not his declared successor. Trajan's reaction to this

40. See for example F. Clementi, "I mercati traianei e la Via Biberatica," Roma, 8 (1930), 505; Martin (above, n. 3), col. 512; Cultrera (above, n. 26), p. 680; Paribeni (above, n. 4), p. 129; Bianchi Bandinelli, "Apollodoros" (above, n. 33), p. 479; Rostovtzeff, 2, 694, n. 3; cf. OCD, p. 70 (7). In addition to the attributions in Dio, the proposed list now stands as follows: the Markets of Trajan, Trajan's Column, the frieze on the Arch of Constantine, a Circus-Naumachia, and the Pantheon (all in Rome); Porto, works at Ostia, the harbor at Centumcellae (Civitavecchia), the arches at Ancona and Benevento, and the Terracina road cuts; the monument at Adamklissi near the mouth of the Danube and road cuts in Dacia; and a walled enclosure in Damascus.

41. See Paribeni (above, n. 4), p. 125.

42. Martin (above, n. 3), col. 512; cf. Bloch, p. 116: "Apollodoro di Damasco, che forse non fu estraneo al grandioso [Pantheon] progetto."

43. Procopius, On the Buildings 1.1.66–78 (cf. 1.1.50) contains another such confrontation; cf. Paribeni (above, n. 35), 2, Fig. 16; and the splendid scene in E. Waugh, Helena (Boston, 1950), pp. 158–63.

rebuff is not revealed. The text then records that Hadrian had been drawing pumpkins or something like pumpkins, an activity Apollodoros clearly feels to be childish. The vegetable in question is the same as the Latin *curcubita* or round gourd, paneled and gored with convex forms between its meridian curves.[44] Recently it has been suggested that Hadrian's drawings were of gored or umbrella-shaped domes, of the kind seen in several Hadrianic buildings, for example the vestibule of the so-called Piazza d'Oro at Hadrian's Villa. The interior shapes of these vaults strongly resemble the outer surfaces of pumpkins.[45]

The second half of the passage, which describes Apollodoros' criticism of the design of the Temple of Venus and Rome, raises several points. A drawing, or probably more than one drawing (because of the implication that Apollodoros inspected a section or elevation), was sent to him by Hadrian. The text does not say directly that Hadrian himself designed the temple, but this may be implied by the fact that the plan was in his possession.[46] Again the high standing of Apollodoros is emphasized. Hadrian bothers to solicit his opinion or boast to him, depending upon how one reads between Dio's lines, and there is an oblique reference to his previous indispensability. By first referring to the design as one under consideration and then speaking of a mistake that could not be righted the text seems to be ambiguous about when, with respect to the construction of the temple, Apollodoros was consulted. But the characterization of Hadrian as unable

44. "Draw your pumpkins": τὰς κολοκύντας γράφε, from κολοκύντη (κολοκύνθη, κολοκύνθα). E. Cary, the Loeb translator (*8*, p. 431), in giving "gourds," does not, I think, properly convey the shape of the vegetable in question; the long gourd is the σικύα. Martin, or his translator (above, n. 3), p. 511, says "nasturtiums."

45. The idea is Professor Frank E. Brown's, and he has generously allowed me to mention it here; his paper ("Hadrianic Architecture") will appear in a *Festschrift* for the late Karl Lehmann, announced in New York in 1964. A pumpkin-like dome of Hadrianic date can be seen in the remains of the palace in the Gardens of Sallust in Rome: K. Lehmann-Hartleben and I. Lindros, "Il palazzo degli Orti Sallustiani," *OpusArch*, 1 (1935), 196–227; Nash, *1*, 496. At least two remain at Hadrian's Villa: S. Aurigemma, *Villa Adriana* (Rome, 1961), Figs. 80–83, 164; cf. Durm, Figs. 314, 315, 317. The vaults of the so-called Temple of Venus and its vestibule at Baia were of this type; F. Rakob, "Litus beatae veneris aureum. Untersuchungen am 'Venustempel' in Baiae," *RM*, 68 (1961), 114–49; cf. Lugli, *Tecnica*, 2, Tav. CCVIII.2. There is another example at Baia just to the southwest of the so-called Temple of Mercury, an octagonal gored or scalloped vault which

on the basis of its construction would appear to be of Hadrianic date; as far as I know it has not been published. At Bulla Regia, just east of the southeast corner of the Baths marked B on no. 26 (Fernana) in the *Atlas archéologique de la Tunisie* (Paris, 1893), there is a similar octagonal gored vault, also apparently unpublished, that belongs to the same family of vaulted forms.

46. The passage has been cited to show that Hadrian drew the plans and was an architect: Platner-Ashby, p. 553; Promis, "Gli architetti" (above, n. 2), p. 177, who was persuaded that Hadrian was a Greek-trained architect; cf. Mac-Mullen (above, n. 1), p. 227, n. 38. The modern concept that Hadrian was a practicing architect stems in large part from the championship of Rivoira, p. 118; id. (above, n. 1), 2, 104–08, and his articles "Di Adriano architetto e dei monumenti adrianei," *Reale Accademia dei Lincei, Rendiconti*, 18 (1909), 172–77, and "Adriano architetto e i monumenti adrianei," *Nuova antologia* (April 16, 1910), 8 pp.; see for example *CAH*, 11, 797; R. Vighi, *The Pantheon* (Rome, 1957), p. 11; J. Finch, *The Story of Engineering* (New York, 1960), p. 72. For the temple, see G. A. S. Snijder, "Kaiser Hadrian und der Tempel der Venus und Rome," *JDAI*, 55 (1940), 1–11.

to right the mistake and rising in wrath to slay the man can be attributed to Dio's prejudice. The remains of the temple sit upon a high terrace whose side toward the Flavian Amphitheatre contains a number of rooms, and it may be that Hadrian made use of Apollodoros' criticism.[47] The first phrase, referring to a "proposed structure," is probably accurate; if so Hadrian forwarded the drawings sometime in the mid-120s.[48]

The conclusion that Hadrian was learned in architectural matters is inescapable. The texts, his buildings, and the nature of his personality all bear this out. Spartianus says that he "was greatly interested in poetry and letters. He was very expert in arithmetic, geometry, and painting. He . . . wrote much verse . . . "[49] Dio records that he modeled and painted.[50] Besides his predisposition toward the arts he apparently felt, as so many English aristocrats of the eighteenth century were to feel, that architecture was a subject an educated, sophisticated man commanded. But whether he designed buildings and saw them through to completion, performing all the functions of a professional architect, is another matter. None of the texts that speak of his many talents say so, though Spartianus records that he carried out or planned semi-architectural projects with the aid of professionals (see p. 130). The pumpkin drawings and the temple plans show how close he was to architecture, and Apollodoros' rude dismissal ("you don't understand any of these matters") could have been prompted by a tactless display of knowledge as readily as by a show of ignorance. If he did actually design buildings in Rome, Ostia, or Tivoli, their construction was supervised by others, for during his reign he was out of Italy for many years.

Hadrian's relationship to architecture was twofold. On the one hand he was a brilliant dilettante, an ἀρχιτέκτων μουσικός, and on the other, in virtue of his position, an active participant in the planning of state programs and probably in the decisions governing the designs of particular buildings as well.[51] He "enrolled by cohorts and centuries, on the model of the legions, builders, geometers, architects, and every sort of expert in construction or decoration."[52] These were the men who did the day-to-day work. Hadrian ordered, suggested, and criticized, shaping buildings more by the force of his intellect and personality than by any painstaking professional procedures for which in any event he had little or no time. He seems to have been deeply curious about design, and something in his strange, quick nature was fed by a steady multiplication of different architectural forms. He asked for buildings continually, collecting them as other men collected sculpture or gems. Through his passion for building he influenced architecture profoundly,

47. Suggested for example by J. H. Middleton, *The Remains of Ancient Rome*, 2 (London, 1892), 219; and W. J. Anderson et al., *The Architecture of Ancient Rome* (2nd ed. London, 1927), p. 74.

48. See above, Chap. 5, n. 5.

49. *SHA, Hadrian* 14.8–10.

50. 69.3.2.

51. In this sense Rivoira's thesis (see above, n. 46) is probably correct; see also Dio Cassius, 69.5.2–3.

52. The anonymous fourth-century *Epitome de Caesaribus*, as quoted by MacMullen (above, n. 1), p. 215; the *Epitome*, usually published together with Aurelius Victor, used to be thought his work.

not the least because he was able to manipulate so much talent, manpower, and money in its favor.

ARCHITECTURAL PRACTICE AND METHODS

Numerous inscriptions and a few general references in the texts confirm what is suggested by the magnitude of building activity on three continents—the Roman architectural profession was a large and honorable one.[53] Many architects of the first and second centuries were imperial freedmen, and many were Greeks.[54] In Trajan's time the assignments of some of these men were controlled by the government.[55] Hadrian's organization of a corps of architects and specialists along paramilitary lines has already been noted. It appears that there were three main groups—military specialists, men in private practice, and civil servants. Tacitus and Martial respected the profession, and Vitruvius was very proud of it. He speaks of

> so great a profession as this . . . only persons can justly claim to be architects who from boyhood have mounted by the steps of their studies and, being trained generally in the knowledge of arts and sciences, have reached the temple of architecture at the top.[56]

A youth marked for architecture studied the liberal arts while serving an apprenticeship to a master, or was trained in the army.[57] In the latter case there was a good deal of emphasis upon practical engineering and weaponry as well as upon functional design and permanent structure. The influence of military needs and training upon Roman architecture generally has perhaps been exaggerated, though military architects did lay out towns and design civil buildings in the provinces.[58] The distinction between architect and engineer is often hard to draw, and many an *architectus* of the inscriptions was probably an expert in construction and public works projects rather than a designer. On the other

53. For lists of names, see above, n. 2. For the rank and titles of the many military architects, see Vegetius, *On Military Matters* 1.7, 2.11; *RE*, 2 (1896), cols. 551–52; A. von Domaszewski, "Die Rangordnung des römischen Heeres," *Bonner Jahrbücher*, *117* (1908), 25–26; cf. MacMullen (above, n. 1), pp. 214–17.

54. Freedmen appear frequently in the inscriptions. Trajan reminds Pliny the Younger (*Letters* 10.40) that "it is usually from Greece that [architects] come [to Rome]."

55. Pliny the Younger, *Letters* 10.39–42; cf. 10.62. See also *ESAR*, 5, 72.

56. 1.1.11.

57. See F. E. Brown, "Vitruvius and the Liberal Art of Architecture," *Bucknell Review*, 11.4 (1963), 99–107, for Vitruvius' objectives in writing his *Ten Books* and the cultural background of

his ideas and beliefs. See also M. L. Clarke, "The Architects of Greece and Rome," *Architectural History*, 6 (1963), 9–22; cf. G. Downey, "Byzantine Architects, Their Training and Methods," *Byzantion*, 18 (1946–48), 99–118 but esp. 108; see also below, n. 61. For the army and architecture, see above, n. 53; C. Germain de Montauzan, *Essai sur la science et l'art de l'ingénieur* (Paris, 1909), pp. 115–17; Paribeni (above, n. 4), p. 127; R. MacMullen, *Soldier and Civilian in the Later Roman Empire* (Cambridge, Mass., 1963), pp. 22–48 and citations. There is some evidence that experienced men were enrolled in the Praetorian Guard: *CIL* 10.1757, 11.20, 630; and see M. Durry, *Les cohortes prétoriennes* (Paris, 1938), p. 115.

58. See for example I. A. Richmond, *Roman Britain* (Harmondsworth, 1955), p. 88.

hand every Roman architect who was an artist also had to be a practical builder. The broad base of the profession was composed of men of great personal experience of materials and construction, and as in any period the number of truly gifted and original designers was small.

Vitruvius insists upon the necessity of wide knowledge.

> The science of the architect depends upon many disciplines and various kinds of knowledge inherent in other arts. The architect's own contribution is in craftsmanship and technology. Craftsmanship is continued and familiar practice, which is carried out by the hands in such material as is necessary for the purpose of a design. Technology sets forth and explains things wrought in accordance with technical skill and method.[59]

He adds that the architect

> should be a man of letters, a skillful draftsman, a mathematician, familiar with scientific thought, a diligent student of philosophy, acquainted with music, not ignorant of medicine, knowledgeable about the opinions of the jurists, and familiar with astronomy and the theory of the heavens.[60]

This second passage should be taken at face value, not as mere rhetoric.[61] Vitruvius in his following paragraphs amply justifies each specification. He is speaking of what the *best* professionals must always know, for wide general knowledge brings better solutions more quickly. Criticism of this passage is in any event repudiated by the appropriateness of the design, functional dispositions, orientation, and effects of great Roman buildings.

Plans, elevations, perspective views, and colored renderings were made then as now. Two Vitruvian passages are particularly relevant.

> The ways of setting things out (*species dispositionis*) are these: plan (*ichnographia*), elevation (*orthographia*) and perspective (*scaenographia*). Plan calls for the competent use of compass and rule, and with these the proper dispositions are made at the sites (*e qua capientur formarum in solis aerearum descriptiones*). Elevation, however, is the image of the standing façade, a slightly shaded drawing showing the finished appearance. Perspective also is the shading of the façade, and of the retreating sides, with all of the lines verging to a point that is the center of a circle.[62]

59. 1.1.1.

60. 1.1.3.

61. MacMullen (above, n. 1), p. 211, finds Vitruvius' requirements somewhat ridiculous; but see Vitruvius, 1.1.4–17, and Brown (above, n. 57). On architectural training, see Germain de Montauzan (above, n. 57), pp. 111–14, 116; C. Barbagallo, *Lo stato e l'instruzione publica* (Catania, 1911), p. 188, n. 2, pp. 196–97, 220–21, 230, 390–91; H. I. Marrou, *A History of Education in Antiquity* (3rd ed. London, 1956), pp. 310–12; cf. Briggs (above, n. 4), pp. 30–32.

62. 1.2.2.

An architect must be a man of letters that he may keep a record of useful precedents. By his skill in draftsmanship he will find it easy by colored drawings to represent the effect desired. Mathematics again furnishes many resources to architecture. It teaches the use of rule and compass and thus facilitates the laying-out of buildings on their sites by the use of set-squares, levels, and alignments. By optics, in buildings, light is duly drawn from certain aspects of the sky. By arithmetic, the cost of a building is summed up; the methods of mensuration are indicated; while the difficult problems of symmetry are solved by geometrical rules and methods.[63]

Another text, which may date from the High Empire, refers to "the suitable method of drawing images of buildings."[64]

Thus the plans that have been preserved in mosaic and on marble represent only one of the graphic devices used by Roman architects. Vitruvius' perspective, shaded, and colored drawings were made on ephemeral materials, but the techniques employed can be seen in numerous Roman paintings and mosaics and on coins (see Plates 25 and 51).[65] Drawing instruments have been found for example at Herculaneum, and like so many ancient hand tools they differ very little from their modern counterparts in design.[66] Set squares and site tools appear on several tomb reliefs, and there is a wonderful mosaic in the Bardo Museum in Tunis of an architect and his assistants (Plate 127).[67] A column is being carted to the site, mortar is being mixed, and a carver is shaping or fluting a colonnette. The architect appears at the top of the panel, holding his five-foot measuring stick in one hand while gesturing with the other toward a wreathed inscription, now

63. 1.1.4. Vitruvius does not give the rules and methods mentioned in the last phrase—perhaps he assumed that they would be familiar to his readers.

64. *Heronis Alexandrini opera quae supersunt omnia*, ed. W. Schmidt and J. L. Heiberg, 4 (Leipzig, 1912), 106–07. L. Grasberger, *Erziehung und Unterricht im klassischen Altertum*, 2, 343–50, has collected the evidence for the teaching of drawing, according to Marrou (above, n. 61), p. 393. See also Downey's article cited above, n. 57.

65. On perspective see (in addition to the quotation on p. 138 above) Vitruvius, 7.Praef.11 (cf. the Loeb edition, *1*, p. x); P. W. Lehmann, *Roman Wall Paintings from Boscoreale in the Metropolitan Museum of Art* (Cambridge, Mass., 1953), chapter on the cubiculum; J. White, *Perspective in Ancient Drawing and Painting* (London, 1956), pp. 43–60.

66. Illustrated in H. W. Dickinson, "A Brief History of Draughtsmen's Instruments," *Transactions of the Newcomen Society*, 27 (1949–51), 73–83, on Pl. XVI.1. See also Daremberg and Saglio (above, n. 4), *1*, Figs. 463–66 on p. 381; Rivoira, Fig. 92; M. F. Squarciapino, "Piccolo corpus dei mattoni scolpiti ostiensi," *BC*, 76 (1956–58), 186–88 and Tav. II; F. Kretzschmer, *Bilddokumente römischer Technik* (Düsseldorf, 1958), pp. 11–12 and Bild. 13–17, 30, 35, 45; Boëthius, p. 173; C. Casalone, "Note sulle pitture dell'ipogeo di Trebio Giusto a Roma," *Cahiers archéologiques*, *12* (1962), Fig. 4 and p. 59; and the materials in C. Merckel, *Die Ingenieurtechnik im Alterthum* (Berlin, 1899); A. Neuberger, *Die Technik des Altertums* (4th ed. Leipzig, n.d.); H. Schöne, "Die Dioptra des Heron," *JDAI*, *14* (1899), 91–103; E. N. Stone, "Roman Surveying Instruments," *University of Washington Publications in Language and Literature*, 4 (1928), 215–42.

67. It is probably Early Christian in date; see the *Catalogue du Musée Alaoui*, *Supplément* (Paris, 1910), no. A-264 (p. 20), and Pl. IX. There is a copy in Rome: C. Pietrangeli et al., *Museo della civiltà romana, Catalogo* (Rome, 1958), p. 609, no. 5.

lost. Beside him are a capital, a set square, a plumb bob with its cord, and a stake for fixing setting-out lines in position.

In addition to the marble plan of Rome, several other architects' plans have been preserved on stone.[68] There is also in existence part of a mosaic plan of a building composed of curvilinear rooms (Plate 128).[69] It is a bath, with the pools and basins shown in blue tesserae and the dimensions of the rooms given in mosaic numerals. At first some of the curves appear to be non-segmental, but if allowance is made for the slightly irregular setting of the tesserae it will be seen that they are segments of circles like all the curves of Roman plans. The shape of the rooms marked with the numerals VII and XII, for example, is derived from a four-center oval of the kind used to determine the plans of the amphitheatres, a shape easily constructed with rule and compasses on paper and laid out with stakes and lines on the site. Surely Roman working plans were dimensioned. The passages quoted from Vitruvius imply it, and it seems proper to assume that they appear on the mosaic plan because the mosaicist faithfully copied the intent of the original drawing.

Major measurements in Roman buildings are usually multiples of five Roman feet, and smaller dimensions are quite often free of fractions.[70] For example, the octagon of the Domus Aurea wing was constructed within a circumscribed diameter of fifty feet, the interior of Domitian's basilica is approximately seventy by one hundred feet, and his state triclinium is one hundred feet wide with piers measuring six feet by ten. The main hall of the aula of Trajan's Markets is one hundred and fifteen by thirty feet in plan and forty feet high to the crown line of the vault. Finally, the porch of the Pantheon is sixty-five feet deep and the controlling dimension of the rotunda and dome is one hundred and fifty feet. Because of this habit, sub-dimensioning was simplified. Tiles and bricks were made to standard two, one, and one-half foot lengths. It is pertinent to note that though Vitruvius mentions the golden section he also includes the proportion $1:\sqrt{2}$, which is easier to lay out on the ground. He theorizes in terms of proportional or modular units, but the passages quoted show that these were transposed into numerical dimensions as plans and other drawings were prepared.[71]

68. *FUR*, I, 207–10 and Tav. Q. For one of the few extant Roman architectural "models," a raised plan in marble of a pseudo-peripteral tetrastyle temple, see M. F. Squarciapino, *Museo ostiense* (Rome, 1962), p. 18, no. 189; it could be a votive offering by or for an architect, but more probably it records the erection of a temple or chapel by an Ostian family. See also Crema, Fig. 330.

69. *FUR*, I, 209, and citations.

70. As noted earlier, the Roman foot = 0.295 m. It is recorded for example on the monument to Statilius Aper in the Conservatori Museum; see A. E. Berriman, *Historical Metrology* (London and New York, 1953), pp. 121–23. It appears also on the face of the great Trajanic road-cut at Terra-

cina, where ten-foot vertical intervals are marked and numbered; see G. Lugli, *Anxur-Tarracina* (Rome, 1926; = *Forma italiae*, I, part 1.1), cols. 210–12 and Fig. 29. A number of sources are collected in F. Hultsch, *Griechische und römische Metrologie* (Berlin, 1882), pp. 74–79. Duodecimal systems were also used, as usual for the equal ease of obtaining thirds and quarters; see Vitruvius, 8.6.3 and 8.6.7, for example. The hexagonal Trajanic harbor at Porto is inscribed within a diameter of 2400 Roman feet and its sides are therefore 1200 feet long; see the plan in *Rend-PontAcc, 23–24* (1947–49), 195.

71. The examples set for students by Hero of Alexandria do give measurements; see above, n. 64 and T. H. Martin, *Recherches sur la vie et les*

The architect himself, or surveyors and levelers working under his supervision, laid out his plan upon a cleared site or artificial terrace using instruments.[72] The positions of the major masses could be cross-checked by triangulating with lines. Once these main positions were established, experienced foremen could derive the sub-dimensions from the architect's drawings (the Roman habit of symmetry made the location of many secondary positions self-evident). From the point of view of dimensioning, the remaining work, such as the fitting of architectural sculpture, would have followed automatically. The economy of all this, the orderly interworking of planning, labor, and the supply of materials, will be discussed in the next chapter.

The description Frontinus gives of his staff conveys some idea of what the office of a *praefectus fabrum* was like. Frontinus began a term as director of the municipal water board in Rome in 97 and later wrote a manual of the duties of that officer and his assistants.[73] He records that in addition to the *curator aquarum* or director, some two dozen categories of administrators and practical specialists were gathered in the *statio aquarum* or central office. Engineers, architects, assistant directors, secretaries, clerks, and slaves from the public roll are all specifically named. Measurers, levelers, pipe makers, keepers of reservoirs, inspectors, and specialists in repaving streets disrupted during laying or repairing mains are also mentioned. Even the men who crushed discarded terra cotta for the hydraulic cement used to line conduits and tanks are included. The title or designation of each kind of specialist and artisan is given.[74] This information is important because it shows how well organized and prepared the government was when it undertook major works. When Trajan decided to build the Markets, or Hadrian the Pantheon, the architect had at his disposal a trained hierarchy of assistants under whose supervision construction took place. If Frontinus had such an elaborate staff, the presiding architects of state programs would not have been provided with less. The organization required in building the Forum and Markets of Trajan or in excavating the vast hexagonal port by the mouth of the Tiber made this almost inevitable, a conclusion also indicated by the strong Roman disposition to centralized authority and chains of command. Under Trajan and Hadrian if not under Nero and the Flavians there quite probably was a ministry or office of works presided over by a *praefectus* or *curator*, a man like Apollodoros. This hypothesis fits with the available evidence, but apparently there is no direct confirmation of it in the sources.[75]

What a major Roman architect of the imperial period had at his disposal in addition to his own talent and energy was the assistance of the government. The attitudes of the government were particularly suited to contribute to the success of the kind of designs

ouvrages d'Héron d'Alexandrie (Paris, 1854; = *Mémoires présentés . . . à l'Académie des inscriptions et belles lettres*, 4).

72. See above, n. 66.

73. See T. Ashby, *The Aqueducts of Ancient Rome* (Oxford, 1935), Part I.

74. See for example Frontinus, *Concerning the Aqueducts* 25, 96, 99, 100, 117.

75. Cf. Strabo, 575; and see Germain de Montauzan (above, n. 57), p. 112, n. 3; O. Hirschfeld, *Die kaiserlichen Verwaltungsbeamten von Augustus bis auf Diocletian* (2nd ed. Berlin, 1905), p. 266.

under discussion. The emperors' preferences undoubtedly played a part in this. Once a monumental vaulted design was approved the fairly orderly machinery of the huge official establishment came into play. Money, materials, and labor were forthcoming from an administration habituated to reaching its objectives. Of the things necessary to see a great building through to completion, those the government could most readily and efficiently supply were labor and materials. From the point of view of putting materials into place during actual construction, the great vaulted buildings, constructed of tens of thousands of bricks and untold basketsful of mortar, were chiefly the product of semi-skilled and unskilled labor. In the provinces the ordinary soldier often baked and laid brick, cut stone and wood, and hauled and carried all kinds of materials. Any able-bodied man could if properly supervised mix and carry mortar, lay aggregate, and move materials from point to point. In addition to labor the government often supplied or procured materials, arranged any necessary subcontracting for lime, bricks, and the like, and saw to the crucial matter of properly assembling materials at the site. Of the four major requirements for the erection of a great public vaulted building—architect, master carpenter, labor force, and the proper preparation and assembly of materials—the established government offices controlled or supervised at least two.

In vaulted architecture the architect was able to design more freely, to move more rapidly to new forms, than in traditional, trabeated architecture. He could be quite independent of sculptors and decorators. He was in direct control of the design and construction of the building, unlike the classical Greek architect who had been in a sense himself a master sculptor and who, though he was called chief artisan, was more in the position of a first among equals. In vaulted work the architect assumed an importance unknown in earlier times. The visual and spatial possibilities and structural character of the new architecture first diverted and then converted much first-rate talent in both Rome and the provinces. The new style offered an opportunity for visual expressions previously unknown, and in it the architect gained greater control of the building art by being largely freed from dependence on sculptors and stonecutters. These attractions, from the point of view of the architect, also help to explain the rapid development and acceptance of vaulted architecture. Designing and building with columns, entablatures, and beams did not cease, but from the late first century onward traditional designers were never again the sole masters of monumental architecture.

VII

ECONOMY OF CONSTRUCTION

ARCHITECTURE properly includes the art of building, and to omit it would be to suggest a division of knowledge and responsibility that Roman imperial architects would not have recognized. Labor, materials, and methods of building were efficiently organized in an economy of construction second only to principles of design in the formation of the new architecture. Roman attitudes toward making, assembling, and using materials produced the orderly rhythms of preparation and construction essential to success in large buildings of brick and concrete. The great architects had at their disposal ready trains of supply and assembly that reached from the distant clay pits and quarries to the tops of their towering scaffolds, where brick and aggregate, by reversing the processes of nature, were bound by mortar into rock-like structure.

Besides the primary evidence in the buildings themselves, there are wall paintings, reliefs, inscriptions, and texts that yield some information about building processes and the preparation and manufacture of materials. The modern literature about Roman materials and walls is very large and has all but overwhelmed the study of the architecture itself. There are useful, detailed books and thousands of pertinent passages in the reports and notices of excavations in thirty modern countries. The labor that awaits those who would knit the facts into a reliable and useful fabric of comparisons and deductions is immense, but for Rome and its vicinity the evidence for materials has been published in an orderly way.[1] Roman vaults, methods of building, and economy of construction have not been as fully treated as materials.[2]

---

1. By Lugli, *Tecnica*, and Blake, *1, 2*. For Miss Blake's method, see important reviews in *JSAH*, 7 (1948), 33–36; *AB, 33* (1951), 133–39; *AJA*, 65 (1961), 327–29. I understand that the manuscript of her third volume, dealing with the period from Trajan to Constantine and largely completed before her death, is being prepared for publication. Both she and Lugli are chiefly concerned with walls, giving descriptions, classifications of facings, and criteria for dating; the pioneer work in this last category, still useful, is E. B. Van Deman, "Methods of Determining the Date of Roman Concrete Monuments," *AJA*, 16 (1912), 230–51, 387–432.

2. See above, Chap. 1, n. 42, and Chap. 3, n. 46. J. H. Middleton, *The Remains of Ancient Rome, 1* (London, 1892), Chap. II, and G. Giovannoni, "Building and Engineering," in *The Legacy of Rome*, ed. C. Bailey (Oxford, 1951), form a convenient introduction to these subjects.

The labor force formed the base of this economy. Unskilled workmen were enrolled or impressed in gangs, and craftsmen and semiskilled workers were organized according to their specialties into corporations or guilds (neither term is very satisfactory; what had begun as mutual assistance associations and funeral colleges were increasingly regulated by the government as the *étatisation* of society deepened).[3] Statius, enthusiastically describing Domitian's new road across the Volturno marshes into Naples, gives a glimpse of Roman divisions of labor and orderly method.

> The first work was to prepare furrows and mark out the borders of the road, and to hollow out the ground with deep excavation; then to fill up the excavated trench with other material, and to make foundations ready for the road's arched bridge, lest the soil give way and a treacherous bed provide an unstable base for the heavily loaded stones; then to bind it with blocks, set close on either side, and with frequent wedges. How many gangs are at work together! Some cut down the forest and strip the mountain sides, some shape beams and boulders with iron tools; others [cement] the stones together . . . others work to dry up the pools and [dig canals] to lead the minor streams far away. These men could cut the Athos peninsula . . .[4]

The inscriptions about Roman corporations or guilds have been quite thoroughly canvased. Among the corporations connected with construction the following are known:

> *fabri*—general construction workers
> *fabri aerarii*—bronzeworkers
> *fabri ferrarii*—ironworkers, blacksmiths
> *fabri tignarii* (*tignuarii*)—carpenters
> *figuli*—potters and brickmakers
> *marmorarii*—marbleworkers
> *pavimentarii*—layers of pavements
> *sectores serrarii*—sawyers of stone
> *vectuarii* (*vectores*)—carters (and makers?) of lime

There was even a *collegium subrutorum* or guild of demolition experts.[5] During the period under discussion, labor of all kinds seems to have been plentiful in Rome.[6] The

---

A. Choisy, *L'art de bâtir chez les Romains* (Paris, 1873), should be used with some caution but contains much of value. Standard Italian works, in addition to Lugli, include Giovannoni; G. Cozzo, *Ingegneria romana* (Rome, 1928); and C. Venanzi, *Caratteri costruttivi dei monumenti. I. Strutture murarie a Roma e nel Lazio. Parte prima* (Rome, 1953). See also G. Guerra, *Statica e tecnica costruttiva delle cupole antiche e moderne* (Naples, 1958); J. Le Gall, "Modes de construction et techniques dans l'architecture romaine," *Revue archéologique*, 1 (1959), 181–202 (a

discussion of Lugli's *Tecnica*).

3. Rostovtzeff, 1, 379–92, 462; Meiggs, p. 319; cf. *ESAR*, 5, 246–52. The fundamental work on the guilds is J. P. Waltzing, *Étude historique sur les corporations professionnelles chez les Romains* (4 vols. Louvain, 1895–1900).

4. *Silvae* 4.3.40–58.

5. The list is from Waltzing (above, n. 3), 2, 117; the *collegium subrutorum* appears in *CIL* 6.940. Cf. Meiggs, pp. 311–36, esp. p. 319.

6. *ESAR*, 5, 234–36.

proportion of freemen to slaves is not known; we have no document such as the building contract for the north porch of the Erechtheion in Athens, which records that out of a hundred and seven men at work at least forty-two were metics (registered aliens) and twenty were slaves (all of the latter were masons or carpenters).[7] Whatever their status Roman laborers and craftsmen were bonded firmly in groups to which their individualities were largely submerged, just as the small units of materials they put into position were essential but standardized parts of a coherent structural whole. This shaping of manpower and knowledge into a system both orderly and flexible explains certain characteristics of the new architecture. The imperial architect could command a large and well-organized labor force, and with its help he gave monumentality to his ideas and permanence to his buildings.

MATERIALS

In all vaulted buildings of imperial date, with the exception of some provincial work in cut stone, materials were used in a consistent way. Small individual structural elements were combined with mortar to obtain, after the fabric had dried out and cured, structurally continuous and enduring solids. Piers, walls, and vaults were made of concrete, and brick facing was used on piers and non-foundation walls. Wood and stone were as important in erecting buildings as lime, sand, and brick, and a fair amount of metal was used, though not in structural members. These materials will be considered in an approximately ascending order of their significance.

The extensive use of metal in ancient architecture is sometimes overlooked. In addition to decorative elements such as bronze capitals, rosettes, and cornices, metalworkers and foundrymen made doors, conduits, pipes, and a wide variety of fittings and hardware.[8] Metal roof tiles, of the kind used on the Basilica Ulpia and the Pantheon, were not uncommon. Within the structural fabric of ancient stone buildings massive iron clamps, often secured in lead, were frequently used.[9] The timbers of the roof of the Pantheon porch may have been encased in metal, and there were probably other instances of protecting wooden members with metal sheathing. For hanging ceilings of cement and tile, Vitruvius prescribes the use of large iron bars, hung from iron hooks in the beams above, to carry the suspended weight.[10] In the piers and walls of Roman vaulted buildings a great deal of iron and bronze was used, in the form of cramps and plugs, to insure a permanent bond between marble facing, setting beds of cement, and the brick-faced structure proper (Plate 129, a detail of a Domus Flavia wall). Metal was

---

7. R. H. Randall, Jr., "The Erechtheum Workmen," *AJA*, 57 (1953), 199–210.

8. See for example Durm, pp. 344–52; *Oxford History of Technology*, 2 (1956), 236, 419; F. Kretzschmer, *Bilddokumente römischer Technik* (Düsseldorf, 1958), pp. 53–58; R. Calza and E. Nash, *Ostia* (Florence, 1959), Fig. 80.

9. Vitruvius 2.8.4; cf. 1.5.3. See also Middleton (above, n. 2), *1*, 40; W. B. Dinsmoor, *The Architecture of Ancient Greece* (London, 1950), pp. 104–05, 174; Blake, 2, 90, 92, 93.

10. 5.10.3; cf. Middleton (above, n. 2), 2, 119–20.

also employed to hold terra-cotta elements—such as the vertical flues of radiant-heated rooms—in position while setting beds and facing materials were applied and the mortar dried out. None of these metal fixtures were visible in finished buildings. In spite of the results of natural decomposition and systematic scavenging, their positions can be located by examining exposed piers and walls for embedded stumps and for the holes that mark their original locations.

The brick facing was often studded with large nails and spikes to provide purchase for the thick layers of stucco finishes or the cement beds for marble revetments, whichever was to be applied. These nails, usually of iron though sometimes of bronze, were driven into the mortar joints between the bricks.[11] Flues and down-drain pipes were on occasion positioned and held by heavy iron holdfasts or T-shaped cramps driven deeply into the wall fabric. Long cramps of iron or bronze, their outer ends turned down, were sometimes used to position and fasten sheets of marble to the walls. These cramps were pounded into the structural wall, and sometimes fixed there with lead, before the cement bed for the revetment was applied. They thus passed all the way through the bed, which was often 0.20 m. or more thick. Their turned and flattened ends were fitted into slots cut into the thin edge of the marble sheets.[12] Bronze wedges were often used to fix marble plugs in the walls, another kind of key for the application of stucco or cement (Plate 130a, a detail of a Domus Augustana wall, where the stub of a bronze wedge is visible against the right side of the broken marble plug). Iron nails were used to construct the falsework of wood essential in making vaulted buildings.[13]

Because of the relationship between structure and décor and the indispensability of falsework, metal was important to the economy of construction. Raking joints between bricks would not have keyed the thick cement and stucco beds to the structure permanently, and nailing obviated much arduous labor in making falsework secure and stable. Hydraulic installations required pipes and a variety of valves and fittings. These metal products, mostly small in size and hand made in quantity, suggest that conservation of labor was not an important objective. Rapid and efficient construction required an ample supply of materials prepared in advance. That a variety of humble metal units were first produced in quantity in the workshops and then supplied in a finished state to the site is a good indication of Roman attitudes toward the economy of vaulted design.

11. Vitruvius obviously considers nails commonplace; see for example 7.3.1. The New York *Times* for October 11, 1961, carried a dispatch from Glasgow saying that nearly a million Roman nails, 6 to 16 inches long and weighing 7 tons in all, had been found at the site of the Roman fort built at Inchtuthill in 83. They have been explained as the result of a make-work policy (by L. S. de Camp, *The Ancient Engineers* [New York, 1963], pp. 188–89) but probably were the stock of a construction depot.

12. See for example *FUR*, *1*, Tav. O; cf. Middleton (above, n. 2), *1*, 87, *2*, 121, 124–35.

13. Cf. Blake, *2*, 23–24. Here falsework is used to mean all temporary woodwork, for whatever purpose; shuttering, the wooden walls against which concrete was poured, usually for foundations; formwork, the shaped woodwork upon which vaults were poured; scaffolding, the workmen's platforms; and framing, the supports for formwork and scaffolding.

Wood was the other unseen material. The master carpenters and their assistants are the forgotten men of imperial architecture. Their materials and products, being ephemeral, are easily ignored. But without a mastery of construction in wood, which was sometimes of a very complicated kind, Roman vaulted architecture could not have developed as it did. The entire structural process was dependent upon woodwork. Foundation walls were cast against wood shuttering. Walls could be laid up and vaults poured only with the aid of scaffolding, and the forms for all but the smallest vaults, arches, coffers, and niches had to be built first in wood (impressions left by formwork boards, some of them modern, are visible in Plate 29). Supplying and cutting timber, and assembling wooden frames and forms, was utterly essential.

Posts, beams, and boards were in many cases necessarily cut to standard dimensions. The impressions of the boards used in making shuttering for foundation walls often measure just shy of one Roman foot in width (Plate 21a, left).[14] The boards and their supporting vertical posts would have been reused, a procedure facilitated by standard dimensions. It is reasonably certain that shuttering frames were in some cases moved up as the previous pours of a high foundation wall gained bearing strength.[15] If this is correct, standard dimensioning would have been essential in order to fit the framing to the finished portion of wall below. Making certain kinds of vaults, especially barrel vaults, involved similar requirements. To build a long, vaulted cryptoporticus of the kind seen on the Palatine or at Domitian's villa at Albano it was not necessary to provide fifty or a hundred running meters of formwork and supports. Only one or two relatively short sections were necessary, which after the mortar had gained sufficient strength could be lowered slightly (the decentering process) and moved into the next position. The tabernae of the Markets of Trajan or the many reduplicated storerooms of Porto could have been vaulted with the use of a small number of efficiently designed wooden frames and forms that needed only partial disassembly before being moved to the next location. For similar reasons it is quite probable that scaffolding and framing members were somewhat standardized. This is borne out by the nature of the horizontal beams that were socketed into rising walls and that supported, together with vertical frames, the temporary wooden floorings for the masons and their assistants (Plate 130b). In many cases the socket or putlog holes can be seen, and their regularity of size and pattern, especially in second-century construction, argues for a certain standardization of scaffolding measurements (Plates 49, 52, 54, and 129). Thus planned control over cutting falsework beams and boards can be inferred, and perhaps a certain interchangeability of key members as well. The use of wood was not limited to structural falsework. Ladders and elaborate ramp systems for battalions of hod and mortarmen, tripods and gan-

14. See the useful drawings in Durm, p. 211, where in my experience, however, the measurements given are atypical.

15. This is implied by Middleton (above, n.

2), *1*, 49, and seems to be borne out by such evidence as the great height of the vertical post-grooves on the northeast or Velia side of the Domus Aurea structure of Pl. 21b here.

tries for lifts and cranes, and frames for various kinds of tackle and rigging all had to be constructed.

Timberwork and carpentry for architectural purposes were well understood crafts before the time of Nero. By then large roof trusses were not uncommon and elaborate scaffolding was normal. Shipwrights and military technicians had solved many difficult problems of construction in wood.[16] The references by Seneca and Suetonius to revolving machinery and movable paneling indicate the degree of complexity of fabrications in wood and metal that had been mastered by the middle of the first century. But monumental vaulted construction involved new problems in carpentry for which there was no direct precedent. The repetition of a given type and size of arch or vault within one building, a common occurrence, meant that the necessary carpentry was studied not only with respect to the needed architectural form, but also, because of the advantages of repeated use, as a problem in efficient design. The increasing complexity of vault shapes depended to some extent upon the development of formwork. Spherical domes and semidomes could be approximated in wood, their inner surfaces rendered geometrically more exact with stucco or cement, but shapes such as those of perspective coffers sunken in vaults of double curvature, annular vaults intersected by cylindrical shapes, and gored or pumpkin domes posed different orders of problems, all of which were solved by Roman carpenters. The distinctive forms of mature vaulted architecture were in some measure the creation of these men. No design could be carried out that outstripped their capacities or the limits of their material.

Quarrying, transporting, and cutting stone comprised a major Roman industry.[17] The titles and functions of a number of supervisory officials are known, as well as the designations of many classes of workmen. The list of the latter runs from those who sawed and roughed out the blocks (*caesores, quadratarii*) to polishers (*politores*) and cutters of inscriptions (*characterarii*).[18] Quarry blocks, serially numbered, were sometimes inscribed with the names of the quarry superintendent and the reigning emperor.[19] Stone was commonly moved great distances. That for the columns of the Pantheon portico, which came from a quarry near the Gulf of Suez, is wholly typical in this respect. By the second century the many colored marbles of the Mediterranean provinces were all available in Rome. The stupendous quantity of material quarried and finished both locally and abroad can be inferred from the figures of those who have given themselves the pleasure of computing approximately the volume of marble used in Trajan's Forum and the number of cartloads of travertine and other materials required for the Flavian Amphitheatre—26,000 cubic meters and 292,000 Roman cartloads, respectively.[20]

16. See Vitruvius, Book 10; L. Casson, *The Ancient Mariners* (New York, 1959), passim; cf. above, Chap. 2, nn. 16, 24.

17. The standard work is C. Dubois, *Étude sur l'administration et l'exploitation des carrières . . . dans le monde romain* (Paris, 1908). See also Rostovtzeff, *1*, 340–42, and the discussion and citations in 2, 688–91.

18. Middleton (above, n. 2), *1*, 25–26; *ESAR*, 4, 693–95.

19. Middleton (above, n. 2), *1*, 25 and n. 2.

20. *ESAR*, 5, 67–68, 221–22, with citations.

The use of stone in vaulted buildings is largely self-explanatory. Stone vaulting was almost entirely abandoned in Rome during the imperial period, but it appeared in some quantity in provinces where materials for concrete were unobtainable or of poor quality, or where a tradition of vaulting in stone was firmly established.[21] Vaulted construction with stone voussoirs and concrete combined can be seen in late Republican buildings such as the sanctuary at Palestrina. This mixed work was not at all common in and near Rome during the imperial period, though it is seen in an important exception, the Flavian Amphitheatre.[22] The use of stone for decorative purposes will be discussed in the next chapter. Among structural uses, that of stone for piers was rare, but again the Flavian Amphitheatre is an exception. At first, structurally indispensable stone columns were almost as unusual, but they became more common in Hadrian's time. The monolithic marble shafts that screen the interior niches of the Pantheon are of this type (Plate 105). Large stone consoles, set deeply into piers or walls and cantilivered out into space, were used as imposts or footings for vaults and arches. They were employed to decrease lateral spans (Plate 92) and to help support the shallow vaults of exterior balconies (Plate 84, left center, and Plate 90). Stone impost blocks were used within the structural fabric of the Pantheon (Plates 105 and 106). Finally, small stone brackets, functioning visually rather like the dentils of the orders, were often used to support terracotta cornices (Plate 112). These consoles and brackets were often made of travertine, a handsome local stone tinged with tan and gray that was also used to face a number of public buildings. The consoles and brackets, now often broken off at their wallplanes, contrasted sharply in color and texture with the brick or stucco of the walls.

Stone aggregate is a necessary part of concrete because mortar by itself cannot sufficiently resist the crushing force of great weights. Aggregate gives concrete its necessary structural body by increasing the density of the mass. It also reduces the amount of lime that must be burnt and slaked. The Romans used several kinds of stone for aggregates, ranging in weight from selce, a very heavy lava stone used in foundation walls, to lightweight tufa (a local, granular stone) and pumice, both used in vaults. Other kinds of stone, as well as broken bricks and tiles, were also used. All of these materials were found in and near Rome. Architectural sculptures and other stone members of demolished buildings were sometimes broken up and used as aggregate (the foundation walls of the Domus Aurea structures on the Palatine contain broken refuse from the great fire of 64). In many structures different aggregates were used according to the loads to be carried. Certain vaults of the Flavian Amphitheatre contain pumice, and the five

21. On the contrast between concrete vaulting in Italy and stone or rubble vaulting in Asia Minor, see J. B. Ward Perkins in *The Great Palace of the Byzantine Emperors, Second Report*, ed. D. T. Rice (Edinburgh, 1958), pp. 83–89 and Pls. 27–28. A number of monumental stone vaults of imperial date can still be seen in the eastern provinces in buildings derived from Italian designs, for example in the two major baths at Hierapolis in Phrygia, one of which is discussed and illustrated by P. Verzone, "Le chiese di Hierapolis in Asia Minore," *Cahiers archéologiques*, 8 (1956), 40–45.

22. Blake, 2, 92–93.

kinds of aggregate in the walls and dome of the Pantheon were separated into five horizontal zones, each containing a lighter aggregate than the one below.[23] In foundations the aggregate often occupies two thirds of the total volume of the fabric.

Aggregate was added to the mortar during the actual construction of the wall or vault. Often the stones were spaced at random, having been dumped into the forms and left untouched (Plate 10a), though sometimes they were raked out. In Trajanic and Hadrianic work they were frequently laid by hand in regular rows, spaced evenly in the mortar both horizontally and vertically in order to distribute evenly resistance to load (Plate 78).[24] The stone in such cases is usually a yellowish tufa, roughly shaped into loaf forms about a half-foot in length. Such aggregate takes up about half the volume of the concrete of walls and vaults. It is always completely surrounded by mortar, with the exception of the exposed irregular sides of pieces laid against wooden shuttering or formwork (Plate 78). A good measure of systematic control over making and using aggregates was necessary. Again single, small pieces of material were processed by hand, both when they were broken and roughly shaped and when they were placed in the mortar, and again the required quantities were vast. The method by which the right amount was brought to the proper place in due order was essential to the uninterrupted, secure construction of large vaulted buildings. The attention the Romans were willing to pay to so modest a material indicates how closely the nature of imperial architecture was connected with their habit of undertaking to place all things in orderly relationships.

Many structural and decorative elements of kiln-fired terra cotta were manufactured. From clay beds to finished buildings several processes and kinds of specialists were involved. The clay had to be extracted, aged, and prepared. Sometimes straw was added, and on occasion pozzolana or crushed brick. The various shapes were formed, dried somewhat, fired, stored, aged, and inventoried (at the brickyard a master potter or *figulus* was in charge). When needed the tiles, bricks, flues, pipes, and the like were carted to the site. The industry required wood for the forms and charcoal for the kilns, experts in the design, construction, and use of kilns, and the personnel for making the many items that were in regular use.[25] Immense amounts of terra cottas were prefabricated by hand, mostly on the estates of the emperors and the great landowners. It was a profitable business, and stocks were laid up to age in expectation of future requirements.[26] Toward the end of the period the industry came increasingly under direct government control, partly because many estates became for one reason or another imperial property.[27]

The basic product was the thin, square brick or tile, made in many sizes. Before firing

23. See above, Chap. 5, n. 37.

24. G. De Angelis d'Ossat, "La forma e la costruzione delle cupole nell'architettura romana," *Atti*, 3, 241–42, 245.

25. For the brick industry, see *ESAR*, 5, 207–09; Bloch, pp. 334–40; cf. R. MacMullen, "Three Notes on Imperial Estates," *Classical Quarterly*,

12 (1962), 277–82.

26. H. Bloch, "The Serapeum of Ostia and the Brickstamps of 123 A.D. . . .," *AJA*, 63 (1959), 234, 237.

27. Meiggs, pp. 67–68; cf. Bloch, pp. 324–25, 336.

the standard shapes were two feet on a side (*bipedales*), one and a half feet (*sesqui-pedales*), and so on, and about one-eighth to one-tenth as thick as they were broad (Plates 112, 129, and 131). They were almost universally of excellent quality—very hard, fairly true, and sharply edged—and ranged in color from magenta-brown through a deep reddish-brown to light yellow. Roof tiles, both flat (with flanges) and curved, and small bricks for use, long edge up, in pavements of herringbone pattern, were manufactured. Many hollow shapes, round and rectangular in section, some flanged for joining and some perforated for cross-circulation, were produced for drains and flues. More specialized items such as chimney pots and two-foot voussoir tiles, slightly wedge-shaped, were available (see Plates 60 and 131a for the latter). The *tegula mamata*, a facing tile with small bosses projecting from its inner side, was made to provide narrow air and drainage spaces between structure and finish materials in damp locations. Hexagonal and curved tiles and bricks were made (Plate 61). Finally, decorative terra cottas in a wide variety of earth colors appear in the buildings. These range from simple moldings to elaborate capitals (Plate 88, top right, and Plate 132), and include small pieces of basic geometric shapes made for inlays.[28]

Perhaps for purposes of inventory or taxation, a proportion of bricks and tiles were stamped while in the forms with the name of the yard and its master potter.[29] As time passed these stamps tended to include more and more information, though it was given in very abbreviated form. In the second and early third centuries the names of consuls in office when the brick was made were often added. The text of a late stamp shows the fully developed style (only the upper-case letters appear on the brick):

OP[us] DOL[iare] EX PR[aedis] C. FUL[vi] PLAUT[iani] PR[aefecti]
PR[aetorio] C[larissimi] V[iri] CO[n]S[ulis] II [ex] FIG[linis] TER[entianis]
A L[ucio] AEL[io] PHIDEL[i]

"Brick from the estates of His Excellency C. Fulvis Plautianus, Prefect of the Praetorian Guard, Consul for the second time, from the Terentian Brickyard, made by L. Aelius Phidelis." The date is 203–05, and the inscription is stamped in circular form, about four inches across, around the figure of an eagle, the trade-mark of the *figlinae teren-tianae*.[30]

28. Types and shapes of terra-cotta products: Vitruvius, 2.3.3, 5.10.2, 7.4.2; Durm, pp. 183–90; Meiggs, Pls. XI, XVb (left), XXXIIb; Lugli, *Tecnica*, 1, 541–52; J. Toynbee and J. B. Ward Perkins, *The Shrine of St. Peter and the Vatican Excavations* (London, 1956), Pls. 10, 11; H. J. M. Green, "An Architectural Survey of the Roman Baths at Godmanchester, Part Three . . .," *The Archaeological Newsletter*, 6 (1960), 277, where with respect to the wide distribution of terra-cotta flue tiles carrying a particular stamp it is said that "it almost looks as if the firm had a contract for this type of work." The two-foot square structural tiles weigh about 18–21 kg. (40–46 lbs.).

29. See the illustrations in Bloch, Tav. Agg. A and B between pp. 22–23; and in Lugli, *Tecnica*, 1, 554–55. On the use of brick stamps for dating, see Meiggs, pp. 540–41. Some of the bricks used in the consolidation of the Domus Augustana fabric during the 1930s are stamped A/XII/M/EF (the twelfth year of fascism, M[ussolini?]).

30. The inscription is taken from H. Bloch, "The Roman Brick Industry and Its Relationship to Roman Architecture," *JSAH*, 1 (1941), 8.

The various colors of Roman bricks and decorative terra cottas are important. By using different kinds of clay and by varying the length of firing, colors were deliberately produced for visual purposes. Contrasts of color were common. At Ostia, for example, external pilasters of dark red and capitals and moldings of yellow, all of terra cotta, appear in Trajanic and Hadrianic tombs and buildings. At Isola Sacra, near Ostia, there are many examples of multicolored decorative terra-cotta inserts in external walls. If these details were meant to be stuccoed over, it is difficult to understand why pieces of various colors were produced and then carefully assembled in architectural and decorative patterns. It is apparent that at least some terra-cotta exterior surfaces were meant to be seen.[31]

In and near Rome, and in those parts of the provinces where suitable materials were available, terra cotta manufacture became an industry. Huge quantities were made by co-ordinating the several production processes, a high degree of standardization was achieved, and stocks were laid up in excess and in ignorance of requirements. The standard tile and brick sizes and the fixed shapes and sizes of terra-cotta fittings and parts facilitated planning and helped architects and builders to increase the efficiency of construction. Layout and dimensioning were simplified. The extensive interchangeability of terra-cotta parts, so obvious today, was a radical innovation. They were fully utilized in the economy of building, to the extent that each brick was put to more than one use during construction, as will be seen.

Metal, wood, stone, and terra cotta were all used, temporarily or permanently, in connection with mortar. The word is used here to indicate all materials of mixed composition that were in a semi-fluid state at the time of actual use in construction: the mortar for brickwork, the mix in which aggregates were placed to make concrete, and the various types of aggregate-free cements such as *opus signinum*, a mortar containing both crushed brick and pozzolana that was used to line structures carrying or containing water and to protect the exteriors of vaults.[32] Plasters and stuccoes, being non-structural, belong in another category. They were used chiefly for facings, interior moldings, and decorative reliefs.

In Roman times mortar was already of great antiquity. Greek mortars were famous for their strength and quality. Before developing concrete the Romans had used mortars for many purposes, for example to level courses of stones not cut and finished precisely.[33] By the second century B.C. the properties of mortar were quite fully understood and the development of true concrete construction was well underway. When in the next century kiln-fired brick began to replace unfired brick, and pozzolana came into regular use, mortar became an essential material. The lengthy modern discussions of the various types of Roman wall facings are somewhat misleading, for mortar is the most important struc-

31. See above, Chap. 4, n. 24.   Blake, *1*, Chap. 9.
32. Roman mortars are discussed in detail by   33. Blake, *1*, 145.

tural material in Roman non-trabeated architecture. Facings changed, and the changes give some indication of date, but the facings are not the walls themselves.

Vitruvius says that in making mortar, sea sand should be avoided. Good sands, he adds, crackle when rubbed and do not stain white cloth.[34] Lime, after burning, should be set aside to age.[35] By his day the Romans had mastered the use of pozzolana, which they added to the dry mix in lieu of part of the sand. Pozzolana is a friable volcanic material, found in thick beds of chunks and gravel-sized pieces in Latium and Campania and easily reduced to usable form.[36] It often has a distinct reddish or yellowish hue and has the property of forming hydraulic silicates in combination with lime, quartz sand, and water. The importance of pozzolana can be exaggerated, for some large Roman concrete buildings were built without it, but mortar made with it will set readily underwater, an advantage Roman engineers made good use of. The architects and builders of the high empire must have been convinced that pozzolana improved their concrete, for it was used in all the buildings described above and is rarely absent from high imperial construction in Rome and its environs.

Making mortars and using them in the building processes was in effect a process of dehydration—the burning of lime—and subsequent hydration. Because water could be added to the granular substances at the convenience of the builders, the construction of walls and vaults was much facilitated. The amorphous, dry ingredients could be easily measured and divided into manageable quantities. No highly skilled labor was required. The amounts of mortar needed for use during a given period of time could be readily calculated, and the consecutive steps of preparation and use suited Roman habits of orderly procedure. Mortar gave the architect the basis for structural materials that could be cast in a variety of architectural shapes, and its importance lies in its inherent potential of form. Doubtless there was a long period of trial and experiment. By the early first century the basic problems had been mastered and sound knowledge accumulated empirically. The ruin of part of old Rome in the summer of 64 provided the first city-wide opportunity for the use of mortar, which for nearly three centuries thereafter was the essential substance of vaulted architecture in the capital.

The ultimate synthetic product of Roman experiments with mortars, aggregates, and structural problems was the durable concrete of imperial times. Enough has been said in the preceding paragraphs about aggregate and mortar to convey the nature of its composition and something of its properties.[37] Basically it was a material for casting on a monumental scale. When correctly made and poured it could provide structurally con-

34. 2.4.1. For Roman screening of sand, see N. Davey, *A History of Building Materials* (London, 1961), p. 127.

35. 7.2.2. The flare kiln used for burning limestone today is almost exactly like the kiln described by Cato, *On Agriculture* 38.

36. Vitruvius, 2.6; Strabo, 5.4; A. Maffei, *EncIt* s.v. "Pozzolana"; L. Crema, "La volta nell'architettura romana," *L'Ingegnere*, 16 (1942), 941; Blake, *1*, 42–43.

37. For technical discussions, see G. Vacchelli, *Le costruzione in calcestruzzo ed in cemento armato* (Milan, 1909); Blake, *1*, 314–18 (with citations).

tinuous solids from foundations up to the crowns of vaults. The necessity of repeating bearing surfaces was much reduced. Ideally speaking, seamless and jointless structures were made possible. Architects and builders were largely freed from the necessity of thinking and planning in terms of beams and isolated bearing points, and could concentrate upon less fragmented structural and visual forms. Inevitably this led to an architecture more modeled than assembled, and it helps to explain the proliferation of curves in both plans and sections from the middle of the first century onward.

In the economy of vaulted design, shapeless raw materials were transposed into building solids by inverting natural processes.[38] Sand, lime, and pozzolana were made into rock, and clay was baked almost as hard as stone. But the small scale of the individual bricks, and the timing of bringing together the ingredients of mortar, meant that the new materials were pliant and flexible. They were the chief structural resources the great architects of the period had in mind when designing, the equivalent of stone for the Greek masters and steel and reinforced concrete for architects today.

In the use of materials two essential features stand out. One is organization, the result of applying administrative talent to problems of reliable procurement and methodical sequences of construction. Order and system were brought into complex situations involving the mutual adjustment of many variables and the fairly efficient deployment of thousands of men. The Romans learned much about such things from their predecessors, but the mastery of the economy of vaulted construction was peculiarly their own. From this point of view the method of erecting the Palace of Domitian or the Pantheon was as characteristic of Roman civilization as the law or the army. The second and more significant point concerns the inherent connection between the nature of the materials and the space-geometry of the buildings. Roman builders did not subtract from materials to obtain form, as a stonecutter does when he fashions a squared block or a cornice, but added materials together, binding them freely with mortar and building up steadily around and over a space to give it definition. It was in this sense that bricks and concrete were flexible, occupying and forming with ready adaptability the volumetric boundaries conceived by the architect.

METHODS

The building process was largely derived from the nature of the materials, which, because the fabric had to dry out and cure, were unfinished at the moment of use. In order to obtain secure and stable buildings, construction had to proceed according to rhythms of work determined by the setting time of the mortar. The speed with which a portion of newly made structure reached sufficient bearing strength was the key factor both in planning construction and in actual building. Brick-faced walls and piers were built, without

---

38. Vitruvius is at some pains to explain the properties of lime and pozzolana in 2.5.2 and 2.6; for the place of such subjects in his scheme of architecture, see F. E. Brown, "Vitruvius and the Liberal Art of Architecture," *Bucknell Review,* *11.4* (1963), 105.

shuttering, a horizontal layer at a time, and as soon as a layer could bear enough weight the process was repeated and the building rose another few feet. For both stability and efficiency, timing was all.

In order to obtain better siting or footings the Romans were willing to alter natural contours extensively. Valleys were filled and hills were cut back. By Flavian times it was normal practice to place important buildings on level vaulted terraces or deep concrete mats.[39] Long experience with roads, aqueducts, bridges, ports, and other massive utilitarian works provided a sound knowledge of sinking foundations for stable arcuate and vaulted construction. Foundations tended to be deep and extremely substantial. The Esquiline Wing of the Domus Aurea stands upon a vast, thick sheet of concrete, poured in part at least over pre-existing houses. This increased the elevation of the building on the hillside and gave it a substantial base. Rabirius, to obtain his two desired floor levels (Figure 5, p. 50), filled depressions, cut the Palatine rock back where necessary, and extended his upper platform to the desired limits on lofty vaulted substructures. Again, earlier buildings were filled in or their structure utilized.[40] The vertical staging of Trajan's Markets (Plate 75) is composed of vaulted terraces that rise as much as four stories above the slope of the Quirinal. The Pantheon rotunda and drum stand upon a massive ring of concrete (Plate 105). Because of these precautions, evidence of settlement in these buildings is rare. They were quite well prepared to meet the threat of outside forces such as earthquake, subsidence, or extraordinary wind pressure.

The care taken in monumental building to obtain firm footings and to distribute loads fairly evenly is also evident in the supports for bearing walls. The normal practice was to excavate to a depth of two or more meters—foundation walls five and six meters deep are not unknown—and then pour the concrete wall between wooden shutterings. Many of these walls can be examined today. Some have been exposed to the weather for many years, but the negative forms of the shuttering posts (usually placed on the wall side) and of the boards as well are sometimes so clear that the grain of the rough-sawn wood can still be read.

Foundation walls were rarely faced. Once the concrete had cured sufficiently the shuttering was removed and the brick-faced wall was begun above ground level. It is not likely that shuttering, properly shored, was much used to help support faced walls, although a contrary opinion has been held.[41] The use of shuttering against brick facing would have been difficult. First, the brick wall would have to be built up to a sufficient height to take advantage of vertical timbers long enough to give support to a considerable number of horizontal shutters. Short vertical timbers, supporting only a few boards,

39. G. Lugli, "Nuove forme dall'architettura romana nell'età dei Flavi," *Atti*, 3, 95–102, discusses this among other innovations of Flavian times.

40. Lugli, *Roma*, pp. 493–508; A. Bartoli, "Scavi del Palatino (Domus Augustana)," *NS* (1929), 26. Very recently an immense concrete foundation of imperial date, 11 m. high, has been found about 50 m. west of no. 13 on Pl. 40 here; it is saw-toothed in plan (cf. Vitruvius, 6.8.7).

41. Middleton (above, n. 2), *1*, 57–58; cf. Blake, *1*, 294.

would not have kept the wall true. If high shuttering were put up first, the bricks would have had to be laid from the inside, a very unlikely procedure even for thick walls. Since the brick facing is always very shallow, a mere skin a brick or half-brick deep on the surface of the concrete, it would have become increasingly unstable as it rose without its intended concrete core, and extremely difficult to keep true even if erected from inside up against the shuttering boards. Finally, the risk would be run of having the lower courses of mason's mortar stiffen too much before the concrete was poured in, preventing the two mortars, which were applied separately, from setting together properly.

The only woodwork that seems to have been required for building brick-faced walls was the scaffolding for the masons and the ladder and ramp systems needed for bringing up bricks, mortar, and aggregate. Since the brick facings did not function structurally once the mortar had hardened, and since shuttering was impractical, speed of erection and accuracy of construction were functions of the stiffening and drying rate of mortar. The unrestored portions of the walls of such buildings as the Markets and the Pantheon, being absolutely uniform, give no indication of the levels at which construction may have been temporarily halted for drying, for the assembly of new scaffolding, or for the end of the working day. If the mixing of mortar and its delivery to the masons, and to the mouth of the wall, were timed so that it would start to stiffen shortly after it was put in place, then perhaps both of the brick skins and the concrete core could all go up more or less together. The operation could then continue for some distance before it was necessary to halt and allow the wall to gain enough strength to carry an additional load safely and without risking distortion.

The vertical distance between halts that might be accomplished under these circumstances cannot be calculated because the most important variables are unknown. It is likely that the mortars stiffened rapidly. The rows of putlog holes for the horizontal members of the scaffolding indicate that about twenty to twenty-five rows of bricks were laid from a given level (Plates 49, 52, 54, and 129). The so-called bonding courses, discussed below, may possibly mark the end of a day's work. What is more important is that true and stable walls and piers could be built accurately by this leap-frog method. Concrete was poured between low, thin retaining walls of brick, and as soon as it set sufficiently to bear the load of the next layer, the process was repeated. Nice adjustments in timing and the supply of materials were required if the labor force was to be used with efficiency. The best masons and practical builders alone could not make the system work, for the details as well as the broad outlines of the planning had to be completed in advance. In practice this probably meant that everyone knew their job from long experience. Even so the Roman genius for order and system lay behind all the day-to-day work.

The facing bricks, from Nero's time onward, were usually sawn or broken into triangles before they were used.[42] Laying and jointing, especially in the principal Trajanic and Hadrianic monuments, can only be characterized as nearly perfect (see Plates 78,

42. Blake, 2, 162–63, gives a good summary of this development; cf. Lugli, *Tecnica, 1,* 584.

88, 95, and III, for example). Yet much of this meticulous work was not intended to be seen. Presumably it cannot have been done to protect the concrete, for foundation walls were usually left unfaced and many of them, little damaged by nature, still support their original loads. Also, inside walls as well as peripheral walls were faced. The facing did not provide a sufficiently rough surface for stucco or cement to adhere to satisfactorily, and the hardness of the bricks and the pozzolana mortar made it difficult to attach anything to the wall at all. Yet the bricks were necessary. They formed temporary, low formwork while the wall was going up in stages. At the lower levels this could have been done more easily and economically with shuttering properly shored. But the higher the wall went the more difficult this would have become and, above a certain height, it would have been all but impossible. Walls fifteen and twenty meters high were built, and for these heights no shoring or other form of counterpressure could have been readily provided. Also, the triangular bricks exposed rough and somewhat porous surfaces for marriage with the mortar of the interior concrete core, for by laying the bricks in simple bond a pocketed interior wall of irregular points was produced. In this sense bricks were used simply as another form of aggregate. Since they were evenly dressed on the outside, the task of keeping the wall in alignment was facilitated.

Early Roman experiments with concrete evolved from the use of relatively uncompacted rubble fills placed between ashlar or other types of stone walls. Facing materials grew thinner and progressively less structural, and cores became increasingly able to bear heavier loads. This evolution intersected the discovery of pozzolana mortars and, later, the quantity production of high-quality kiln-fired brick; the builders of the imperial age made the most out of combining tradition and invention. The multiplicity of functions assigned to brick facing, which in some cases included a purely aesthetic and visual role, is typical of the economy of vaulted design. The reciprocities established among materials and their functions both during and after actual construction were ingenious. Orderly procedures are necessary to all successful monumental construction, but the Romans mass-produced building materials and investigated their efficient and appropriate uses to a greater degree than any pre-industrial people. The ancient Latin principle of order, the instinctive habit of trying to put men and things in their proper places of service, lay behind this.

Concrete was similarly regarded. Mortar was readily divisible into any usable quantity, and aggregate was almost as easily gathered into suitable amounts. Because of this the apportionment of work and sequences of construction were simplified. Work did not have to stop or slow down for such things as a split entablature block or the complex procedure of decentering a great stone arch or vault. Crews of handlers and riggers did not repeatedly have to stand idle during delicate operations such as the accurate positioning of heavy column drums. Behind the construction of vaulted buildings lay an ideal of smoothly dovetailed, uninterrupted functions. While one zone or layer of wall was curing another could be built, and the various processes of construction were carried forward in cyclical rhythms.

In essence, Roman wall-making depended upon making and laying brick and upon shoveling and carrying. The men who constructed the Markets or the Pantheon must have found this work nearly endless, but the walls they built are striking examples of Roman order both as products of methodical construction and as visible forms. Some of the actual processes can be traced in the plates. In both Plates 127 and 130b the preparation of small amounts of mortar is shown. In the former, water is being poured from an amphora-like container and mixed with sand and lime piled inside a ring of earth; the baskets for carrying it to the mouth of the wall are nearby. In the latter a workman is mixing mortar beside the scaffolding, while others carry mortar and bricks to the masons who are working on both sides of the wall. Plate 21a, left, shows foundation walls, and Plates 46 and 53 concrete cores. In Plate 129 other aspects of construction are revealed. Putlog holes for scaffolding appear near the top of the photograph, and to the left, part of the setting bed for the marble revetment can be seen (compare Plates 27, 47, and 66, where the shims, or their negatives, used for aligning the marble sheets on the cement beds, are visible). At the bottom is a colored marble base molding with its pavement-level band, restored from broken fragments found on the site. At top center a broken marble plug is visible, and just below the right-hand putlog hole the edge of a two-foot tile, one of a "bonding" course running through the wall, can be seen. Plate 133, which shows the remains of an engaged column in the Hippodromos of Domitian's palace, will suggest how consistently the principles of this economy were applied. The core of the column was built up of concrete structurally continuous with the wall, then roughed out to three-quarters round with mortar and broken pieces of brick. This irregular surface was then smoothed with cement to form a setting bed for the thin sheets of colored marble, fluted and pre-cut in strips, and the ring of base moldings.[43]

At the top of the walls the work of the brickmasons ceased. Construction was continued by the gangs who poured concrete, but the execution of the architect's design became the responsibility of the carpenters. Their formwork and its underpinnings not only had to support the concrete, which weighed from one and a half to two metric tons per cubic meter, but also had to be designed to prevent any unequal loading during construction from causing distortions of shape. The construction of formwork for barrel vaults, in contrast to that for surfaces of double curvature, was relatively simple. For large vaults the radius-curve for the formwork would first have been lofted full scale on the ground; the tradition that the rib-curves for S. Peter's dome were laid out on the pavement of S. Paolo fuori le mura comes to mind. If coffers were called for, their forms had to be positioned firmly and accurately on the cylindrical, spherical, or annular surface of the formwork (Plates 10b, 70, and 110). Removing the falsework of a large vault must have been fairly specialized work. After the formwork proper was taken down its framing and supports were used by the men who finished and decorated the under-

---

43. The pieces of marble veneer were called *crustae*. See Pliny the Elder, *Natural History* 36.48, on the evolution of marble revetment.

surface of the vault. When their work was done the frame of massive timbers and shores was dismantled. The brickmasons' scaffolding on the insides of the walls was turned over to the decorators for finishing off the interior surfaces. This scaffolding may have been an integral part of the supporting structure for the vault formwork; if not, it remained in place while the vault was being made.

Some effort was made to reduce the amount of formwork and simplify its construction. It became increasingly common during the period under discussion to make the vault form of tiles or thin bricks laid flat upon a framework of wood. This was done for surfaces of both single and double curvature; some of the tiles used to form the partispherical vault over the great niche at position 5 in the Pantheon can still be seen in position. Once in a while a roughly built arch of bricks appears embedded in a vault, though this is rare until after Hadrian's time. These arches look like ribs, but they show more mortar than brick and are structurally one with the concrete mass of their vaults. They may possibly have been built in an attempt to reduce the quantity of formwork, but since they usually appear in vaults divided into sections by tiles set on end toward the center of the void below, it is more likely that they were used to compartmentalize the mass temporarily, which made it easier to pour and compact the concrete.[44]

The possible complexity of the carpenters' tasks is illustrated by the Domus Aurea octagon and its dependencies (Plates 29–34). Groin, barrel, ramping, niche, and more or less elliptical vaults were called for in addition to the central canopy with its wide oculus. A complicated though generally symmetrical set of forms was planned for the superstructure. In addition, the builders were asked to form the exterior of the central vault of flat and rather steeply inclined panels, partly in order to increase the light reaching the radially disposed rectangular chambers. Because of this the haunches of the dome could not be loaded with stabilizing masses of masonry as was usually done for large vaults. Almost all of these many surfaces had first to be built of wood, and few if any supports could be removed until the brick oculus ring was closed and the exterior superstructure completed.

The fifty-foot diameter defined by the inner angles of the piers was sufficiently small to allow thick horizontal cross timbers to be used as supports for the last zone of formwork. The loss of the original décor has revealed the holes into which they were socketed (Plate 29), showing that the fabric below them, after gaining bearing strength, served as an aid to construction (beams resting upon side walls were often used to support the formwork for barrel vaults). Since concrete must be put into position in a

44. See the sensible remarks by Ward Perkins (above, n. 21), p. 81; and by Cozzo (above, n. 2), pp. 178–79. They agree that these ribs did not function independently once the concrete had cured. In some cases tiles project from the undersurface of the concrete, perhaps to give purchase to stucco; this can be seen in the Large Baths at Hadrian's Villa (see Lugli, *Tecnica*, 2, Tav. CCIV–CCV). J. Fitchen, in his *Construction of Gothic Cathedrals* (Oxford, 1961), where there is much useful information about Roman construction, implies on p. 66 that flat tile formwork (laid on wood framing) was standard in Roman times, but actually tiles were not used as frequently as wooden formwork.

semi-fluid state and will slump without support, the extrados panels of the octagon, which rise at an angle of approximately 60° from the horizontal, were poured against formwork. Experience with problems of this kind seems to have taught Roman builders that certain juxtapositions of forms did not readily lend themselves to an efficient economy of construction. The structure of the octagon is very ingenious, but the kind of geometric membering it displays does not seem to have been repeated. One of the reasons for this may have been the problem of access to the wood forms. Most if not all of the structure had to be poured from outside the timberwork. This was more or less normal procedure, but at the Domus Aurea the complications of the formwork and its supports would have been barriers to efficient and smooth rhythms of work.

The piers and panels of the central octagonal vault are quite thin. The widths of its supports, in relationship to span and weight, are noticeably smaller than in most later buildings, where bulk of material seems to some extent to replace ingenuity of structural design (on this more below).[45] Experience led to less complex procedures, and the results are evident in the simple, bold forms of many post-Neronian buildings. Rabirius designed and built curvilinear, paneled forms, but his structures, relatively speaking, were continuous and unfragmented in form. Most extant Trajanic vaulted buildings are characterized by a direct, clear geometry. The complexities of shape seen in Hadrianic pumpkin vaults are those of surface, not structure. Their undulations were sculptured, in the sense that they were obtained by pouring concrete against complex forms, and behind and above them considerable masses of stabilizing masonry are always found.

Once the formwork of a vault was in position the actual construction was relatively simple. Mortar and aggregate were raised to the pouring level and put into position.[46] Usually the extrados was given a coat of waterproof pozzolana cement, though terracotta tiles were sometimes laid directly upon the concrete (Plate 81), and the huge Pantheon vault was finished with a thin covering of brick. If an oculus was required a stout wheel-form was built. This was positioned horizontally at the open crown of the vault, and rings of bricks, set vertically, were laid around its circumference (Plates 33a and 105). The last pours of concrete then brought the fabric of the vault up to this brickwork, and construction was complete. After a period of drying and curing the

45. For a discussion of the relationships between span and supports in Roman vaults, see F. Rakob in *Gnomon*, 33 (1961), 243–50.

46. These materials were carried up in baskets (see Pls. 127, 130b here). The wheelbarrow, which was in use in China in the third century, did not appear in the west until many centuries later; J. Needham, *Science and Civilization in China* (Cambridge, 1954), *1*, 118; *Oxford History of Technology*, 2 (1956), 642. For cranes, etc., see Vitruvius, 10.2; Kretzschmer (above, n. 8), pp. 23–26; J. Rougé, " 'Ad ciconias nixas'," *Revue des études anciennes*, 59 (1957), 320–28

(a study of *CIL* 6.1785, concluding that the inscription refers to a guild of crane operators; I owe this reference to the courtesy of Professor Lionel Casson); A. G. Drachmann, *The Mechanical Technology of Greek and Roman Antiquity* (Copenhagen, 1963), pp. 142–48, 199. For the huge construction crane, operated by a treadmill, that appears on a relief from the tomb of the Haterii, see A. F. Burstall, *A History of Mechanical Engineering* (London, 1963), p. 88; cf. F. Castagnoli, "Gli edifici rappresentati in un rilievo del sepolcro degli Haterii," *BC*, 69 (1941), 59–69.

formwork could be dismantled and the structure given over to the decorators and marbleworkers.

STRUCTURAL FEATURES

Roman engineering was empirical, based upon deductions made from observation and experience. Not all of these deductions can be reached today by studying the buildings, and important data for the analysis of vaulted-style structure and statics are missing. The drying times and curing rates of the mortars, crucial factors in obtaining stability and in the economy of construction as well, are unknown. The true physical composition and precise structural nature of the concrete itself is uncertain.[47] Yet the basic structural principle is clear: stability depended not upon pressure or friction, as in unmortared arches or vaults of cut stone, but upon something very different, the cohesion and homogeneity of the cured concrete mass.[48]

This principle and its application explain many features of vaulted-style construction.[49] The concrete cores, invisible once the buildings were finished, were in theory continuous bearing solids. Vaults were cast by pouring down upon wooden forms in order to fill up the volumes and obtain the surfaces the forms described, and this was done without any thought of voussoirs or other discrete internal divisions of structure. These vaults were physically continuous with their piers and walls, for there were no intervening bearing surfaces. But in practice the problems raised by giving shape and support to the initially formless concrete led to methods of construction that made the finished fabric structurally less simple than theory indicated. In addition, the procedures followed by the builders often caused the ideal continuity of the fabric, inherent in the basic principle, to be interrupted. By using brick to give shape to the concrete walls and piers until they hardened to bearing strength, certain secondary structural problems were introduced. At the beginning these bricks functioned as shuttering, but as the mortar

47. For the technical literature, see above, nn. 36, 37, and Chap. 3, nn. 45, 46. On the drying rate of mortars see Vitruvius, 2.4.2; Frontinus, *Aqueducts* 123; Ward Perkins (above, n. 21), p. 79; cf. *AJA*, 65 (1961), 328; Blake, *1*, 316, 352; Fitchen (above, n. 44), pp. 262–65. I have never seen anything resembling an expansion joint, even in the largest structures. There is no evidence as to whether the concrete was ever compacted after being tipped into the brick or wood forms, but cf. Vitruvius, 7.1.3. The question of the monolithic character of Roman imperial concrete is much debated. In general it appears that small thick vaults can properly be spoken of as monoliths, but large and relatively thin vaults probably cannot; see Ward Perkins, p. 80; cf. Fitchen, pp. 64–65 and citations.

48. In the strictest terms these buildings are not entirely in compression, for there is a certain amount of beam and tie action within them.

49. Among them the "hanging" quality of certain vaults which have partly fallen, for example in the Large Baths of Hadrian's Villa (S. Aurigemma, *Villa Adriana* [Rome, 1961], pp. 90–95), and the large flat slabs of concrete flooring that just may have been used to span small distances but which are more probably the layered pieces of floors of upper stories which have separated from the vault concrete. These slabs can be seen for example at Hadrian's Villa in the three-apsed hall by the Poikele, and in the lower level of the Domus Augustana; cf. Vitruvius, 7.1.3. See also Middleton (above, n. 2), *1*, 64, 70–72, *2*, 121, 245.

cured they became an inseparable part of the structure, preserving the concrete core within a thin, weatherproof crust to which new outer finishes could be applied when needed. It is this duality of function that accounts for several distinctive features of Roman brickwork.

First, the bricks in the horizontal courses and arch-forms of walls are only skin deep (except for the so-called bonding courses and the rare cases when the arches, as in the Pantheon rotunda, are actually the visible ends of brick vaults). This is clear for example in Plate 26, where most of the bricks of the shallow arch over the alcove have fallen or have been robbed out and the structural concrete is visible in a plane just behind the surface of the original brick facing (seen at the left). In Plate 131a the exceptionally strong bond between the surface brick and the concrete core is apparent. When the wall was cracked in an earthquake or by subsidence the brick arch was broken with it. The crack did not travel around the periphery of the arch, as it might well have done if the arch were actually part of a vault passing back through the wall. This leads to the second point: the many arches embedded in brick walls are structurally one with the finished fabric (see also Plates 15 and 38). They are usually called relieving arches, but they could only have performed as such while the wall was going up and for a certain period thereafter. These arches were an aid to construction, just as the horizontal brickwork was, and like the brickwork they became in time an integral part of the bearing fabric. Their function seems to have been to help insure stability in the plane of the wall during drying and curing.[50] Thirdly, building around openings, and distributing loads toward the sides of openings during construction, led to the introduction of various types of flat and segmental brick arches. Plates 26, 34, and 59 show flat arches over openings (that in Plate 59 is curved in plan, a fairly common occurrence). These arches are also only skin deep, for the concrete of the wall or vault above reaches right down to the upper limit of the opening.[51] On Plates 111, 112a, and 113 examples of segmental and semicircular arches over openings can be seen. Almost all of these various arches were made of two-foot tiles broken in half and set voussoir-like, in groups of three to six, between full-sized tiles reaching back into the body of the concrete core.

The "bonding" courses of two-foot tiles reaching through the walls are more puzzling. They appear in much, but not all, high imperial concrete construction (see for example Plates 53 and 129). The vertical spread between them normally varies from fifteen to twenty-five courses, though at the Pantheon they appear regularly every twenty-eight courses or 1.20 meters apart. It has often been said that they reinforced or helped to

---

50. For the function of brick facing as formwork, see I. A. Richmond in *PBSR*, 10 (1927), 14, followed by J. B. Ward Perkins in *AJA*, 65 (1961), 328. For the so-called relieving arches, see Ward Perkins (above, n. 21), p. 81; id., "Roman Concrete and Roman Palaces," *The Listener*, 56 (1956), 702; cf. Rivoira, Fig. 79b on p. 73, and Meiggs, p. 544. The hold of the economy of construction was so strong that in provincial vaulted work, stones were sometimes cut to shapes resembling bipedales and used as voussoirs in such arches, as in the baths of Mactaris (Maktar) in Tunisia.

51. For illustrations, see Rivoira, Fig. 79b on p. 73; Venanzi (above, n. 2), Fig. 1 on p. 29.

solidify the fabric, and sometimes they are referred to as leveling or settling courses.[52] Because they interrupted the structural continuity of the concrete and formed surfaces upon which the bearing mass might pivot if the building moved, it does not seem correct to call them bonding courses, although Roman builders may have thought they were. Plate 131b, a detail of a pier in the Piccolo Mercato at Ostia (built ca. 120) helps make this clear: an earthquake moved the superstructure, and the upper part of the pier twisted upon the flat concrete surface made by the tiles. These through courses could have been used somehow for leveling and compacting a day's pour, or they may simply mark the end of an assigned portion of work. There is evidence that they were sometimes employed during construction to distribute the load from the horizontal scaffolding beams more widely upon the uncured wall, for in a number of buildings the tiles are used to form the lower surface of the putlog holes (see Plate 129, and compare Plate 38, left middle ground, where much of the facing is modern).

Thus, although concrete did most of the work, bricks were essential both to construction and structure proper, and in thin walls the facings are probably as important structurally as the concrete. In monumental buildings the facings were falsework, weatherproofing, and structure all in one, and their various infixed devices were developed to solve the problems inherent in constructing permanent formwork, inseparably bonded to the main structure, at great scale. In much more or less routine work the structural problems were far less difficult. The economy of vaulted construction encouraged the serial reduplication of barrel-vaulted spaces, side by side or stacked vertically, with uniform dimensions. In vertical stacks the concrete fill necessary to obtain the horizontal floor of an upper level automatically loaded the haunches of the vault below (Plate 93, right), a simple and easily realized structural concept that was used very frequently in insulae and various kinds of commercial buildings. But when the spans of the vaults reached considerable size the structural problems were much magnified. The economy of construction remained the same, however, for what had begun so long before in buildings like the Porticus Aemilia had developed into a sure instrument of building applicable to tabernae and palaces alike.

All structures require maintenance, but Roman vaulted buildings because of their impervious solidity must have been fairly easy to keep up. Many were restuccoed and repainted every few years just as so many Roman buildings are even today. There is some

52. Many writers say or imply that they strengthened the structure, for example Blake, *1*, 292, 303, 2, 102–41, following Van Deman (above, n. 1), pp. 413, 417, 421; and M. Petrignani, "La Domus Flavia," *BollCentro*, 16 (1960), 62. Middleton (above, n. 2), *1*, 58, observes that they were useless in this respect; G. Carettoni, "Costruzioni sotto l'angolo sud-orientale della Domus Flavia," *NS, 3* (1949), 61, that they were probably used to prevent undue settlement as the fabric cured; and Venanzi (above, n. 2), 27, that they weakened walls rather than strengthened them. Vitruvius, 2.4.2, implies that in his day concrete walls were normally built up without interruption. Cf. the discussion in Lugli, *Tecnica*, *1*, 570–72, and his illustrations in 2, Tav. CLXV.-1–4. For the use of "bonding" courses at Ostia, see Meiggs, p. 544. Again a similar feature in stone appears in the provinces, for example in the Baths of Antoninus Pius at Carthage.

evidence that public structures were looked after in ancient times in an orderly way. The jurist Ulpian (ca. 160–228) is quoted in Justinian's Code to the effect that the maintenance of official buildings is to be supported by tax money. Another passage from the same source says that

> [the provincial governor] ought to go round the temples and public works to examine whether they are in proper repair, or require in any way to be restored, and, if there are any which are only in course of construction, he ought to see that they are completed so far as the resources of the municipality admit. He ought also to appoint in the regular form superintendents of the works [curatores operum], and, if necessary, provide military attendants to support them.[53]

There is a somewhat similar passage in the Theodosian Code where governors are urged to render prompt reports on such matters.[54] This, together with Ulpian's reference to "the regular form," suggests that maintenance was very much a continuing concern of the government.[55]

RELATIONSHIPS BETWEEN STRUCTURE AND DESIGN

In many respects design and structure cannot be separated. The way Roman vaulted buildings were erected resulted in specific technical features and in stylistic characteristics as well.[56] The question of whether in this respect design or structure came first is an artificial one because to a great degree they were the same. As far as construction was concerned, it was the necessity of putting nearly the entire structure into compression that most influenced design, but this in turn came about partly because of the wish or need for large unobstructed spaces roofed by vaults.

Compared to the body of modern theory, Roman knowledge of statics was rudimentary, yet with respect to the economy of construction it was entirely adequate. Though Roman architects and builders achieved permanence and stability more through weight than by refined calculation, their amounts of masonry do not seem so excessive as some modern writers have thought.[57] It is not only that they made use of lightweight materials such as pumice, for superfluous structure was eliminated by a variety of other means.

53. *Digest* 1.16.7.1, quoted by R. MacMullen, "Roman Imperial Building in the Provinces," *Harvard Studies in Classical Philology*, 64 (1959), 209.

54. 15.1.2.

55. There is a good deal of epigraphical evidence; see *ESAR*, 5, 95–101, for example; cf. A. J. B. Wace, "The Greeks and Romans as Archaeologists," *Bulletin de la société d'archéologie d'Alexandrie*, 38 (1949), 32–35.

56. For discussions of these relationships, see the works cited above, Chap. 1, n. 42.

57. Fitchen (above, n. 44), p. 66, says that the Romans were interested in massiveness, not lightness of construction; cf. K. Lehmann, "Piranesi as Interpreter of Roman Architecture," *Piranesi* (Northampton, Mass., 1961), pp. 89–90, who says that "the bold Roman experimental structural technique achieved what it did through exaggerated caution, among other things, in building huge substructions," and speaks of the "overwhelming size and bulk of Roman buildings." The Romans' greatest lack with respect to construction was knowledge of applied mathematics.

The economy of structure in the Domus Aurea octagon and the aula Traiana super-structure appears also in the Pantheon, where the vast bulk intimated by the rotunda exterior is in fact reduced by half by the key chambers and niches, and the work of supporting the great dome is chiefly accomplished by the eight piers. The upper part of the Pantheon dome is quite thin, and anticipates to a certain extent the modern practice of obtaining stiffness and stability in thin vaults by giving them surfaces of double curvature (Plate 105). The groin vault was popular because it required supports of minimum silhouette, which meant that ample light could be admitted up under the roof where it is most needed in a vaulted interior. Conversely, the cloister vault was soon abandoned because it required too much structure (Figure 1, h, p. 17).

There are other reasons for the rather bulky outlines of large Roman vaulted buildings. Some of the masonry masses were required to get the building up as well as to insure its stability after the fabric had dried and cured. Because the Romans were unable or for some reason unwilling to construct anti-tension devices, such as tie rods for their barrel vaults or continuous metal rings around the haunches of their free-standing domes, it was essential to attempt to convert all tension forces into compression. This was usually done by placing stabilizing masses high above the pavement, over walls or piers and the lower zones of vaults (see Plates 80 and 105, for example). All these masses can properly be called buttresses, for a buttress, however designed, is a device to counteract tension. Until the vault was closed and the structure had aged somewhat these buttresses helped keep the structure in equilibrium. There is little doubt that once the concrete had become strong enough to support the structure some of this concrete could safely be cut away. Naturally this was never done by the Romans, though one section of the buttress of the Markets semidome in Plate 80 was almost entirely cut away at some time unknown without any apparent effect upon the stability of the structure. Thus the apparently excessive bulkiness of the buildings, largely confined to their superstructures, was to some extent inherent in the nature of the materials and the economy of construction. The fact that this method of building also lessened the spans of vaults, by effectively raising the walls or piers higher than the visual impost levels, has already been discussed.[58] This makes the vaults look wider than they really are.

In broader terms this economy of construction and its attendant structural system affected design for both good and ill. So much was predetermined that the architects, while gaining many practical advantages, lost some freedom of design. Only the more gifted men were able to bend the system to their will and obtain from it highly original buildings. Few new methods or materials were introduced after Domitian's time, and irrespective of design the erection and structure of the great majority of vaulted concrete buildings of the next two centuries can be explained in the same way. Thus certain directions were closed to imperial architecture. By reducing the processes of construction to an orderly uniformity never again achieved in monumental architecture, the Romans

58. See pp. 57 and 109, and above, Chap. 3, n. 45, Chap. 5, n. 36.

limited the possibilities of design. They restricted themselves almost completely to shapes that could be made in wood, which meant in effect that they used only flat planes and surfaces generated by circles. Exceptions to this appeared but they were negligible in quantity and influence. One reason the dome was so popular was that it was the most expressive and at the same time the most complex form that their economy and structural method could produce on a large scale.

On the other hand the system had many advantages. Once it was perfected, stability was to a great extent a foregone conclusion. In a sense a structure grew out of itself because of the relationships among facings, cores, and compression devices (paradoxically, the bulkiness of vaulted designs was the result of a rather clever and economical way of building). The system helped in answering quite readily and efficiently the need for great quantities of construction. The way buildings were put up assisted in making the act of architecture a social one, no inconsiderable achievement and until then unknown in the ancient world. The Romans were able to build functional, permanent structures of many types by means of one architectural technology. Partly because of this, great buildings for public use became commonplace, and architecture of some consequence was brought into daily life and to ordinary towns far more than in the past. In this the economy of construction was an essential force. Its simplicity and method, synchronized to the needs and purposes of an age of cities, facilitated planning and realizing public building programs. Because of these things, and because of what the buildings inspired in later generations, the economy of imperial construction is a significant part of the history of architecture.

Behind it lay the attitudes and talents of the new architects. The predetermined order and timing of events meant that they had to direct large groups of men and insure that they did their work without appreciable error. Each of these workmen, like each brick in the walls they made, performed as a soldier under orders. The economy of the new architecture derived maximum efficiency and utility from each element in relation to its neighbors, an expression of an inherent Latin trait. The unknown military tribune, who at the battle of Cynoscephalae in 197 B.C. "judged on the spur of the moment what ought to be done" and detached twenty maniples with which he broke the phalanx of Philip V, expressed the same trait.[59] He had the training to give him judgment, and the materials of his contribution to Flamininus' victory were prepared to respond in an orderly way to his decision. Under difficult conditions he was able to move two thousand infantry quickly, efficiently, and successfully. So it was also with imperial architects, their materials and men.

59. Polybius, 18.26.1–5.

VIII

THE NEW ARCHITECTURE

WHAT THE PALACES, the Markets, and the Pantheon show above all else is the maturity of the concept of monumental interior space. The strength and dynamism of imperial civilization were so great that the need for a suitable architecture could not be denied. The Romans, always building, quite naturally sought for forms that would express this ecumenical experience. Vaults were not in any way new when Severus, Rabirius, and their contemporaries gave architecture a fresh beginning with their great buildings. Yet they fashioned the new style with vaulted spaces, and in the last analysis it is the meaning and effects of these spaces that more than anything else give the style its identification and individuality. In Timgad as in Tralles, at Baia as at Bosra, the Roman stewardship of all antiquity and the imperial hope for one inclusive society—coerced or free—were proclaimed by an architecture of splendid interior spaces.

Rome itself was the nexus where many strains of design and technology were gathered together. There, seen in the light of imperial social and political aims, these strains were adapted and reworked as the new style evolved. The forms and effects of this architecture served the capital and the provinces alike until during the fourth and fifth centuries they were gradually translated into the artistic languages of the early middle ages. In this way Roman concepts of interior space lived on in both East and West. The palaces, Markets, and Pantheon alone cannot carry the whole burden of this complicated story, but they record accurately its first and in many ways most creative chapter and vividly mark the stylistic and emotional distance between the new architecture and that of the past. The inherent value of these buildings as examples is magnified by the long life, after the dissolution of imperial authority in the West, of their architectural principles and the associations evoked by their forms.

CHARACTERISTICS OF DESIGN

The transcendent characteristic of the new architecture was its space-shaping, space-bordering quality. Whatever the décor, however integrated the trabeation, this quality predominated. Its omnipresent, generative force was the circular curve, occasionally modulated to polygonal shape, upon which progressive architects based their volumetric and spatial creations and with which they resolved and fixed their axes and vistas. The curve gave them the radial focus that more than anything else established the viewer's relationship to their designs. Not only the major vaulted spaces, but their entrances, openings, niches, and décor were evolved from a preoccupation—almost an obsession—with the embracing and focusing qualities of circular lines and surfaces. The indispensable curve gave Roman vaulted architecture its overwhelming sense of place, and its use in three dimensions as the boundary of architectural space is the quintessential feature of the style. Although the formal structure of the style was geometric, a number of shapes were used together in every building. Even the Pantheon, the most unitary of Roman monumental designs, is composed of triangles, a prismatic block, a cylinder, a hemisphere, and apsidal recesses. The imperial architect, unlike a designer such as Ledoux, was not attracted by basic, unadorned geometric shapes standing alone as buildings. Shapes in combination interested him, shapes arranged significantly and harmonically as to scale and meaning, and articulated by an elaborate but consistent system of decoration and well thought-out lighting.

Although in this way Roman design "became absolutely emancipated from precedent, and was pursued as research into the possibilities of form and combination,"[1] the ancient principle of symmetry was not abandoned. Few vaulted-style buildings erected before Hadrian's death in 138 depart to any considerable extent from a basic, underlying frame of mirror or bilateral symmetry. The geometric interior volumes were themselves symmetrical, and were combined symmetrically in plan. Eccentricity of plan and therefore of elevation was extremely rare. Dominant axes and balanced silhouettes, and the almost complete lack of any noncircular curves, explain as much as the solidity of their construction the impression of strength and permanence these buildings give. The stability implied by simple geometric forms was exploited to the full, both through the persistent revelation of their inherent symmetry and by combining them, as for example when a semidomed apse was placed at the end of a barrel-vaulted room. This hyper-symmetry, this unwillingness ever to admit any ambiguity of axis, was so positive a force that even the external axes leading to the entrances of monumental buildings were defined by courtyards or other axially parallel features. By such means even open spaces could be given a certain feeling of interiorness. Unlike the projected axes of Greek monumental architecture, which frequently passed unhindered out across the natural landscape, the center lines of Roman buildings tended to be stopped and fixed by architectural solids nearby—an apse, a nymphaeum, even a gate would do (in a space of

1. W. R. Lethaby, *Architecture, an Introduction to the History and Theory of the Art of Building* (3rd ed. Oxford, 1955), p. 94. Cf. G. Lugli, "Nuove forme dall'architettura romana nell'età dei Flavi," *Atti, 3,* 101–02, who speaks of the work of late first-century architects as "un movimento spontaneo in rapporto con la transformazione politica e civile della vita sociale che eleva di un balzo l'architettura romana al primo piano delle arti, le addita nuova vie da seguire, le propone nuovi temi che formeranno poi la preoccupazione di lunghe generazione di artisti"; and L. Crema, *Significato della architettura romana . . .* (Rome, 1959; = *BollCentro, 15*), pp. 14–22.

centralized plan, another major axis was self-contained within the building itself). Embracing, curved shapes were used to catch and cup the central lines of architectural force as the basin of a fountain catches its jet of water. Against a vertical half-cylinder capped by a shell-form or semidome the movement of an axis was both marked and resolved. The parallel side walls or other bordering features of a central axis, whether of a single space or a large composition of many elements, were almost always exactly alike. As in the atrium house the path along a controlling axis might be interrupted, but this rarely diluted its visual and directive power. The deviations introduced were only temporary, for no real choice of routes was offered and the compelling symmetry of the design was unaffected (see Figure 3, p. 22, for example).

Centered at the end of the axis was the visual or physical goal, a concave feature or enclosed volume (Plates 25–27, 74, and 95). The tablinum or family office of the ancient house, the cella of the temple, the niche of a garden fountain, and the rotunda of the Pantheon were all alike in this respect. This relationship between axis and terminal hollow was sometimes contained wholly within a building, as in Domitian's state halls upon the Palatine where apsidal recesses focused all attention (Figure 6, p. 58, and Plates 44 and 49). Curving apses and niches were subordinate features only in scale, for they were essential elements of design, not only fixing axes but expanding the larger volumes and lessening the physical substantiality of structure (Plates 56, 59, 60, and 107).[2] From the standpoint of their effects upon the viewer these curving recesses were rather like vaults set up on end, moving the flowing boundary of the room away from him and shaping the space about him with similar surfaces. They were often missing in purely functional designs, where, however, vaulted spaces and the axis of the underlying frame of symmetry were always present.[3]

Axis, symmetry, and vaulted terminal volumes became in a sense the formula for design. Partly for the technological reasons discussed above, there was a good deal of sameness to imperial vaulted architecture, though this was not without its advantages. Originality came in the way the formula was handled. Once the practicality of the style for utilitarian purposes was fully apparent, few innovations were made in that direction. But palaces, villas, baths, and other urban building types offered a greater opportunity for imaginative solutions, and one is tempted to divide the style, at least in Hadrian's time, into two categories of design. The first and more conservative was characterized by the serial reduplication of simple, uniform vaulted units to make solidly built terraces, insulae, and a number of commercial building types.[4] The second was marked by

2. On the evolution and function of Roman apses and niches, see the very useful work of Tamm, pp. 147–79.

3. In general, the more monumental the building the more insistent the symmetry around the controlling axis of the plan. The study of asymmetrical planning in vaulted imperial buildings can best be developed from post-Hadrianic evidence.

4. Rooms in concrete-walled insulae were by no means all vaulted; many were covered by the floor of beams and planks (*contignatio*) of the space above. A restored contignatio can be seen in R. Calza and E. Nash, *Ostia* (Florence, 1959), Fig. 29.

a variety of shapes within one building, by the diverse heights of individual vaulted volumes, and frequently by the carefully designed combination and interplay of exterior and interior spaces—in short, by more complex and ingenious design.

The first category was essentially architectural engineering raised to the level of architecture through simplicity of form (Plate 90). The second arose in part from the realization that each vaulted element could be a more or less independent structural entity and could therefore be given its own character. During Rabirius' time it became increasingly apparent that the various internal spaces of a building need not conform to a common roof line. By using arched openings in a variety of ways, by building groin vaults, and by capitalizing on the cohesiveness of concrete, horizontally continuous supporting walls could be eliminated. These developments in turn opened up entirely new possibilities for composition and lighting. The solid sides and tops of vaulted structures could be partly eliminated. Spatially interpenetrated design, brilliantly begun by Severus in his octagonal atrium for the Domus Aurea, was enthusiastically pursued and was one of the main features of post-Hadrianic architecture. Vaults as well as arches could be carried on columns (Plates 35 and 36), and it was in the second century that the orders were fully absorbed in a creative synthesis of old and new.

The architects' freedom in using and manipulating light was radically expanded. From the Porticus Aemilia onward the relationship of light to the character and effects of vaulted spaces was investigated with growing competence. The direction and amount of daylight admitted to interiors, once the style had matured, was little hampered by structural requirements. Dependence upon vertical openings of rectangular outline disappeared along with dependence upon a structural system composed of many bearing elements arranged in rectilinear patterns. Slanting and horizontal openings were possible. Walls were not needed under the turning ends of barrel vaults, and the openings at the ends of large interior spaces could be greatly increased. The introduction of huge groin vaults compounded this advantage (Plate 73, central hall, and Plate 93). The economy of construction led to an increased use of piers (Plates 47, 85, and 94). The most spectacular effects were created by oculi, which as windows were ambiguous features exactly suited to the illusionistic nature of vaulted design. An oculus centered in the crown of a dome caused the vaulted space to appear both roofed and open, and by showing only the sky strengthened the sense of interior containment and place produced by the peripheral walls or piers and the spreading vault itself (Plates 29 and 125).

Light sources were usually placed well above eye level (Plates 78 and 92). This was done principally to light the vaults adequately and insure their visual effectiveness, and to eliminate views that would detract from the illusion of independent, autochthonous places. Oculi are extreme cases of this principle. Sometimes openings were elevated because of neighboring or surrounding structure, but the principle of design remained the same (Plates 28, 33, 36, and 135). Eye-level windows usually gave onto more architecture—a fountain, a peristyle, or some other man-made feature axially related to the vaulted interior (Plate 40, numbers 12–14, and Plate 58, numbers 11–13). Few openings were windows in the conventional sense. They were primarily elements of design, far more important as sources of form, in the sense that they illuminated interior surfaces, than as openings to the outer world. Their positions were carefully plotted with respect to the spaces they were to light, and with them imperial designers gained some of their most original and striking effects. The Domus Aurea octagon and the Pantheon are probably the best-known examples, but there were many others, hardly less spectacular, as several of the plates will suggest (see Plates 35, 38, 78, 85, and 135).

Thus these buildings had in common a fairly simple geometry of form raised in three dimensions from symmetrical plans (to a certain extent the design of Trajan's Markets departed from this east of the Via Biberatica, but each of the six major divisions themselves conformed to the basic principle insofar as the contours of the site permitted). Also, in every mature vaulted design, direction and place were very powerfully expressed. The simplest structures accomplished this through the effects of a single barrel vault, the more complex by assemblies of shapes and spaces leading to a large vaulted interior. An environment of controlling forms pre-empted attention and rigorously limited freedom of movement, characteristics inherited from the past. For centuries the open sacred precinct, with its altar and its looming cult building beyond, had given form and direction to the most fundamental rituals of Roman life. The early imperial fora, with their elevated marble temples dominating elongated enclosures, expressed the same principles in more sophisticated fashion. In the vaulted style the evolution of this traditional directionalism and focus was brought to its logical conclusion. One was now either guided toward a focal concavity or brought into an axially terminal space, a large and well-lighted architectural volume from which the natural world was excluded, where enveloping and radially focused surfaces suggested permanence, stability, and security.

DECOR AND ARCHITECTURAL FORM

The artistic evaluation of vaulted-style decoration, like the study of its presumed Hellenistic origins, has yet to be made. Because of the nature of the decorative materials and the literal delapidation of the buildings, the amount of evidence is quite meager. Mosaic pavements are very common, and a fair amount of painting remains, but apparently no monumental vaulted interior exists in its original condition. All that can usually be found are bits and pieces of marble, mosaic, and stucco, sometimes in their original positions but more frequently broken up and scattered about. Even the Pantheon, unique in its state of preservation, has suffered significant losses such as the decoration of the attic zone and dome. The difficulties caused by this fragmentary nature of the evidence are increased by an understandable tendency to think of Roman décor in terms of Campanian houses and villas, where the walls of box-like rooms were covered with paintings. This explains in part why the paintings of the service rooms and corridors of the Domus Aurea wing have been thought typical of Neronian monumental décor. As paintings they are typical enough, but painting was not always used in the emperor's rooms, where precedence was normally given to marbles, stucco work, mosaic, and the gilding that gave the palace its name. Together with painting, sculpture, and water, these were the techniques and materials of high imperial decoration.

As far as vaulted design is concerned, the axiom that Roman decoration was unrelated to architectural form needs revision.[5] It is true that the classical vocabulary of the orders was not successfully adapted to the new architecture immediately, and there are cases of artificial and rather unsightly combinations of trabeation with vaulted interiors. But gradually traditional elements were brought into harmony with the principles and imagery of imperial design, and by Hadrian's time the orders, freed from the linear rigidity of the past, were fused with a decorative system that had been evolved specifically for vaulted architecture.

This system was determined by the characteristics of architectural design. Based upon the reduplication of the primary building shapes, décor served the same objectives. It consisted of linings or sheaths of essentially nonstructural materials cemented directly to the structural fabric. Like the materials of construction these colored marbles, stuccoes, mosaics, and paintings were either in a plastic condition at the time of application or of small size in contrast to the expanses of surface they were to cover. Any rough construction was disguised. The space-borders of the interiors were not significantly altered, though the shadows cast by the low projections of marble base moldings and stucco cornices and reliefs sharpened the definition and strengthened the bold lines of the geometry of design. The mass and weight of the structural solids were depreciated and the impression of a seamless envelope of space was increased. Finally, the play of light upon the highly polished marble, the fractured and somewhat irregular surface of mosaic, and the vividly colored paintings and accents of gilding brought to life the purely spatial reality of the architecture.

The lack of a complete ensemble makes it necessary to consider these techniques and materials separately. The pavements of monumental buildings were usually laid in geometric patterns of colored marbles (Plates 49, 98, and 107; compare Plate 77). Otherwise marble mosaics were used, sometimes of a single color, as in the tabernae of Trajan's Markets, but more often polychrome.[6] Walls and piers were revetted with colored marbles or decorated with painting, more rarely with stucco work (marbles, Plates 104, 108, 129, and 133; painting, Plate 63, right; stuccoes, Plate 15, on the arch of the

5. Expressed for example by R. Carpenter, "Art in Transition," in *The Age of Diocletian, A Symposium* (New York, 1953), p. 75; cf. D. S. Robertson, *A Handbook of Greek and Roman Architecture* (2nd ed. Cambridge, 1945), p. 245.

6. For marble and mosaic pavements, see B. Nogara, *I mosaici antichi conservati nei palazzi pontifici del Vaticano e del Laterano* (Milan, 1910); M. E. Blake, "The Pavements of the Roman Buildings of the Republic and Early Empire," *MAAR*, 8 (1930), 1–159; id., "Roman Mosaics of the Second Century in Italy," *MAAR*, 13 (1936), 67–214; S. Aurigemma, *Tripolitania, I mosaici* (Rome, 1960; = *L'Italia in Africa, 1.1*); id., *Villa Adriana* (Rome, 1961), Figs. 59, 158, 183–89, and (in color) Tav. VIII, XIV–XXII, XXIII–XXXII; G. Becatti, *Mosaici e pavimenti marmorei* (2 vols. Rome, 1961; = *Scavi di Ostia, 4*).

bridge, and Plate 34, fragments on the under-surfaces of the inner chamber vaults).[7] Painting and marblework were often combined in one room (Plate 27, where the general pattern of the marble revetment of the apse is preserved by the shims and marks in the setting bed, and the vault and the wall above are painted; compare Plates 47 and 66). Vaults were finished with painting or stuccoes, sometimes with mosaic; again the techniques were often combined. In every case the surface was organized by linear divisions—the rows of the marble cubes (tesserae) of the mosaics, the patterns of the floor and wall marbles, and the division of the wall and vault surfaces into geometric designs with painting and stucco. Squares, circles, and oblongs predominated, shapes that echoed the primary forms of the architecture.

Glass was also used, as in the pavement of the Domus Transitoria rotunda, and in the mosaics, long since fallen, that decorated some of the vaults and pools of Domitian's palace. Bright orange, light green, sea-blue, and blue-black tesserae, made by cracking sheets of pigmented glass into roughly cubical, light-catching shapes, can still be found at the Domus Augustana (lying in the nymphaeum at number 2 on Plate 58, for example), at Hadrian's Villa, and at Ostia.[8] These mosaics were sometimes placed under water or up in the vaults beside pools or over fountains, but their effects, like those created by the enlivening surfaces and jets of water, are lost to us. The elder Pliny, writing during Vespasian's reign, introduced his discussion of glass with remarks about this technique.

> Tessellated pavements in color came into use as early as Sulla's time [138–78 B.C.]. At all events, there exists even today one made of very small cubes which he installed in the Temple of Fortune at Palestrina. After that, mosaic was extended from floors to vaulted ceilings, and today these are made of glass, a recent invention.[9]

Vault mosaics of marble tesserae were also fairly common, to judge from the fragments that remain.[10]

7. For marbles, see F. Corsi, *Delle pietre antiche* (3rd ed. Rome, 1845); H. W. Pullen, *Handbook of Roman Marbles* (London, 1894); Lanciani, pp. 623–25; *I marmi italiani* (Rome, 1939); Blake, *1*, 56–60; and the works cited above, n. 6, and below, n. 13. For painting, F. Wirth, *Römische Wandmalerei . . .* (Berlin, 1934); A. Maiuri, *Roman Painting* (Geneva, 1953); M. Borda, *La pittura romana* (Milan, 1958). For stuccoes, of which Vitruvius (7.3.9–10) says that the polished flat surfaces should reflect mirror images, see G. Ferrari, *Lo stucco nell'arte italiana* (Milan, 1910); E. L. Wadsworth, "Stucco Reliefs of the First and Second Centuries Still Extant in Rome," *MAAR, 4* (1924), 9–102; M. Brion, *Pompeii and Hercu-laneum* (London, 1960), Fig. 43. High on the façade of the Domus Aurea, between nos. 21 and 22 on Pl. 24 here, there are figured plaques of stucco, painted red and blue, above a stucco cornice.

8. For other examples, see above, Chap. 2, n. 45; Blake, *2*, 58, 139, 149; J. Toynbee and J. Ward Perkins, *The Shrine of St. Peter and the Vatican Excavations* (London, 1956), pp. 72–73 and Pl. 32.

9. *Natural History* 36.64. In the same paragraph he speaks of decoration in encaustic, and in 36.24 of a theatre stage of the first century B.C. whose middle story was of glass and uppermost of gilded timbers.

10. For an example, see above, Chap. 2, n. 66.

What resulted was a shell of color, fitted around inside the architectural space. In this manner the vaulted style first turned architecture inside out, and by excluding the natural world created illusions of places governed solely by the will of man. Imagination is required to recreate this effect in the mind's eye, and it is necessary to fall back upon analogous evidence. The painted and stuccoed vault decoration in some pagan tombs of imperial date are useful. For example, a vault is preserved in the tomb of the Pancratii, beside the Via Latina just outside Rome, which gives an idea of the beauty and brilliant color of this kind of decoration.[11] The entire surface is divided by low stucco moldings into a variety of comparatively small geometric shapes containing figures in low relief, painted scenes, and abstract designs. Red, white, blue, and yellow predominate. There are several magnificently colored and decorated vaults in the Roman tombs under S. Peter's, and certain vault-paintings in the earlier catacombs, with their linear divisions of surface, also reflect high imperial principles.[12] The extraordinary variety of marbles quarried for the Romans in Italy and the provinces can be seen, the stones recut and reused, in the splendid baroque churches of Rome.[13] The available range of colors and tones in marble was quite extensive, and the architect could specify dark red and deep green porphyries and tinted granites as well. He used these colors not only to create sensations of great luxury but also to charge his interiors with brilliant effects of light. Early Christian and Byzantine mosaics are probably separated from first- and second-century work by too great an artistic distance to be used analogously, though they display the sheath-like and light-gathering properties of the mosaics that once lined many Roman vaults. Rather suprisingly, a fair number of stucco-work scenes and fragments have survived other than in tombs. They can be examined for example in the underground basilica just outside the Porta Maggiore, in the Domus Aurea wing, in a Palatine cryptoporticus, at the imperial villas of Albano and Tivoli, and in the National Museum in Rome.[14]

There was also a secondary system of interior decoration, which at first may seem to have been at variance with the principle of surface-lining. This system was characterized by architectural constructions (composed from the traditional vocabulary of the columnar orders) built against interior walls or placed free-standing out in the vaulted spaces themselves. In monumental buildings they were usually made of or faced with colored

11. For the Tomb of the Pancratii, see Wadsworth (above, n. 7), pp. 73–78 and Pls. XXV–XXXV (cf. pp. 69–72 and Pls. XX–XXIV, the Tomb of the Valerii, nearby on the Via Latina); Borda (above, n. 7), Tav. 7 (color). For other examples of decorated vaults see Aurigemma, *Villa* (above, n. 6), Figs. 24, 60, 85, 96, 195; the fundamental article by K. Lehmann, "The Dome of Heaven," *AB*, 27 (1945), 1–27; Nash, *2*, Figs. 1073–74, 1076, 1079–84, 1121–22, 1149; Calza and Nash (above, n. 4), Fig. 37.

12. Toynbee and Ward Perkins (above, n. 8), pp. 63–104 and Pls. 2–6, 12–15; J. Wilpert, *Roma sotterranea, Le pitture delle catacombe romane*, 2 (Rome, 1903).

13. See the color plates in E. Lavagnini, *Altari barocchi in Roma* (Rome, 1959); for the use of colored marbles in bath buildings see Lucian, *Hippias*, and Seneca's letter *On Scipio's Villa*.

14. See Wadsworth (above, n. 7).

marbles, and in lesser structures they were of painted stucco. The most common form was the aedicula, which duplicated the sheltering sensation of the vault overhead, helped to establish scale, and was often used to focus attention upon a shrine, a statue, or a fountain (Plates 104 and 132, and compare Plate 51; Plate 62, center, shows the holes for the stone consoles that helped support the aediculae that once enframed the three wall niches).[15] Other examples are the column screens that were placed with their entablatures across otherwise unobstructed spaces (Figure 3, p. 22), and what are here called for convenience baroque walls, where columns, usually carrying ressauts, were set alongside vertical surfaces brought forward and back by spur walls alternating with niches or recesses (Plate 21a, Plate 45, left interior, and Figure 6, C, p. 58). Columns were also set in front of piers in line (Plate 47, where the breaks in the base molding indicate column positions). When these additive architectural forms were small in scale the differences between the two systems, though diminished, were still apparent. A low relief in stucco depicting an aedicula, with figures and with structural members displayed in approximate perspective, belonged to the first or surface system, but a small aedicula enframing a niche centered in the end wall of a vaulted room belonged to the second. In the first case, space was intimated by an illusion based upon the techniques of painting; in the second an actual space, however small, was bounded and defined. In general, decorative work in terra cotta belonged to the first system (Plates 87, 95, and 132).

What linked these two methods was their common derivation from the principles and objectives of vaulted design. Both were used to enhance the definition of interior space and to hide or obscure the physical reality of structural masses. Aediculae fixed axes and gave the viewer points of reference to use in establishing his relationship to the shape and character of the main architectural volumes. Column screens suggested spatial boundaries without wholly closing off the spaces or views on either side. Baroque walls, which in some cases were composed by joining several aediculae in an interior façade, clothed bearing masses with nonfunctional constructions of broken surfaces that produced deep shadows. The enframing designs of both systems were based upon linear divisions and outlines, and both modulated the simple geometry of the structural shapes to articulated envelopes of color and light. The lines and patterns of these decorative envelopes, activated by illumination coming from openings revealing only the sky or contiguous man-made spaces, in a sense substituted for windows. Had conventional, eye-level openings been used they would have destroyed the illusion of self-contained and independent places the imperial architect sought. Plain and undecorated rectangular, cylindrical, and spherical surfaces alone could not create this illusion, for they were too expressive of weight and structure. It was necessary to reduce and if possible eliminate the sensations evoked by these palpable realities, and this necessity accounts for the intimate connection, both physical and artistic, of décor with architectural form.

15. See above, n. 2; cf. the essay on the aedicula by J. Summerson, *Heavenly Mansions* (New York, 1963), pp. 1–28.

There is no single existing building where the application and effects of these principles can be studied. The statues and marbles have been broken up, carted off, or burned for lime. Some of the paintings are now in museums, torn from their contexts, and most of the relatively few left in the buildings are illegible or badly damaged. The mosaics have fallen and most of the stucco work has crumbled away. The nature of decorative planting can only be conjectured (Plates 42 and 68). The aqueducts have not functioned for some fourteen hundred years and the hydraulic fittings and their adjacent metal pipes were dug out and melted down long ago. A very few pools have been restored but most of those that have been cleared are dry (Plate 66), and the fountains are nothing without the play of water (Plates 48 and 50). In spite of all the differences between Roman and medieval architecture, perhaps the courts and pavilions of the Alhambra or the interiors of two or three small Constantinopolitan churches (painstakingly cleaned and consolidated in recent years) come nearer to conveying the effects of vaulted-style decoration than any other buildings still standing.

The great cores of brick and concrete, stripped and bare, upon which much of our understanding of Roman vaulted architecture must depend, were built to enclose enclosures of space. The interior linings were as integral a part of the style as the design of the supporting fabric that determined their general form. Decorative methods were fundamentally cosmetic in nature but thoroughly consistent with the principles of architectural design.[16] The coffers of the Pantheon and the humblest stuccoes of a vaulted tomb, whatever their iconographic significance, fulfilled the same artistic and sensory purposes. Imperial décor was not simply the expression of an arriviste taste for glittering and luxurious surroundings, for its main function was to heighten the impressions and illusions vaulted spaces were intended to convey.

INTENDED INSTRUCTION OF THE SENSES

Some of the sensory implications of axis and symmetry, and of the radial focus of curving surfaces upon the path and visual objective of the observer, have already been described. The chief key to the kind of sensory reaction or emotional response evoked by these buildings was the capacity of their concave shapes to induce an impression of expanding or rising hollowness. In this respect the concavity of a rounded niche or apse and of a vault overhead served the same purposes. Both enlarged and shaped the primary space with their unbroken concave surfaces, unifying and individualizing it in a way impossible with flat roofs and sides joined at right angles. And by reinforcing the

16. It is the exterior use of the traditional orders (in free-standing and large-scale forms such as monumental temple fronts, colonnades) and colonnades for peristyles and courts, that sometimes seems inconsistent with the principles of vaulted design. In these the various parts of the orders—bases, shafts, and capitals and entablatures—were often of different materials and colors; cf. Pl. 97 here, where the bases are of white marble and the shafts of tinted granite. For examples of the consistency of interior decoration in more traditional buildings, see Brion (above, n. 7), Figs. 8, 33, 43, 76, 81.

embracing, containing qualities of interior space these concave shapes heightened the sense of place, the expression of a specific and suitable location for a particular purpose, that had always dominated Latin architecture.

A Roman vault, with its continuous surfaces in a posture of expansion against the force of gravity, obscured the way in which a building was built and what made it stand. This resulted in a psychological as well as a volumetric increase in the height of an interior space because of the sensory and kinesthetic responses awakened by a shape that apparently contradicted the effects of gravity. By receding from the observer the concave surface of a vault made the size of a large space difficult to comprehend. An ambiguity of dimension, a certain incommensurability, was created, which through the agency of the properties of concavity worked toward an illusion of the expansion of space. The real or implied tangency between a vault and its vertical supporting system assisted in this, for there was no obvious connection between them (Plate 3). In most monumental architecture before Nero's time a support could be expected to read as such, but in vaulted buildings this was no longer the case. However un-architecturally minded an observer might be, he could not be free of the sensation induced by the presence of structural material curving overhead. At the same time the realities of that structure were not made clear to him. This effect of ambiguity and suggestion of incommensurability was completed by the continuity of the vault surfaces. They never came to any kind of linear or angled change of direction but simply continued curving steadily up and across the space, so there was no reference point or structural angle from which the senses could derive an impression of load or structural membering (Plates 60, 78, and 105). Groin vaults functioned similarly because of the visual ascendancy of their transverse curves (Plate 92).

A space was also individualized by a vault by means of the difference between its shape and area and those of the level surface beneath the observer's feet. In a flat-roofed room or hall the floor and ceiling are parallel, but in a Roman vaulted interior the ceiling outline is translated from the impost outline to an invisible central point or line (visible lines in the case of intersecting vaults). The particularity of each volume was preserved when the Romans duplicated vaulted spaces horizontally or vertically within a building because the roof of each space rose above the maximum height of the vertical structure rather than conforming to a common, level plane (Plates 1b and 2, and Plate 93, right). In buildings of more sophisticated design, such as the Domus Augustana, the individual spaces and their vaults were of different sizes and heights. In both kinds of design one was led through a series of spaces, each with one or more of its bounding surfaces hollowed away from him. In whatever manner these spaces were interconnected, each one seemed an unshakably fixed place because the multiple radii of its curves, unseen but instantly operative upon the senses, projected into the space being experienced and traversed. The observer and the bounding surfaces were joined in a geometry of place, and the individuality of each room or hall was insured by the rising, continuous surface overhead.

These concavities performed still another function. They described at large scale in a generalized architectural metaphor the invisible envelope determined by the maximum reach of the human limbs. This furthered the sense of place by suggesting, however subtly, an affinity between the observer's potential for action and the architectural forms. Vaulted spaces were more receptive to the imagined projection of the body's normal movements and gestures than the prismatic volumes of flat-roofed interiors.

Possibly the physical scale of man was suggested, consciously or not, in order to help in regulating and controlling his environment by claiming his sensory sympathies before dictating his course of action. Certainly the plans of vaulted buildings make it clear that freedom of choice as to direction and path was severely limited. No access to nature was allowed unless nature had been brought into a garden court or other firmly bounded architectural setting and forced to conform to the Roman drive to order all things. The implications of incommensurability reinforced this control. Of these effects domed buildings were the ultimate examples, for their visible surfaces of double curvature and the basic form of the surrounding cylinders below contained no referential lines or points whatsoever. In such a building the sensation of a fixed and immutable place was inescapable, and the bigger the space the more potent the effect. Only the vertical axis had commanding direction, and along that the observer could not travel. He was thus fixed in a localized, discrete quantity of space, shaped to surround and protect him for the moment with an illusion of completion and perfection.

Since the effects of vaulted interiors could not be disturbed by any view of the terrestrial world or any implication of its chaotic presence, the eye and the kinesthetic sense were of necessity alerted and instructed by the decoration as well as by the primary architectural forms. The importance of lighting and the effects created by the use of water can hardly be exaggerated. The principles governing the use of daytime light have already been described. By appearing to eat into structural solids, the natural halation of light at the edges of the elevated openings furthered the sensation of desubstantiality prompted by the return of light from brilliant and polished surfaces (Plates 36 and 125). The sound and motion of water and its silvery, coruscating reflection of light were rarely beyond sight and hearing. Domitian's palace, for example, contained at least fourteen major pools and fountains, many of them occupying sizable rooms. The curved surfaces that bring water most fully to life were indigenous to vaulted architecture. Pools, simple fountains, elaborate nymphaea with many jets and streams, artificial grottoes, water stairs (Plate 21a, top right), and rigoles (stepped troughs producing continuous movement and susurration) added these dimensions of motion and sound. In a great palace or villa the eye and ear were invited to contemplate not everyday scenes but a παράδεισος or ideal place, a color-strewn, enclosed, and contrived world where a satisfactory present and an untroubled future might seem equally assured.

Vaulted architecture, like state sculpture, was rhetorical. It was intended to carry conviction, even to coerce belief.[17] Its fluidity of line, surface, and space was illusory not

17. See for example the remarks by R. Brilliant, *Gesture and Rank in Roman Art* (Copenhagen, 1963; = *Memoirs of the Connecticut Academy of Arts and Sciences, 14*), p. 105.

only in the visual sense but also because it implied a freedom of action which in fact it denied. On every side there were walls or structural screens the openings in which led, in the interior of a building, either to other vaulted spaces or to courts open only to the sky. Choice was limited to positions within the prescribed spaces. Almost always one came out the way one went in; most vaulted-style plans are culs-de-sac. By these means the senses were instructed by an architecture "which expresses its moral order by an environment which cannot be disobeyed."[18]

Perhaps the concavities large and small were more than anything else the result of attempting to express permanence. The curves above and roundabout may have been architectural expressions of the spirit that produced the regulatory bodies of traditional law and precedent. Both niches and vaults described by implication what the Romans prized so much—stability and direction. In this sense niches, because of their embracing and sheltering forms, strongly suggested permanence. The vaults also embraced and sheltered, implying protection and security, and those of great size inspired a certain feeling of awe because of their apparent structural ambiguity. Both niches and vaults intimated that order could be brought out of the uncertainties of existence as well as out of the limitlessness of space (Plate 132 shows a good example, at fairly small scale, of these qualities). The vaulted style, with its relatively seamless continuity of surface, its tendency to rhetorical persuasion, and its capacity to call up strong sensations of fixed and ordered places, reflected both the claims and the realities of imperial society.

IMPERIAL CIVILIZATION AND ARCHITECTURE

In May of the year 357 the emperor Constantius II, who had spent his life outside Italy, visited Rome. Accompanied by his staff he systematically inspected the great monuments. The Capitoline temples, the Flavian Amphitheatre, the Pantheon, the imperial baths, and the towering commemorative columns of past rulers astonished him, and he despaired of adorning the ancient city. At the sight of Trajan's Forum his feelings broke through his usual reserve. With him as a junior officer was the future historian Ammianus Marcellinus, who later recalled the event.

> But when the emperor came to the Forum of Trajan, a structure unique under the heavens, as we believe, and even admired by all the gods, he stood fast in amazement, turning his attention to the gigantic complex about him, defying description and never again to be imitated by mortal men. Therefore abandoning all hope of attempting anything like it he said he would and could copy Trajan's horse alone, which stands in the center of the Forum and carries the effigy of that emperor. To this the Persian prince Ormisdas, who was standing near him . . . replied with native wit, "First, Sire, build a like stable if you can . . ."[19]

What Constantius saw, what so moved him, was a definition of the Empire of another day in the language of architecture and sculpture. In Trajan's grand scheme Roman and

18. F. E. Brown, "Roman Architecture," *College Art Journal*, 17 (1958), 114.

19. 16.10.15–16; cf. above, Chap. 5, n. 62.

Greek forms were mingled in an expression of the nature of Rome's world at the moment of its widest imperial expansion. The triumphal arch, the vast marble-paved and colonnaded court of the Forum proper, and the majestic Basilica Ulpia spoke of Latin ways in recognizably traditional images (Plates 74 and 126).[20] The reliefs of the marvelous column celebrated conquest, but with as much emphasis upon the work of colonization as upon battles; the ancient gods were ignored. Beyond the Forum court where Constantius stood in amazement rose the Markets, whose inflected shapes contrasted sharply with the horizontally defined architecture below (Plate 75). All the elements of imperial state art, ancient and modern, were assembled here in a single program. The most significant feature for the history of architecture is the prominence given the vaulted style. By Trajan's time it had become an accepted and often preferred manner of building, a response in architectural form to the needs and motivations of imperial society. That society, which appears to have been working toward a unified Mediterranean-European culture, made demands upon architecture unknown to the nations and city-states of the past. These demands were answered in part by a style based upon the phrasing of fundamental qualities of Roman-ness in nontraditional ways. The vaulted style was the uniquely imperial style in that it reached definition under the particular conditions of imperial civilization. It had not existed before, and it is reasonable to suppose that it may have expressed the character of that civilization. Discussions of this kind are bound to be somewhat speculative, but since the programs, technology, and economy of these buildings seem to have been clearly related to the aims and resources of Roman society and were not simply adaptations of earlier or foreign ideas, it may be worthwhile to consider the matter.

It is unlikely that the style was an autonomous artistic phenomenon, unrelated to the culture of its time. The sensory apprehension of its shapes effected the same kind of relationship between the viewer and the building as Roman architecture had always done. These relationships—of place, position, and direction—were as old as the clearing of the first open ceremonial space because the making of buildings by the Romans was always a function of their will to order their experience. From the earliest times they created social and political mechanisms that excluded as far as possible the incompre-

20. For the decoration of the Forum, see M. E. Bertoldi, *Ricerche sulla decorazione architettonica del Foro Traiano* (Rome, 1962; = *Studi miscellanei, 3*), who dates the sculpture to the years 112–19 (pp. 4, 32); see also Zorzi, p. 62 and Fig. 75; A. Bartoli, "La recinzione meridionale del Foro Traiano," *MemPontAcc, 1.2* (1924), 177–91; Crema, Fig. 417; and see above, Chap. 4, n. 1. The restorations by L. Canina, *Gli edifizi di Roma antica, 3* (Rome, 1848), Pls. 111–25, often reproduced, could now be restudied and made considerably more accurate; cf. T. Ashby in the preface to his revision of W. J. Anderson and R. P. Spiers, *The Architecture of Ancient Rome* (London, 1927), p. viii: "Is it too much to hope that Roman architecture may at length be emancipated from Canina?" The most accurate plan of the Forum area is that by I. Gismondi in *BC, 61* (1933), Tav. Agg. A. opp. p. 256; it is reproduced in *CAH, 11,* opp. p. 775, and Pl. 74 here is based upon it. Cf. E. Gjerstad, "Die Ursprungsgeschichte der römischen Kaiserfora," *OpusArch, 3* (1944), 40–72; P. H. von Blanckenhagen, "The Imperial Fora," *JSAH, 13* (1954), 21–26; above, Chap. 4, n. 12.

hensible, the disruptive, and the adventitious, and in the broadest terms this was the foundation of their civilization. Relationships were firmly established among most aspects of experience by traditions built upon ceremony, precedent, and statute. Whenever possible, uncertainties were bridged over and viable connections established by formulas that in time made a network of bridges connecting the diverse elements of existence. Speculation about the nature of existence and the exploration of the unfamiliar, when they occurred, were usually expanded from this frame of prescribed acts and rules. The Romans were hardly unique in this sense, but given their great drive to organization and order it is unlikely that their architecture would have been unaffected by these historical characteristics. The Roman was bounded by this way of life, and often severely limited by it, but with it he fashioned his particular achievements, among them many Western institutions and an original and highly influential architectural style.

The vaulted style was infused with the same hortatory quality found in official statuary and reliefs, upon coins, and in the panegyrical literature. This insistent rhetoric of Roman state art reflects the sharp paternalism upon which the coherence and preservation of society was thought to depend. In the buildings this quality is evident in the way the senses were instructed by axis, symmetry, and the properties of concavity. These characteristics of design and sensory instruction also reflected the balance and order, the almost choreographic clarity, of Roman ritual and liturgy. In these ways the vaulted style was a mimesis of the state, a metaphor in tangible form upon its traditions and its claims to all-embracing sovereignty. Naturally it arose in Rome, the center of these traditions and claims, where after Nero's time it was used to create an *urbs pro maiestate imperii ornata*.[21]

All of the great vaulted buildings were charged with the property of expressing unity. Encouragement to individualism was missing because choice was missing. Vaulted architecture was no more permissive than the state itself. Axis, symmetry, and the terminal feature or volume kept everyone *en face* in fact or in mind with the focal, symbolic shape; there were no true alternatives. Roman architecture might be defined as a body of law in masonry, governing human responses by didactic forms whose expressive force was intended to be recognized or apprehended immediately by the sensory faculties. Grace and elegance were sacrificed to this drive to persuade one and all to conform, and this could explain the preoccupation with the primary geometric shapes so readily yielded by the economy of imperial construction. The age of truly personal expression in architecture lay in the future, for the architecture of Rome, like that of Egypt and Greece, spoke of a particular way of life and the institutions it fostered rather than of the independent opportunity and taste of any single individual.

The nature of imperial society was also expressed in the very orderly way in which diverse human and natural resources were directed toward the end in view. The success of the solution to these essentially logistical problems is evident in the ability of the Ro-

21. The phrase is from Suetonius, *Augustus* 28.3.

mans, during the first and second centuries, to erect large numbers of buildings simultaneously without straining either their knowledge or their economy of construction. Their capacity to move almost as one man toward a desired goal was exploited in an atmosphere of bureaucratic expansion and increasing state regulation, but this made possible that supple manipulation and control of each unit of action and substance that insured the continuity of the necessary rhythms of construction. Bricks and aggregate were deployed through the buildings like maniples and centuries of infantry in the sense that each anonymous unit obeyed the commands of the architect and was dependent upon the proper functioning of exactly similar units assembled in a strictly disciplined order. The hundred foremen, each directing a gang of a hundred men, who are said to have supervised the construction of Hagia Sophia, were the inheritors in Justinian's age of Roman working methods.[22]

The government influenced the new architecture in other practical ways. It largely controlled finances, could focus talent and labor upon architectural objectives if and when it chose, and concerned itself with building codes and schedules of maintenance. Apparently a fair proportion of architects and builders were trained during military service, and many were kept on the government rolls either in the army or in the civil service to be posted to various locations around the Empire as the need arose. The guilds, at first only supervised by the government, were gradually absorbed into its ever expanding, infinitely graded hierarchy. The government was in a position to orchestrate the architectural resources of the whole realm. Sparse as the written evidence is, it suggests that this was done for architecture as for law, the administration, and the army.

That the emperors and their governments used the vaulted style as an instrument of propaganda can hardly be doubted. All official architecture was used in this way. The proliferation in the provinces of large baths based upon first- and early second-century designs in Rome is the most obvious case, but many other vaulted building types were used in the provinces, such as markets, warehouses, amphitheatres, and municipal nymphaea. Districts and towns in Italy were embellished with an apparent generosity that the emperors surely regarded as a sound investment in the future of the state. Though the financial resources of the Empire were primitively managed there was always money for building after the armies and the supply of Rome had been provided for. The doors of the treasuries were open to provincial governments as well. Astute provincial officials and citizens knew how to take advantage of the government's predisposition to build.[23] The pax romana kept communications open, allowing the style to spread and change as it was conditioned, in both Rome and the provinces, by non-Latin concepts.

What happened in Rome and many imperial cities during the years 54 to 138 is very much like what is happening in industrial countries today. Even making necessary allowances for the profound technological changes of the last two centuries, the Roman ex-

22. A. Banduri, *Imperium orientale, sive antiquitates Constantinopolitanae*, in the *Corpus Byzantinae Historiae*, 25.1 (Paris, 1711), 69.

23. See R. MacMullen, "Roman Imperial Building in the Provinces," *Harvard Studies in Classical Philology*, 54 (1959), 209–10.

perience of architecture and building in the High Empire was more like our own than that of any other age. Both periods are marked by a drive to surpass the old led by men who want the new. Both are concerned with the visual as well as the social condition of the municipality. Today, when imitation Georgian and nondescript buildings are razed by the block and replaced by innumerable variations on the rectilinear silhouette, something of what happened in Rome, Ostia, Leptis Magna, Pergamon, or a hundred other cities of the Empire is taking place. Even the smallest town was given some architectural token to represent the imperial peace. In general the Romans built more slowly and more permanently than we, but they had the same compulsion to make their cities conform, in their public buildings at least, to the modern age. And the modern age was the new imperial order, which uprooted hundreds, sometimes thousands, of families to make way for new housing and municipal buildings.

Unlike the Egyptians and the Greeks, the Romans of the Empire built most of their major buildings for the social commonwealth. The importance of the temple, from the architectural point of view, was challenged by the attention given to secular buildings. Since imperial society and the state were shaped in the same image, the new vaulted architecture was essentially social in nature. The concept that Roman architecture is basically utilitarian, so popular for so long, is correct with respect to its emphasis upon social utility. What the Romans wanted were places where they might either act upon or debate and consider the very real and never entirely solved problems that arise among men. Roman architecture is the tangible shape of an innermost Roman trait—the desire for the adjustment of one thing with another. For the Romans this adjustment had to take place in a prescribed place ordered in such a way as to facilitate the means adopted. Because the Romans persisted in interpreting this need, the skyline and visual register of central Rome changed ceaselessly for more than two hundred years and the ancient cities of earlier societies, in many cases already extremely rich architecturally, were rebuilt or enlarged with Roman designs. In less ancient lands miniature Romes sprang up. London and Dougga, Ostia and Dura, whatever their rank in the multinational fabric of Roman imperial civilization, all make this clear: neither earlier styles nor traditional forms could alone express and house what Rome hoped to accomplish.

Western Europe and the lands around the Mediterranean still brim with architectural documents of these intentions. The principles of this architecture, for centuries an effective instrument of Roman culture, were not lost when the political framework of ancient society collapsed. They survived the transition to the early middle ages, and together with Roman literature and law have continued ever since to give inspiration and instruction. And Roman architecture has never ceased to be relevant to the study of the nature and meaning of architectural form, for it was an expressive and powerful art, defining a critically important experience of Mediterranean and Western man.

IX

SUPPLEMENT

THE COMPLEXITIES of the story of Greek and Roman architecture are more apparent today than they were a decade or two ago, and it is becoming clear that the varieties of architectural form in antiquity are greater than those found in any of the grand styles of Western art until the nineteenth century. To call all the buildings put up between the sixth century B.C. and the early fourth century A.D. classical is to stretch that literary concept beyond even its permissive boundaries, for it implies a continuity of governing principles and a homogeneity of design the evidence cannot support. The preceding chapters call attention to this artistic diversity by emphasizing the special qualities of vaulted design; this one brings aspects of that material up to date and includes additional suggestions about its implications for the study of Roman architecture.

*   *   *   *

Chapter I, Background. The most important recent surveys of Roman imperial architecture are those by Ward-Perkins and Rakob.[1] Discussion of many sites and topics can be found in the *Enciclopedia dell'arte antica,* and the *Princeton Encyclopedia of Classical Sites* includes nearly every known Roman settlement; both have bibliog-

---

1. A. Boëthius and J. B. Ward-Perkins, *Etruscan and Roman Architecture* (Harmondsworth, 1970), Parts II–IV (Boëthius' portion, Part I, has been revised by R. Ling and T. Rasmussen and entitled *Etruscan and Early Roman Architecture* [1978]; Ward-Perkins' revision of his section of the original edition has been announced [*Roman Imperial Architecture*]; unfortunately neither of the two extant volumes has an analytical index). Recently, Ward-Perkins has published a briefer version of his studies: *Roman Architecture* (New York, 1977). F. Rakob's survey appears in vol. 2 of the *Propyläen Kunstge-* schichte: *Das römische Weltreich,* by T. Kraus and others (Berlin, 1967), pp. 153–201 and Plates 12–115. His work in the archaeology of Roman architecture has continued with "Das Quellenheiligtum in Zaghouan und die römische Wasserleitung nach Karthago," *RM,* 81.1 (1974), 41–89, "Die Principia des römischen Legionslagers in Lambaesis . . . ," *RM,* 81.2 (1974), 253–80 (with S. Storz), and "Hellenismus in Mittelitalien. Bautypen und Bautechnik," *Hellenismus in Mittelitalien,* I (1976), pp. 366–86 (= *Abhandlungen . . . Göttingen, Phil.-Hist. Klasse,* 97.1).

raphies for all entries.[2] Nash's invaluable *Pictorial Dictionary of Ancient Rome* was issued in a revised edition in 1968, and the third volume of Blake's detailed study of structural techniques in Rome and its vicinity appeared in 1973.[3] Many standard and antiquarian works have been reprinted in recent years; among these is Desgodetz' remarkable *Édifices antiques de Rome*.[4] There are new archaeological guides to the capital, and valuable collections of texts and inscriptions have appeared in translation.[5] The publication of the excavations at Ostia continues, and a revised edition of Meiggs' standard work appeared in 1973.[6] Reference will be made below to recent works on particular sites, buildings, and topics that figure in the text.

Discussions of vaulting as a structural technique, which reached a kind of crescendo toward the middle of this century, have abated somewhat and have become more sober and reliable than they were when they were used as ammunition in the *Orient oder Rom* controversy and related polemics.[7] Both the historical background to early Roman vaulting and its technical characteristics are better understood now.[8] In the place of such structural studies there has been a renewed interest in the complex relationships between later Greek and Roman architecture, but much more work has to be done before those relationships become clear.[9] At the same time the relevant monuments of the later Republican period have been re-studied; previous identifications have in some cases been questioned.[10] The Sanctuary of Fortune at Palestrina has continued to attract the attention of scholars, but its date has not yet been securely fixed.[11] Baia has at last begun to receive its due, and although no comprehensive excavation report on this important site has appeared, it is now possible to gain a

2. *Enciclopedia*: 7 vols. and supplements (Rome, 1958–73); the *Princeton Encyclopedia* appeared in 1976, edited by R. Stillwell, W. L. MacDonald, and M. H. McAllister.

3. E. Nash: 2 vols. (2nd ed. London, 1968); M. E. Blake, *Roman Construction in Italy from Nerva through the Antonines* (Philadelphia, 1973), ed. and completed by D. T. Bishop.

4. Reprint of the 1682 ed. (Westmead, 1969). Fundamental works by Ashby, Lanciani, Richmond, Tomassetti, and others have also been reprinted in recent years.

5. G. Lugli, *Itinerario di Roma antica* (Milan, 1970; a number of his articles appear in his *Studi minori di topografia antica* [Rome, 1965]); F. Coarelli, *Guida archeologica di Roma* (Verona, 1975). D. R. Dudley, *Urbs Roma. A Source Book of Classical Texts . . .* (London, 1967), is very useful, as is J. J. Pollitt, *The Art of Rome, c. 753 B.C.–337 A.D. Sources and Documents* (Englewood Cliffs, N.J., 1966).

6. Ten vols. of the *Scavi di Ostia* had appeared by 1980; the second edition of Meiggs' book was published by the Oxford University Press. Cf. J. E. Packer, *The Insulae of Imperial Ostia* (Rome, 1971; = *MAAR, 31*).

7. See Ward Perkins, cited in n. 57 to Chapter 2, above; cf. Rivoira's aggressive defense of Roman originality.

8. See for example T. D. Boyd, "The Arch and the Vault in Greek Architecture," *AJA, 81.2* (1978), 83–100; R. Mainstone, *Developments in Structural Form* (London, 1975), passim, but esp. Chapters 6 and 7; P. Sanpaolesi, "Strutture a cupola autoportanti," *Palladio, 21* (1971), 3–64; and C. F. Giuliani, "Volte e cupole a doppia calotta in età adrianea," *RM, 82.2* (1975), 329–42; cf. *AJA, 78.2* (1974), 173–74.

9. To the works cited in nn. 15–18 to Chapter 1, above, add the articles in *Hellenismus in Mittelitalien*, cited in n. 1 here.

10. For example, the "Market" at Tivoli; see C. F. Giuliani, *Tibur, Pars prima* (Rome, 1970), pp. 218–22.

11. See F. Coarelli, ed., *Studi su Praeneste* (Perugia, 1978); id., "Public Building in Rome between the Second Punic War and Sulla," *PBSR, 45* (1977), 1–23; cf. M. P. Muzzioli, *Praeneste. Pars altera* (Rome, 1970). A late second century B.C. date for Palestrina is now being emphasized.

fairly thorough understanding of its buildings from the printed page.[12] To the list of rusticated, mannered designs can be added arches of the Aqua Virgo of 19 B.C. that can be seen by the Via del Nazareno.[13]

Chapter II, Nero's Palaces. Studies of various aspects of Nero's reign and personality continue to multiply.[14] The nature and degree of his devotion to the arts has been argued in recent years in some detail, and the deliberately slanted manner in which the Domus Aurea was represented in the literary tradition has been the subject of a careful study.[15] Chiefly because of its presumed connection with the fledgling Christian community in Rome, the Great Fire of A.D. 64 has been discussed repeatedly.[16] But these works are concerned only incidentally with archaeological and architectural problems, and the study of the physical effects and urban legacy of the fire languishes. On the other hand the *insula,* whose evolution seems to have been so markedly accelerated by the fire, continues to be a focus of attention.[17] But the centerpiece of Neronian architecture remains the Esquiline wing of the Domus Aurea, whose position on the cutting edge of the revolutionary developments in Roman architecture appears to be secure. It is important to note that it is a relatively new addition to the roster of the great imperial monuments of Rome, first gaining attention because of its paintings and their profound art-historical significance, with interest in its radical architectural nature surfacing only some fifty years ago.[18] Recent studies have dealt with specific aspects of the wing rather more than with the principles of its conception and design, the celebrated octagon and its dependencies attracting the most attention.[19]

12. See the *Atti dei convegni Linci, 33* (1977): *I Campi flegrei nell'archeologia e nella storia,* esp. the articles by Giuliani, Mingazzini, and Sgobbo; M. Boriello and A. D'Ambrosio, *Baiae-Misenum* (Florence, 1979); and Rakob's article cited in n. 45, Chapter 6, above.

13. Nash, *I,* pp. 55–56.

14. See the references in A. Garzetti, *From Tiberius to the Antonines . . .* (2nd ed. London, 1974), pp. 605–12 and 742–46.

15. G. C. Picard, *Augustus and Nero* (London, 1966), pp. 87–113; M. F. Gyles, "Nero, qualis artifex?" *Classical Journal,* 57 (1962), 193–200; P. M. Frazer, "Nero the Artist–Criminal," *Classical Journal,* 72 (1966), 17–20; M. P. O. Morford, "The Distortion of the Domus Aurea Tradition," *Eranos,* 66 (1968), 158–79.

16. C. Saumagne, "Les incendiaires de Rome . . . ," *Revue Historique,* 227 (1962), 337–60; cf. J. Beaujeu, *L'incendie de Rome en 64 . . .* (Brussels, 1960; = *Collection Latomus,* 49); and further citations in Garzetti (n. 14, above), pp. 745–46.

17. Meiggs (n. 6, above), Chapter 12 and pp. 569–70; Packer (n. 6, above).

18. The story begins in 1913 with Weege's work (see n. 29, Chapter 2, above), but it was only in the 1930s that the architecture of the wing began to attract

much attention. To the publications cited in n. 48 to Chapter 2, above, add N. Dacos, *La découverte de la Domus Aurea . . .* (Paris, 1968).

19. N. Neuerburg, *L'architetture delle fontane e dei ninfei nell'Italia antica* (Naples, 1965; = *Memorie dell'accademia di archeologia lettere e belle arti di Napoli, 5*), pp. 97 and 200 (the water-stair); G. Zander, "Nuovi studi e ricerche su la Domus Aurea," *Palladio, 15.1–4* (1965), 157–59; G. Wataghin Cantino, "Observations on the Domus Aurea," *Mesopotamia, 1* (1966), 109–18; H. Lavagne, "Le nymphée au Polyphéme de la Domus Aurea," *Mélanges d'archéologie et d'histoire de l'École française de Rome, 82* (1970), 673–722; H. Prückner and S. Storz, "Beobachtungen im Oktagon der Domus Aurea," *RM, 81.2* (1974), 323–39; D. Bizzari Vivarelli, "Un ninfeo sotto il parco di Traiano," *Mélanges. . . , 88* (1976), 719–57; A. Aiardi, "Per un interpretazione della Domus Aurea," *Parola del passato, 33* (1978), 90–103; for Minori, see N. Franciosa, *La Villa di Minori* (Minori, 1968); for the degree of sophistication reached in the construction of ancient "machinery," see D. de S. Price, *Gears from the Greeks* (Philadelphia, 1974; = *Transactions of the American Philosophical Society,* 64.7).

Chapter III, Domitian's Palace. The existing fragments of this great creation remain enigmatic. In contrast to the Domus Aurea wing or the Markets of Trajan, not much material is available and the study of the Palatine therefore proceeds slowly. Later additions to Rabirius' buildings have been published, and the mosaics found on the hill as well, but the full-scale scholarly attack that the importance of the site warrants has not yet been mounted.[20] An attempt has been made to assign the Domus Augustana to an architect other than Rabirius.[21] More has been written about the sestertius of A.D. 95/96, which has been put to use once again in an attempt to establish the main lines of the design of the Domus Flavia.[22] The question of the existence of vaults over the state halls would seem to remain moot; the evidence is probably insufficient for proof one way or the other.[23] The viability and apparently enormous influence of the forms and spaces Rabirius created do not seem to have been investigated further, though the post–Rabirian habit of including circus-shaped courts or buildings in imperial residences and villas has.[24] The idea that the Domus Flavia and Augustana are peristyle palaces, correct as a description of the nature of their central courtyards but inadequate as a definition of their overall architectural character, persists.[25]

Chapter IV, Trajan's Markets. The richness of the visual material for knowledge of the Markets before the modern excavations is gradually being revealed, but the significance of the complex in the history of architecture has not been much discussed.[26] Other major structures of Trajan's time have fared better, such as his huge baths on the Esquiline.[27] The architectural sculpture of his Forum has also received attention,

20. J. J. Herrmann, Jr., "Observations on the Baths of Maxentius in the Palace," *RM*, 83 (1976), 403–24; H. Finsen, *La résidence de Domitien sur le Palatin* (Copenhagen, 1969; = *Analecta romana instituti Danici, 5, Supplementum*); M. L. Morricone Matini, *Mosaici antichi in Italia, Regione prima. Roma: Reg. X. Palatium* (Rome, 1967); cf. *BdA*, 50 (1965), 122–23.

21. G. Wataghin Cantino, *La Domus Augustana. Personalità e problemi dell'architettura Flavia* (Turin, 1966; = *Università di Torino, Facolta di lettere e filosofia, archeologia e storia dell'arte, 10*, with bibliography on pp. 97–102). For the two divisions of the palace, see *SHA, Pertinax*, 11.5–13.

22. C. F. Giuliani, "Domus Flavia: una nuova lettura," *RM*, 84 (1977), 91–106; B. Tamm, "Das Gebiet vor dem Rapräsentationspalast des Domitian . . . ," *Opuscula romana*, 6 (1968), 145–91; cf. *Bonner Jahrbücher, 160* (1960), 292.

23. Mainstone (n. 8, above), pp. 115–16; Giuliani (n. 22, above); F. E. Brown, *Roman Architecture* (New York, 1961), p. 40; J. B. Ward-Perkins (1970; n. 1, above), p. 232.

24. A. Frazer, "The Iconography of Emperor Maxentius' Buildings in Via Appia," *AB, 48.3/4* (1966), 385–92; A. Hoffmann, "Das 'Stadion' in der Villa

Hadriana," *Architectura, 8.1* (1978), 1–15.

25. To the citations in n. 81, Chapter 3, above, add A. Boëthius, "Die Atriumhäuser und Ihr Nachlass in der kaiserzeitlichen Palastarchitektur," *OpusArch, 1* (1935), 182–89; and K. M. Swoboda, *Römische una romanische Paläste*, 3rd ed., (Vienna, 1969), p. 276.

26. An exception: S. Giedion, *Architecture and the Phenomena of Transition* (Cambridge, Mass., 1971), pp. 232–37. To the citations in Chapter 4 above, add S. Brinton, "The Great Market of Trajan Revealed," *Apollo* (January, 1930), 52–54; C. Leon, *Apollodoros of Damaskos und die Trajanische Architecktur* (diss. Innsbruck, 1961); R. A. Staccioli, "I mercati traianei," *Capitolium*, 40 (1965), 584–93; H. Plommer, "Trajan's Forum," *Antiquity, 48* (1974), 126–30; and cf. F. Borsi et al., ed., *Roma antica e i disegni . . . di Giovanni Antonio Borsi* (Rome, 1976), Figs. 8 and 9.

27. K. de Fine Licht, *Untersuchungen an den Trajansthermen zu Rom* (Copenhagen, 1974; = *Analecta romana instituti Danici, 7*); id., "Marginalia on Trajan's Baths in Rome," *Studia Romana* (Odense, 1975; = *Festschrift P. Krarup*), pp. 87–95; cf. B. Tamm, "Nero's Gymnasium in Rome," *Stockholm Studies in Classical Archaeology, 7*, 1–41.

and a study of the Basilica Ulpia is underway.[28] But the Markets proper, one of the major urban creations of Western architecture, responsive to the social needs of a huge metropolis and very advanced functionally in comparison with the earlier market buildings of the Greeks and Romans, have not much excited the interest of historians of architecture. One wonders if it is because they are insufficiently "classical."

Chapter V, The Pantheon. Because of its singular variety and quantity, the architecture of Hadrianic times presents many intriguing problems to which scholars continue to gravitate. Our understanding of the relevant but sketchy ancient literature has been improved, and several Hadrianic buildings and sites have been investigated in recent years.[29] There are new books on the Pantheon, as well as a discussion of the possibility of dating it to Trajan's time and attributing its design to Apollodoros.[30] In addition, the Pantheon's predecessors and progeny, and its enormous influence on the history of architecture, have been studied.[31] Interest in the technology of its construction has not abated; the vicissitudes of its fabric over the centuries have attracted attention; and there have been articles and suggestions about other tangible elements of the building.[32]

The more abstract questions about how the Pantheon is to be understood, as a design and as a symbol, have also been explored. Details of the hypothesis that the pediment of the porch contained the representation of an enormous eagle enframed by a beribboned wreath are in print.[33] More is known now about solar orientation

28. C. Leon, *Die Bauornamentik des Trajansforums . . .* (Vienna, 1971; = *Publikationen des Österreichischen Kulturinstituts in Rome, 1 Abt., Band 4*); Professor J. E. Packer, who is investigating the Ulpia, kindly informs me that he reads the *FUR* (Tav. XXVIII) as showing the southwest façade as an open colonnade; Pl. 74 and 126 here are, like the other drawings, not intended to convey any more than a general sense of the configuration of the building.

29. See H. W. Benario, *A Commentary on the Vita Hadriani in the Historia Augusta* (Chico, Calif., 1980; = *American Classical Studies, 7*); and cf. R. Syme, "Hadrian the Intellectual," *Les empereurs romains d'Espagne* (Paris, 1965), pp. 243–53. Some works on Hadrianic sites and buildings: J. H. Oliver, "The Athens of Hadrian," *Empereurs . . . d'Espagne,* pp. 123–33; R. Naumann, *Der Zeustempel von Aizanoi* (Berlin, 1979; = *Denkmäler antiker Architektur, 12*); A. Barattolo, "Nuove ricerche sull'architettura del Tempio di Venere e di Roma . . . ," *RM, 80* (1973), 243–73: Giuliani (n. 8, above); Hoffmann (n. 24, above); and W. L. MacDonald and B. M. Boyle, "The Small Baths at Hadrian's Villa," *JSAH, 39.1* (1980), 5–27.

30. K. de Fine Licht, *The Rotunda in Rome* (Copenhagen, 1968; = *Jutland Historical Society, Publications, 8*); W. L. MacDonald, *The Pantheon—Design, Meaning, and Progeny* (London and Cambridge, Mass., 1976); W.-D. Heilmeyer, "Apollodoros von Damaskos, der Architekt des Pantheon," *JDAI, 90* (1975), 316–47 (but see the remarks by A. C. G. Smith in *PBSR, 46* (1978), 73–78).

31. De Fine Licht, pp. 237–51; MacDonald, Chapters 3 and 5 and the citations there on pp. 143–46; and Giedion (n. 26, above), pp. 152–54.

32. For technology, in addition to the citations in the two previous notes, see Mainstone (n. 8, above), 112–27; Sanpaolesi (n. 8, above); and the drawing of the Pantheon dome under construction in H. and R. Leacroft, *The Buildings of Ancient Rome* (London, 1969), pp. 12–13. For the towers, see H. Hibbard, *Carlo Maderno* (London, 1971), pp. 230–31; and T. Thieme, "Disegni di cantiere per i campanili del Pantheon . . . ," *Palladio, 20* (1970), 73–88; cf. A. Blunt, *Borromini* (London, 1979), p. 225. Other points are considered by L. Crema, "I Pronao del Pantheon," *Hommages à Albert Grenier, 1* (Brussels, 1962; = *Collection Latomus, 58*), pp. 457–61.

33. De Fine Licht (n. 30, above), pp. 45–46.

than before, and questions about the nature of the relationships between Hadrian's building and the Pantheon by Agrippa that once stood on the site are being investigated.[34] Efforts to define the meaning of the great rotunda continue, but it has not yet given up all its secrets.[35]

Chapter VI, Architects. The standing accorded professionals by Cicero and Vitruvius seems not to have been exaggerated. A study of a Roman architectural and artistic family suggests how influential such people were, and an essay for the non-specialist reviews the education and training, as well as the methods, of Roman architects.[36] The attempt to deprive Rabirius of the authorship of the Domus Augustana has been mentioned above.[37] Apollodoros continues to attract attention, as does Hadrian's Temple of Venus and Rome.[38] More information is available now about Hadrianic pumpkin-shaped vaults, and about architects' and surveyors' instruments.[39] Possible connections between the design and forms of vaulted, non-traditional buildings, such as the Markets of Trajan, and the theorems and formulas of Euclid and his school are being discussed.[40]

Chapter VII, Economy of Construction. The means employed by Roman builders to erect stable monumental structures are still not fully understood, but there is some sensible writing on the subject by people knowledgeable in structural matters.[41] There are also detailed analyses of the technology of specific buildings and elements of design.[42] The inscriptions on bricks continue to attract attention, and it may be that the questions surrounding this important subject are close to being resolved.[43] The

34. See the discussion by J. Le Gall, "Les romaines et l'orientation solaire," *Mélanges de l'École française de Rome, Antiquité*, 87 (1975), 287–320; and cf. J. Rykwert, *The Idea of a Town. The Anthropology of Urban Form in Rome, Italy and the Ancient World* (Princeton, 1976), pp. 49 and 55, and nn. 62, 65, and 75 on p. 211 (the sixteen divisions of the Pantheon's plan); cf. also *JSAH*, 29.3 (1970), 263.

35. H. Kähler, "Das Pantheon in Rom," in *Meilensteine Europäischer Kunst*, ed. E. Steingräber (Munich, 1965), pp. 47–75 and 429–31; id., "The Pantheon as Sacral Art," *Bucknell Review*, 15.2 (1967), pp. 41–48; cf. *JSAH*, 39.1 (1980), 97–98.

36. E. Rawson, "Architecture and Sculpture: The Activities of the Cossutii," *PBSR*, 43 (1975), 36–47; W. L. MacDonald, "Roman Architects," in *The Architect: Chapters in the History of the Profession*, ed. S. Kostof (Oxford, 1977), pp. 28–58. See also the entries under "architetto" and Roman architects' names in the *Enciclopedia dell'arte antica* (n. 2, above); and cf. *SHA, Severus Alexander*, 44.4.

37. See n. 21, above.

38. G. Gullini, "Apollodoro e Adriano: Ellenismo a classicismo nell'architettura romana," *BdA*, 53.2–3 (1968), 62–80; Barattolo (n. 29, above); Heilmeyer

(n. 30, above); Leon (n. 26, above); and cf. Garzetti (n. 14, above), pp. 431–32.

39. F. E. Brown's article, "Hadrianic Architecture," referred to in n. 45, Chapter 6, above, is in *Essays in Memory of Karl Lehmann* (New York, 1964), ed. L. F. Sandler, pp. 55–58. For the vaults at Hadrian's Villa, see MacDonald and Boyle (n. 29, above), esp. pp. 23–24; for instruments, O. A. W. Dilke, *The Roman Land Surveyors* (London, 1971), Chapter 5.

40. W. L. MacDonald, "Excavation, Restoration, and Italian Architecture of the 1930s," forthcoming in a volume honoring Henry-Russell Hitchcock.

41. Mainstone (n. 8, above); cf. his "On Construction and Form," *Program* (Spring 1964), 51–70. For construction workers, see P. A. Brunt, "Free Labor and Public Works at Rome," *JRS*, 70 (1980), 81–100.

42. Giuliani (n. 8, above); MacDonald and Boyle (n. 29, above); Sanpaolesi (n. 8, above).

43. To the materials cited in nn. 25–30, Chapter 7, above, add: T. Helen, *Organization of Roman Brick Production in the First and Second Centuries A.D. An Interpretation of Brick Stamps* (Helsinki, 1975), and M. Steinby, "Ziegelstempel von Rom und Umgebung," *RE, Supp. 15* (1978), cols. 1489–1531.

manner in which the labor force was used and the nature of its role—and that of the traditions and professionalism of the *collegia*—in the creation of architectural form need work.

Chapter VIII, The New Architecture. Significant advances have been made in our understanding of the décor of Roman buildings. Vault mosaics, so important to the effects that the new architecture had upon the senses, are now more fully recorded and understood.[44] Knowledge of marble revetment, and of the marbles themselves, has improved.[45] Another important subject that has been studied recently is the Roman niche and its role in architectural design.[46] But attempts to define style have been few and far between, and with good reason, for much essential groundwork remains to be done. The same is largely true of the study of the historical position of the surviving grand monuments of Rome, of their artistic influence and their progeny; these subjects have been put on sound scholarly footing only sporadically. The social and political implications of imperial architecture, so problematical and so difficult to deal with, understandably have also been rather neglected.[47] Hypotheses being in short supply, comments on some of these matters, and about the state of the subject in general, may not be amiss.

*   *   *   *   *

The architectural revolution that took place in the first century A.D. is identified above all by its marked departure from traditional form. Can, then, its monuments be called "classical," the customary designation for the very architecture against whose entrenched authority that revolution took place? Or is it correct to speak of a new style? The matter needs discussion not only for its own sake, but also because of the influence of ancient buildings on style after style in the Western world; it is important to define accurately to what kind of ancient architecture later architects responded. But our general terminology is inexact, indeed confusing, and the identification of the chief formal strains of Roman architecture in particular needs to be reviewed. There the situation is also anything but clear-cut, particularly as the post-medieval tradition of an all-embracing, columniated classicism is so powerful. In addition, the later Greeks, and the Romans especially, adapted the Orders and pedimented temple-fronts to a wide variety of buildings, creating in post–Domus Aurea vaulted designs an impression of a kind of Vitruvian sanctity that can all too easily lead to misapprehensions about their true architectural nature. The complexity of the subject is

44. F. B. Sear, "Roman Wall and Vault Mosaics," *RM, Ergänzungsheft*, 23 (1977).

45. D. Krencker, *Die Trierer Kaiserthermen* (Augsburg, 1929), pp. 306–19; Boëthius and Ward-Perkins (n. 1, above), pp. 260–63; T. Dohrn, "Crustae," *RM*, 72 (1965), 127–41; R. Gnoli, *Marmora romana* (Rome, 1971).

46. G. Hornbostel-Hüttner, *Studien zur römischen Nischenarchitektur* (Leiden, 1979; = *Studies of the Dutch Archaeological and Historical Society*, 9), with a useful analytical index.

47. There are useful observations in Giedion (n. 26, above), passim; and stimulating suggestions in A. Bam-

suggested by comparing, say, the Maison Carrée with the so-called Temple of Venus at Baalbek, or the Basilica Ulpia with that of Maxentius and Constantine; functions aside, they make very uneasy bedfellows, yet all are buildings from the Roman world. So neither "classical architecture" nor "Roman architecture" will do if faith is to be kept with the extraordinarily diversified work of architects of Roman times.

Thus there are two principal roots of the problem of defining Roman architecture. The first is the widely accepted use of the imprecise term "classical"; the second, the formal variety found in the buildings themselves. The late Otto Brendel scrutinized the uses of the word "classical" carefully. He said that if, in discussing classicism in Roman architecture, one seeks a narrow and practical definition,

> the nearest answer seems to be: that which is called "classical" ought to possess some kind of relation or resemblance to the source and origin of all classicism, namely, Greek art at the height of its classical stage, about the second half of the fifth century B.C.

He added that apparently not a great deal ought to be called "classical" in Roman architecture, "if the above, admittedly rather restrictive, definition is applied." And when he asked if Roman architecture implies a special concept of "classical," he said:

> So it seems. There one ought to remember that the use of "classical" as a term of artistic criticism [is] of comparatively recent date. All its applications are modern; to that extent, arbitrary . . . the term was not in [the Roman] vocabulary. . . . Much evidence seems to indicate that among the arts of ancient Rome, architecture was the least classicizing, on the whole. The early Renaissance was probably first to sense a classical element—one not necessarily of the Greek description—in Roman architecture. In their own work one may find the earliest de facto declarations, if not yet the verbal exposition, of Roman architectural monuments as "classical."[48]

So although Roman architecture has its classical side it is quantitatively less than in the figural arts. What makes up the balance? Non-classical architecture, which must be either Roman in origin or the result of the infiltration of architectural ideas and practices from beyond the periphery of the Greco-Roman world. Finally, if Brendel is right, the classical portion of Roman architecture is not necessarily of a Greek kind; that is, there is an identifiable Roman classicism. Thus the architectural critic must try to distinguish clearly between what is Greek and what is Roman even in classical buildings of Roman times. That is not a new idea, of course, but it bears repeating in the present context.

The variety of Roman buildings is well known but has not been the subject of much systematic analysis. The bibliographies in the handbooks are revealing in this

---

mer, *Architektur und Gesellschaft in der Antike* (Vienna, 1974), esp. Chapters 8–11.

48. *JSAH*, 29.3 (1970), 264.

respect. They usually contain a list of general works, and they may have sections on typology, technology, and so on, but few if any stylistic and formal studies appear, partly because the significance of the multiplicity of architectural forms in Roman times has not attracted very much attention. The same bibliographies then often list some of the numerous works dealing with the architecture of regions and provinces, and while this is a useful way to help make a huge mass of often refractory material more tractable, and one that quite properly calls attention to local modes and contributions, it also causes problems. For with respect to the whole of Roman architecture, provincial boundaries are valid artistic boundaries only in particular, limited cases, and grouping together by geography buildings executed in such a variety of different forms over three centuries often isolates them artificially from kindred structures around the Empire. Of course the architecture of major cultures and political periods always defies easy schematization, but that of the wide Roman world, with its evolving, shifting morphology, presents an unusual—perhaps unparalleled—degree of stylistic diversity.

There are other reasons why the study of the subject is somewhat unbalanced, chief among them the sheer quantity of evidence. And buildings from well-known sites sometimes take on unwarranted importance because insufficient comparative material has been analyzed, while some familiar structures have attracted little if any serious discussion. Important excavations, in Rome in particular, remain unpublished. Furthermore, Roman architecture is not often dealt with visually, partly because so many scholars who write about it are first and foremost classicists and archaeologists, and while these disciplines are of course indispensable, they do not fill all needs; approaches based on artistic qualities are sorely lacking. Trajan's Markets are a case in point. Cleared and restored some fifty years ago under conditions that militated against detailed publication, their architectural nature remains all but ignored. Perhaps this is because traditional classical forms are shunned there, or perhaps it is because it is not yet time to see the sprawling, complex Markets as a work of art, a bold and convincing image of the swarming capital they were built to serve. Since architecture is an art, relevant art-historical methods ought to be applied, in order to try to free the monuments from their almost hermetic scholarly isolation and establish more convincingly the reasons why they so powerfully influenced the history of architecture. Sharper definition of their historical position and deeper exploration of their symbolic potential, both much needed, would reveal their intrinsic architectural qualities more fully and make them more intelligible.

But complexities abound. If, for example, working definitions of style are sought, questions about the nature and degree of Greek influence surface immediately. And these are matters still bedeviled by the widely held view that Roman architecture is inferior to, rather than simply different from, Greek architecture. This view embraces convictions such as that about the purity of Greek buildings and the impurity of Roman ones, the debasement of the Orders by the Romans, and other subjective opinions; all of them spring from a false view of the nature of change in art and from mistakenly associating moral standards with aesthetic ones.[49] Such regressive opinions ought to have been disposed of long ago, but like peat fires they smoulder on and probably will never disappear completely. Those who hold them apparently think that architects in Roman times sought to work in a Greek manner and failed (the kind of thinking that has frequently retarded the objective study of Roman sculpture), whereas in fact they almost never sought to design truly Greek buildings. The problem arises, in great part, from the mistake of seeing cosmetic and symbolic applications of versions of the Greek Orders as attempts to make proper Greek architecture, whereas they represent something else entirely. And then there is the fact that when the Romans did use earlier forms they usually adapted Hellenistic ones, which to many proponents of the purity and ascendancy of classical Greek work are also of inferior quality. Even the most conservative Roman building type, the civic temple, has only superficial connections with the grand Greek religious architecture of the sixth and fifth centuries; the study of the two thrives on contrasting them, not on using the later as a foil for the exaltation of the earlier. None of this would be worth more than a line or two, were it not for the pervasiveness of this attitude and the need to see precisely what in Roman architecture descends from the Greeks and what does not. As to the former, it all goes back to Winckelmann, whose role has been neatly characterized by Anita Brookner: after observing that he was largely the creator of the myth of the excellence of the classical past, she adds that he

> pleaded his cause in terms so incantatory that some of his arguments are still persuasive. . . . For Winckelmann, the ancient world was a repository of wise laws, good government, and, above all, physical beauty. Greece was peopled by athletes seven feet tall, marble white, and generally adolescent. There were, of course, no Greek women. Ancient Rome was thought to be a city of bleached white marble fragments, although in its heyday it must have looked more like the Oxford Street façade of Selfridges. The inhabitants of these cities and their provinces were thought to possess the secrets of living beautifully. . . . Winckelmann's error was to persuade himself that one might possess these secrets by "imitating" the Greeks and Romans.[50]

---

49. A connection that R. Scruton, in *The Aesthetics of Architecture* (Princeton, 1979), pp. 252–53, characterizes as a fantasy.

50. The *Times Literary Supplement* (October 18, 1980), 1167, amplified in her *Jacques-Louis David* (New York, 1980), pp. 27–30. See also H. Honour, *Neo-Classicism* (Harmondsworth, 1960), pp. 57–62, who quotes Goethe's remark that "we learn nothing by reading Winckelmann, but we *become* something" (p. 58); and

L. D. Ettlinger, "Winckelmann, or Marble Boys are Better," in *Art the Ape of Nature. Studies in Honor of H. W. Janson* (New York, 1981), pp. 505–11, who reminds us that Winckelmann's view was "a highly personal and historical [one] . . . which settled like a blight on ancient history and classical archeology," and that "his stylistic categories are not drawn from the study of the monuments but taken over from classical theories of rhetoric" (pp. 509–10).

Exactly. And it was he who fathered the equally mythical proposition that the forms of classical Greek art provide the proper standards against which later work must be judged. It was this false start, together with the romantic view of ancient Greece that has flourished since the early nineteenth century, that generated the idea that Greek architecture is somehow inherently superior to Roman, which is an opinion based on emotion and personal taste and nothing more.

The necessity of seeing clearly what in Roman architecture is Greek and what is not could be largely satisfied if the different Roman stylistic groups were defined by establishing, in broad outline, their governing characteristics; it was in the hope of exposing the principles of one of these groups in some detail that the preceding chapters were written. Continuing this process would allow the pieces of the puzzle to be seen more clearly, before attempting to fit them together properly, and might help to make sense out of the profusion of elements of Greek origin found in Roman work by suggesting bases for hypotheses about the reasons for their use and for their formal modalities. Connections between groups formed by the common use of certain elements of design would become clearer, and areas needing study might be revealed. Most important of all, the complexity of the subject would be made somewhat easier to deal with.

*   *   *   *

Architects in imperial times were readier to experiment with their classical and Hellenistic heritage than were their immediate predecessors who, although they began the process that led to the vaulted style, were often content with the Orders as they found them. By Augustus' time the number of basic elements of trabeated design had been increased somewhat from the original four (foundation, wall, Order, and roof), but it was soon expanded to include almost every element now loosely called classical. This expansion was characterized not only by the addition of entirely new forms, such as those found in the vaulted style, but also by deeply creative changes in the way traditional forms were deployed. Today, after centuries of repetition and adaptation, these Roman orchestrations of classical features are so familiar that it can be difficult to see how novel and indeed radical some of them were in their own day. To liberate the hallowed Orders from their Vitruvian stockroom and parade them in fresh versions and combinations on almost every kind of structure, to apply the lineaments of the consecrated temple-front to almost any type of building, was to come close to denying the original principles of properly classical architecture. This process had of course begun before the imperial age, but it was only then that it took flight, altering Western architecture forever and leaving its spare Greek sources behind in a museum-like world of their own. Devising new functions for traditional elements of building was as original, and as significant, as the creation of mature vaulted design. Conservative, somewhat anachronistic work continued to be turned out but in decreasing amounts as its stylistic distance from the newer modes widened; by the second century it had just about run its course.

This evolution of Roman architecture proper was accomplished with some two dozen design elements, each an immediately recognizable, basic feature almost never used alone. They fall into three broad groups: the first consists of elements common to architecture in general, such as walls, roofs, and so on. To these the Greeks added the second group, comprised of the Orders and their extended families of mouldings and other related features. The third group is made up of original Roman elements and others the Romans evolved by expanding upon classical and Hellenistic sources; the elements of vaulted design (see pp. 14–19 and 167–171, above) fall here, as do the new dispositions of the Orders just discussed. The full list of elements in Roman times is as follows:

Apse	Pedestal
Arch	Pier
Attic	Plaque
Balcony	Podium
Corbel	Roof
Doorway	Seating (public buildings)
Entablature	Stair
Exedra, hemicycle	Temple-front, pediment
Floor	Terrace
Foundation	Vault
Moulding	Wall
Niche	Window, oculus
Orders	

With the exception of a few rare forms seen occasionally on elaborate tombs and commemorative monuments, these elements are what architects applied in various combinations to buildings of every kind of function and plan.[51] All substantial buildings of the time were composed with them, and they are the essential building-blocks, so to speak, of classicizing architecture everywhere.

The workable combinations are, by and large, familiar, but an example or two may be ventured. The elaborate stage buildings of Roman theatres are composed of

---

51. Examples of such tombs: those called La Con-nochia near Capua (attenuated, bollard-like diagonal projections) and Absalom's in the Kedron Valley (superstructure in the form of a cone with concave sides), as well as various others at Sarsina, Aquileia, etc. (of concave pyramids); J. M. C. Toynbee, *Death and Burial in the Roman World* (London, 1971), Pl. 37, 38, and 70; H. Gabelmann, *Römische Grabbauten der frühen Kaiserzeit* (Stuttgart, 1979), Abb. 11, 12, 14, 18, 31, etc.

For the other monuments, see for example W. Alzinger, *Die Stadt des siebenten Weltwunders . . . Ephesos* (Vienna, 1962), pp. 52 and 86; G. Kleiner, *Die Ruinen von Milet* (Berlin, 1968), Abb. 36, and cf. Abb. 34. For room shapes and décor, other basic components of Roman design, see Boëthius and Ward-Perkins (n. 1, above), pp. 256 and 260–63; MacDonald and Boyle (n. 29, above), pp. 14–16 and 18–19; and the references in nn. 44 and 45, above.

foundations, walls, podia, pedestals, orders, entablatures, mouldings, pediments, niches, exedra-like recesses of curved or rectangular plan, doorways, and sometimes windows, arches, corbels, and vaults; the same is also more or less true of monumental nymphaea and the elaborate walls found in major baths. In the Markets of Trajan, on the other hand, fewer elements were employed; even less in the late antique Curia; and in certain insulae and small-scale baths, fewer still. If the list is broken down into the traditional and the novel, the number of concave forms in the latter category is worth remarking: arch, vault, exedra, hemicycle, apse, and niche. Also interesting is the number of later elements that function with the Orders: pier, niche, pedestal, podium, and, sometimes, the corbel. In Roman architecture old and new were repeatedly juxtaposed, for example, a temple-front with a vaulted space, or columns with an arch. And the Roman habit of multiplying elements—niches, small-scale temple-fronts, mouldings, and vault-shapes, as well as columns and arches—should be noted.

Rearranging this material into the three broad groups mentioned above produces the following lists:

A. *Common to architecture in general*
    Doorway
    Floor
    Foundation
    Roof
    Stair
    Wall
    Window

B. *Greek creations, primarily*
    Entablature
    Moulding
    Orders
    Pier
    Seating (public buildings)
    Temple-front, pediment

C. *Added, or adapted and strongly emphasized, in Roman times*
    Apse
    Arch
    Attic
    Balcony
    Corbel
    Exedra, hemicycle
    Niche
    Pedestal

Plaque
Podium
Terrace
Vault

Keeping in mind the general appearance of the principal ancient building types, and noting that list C contains almost as many items as A and B together, some propositions can be suggested:

1. All ancient buildings are made up of elements from list A which are usually, but not always, found with others from B or C, or from both B and C; the possible combinations are A alone, A plus B, A plus C, and A plus B plus C.

2. The sources from which the design elements of a building derive provide a general guide to its stylistic category; for example, a properly classical Greek building is composed of elements from A and B, whereas at the opposite end of the stylistic spectrum there is a class of neighborhood Roman baths made up entirely of elements from A and C.

3. The proportionate distribution of elements among the three lists can be used to refine stylistic distinctions to a not inconsiderable degree. Given the first proposition, this means that the presence and number of elements from list B, or list C, or both, will be determining factors.

4. For example, in highly scenic structures such as stage buildings and grand civic nymphaea, almost everything on all three lists is used; whereas the plain, undecorated strip insula is made up of elements from A, sometimes in combination with one or two from C but none whatsoever from B. In the first case, the number of features from C is almost as great, or as great, as those from A and B combined; in the second, fewer than a third of the total number of elements appear.

5. All Roman architecture falls between these two polarities, which are the outer boundaries, so to speak, of the broad spectrum of its formal complexities. These boundaries can be defined as follows (the presence of list A elements being assumed in both cases):

   a. Buildings in which all, or nearly all, of the elements in both B and C appear—in other words, with about half of their design elements from C, which *always appear in combination with others from B;* and

   b. Buildings *with no features whatsoever from B* and only one or two, if any, from C.

Applying these propositions can reveal the historical anatomy of Roman imperial architecture in a general but accurate way. The common use of four basic combinations of elements of design from the historical lists defines its main stylistic groups, which are as follows:

> Classical in the Greek sense (no C elements)
>
> Classical in the Roman sense (some, but non-arcuated, C elements—Brendel's Roman classicism)
>
> The vaulted style (elements from all three lists)
>
> A plain, austere style (no B elements and few, if any, from C).

Refinements are needed, for there are some overlapping and borderline cases. For example, the scenic, highly articulated walls spoken of above may stand alone, without vaults, as in certain civic nymphaea. Such structures include almost every element on all three lists but do not readily fall into any of the four categories. However, most buildings fit readily into one group or another, even the most unusual ones, such as those seen at Hadrian's Villa (where all four groups are very much in evidence).

Perhaps the most significant thing about the Roman styles is that all flourished across the Empire in structures large and small. It is almost equally important to note that no style was restricted to a functional category of buildings and that different styles sometimes appear within a single category—baths, for example, or basilicas. Construction methods could vary within styles, as they did to a lesser degree within building types, though this was sometimes due to local traditions and materials.[52] Thus the three Roman styles are commonly found side by side through the provinces, and although one or another may have been the more visible in a given area, no part of the architectural geography of the Empire was dominated by just one of them.

If the dimension of time is added to the lists of design elements, an increase in the complexity of form becomes apparent. This complexity, paralleled by an expansion in the number of building types, grew more or less steadily from about 200 B.C. onward, to be checked somewhat by an increase in the use of the plain or austere style in the third century. The expansion, in Roman times, of the number of design elements is one of the keys to understanding the nature of Roman architecture. These additions to the established classical repertory simultaneously broadened the design base and altered the character of inherited forms, for example, when a pedestal and a ressaut were added to the base, shaft, and capital of the Corinthian Order. It is this kind of crucial change that analysis by design elements quickly identifies, for it takes the measure of the distance between Greek and Roman principles according to the kinds and number of formal elements present. By these means the often cosmetic appliqué of features originally of Greek derivation can be seen not as the result of attempts to make buildings somehow look Greek, but rather as artistic combinations of old and new features as typical of their time as the mixed society that produced

52. On this point see for example, P. Romanelli, *Topografia e archeologia dell'Africa romana* (Turin, 1970; = *Enciclopedia classica*, 3.10.7), Chapter 5; Boëthius and Ward-Perkins (n. 1, above), pp. 386–89; Blake, passim; and Rakob (1976), n. 1, above.

them. And by these means the degree of Roman originality in a building can be gauged; again, this is a quality that can be seen to have increased with time. Here and there in the fabric of Roman architecture a building will appear that is properly Greek, either put up by a patron whose taste ran to anachronisms or commissioned for some venerable Greek site requiring a harmonious design. But Roman buildings of the second group were in no way Greek, however much traditional detail they might carry, and those in the vaulted and austere styles were uncompromisingly modern.

The most important Roman creation was the architecture resulting from the marriage of the Orders with the essentials of the vaulted style, a union that initially might not seem very promising. But by the end of the first century A.D. the combination was well on its way to full maturity, to becoming a major style in its own right with a long and influential career in the history of Western architecture. Even so, the Romans did not move toward a single, clearly pre-eminent kind of architecture: their cities and towns record unequivocally an architecture almost as varied as the society it served and made up of three quite different styles. That the Greeks had one style and the Romans several has caused much confusion, a situation that putting them together in handbooks does little to alleviate. If the artistic supremacy of Greek buildings is assumed as a matter of course, Roman architecture appears contradictory, or worse, degenerate. But the Greek features of imperial architecture were to the whole as the Greeks and their culture were to society at large—an important and highly visible part, but only a part. The buildings analyzed in the preceding chapters make this clear, for in them the Orders dance to a Roman tune. And the Oxford Street façade of Selfridges does indeed have a strong Roman cast and scale, and for the same reason. Whatever their distant origins, these two ways of making architecture, with vaulted spaces and with walls highly articulated by Roman versions of the Orders, were the ones that the Romans, by bringing them to full maturity, made their own.

APPENDIX

PRINCIPAL DIMENSIONS

(IN METERS)

Dimensions in *italics* are approximate. R = Roman feet. The Roman foot is equivalent to 0.295 meters or 11⅝ English inches. The lengths and widths given are usually those between the inside brick facings.

THE PORTICUS AEMILIA (Plates 1 and 2)

>Overall length: 467.00
>Overall width: 60.00
>Individual chambers: *8.00 x 14.00* and *13.00* high

THE MARKET AT FERENTINO (Plate 3)

>The main hall: *4.40 x 24.00*

THE SANCTUARY OF FORTUNE AT PALESTRINA

The Intermediate-level Eastern Hemicycle (Plates 9 and 10)
>Radius of the colonnade: 4.60
>Overall radius: 8.70
>Span of the annular vault: 3.55
>Height of the vault to its crown: 4.60

THE TABULARIUM (Plate 11)

>Length of the façade: 73.60
>Width of the façade arches: 3.60; height, 7.50

THE MAUSOLEUM OF AUGUSTUS (Plate 12)

>Exterior diameter: 87.00
>Maximum height: *44.00*?

THE "TEMPLE OF MERCURY" AT BAIA (Plate 14)

>Interior diameter: 21.55 (73R)
>Interior height presumably the same

THE CLAUDIANUM (Plates 19 and 20)

>The vaulted chambers: 3.55 x 5.20, and 6.60 high

THE DOMUS TRANSITORIA

The Nymphaeum Court under the Domus Flavia (Figure 2)
>Length of the court: *19.00*
>Width of the court: *8.50*
>Length of the "baroque wall" nymphaeum: *11.00*
>Height of the "baroque wall": *1.60*

Remains under the Temple of Venus and Rome (Figure 3)
>Diameter of the rotunda: *8.00*
>Width of the barrel-vaulted corridors: *4.00*

THE ESQUILINE WING OF THE DOMUS AUREA (Plate 24)

>Overall east–west length of the remains: *218.00*
>Range of room heights: 8.00 to 9.60
>Width of the exterior colonnade (number 1 on Plate 24): 4.20 (*14R*) to the column centers
>Rooms 4 and 6: 7.60 x 8.30 (26 x 28R)
>Room 5: 8.70 x 10.60 (30 x 36R)
>Room 7: 6.10 x 8.60 (21 x 29R)
>The interior court at 8: 23.00 x 53.50
>Room 12: 13.20 x 14.10 (45 x 48R)
>Room 16, excluding the niche: 4.00 x 5.00 (*14 x 17R*)
>Room 18: 9.20 x 9.60 (*32R square*)

Room 22 (excluding the niche): 4.30 x 6.50 (*15 x 22R*)

The five-sided court is 47.00 wide at the façade and 31.00 deep

The Octagon (Plate 30)

Diameter of the circumscribed circle: 14.70 (*50R*)

Diameter of the inscribed circle: 13.50 (*46R*)

Height to the lower plane of the oculus: 9.60

Impost height of the central vault: 5.10 (*17R*)

Vertical rise of the vault: 4.50 (*15R*)

Diameter of the oculus: 6.00 (*20R*)

Maximum exterior height of the octagonal system: *11.80* (*40R*)

Room 24, excluding the niche: 4.50 x 6.80 (*15 x 23R*)

Room 25, excluding the niches: 3.70 x 4.60 (*13 x 16R*)

Room 26, excluding the shallow apse: 6.10 x 8.30 (*21 x 28R*)

DOMITIAN'S PALACE

The Four State Halls (Figure 6; see also p. 57)

Minimum interior height of the Vestibule vault, if built: 44.00 (*150R*)
—of the Basilica: 27.00 (*92R*)
—of the Aula Regia: 34.00 (*115R*)
—of the Triclinium: 32.00 (*108R*)

The Palatine buildings (Figure 5)

Total area of A, B, C, and D: 40,000 sq. m.

Difference in height between CD and AB: 10.15 (*34R*)

The Domus Flavia (Plate 40)

Maximum projection of the artificial terrace northeast from the wall of the Aula Regia: *10.00*

Room 6 on Plate 40: 10.20 x 21.30 (*35 x 72R*)

The peristyle, from wall to wall: 52.10 x 58.00 (*176 x 197R*)
—width of the colonnaded portico to the column centers: 5.80 (*20R*)

The nymphaeum at number 7: 4.40 x 12.00 (*15 x 41R*)

Room 8, circumscribed diameter of the octagon: 12.00 (*41R*)

Fountain room at 12, northeast interior wall: 12.10 (*41R*)

—side by the Triclinium: 31.40 (*106R*)
—north–south diagonal: 33.80 (*115R*)

Room 11, excluding the broad southwest recess: 16.60 x 18.60 (*56 x 63R*)

Elliptical fountain in room 12: 9.00 x 16.00 (*30 x 54R*) overall
—at the highest level: 2.35 x 7.70 (*8 x 26R*)

The Domus Augustana, upper level (Plate 40)

The peristyle, from wall to wall: 52.10 x 58.00 (*176 x 197R*)

Room 20, maximum width: *11.00*

Room 22: 7.00 square

Rooms 24 and 25: 8.50 square (*29R*)

Room 27, by column centers: *14.00* x 15.00

The Domus Augustana, lower level (Plate 58)

Width of staircase at 1: 2.60 (*9R*)

Nymphaeum at 2, excluding the corridor and apse at the northeast: 4.80 x 10.90 (*16 x 37R*)

The octagons at 3 and 5, circumscribed diameter: 8.50 (*29R*); height, 9.60 (*33R*)

Room 4: 7.00 square (*24R*)

Corridor 6 width: *2.30*

The peristyle, from wall to wall: 34.00 x 36.00

Room 8, including the extension into the peristyle: 8.00 (*28R*) x *12.20*

Rooms 11 and 13: 5.10 x 10.40 (*17 x 35R*)

Room 12: 2.70 x 4.80 (*9 x 16R*)

Room 15: 11.50 x 13.40 (*39 x 45R*)

Room 17, excluding the niches: 4.60 x 5.50 (*16 x 19R*)

Width of the exedra colonnade, to the column centers: 5.40 (*18R*)

Chord of the exedra colonnade: 80.00

The Hippodromos (Figure 5 and Plate 41)

From wall to wall, but exclusive of the great southeast exedra: 50.00 x 184.00

TRAJAN'S FORUM (Plate 74)

The axes of the Forum as defined by the inner lines of steps and the inside wall of the triumphal arch: 82.00 x 116.00 (*89.00 x 118.00* overall)
—radius of the hemicycles: *21.00*

The Basilica Ulpia, excluding the great apsidal halls: *55.60 x 117.50*
—span of the central nave: 24.20 on centers
—radius of the great apsidal halls: *20.80*
—overall length: *169.00*

TRAJAN'S MARKETS (Figure 7, and Plates 74 and 76)

Section A1

> Span of the bigger semidomed room: *17.70* (60R)
>
> —interior niches, width: 2.10 (7R)
>
> —thickness of façade wall: 0.890 (3R)

Section A2

> Hemicycle diameter: 56.30 (190R)
>
> Height to the top of the level II cornice: 14.30 (49R)
>
> —to the top of the level I cornice: 7.15 (24R)
>
> Height of the restored level I shop-front (Plate 86): 5.70 (*19R*)
>
> —of the doorway: 2.95 (10R)
>
> Most of the level I shops are 2.85 wide and 2.05 deep (*10 x 7R*)
>
> The aediculae of the level II façade rise 5.90 (20R) above the level II cornice, and are 3.50 wide (12R)
>
> level II internal corridor width: 2.25 (8R)
>
> —façade wall thickness: 1.18 (4R)
>
> Most of the level II shops are 3.60 deep x 5.50 wide (12 x 19R)
>
> Level III terrace width: 3.20 (11R)
>
> Level III shop (radial) depth: 4.30 (15R)
>
> Level III shop wall toward the Via Biberatica, thickness: 0.74 (2½R)

Section A3

> Span of the semidomed room: *14.50* (50R)
>
> Shops by the passageway marked K on Plate 74: 3.00 x 5.10

Section B1

> Width of the Via Biberatica at J on Plate 74: 7.40 (25R)
>
> The aula Traiana interior (Plate 89) is 8.80 x 34.00 (30 x 115R), and 11.80 (40R) high
>
> —the transverse bays, with the exception of the northeastern and southwestern ones, average 5.40 (18R) in width between pier centers
>
> —radius of the longitudinal vault surface: 3.75

Section B2

> Maximum height of the remains above the Via Biberatica: 21.00

THE PANTHEON

The (Lost) Forecourt (Figure 8)

> Height of the modern pavement above the ancient pavement at the south end of the court: *1.40*
>
> —at north end of the present Piazza della Rotunda: 4.00?
>
> The court was 55.00 wide if it was the same width as the rotunda, and it was at least 110.00 long

The Porch (Plates 97–99)

> Plan dimensions, including the great niches: 19.20 x 34.70 (65 x 118R)
>
> Height of the columns: 12.50 (42R)
>
> Diameter of the column bases: 1.48 (5R)
>
> Area of roof: 590.00 sq. m.
>
> Height of doors: 6.30 (21R)

The Rotunda, interior (Plates 98 and 105)

> Barrel-vaulted entrance space just south of the doors: 7.70 wide and 17.40 high (27 x 59R)
>
> Volume of the interior: 70,000 cu. m.
>
> The six interior niche-openings are 8.10 x 10.30 (27 x 35R)
>
> Radius of the hemisphere: 21.65 (73.39R)
>
> Diameter of the cylinder, and height to the lower plane of the oculus: 43.30 (146.78R)
>
> Height from the pavement to the upper surface of the level II cornice: 12.70 (43R)
>
> Height from the upper surface of the level II cornice to that of level III: 8.95 (30R)
>
> The maximum chords of the coffers (taken along theoretical lines of intersection determined by planes passing through the vertical center line of the building) decrease from 3.90 (the lowest horizontal ring) to 2.30 (the highest)
>
> The horizontal bands between rows of coffers are 0.80 wide
>
> The radial bands are 0.80 wide at the bottom but decrease in width as they rise
>
> Unobstructed floor area (without subtracting for the aediculae): 1,470 sq. m.

The Rotunda, structure and exterior (Plates 95 and 105)

> Foundation depth: 4.50/5.00 (an additional ring 3.00 wide was added in Hadrian's time or shortly thereafter)
>
> Inclusive radial width of the cylinder: 6.05 (20R)
>
> Width of the exterior cylinder wall: 1.95 (6½R)

The crowns of the key-chamber semidomes reach within *3.00* of the next level above

The great conical vaults between levels II and III are *1.60* thick and span *8.95* on the interior and *11.60* on the exterior

—those between levels III and IV are 1.20 (4R) thick, span the same distances, but are stepped down under the level IV exterior cornice *1.20* (Plate 105)

The exterior "relieving" arches span *5.00*

The exterior level II cornice is *0.65* below the level II interior cornice

Height between the level III and level IV exterior cornices: *8.20*

The level IV exterior (sloping) terrace is *3.80* (*13R*) wide radially

The original cylindrical wall of the first step-ring is *1.80* (6R) high

The middle five step-rings average 0.90 in height and 0.80 in radial width

The dome above the uppermost step-ring is 1.40 (5R) thick radially (disregarding the coffers); it is covered with a layer of pozzolana cement 0.15 thick

The diameter of the oculus is 8.92 (*30R*)

—area: 62.80 sq. m.

—bronze flashing: 1.75 (6R) wide radially

SELECTED BIBLIOGRAPHY

THE footnotes should be consulted for additional references to the subjects and monuments discussed, as this selection does not include all the titles cited there. For full citations of short titles used here, see the List of Abbreviations on pp. xix–xxi. The entries are arranged under the following headings:

Bibliographies
Texts and Other Non-architectural
    Sources
Handbooks and General Works
Studies of Particular Periods
Italian Sites outside Rome
Rome

Building Types and Forms
Architects and Builders
Materials and Technology
Architecture and the State
Décor
Design and Meaning

BIBLIOGRAPHIES

(see also below, Boëthius and Ward-Perkins, under HANDBOOKS)

Crema. (Index of modern authors, pp. 643–51.)

Fasti archeologici, 1946 (pub. 1948) ff. (Annual of archaeological bibliography; author indices.)

Mostra augustea della romanità, Catologo, Appendice bibliografica, Rome, 1938. (This exhibition, with additions, today comprises the Museo della civiltà romana; see below, Pietrangeli, under HANDBOOKS).

Robertson, D. S., *A Handbook of Greek and Roman Architecture,* corrected 2nd ed. Cambridge, 1945 (pp. 347–78 and addenda [see p. xi]). Reprinted, New York, 1969.

Rounds, D., *Articles on Antiquity in Festschriften,* Cambridge, Mass., 1962. (Thorough index of articles published through 1954.)

TEXTS AND OTHER NON-ARCHITECTURAL SOURCES

Bartoli, A., *I monumenti antichi di Roma nei disegni degli Uffizi di Firenze,* 6 vols. Rome/Florence, 1914–22.

Becatti, *Arte e gusto negli scrittori latini,* Florence, 1951.

Bourne. (Texts and inscriptions of the first century A.D.)

De Ruggiero, E., *Dizionario epigrafico di antichità romane,* Rome, 1895 ff.

Donaldson, T. L., *Architectura Numismatica; or, Architectural Medals of Classical Antiquity,* London, 1859. Reprinted, Chicago, 1966.

Fasolo, V., "Rappresentazioni architettoniche nella pittura romana," *Atti, 3,* 207–13.

FUR. (Much useful material in addition to that on the marble plan itself.)

Piranesi, G. B., *Le antichità romane,* 4 vols. Rome, 1756. (Later Rome and Paris editions and selections; cf. W. L. MacDonald, *Piranesi's Carceri: Sources of Invention,* Northampton, Mass., 1979.)

Pollitt, J. J., *The Art of Rome, c. 753 B.C.–337 A.D.,* New York, 1966.

Promis, C., "Vocaboli latini di architettura posteriori a Vitruvio oppure a lui sconosciuti," *Reale accademia delle scienze di Torino, Memorie, 28* (1876), 207–450.

Rostovtzeff, M. I., "Der hellenistisch-römische Architekturlandschaft," *RM, 26* (1911), 1–186.

Vitruvius, *De architectura libri decem.* (English translations by M. H. Morgan, Cambridge, Mass., 1914, and by F. Granger in the Loeb Classical Library, 2 vols. 1931–34; Morgan's is more satisfactory.) See also:

Boëthius, A., "Vitruvius and the Roman Architecture of his Age," ΔΡΑΓΜΑ, *Martino P. Nilsson . . . dedicatum,* Lund, 1939, pp. 114–43.

Brown, F. E., "Vitruvius and the Liberal Art of Architecture," *Bucknell Review, 11.4* (1963), 99–107.

Choisy, A., *Vitruve,* 4 vols. Paris, 1909.

Nohl, H., *Index Vitruvianus,* Leipzig, 1876. Reprinted, Rome, 1962.

Zorzi. (Palladio's drawings of ancient buildings.)

HANDBOOKS AND GENERAL WORKS

(see also below, DESIGN AND MEANING)

Anderson, W. J., R. P. Spiers, and T. Ashby, *The Architecture of Ancient Rome,* London, 1927.

Atti, 3 (also entitled *Saggi sull'architettura etrusca e Romana*).

Bettini, S., *L'architettura di San Marco,* Padua, 1946 (four chapters on Roman architecture).

Bloch. (Tables of dates of buildings in and near Rome as determined by brick stamps, pp. 348–50; see also Bloch's article in *AJA, 63* [1959], 225–40, on the brick stamps of A.D. 123.)

Boëthius. (Chapters 3 and 4 are on the Domus Aurea and the insula.)

———— "Roman Architecture from Its Classicistic to Its Late Imperial Phase," *Göteborgs Högskolas Årsskrift, 47.8* (1941).

———— "Three Roman Contributions to World Architecture," *Festschrift J. Arvid Hedvall,* Göteborg, 1948, pp. 59–74.

———— and J. B. Ward-Perkins, *Etruscan and Roman Architecture,* Harmondsworth, 1970.

Brown, F. E., "Roman Architecture," *College Art Journal, 17* (1958), 105–14.

———— *Roman Architecture,* New York, 1961.

Cagnat, R., and V. Chapot, *Manuel d'archéologie romaine,* I, Paris, 1916.

Crema.

———— *Significato della architettura romana. . . ,* Rome, 1959 (= *BollCentro, 15*).

Daremberg, C., and E. Saglio, *Dictionnaire des antiquités grecques et romaines,* Paris, 1877 ff.

Durm.

Enciclopedia dell'arte antica, 9 vols. Rome, 1958 ff. (Architects, building types, sites, etc.)

Giedion, S., *Architecture and the Phenomena of Transition, The Three Space Conceptions in Architecture,* Cambridge, Mass., 1971

Kähler, H., *Rom und sein Imperium,* Baden-Baden, 1962. (An English version was published in New York in 1963 as *The Art of Rome and her Empire.*)

Kaschnitz von Weinberg, G., *Die Baukunst im Kaiserreich,* Reinbek bei Hamburg, 1963 (= *Römische Kunst, 4;* introductory).

Lundberg, E., *Arkitekturens Formspråk, 2,* Stockholm, 1951.

Noack, F., *Die Baukunst des Altertums,* Berlin, 1910.

Pietrangeli, C., et al., *Museo della civiltà romana, Catologo,* Rome, 1958.

Rakob, F., "Römische Architektur," in T. Kraus, ed., *Das Römische Weltreich,* Berlin, 1967 (= *Propyläen Kunstgeschichte, 2*).

Rivoira (see above, Chap. 1, n. 42). Reprinted, New York, 1973.

Robertson, D. S. (see the entry above, under BIBLIOGRAPHIES).

Rodenwaldt, G., "Art from Nero to the Antonines," *CAH, 11,* 775–805.

———— "Römische Staatsarchitektur," *Das neue Bild der Antike,* ed. H. Berve, 2 (Leipzig, 1952), 356–73.

Van Deman, E. B., "Methods of Determining the Date of Roman Concrete Monuments," *AJA, 16* (1912), 230–51, 387–432.

Van Essen, C. C., *Précis d'histoire de l'art antique en Italie,* Brussels, 1960 (= *Collection Latomus, 42;* cf. the review in *Gnomon, 33* [1961], 207).

Von Gerkan, A., *Von antiker Architektur und Topographie,* Stuttgart, 1959. (Collected articles and essays.)

Ward Perkins, J. B., "The Italian Element in Late Roman and Early Medieval Architecture," *Proceedings of the British Academy, 33* (1947), 163–94.

———— *Roman Architecture,* New York, 1977.

———— "Roman Concrete and Roman Palaces," *The Listener, 56* (1956), 701–03.

———— *Roman Imperial Architecture,* announced in 1978 (a revision of Parts II–IV of Boëthius and Ward-Perkins, above).

Wheeler, M., *Roman Art and Architecture,* London and New York, 1964. (Popular.)

STUDIES OF PARTICULAR PERIODS

Boëthius. (Chapters 3 and 4 deal with the first and second centuries.)

Brown, F. E., "Hadrianic Architecture," in *Essays in Memory of Karl Lehmann,* New York, 1964, 55–58.

Delbrueck, R., *Hellenistische Bauten in Latium,* 2 vols. Strassburg, 1907. (Palestrina, Tivoli, Cori, the Tabularium, etc.)

Fasolo, F., and G. Gullini, *Il santuario della Fortuna Primigenia a Palestrina,* 2 vols. Rome, 1953. (The Tabularium and the sanctuaries at Tivoli and Terracina, etc., as well as Palestrina.)

Frank, T., *Roman Buildings of the Republic. . .*, Rome, 1924 (= *Papers and Monographs of the American Academy in Rome, 3*).

Gullini, G., *L'architettura romana della fine della repubblica*, Turin, 1962. (Lectures.)

Kähler. (Fundamental for Hadrianic architecture.)

Lugli, G., "Nuove forme dall'architettura romana nell'età dei Flavi," *Atti, 3*, 95–102.

Paribeni, R., *Optimus Princeps, 2* (Messina, 1927), 23–149. (Trajan's works.)

Van Essen, C. C., *Sulla als Bouwheer*, Groningen, 1940.

Von Blanckenhagen, P. H., *Flavische Architektur und Ihre Dekoration*, Berlin, 1940.

ITALIAN SITES OUTSIDE ROME

ALBANO

Lugli, G., "La Villa di Domiziano sui colli Albani," four articles in *BC, 45–48* (1917–20; also collected and printed separately).

Tortorici, E., *Castra Albana*, Rome, 1975.

BAIA

Borriello, M., and A. D'Ambrosio, *Baiae-Misenum*, Florence, 1979.

I campi flegrei, Rome, 1977 (= *Atti dei convegni Lincei, 33*).

D'Ancora, G., *Guida ragionata per le antichità . . . di Pozzuoli e luoghi circonvicini*, Naples, 1792. (Based on Paoli, cited below.)

Maiuri, A., *I campi flegrèi*, 3rd ed. Rome, 1958. (Plan of the excavations, pp. 70–71.)

——— "Il restauro di una sala termale a Baia," *BdA, 10* (1931), 241–52. (The "Temple of Mercury.")

——— "Terme di Baia. Scavi, restauri, e lavori di sistemazione," *BdA, 36* (1951), 359–64.

Paoli, P. A., *Antiquitatum Puteolis, Cumis, Bais existentium reliquiae*, Naples, 1768.

Rakob, F., "Litus beatae veneris aurem. Untersuchungen am 'Venustempel' in Baiae," *RM, 68* (1961), 114–49. (Hadrianic domed buildings.)

THE CAMPAGNA

Ashby, T., *The Roman Campagna in Classical Times*, London and New York, 1927. Reprinted, London and New York, 1970.

Tomassetti, G. and F., *La Campagna romana antica, medioevale e moderna*, 4 vols. Rome, 1910–26. Reprinted, Sala Bolognese, 1976.

CAMPANIA

Brion, M., *Pompeii and Herculaneum*, London, 1960. (Bibliography, pp. 231–32.)

Crova, B., "Le terme romane nella Campania," *Atti, 8*, 271–91.

D'Arms, J., *Romans on the Bay of Naples*, Cambridge, Mass., 1970.

De Franciscis, A., and R. Pane, *Mausolei romani in Campania*, Naples, 1957. (Important drawings and photographs.)

Maiuri, A. (see above under BAIA).

Salinas, R., "Le cupole nell'architettura della Campania," *Atti, 8*, 289–91.

CAPRI

Maiuri, A., *Capri, storia e monumenti*, Rome, 1956.

CIVITAVECCHIA

Bastianelli, S., *Centumcellae (Civitavecchia) Castrum Novum (Torre Chiaruccia)*, Rome, 1954.

FERENTINO

Bartoli, A., "L'acropoli di Ferentino," *BdA, 4* (1949), 293–99.

Boëthius, A., and N. Carlgren, "Die spätrepublikanischen Warenhäuser in Ferentino und Tivoli," *ActaArch, 3* (1932), 181–93.

Gullini, G., "I monumenti dell'acropoli di Ferentino," *ArchClass, 6* (1954), 185–216.

HERCULANEUM

Maiuri, A., *Ercolano. I nuovi scavi (1927–1958)*, 2 vols. Rome, 1958.

ISOLA SACRA

Calza, G., *La necropoli del porto di Roma nell'Isola Sacra*, Rome, 1940.

MINORI

Schiavo, A., "La villa romana di Minori," *Palladio, 3* (1939), 129–33.

OSTIA

Calza, R., and E. Nash, *Ostia*, Florence, 1959.

Meiggs, 2nd ed., 1973. (Fundamental; includes Porto.)

Ostia. (The first volume of the official excavation report; nine more had appeared by 1980.)

Paschetto, L., *Ostia colonia romana*, Rome, 1912.

Thatcher, E. D., "The Open Rooms of the Terme del Foro at Ostia," *MAAR, 24* (1956), 168–264.

PALESTRINA

Fasolo, F., and G. Gullini (see above, under STUDIES OF PARTICULAR PERIODS).

Kähler, H., "Das Fortunaheiligtum von Palestrina Praeneste," *Annales Universitatis Saraviensis* (1958), pp. 189–240.

Lugli, G., "Nota sul santuario della Fortuna Prenestina," *ArchClass*, 6 (1954), 133–47.

Muzzioli, P. A., *Praeneste. Pars Altera*, Rome, 1970.

POMPEII

Brion, M. (see above under CAMPANIA).

Coarelli, F., et al., *Guida archeologica di Pompei*, Verona, 1976.

Maiuri, A., *L'ultima fase edilizia di Pompeii*, Rome, 1942.

PORTO

Lugli, G., and G. Filibeck, *Il porto di Roma imperiale e l'agro portuense*, Rome, 1935.

Scrinari, V., "Strutture portuali relative al 'porto di Claudio' messo in luce . . .," *Rassegna dei lavori pubblici*, 3 (1960), unpaginated.

Testaguzza, O., *Portus*, Rome, 1970.

POZZUOLI

(see also above, CAMPANIA)

Maiuri, A., *Studi e ricerche sull'anfiteatro flavio puteolano*, Naples, 1955 (= *Accademia di archeologia, lettere e belli arti di Napoli, Memorie*, 3).

TERRACINA

Lugli, G., *Anxur-Tarracina*, Rome, 1926.

TIVOLI

Aurigemma, S., *Villa Adriana*, Rome, 1961. (Bibliography, and lists of restoration drawings and vedute, pp. 203–06.)

Boëthius, A., and N. Carlgren (see above under FERENTINO).

Carducci, C., *Tibur*, Rome, 1940.

Clark, E., *Rome and a Villa*, New York, 1952. (Part II: Hadrian's Villa.)

Giuliani, C. F., *Tibvr, Pars prima*, Rome, 1970.

———— *Tibvr. Pars altera*, Rome, 1966.

Gusman, P., *La villa impériale de Tibur*, Paris, 1904.

Hansen, E., *La "Piazza d'Oro" e la sua cupola*, Copenhagen, 1960 (= *Analecta romana instituti Danici, Supplementum, I*; see the critical review in *Gnomon*, 33 [1961], 243–50).

Herter, H., "Die Rundform in Platons *Atlantis* und Ihre Nachwirkung in der Villa Adriana," *Rheinisches Museum für Philologie*, 96 (1953), 1–20.

Kähler. (The fundamental modern study of the Villa.)

MacDonald, W. L., and B. M. Boyle, "The Small Baths at Hadrian's Villa," *JSAH*, 39.1, 1980, 5–27.

Ricerche sull'Architettura di Villa Adriana, Rome, 1975. (= *Quaderni dell'istituto di topografia antica*, 8.)

Vighi, R., *Villa Hadriana*, Rome, 1959. (An illustrated guidebook, trans. J. B. Ward Perkins.)

Winnefeld, H., *Die Villa des Hadrian bei Tivoli*, Berlin, 1895 (= *JDAI, Ergänzungsheft*, 3).

ROME

(see also above, *Mostra augustea*, under BIBLIOGRAPHIES; Bartoli, Piranesi, and Zorzi, under TEXTS; and Pietrangeli, under HANDBOOKS)

Boëthius, A., "The Neronian *'nova urbs.'* Notes on Tacitus' *Annales* . . .," *Skrifter utgivna av Svenska Institutet i Rom*, 2, 1932 (= *Corolla archaeologica . . . Gustavo Adolpho dedicata*), 84–97.

Castagnoli, F., et al., *Topografia e urbanistica di Roma*, Bologna, 1958 (= *Storia di Roma*, 22).

Coarelli, F., *Guida archeologica di Roma*, Verona, 1975.

Desgodetz, A., *Les édifices antiques de Rome*, 2nd ed. Paris, 1779. (Detailed drawings of major buildings; 1st ed., Paris, 1682; other versions pub. London [1771/95, 1848] and Rome [1822]; 1st ed. reprinted, Westmead, 1969.)

Dudley, D. R., *Urbs Roma*, London, 1967.

de Fine Licht, K., *The Rotunda in Rome*, Copenhagen, 1968.

Gatti, G., "Caratteristiche edilizie di un quartiere di Roma del II secolo d. Cr.," *Quaderni, 31–48* (1961; = *Fest. V. Fasolo*), 49–66.

Guattani, G. A., various pioneering works (*Roma antica, Roma descritta ed illustrata, Monumenti antichi inediti*) published in Rome and Bologna from the 1780s onward.

Jordan, H., *Topographie der Stadt Rom im Altertum*, I, parts 1 and 2, and II, Berlin, 1871–85; I, part 3, rev. by C. Huelsen, Berlin, 1907. Reprinted, in 2 vols., Rome, 1970.

Lanciani. (Still a useful introduction to the ancient city.)

———— *Ancient Rome in the Light of Recent Discoveries*, London, n.d.

———— "Segni di terremoti negli edifici di Roma antica," *BC*, 45 (1917), 3–28.

Lugli, *Roma*. (Detailed handbook of the central monuments; includes bibliographies.)

———— *Fontes ad topographiam veteris urbis Romae pertinentes*, Rome, 1952 ff. (Inscriptions and texts, by regions.)

———— *I monumenti antichi di Roma e suburbio*, 3 vols. and a *Supplemento*, Rome, 1930–40. (Lugli's *Roma* is a later, augmented version of Vol. I.)

———— *Itinerario di Roma antica*, Milan, 1970.

MacDonald, W. L., *The Pantheon—Design, Meaning, and Progeny*, Cambridge, Mass., and Harmondsworth, 1976.

Middleton, J. H., *The Remains of Ancient Rome*, 2 vols. London, 1892. (Still useful; basically archaeological.)

Nash. (1300 illustrations; expands and updates the bibliographical entries in Platner-Ashby; there is a German edition; revised English ed., 1968.)

Nibby, A., *Roma nell'anno MDCCCXXXVIII, Parte II, Antica*, Rome, 1839.

Platner-Ashby. (To be used in conjunction with Nash.)

Tamm. (The Palatine.)

Werner, P. C., *De incendiis urbis Romae aetate imperatorum. . .* , Leipzig, 1906.

BUILDING TYPES AND FORMS

(see also above, ITALIAN SITES: De Franciscis and Pane, under CAMPANIA, and Herter, under TIVOLI; and below, Smith, under DESIGN AND MEANING)

Altmann, W., *Die italischen Rundbauten*, Berlin, 1906.

Bieber, M., *The History of the Greek and Roman Theater*, 2nd ed. Princeton, 1961.

Boëthius. (Chapter 4: the insula.)

———— "The Reception Halls of the Roman Emperors," *Annual of the British School at Athens*, 46 (1951), 25–31.

———— and R. M. Riefstahl, "Appunti sul Mercato di Traiano," *Roma*, 9 (1931), 447–58, 501–14; 10 (1932), 159–70.

Callmer, C., "Antike Bibliotheken," *OpusArch*, 3 (1944), 145–68.

Chiolini, P., *I Caratteri distributivi degli antichi edifici*, Milan, 1959.

De Gregori, G., "Biblioteche dell'antichità," *Accademia e biblioteche d'Italia*, 11, no. 1/2 (1937).

Derand, F., *L'architecture des voûtes, ou l'art des traits, et coupe des voûtes*, Paris, 1643.

Girri, G., *La taberna nel quadro urbanistica e sociale di Ostia*, Rome, 1956.

Goethals, E., *Arcs, voûtes, coupoles*, 2 vols. Brussels, 1947.

Hornbostel-Hüttner, G., *Studien zur römischen Nischenarchitektur*, Leiden, 1979 (= *Studies of the Dutch Archaeological Society*, 9).

Krencker, D., et al., *Die Trierer Kaiserthermen*, Augsburg, 1929. (Descriptions, with plans, of baths throughout the Empire.)

Laurenzi, L., "L'origine della copertura voltata e la storia della cupola," *Arte antica e moderna*, 3 (1958), 203–15.

Lugli, G., "Considerazione sull'origine dell'arco a conci radiali," *Palladio*, 2 (1952), 9–31.

Maiuri, A., "L'origine del portico ad arche girate su colonne," *Palladio*, 1 (1937), 121–24.

———— "Portico e peristilo," *Parola del passato*, 1 (1946), 306–22.

Makowiecka, E., *The Origin and Evolution of Architectural Form of Roman Library*, Warsaw, 1978.

Neuerburg, N., *L'architettura delle fontane e dei ninfei nell'Italia antica*, Naples, 1965 (= *Memorie dell'Accademia . . . di Napoli*, 5).

Rakob, F., "Hellenismus in Mittelitalien. Bautypen und Bautechnik," in *Hellenismus in Mittelitalien*, ed. P. Zanker, 2 (Göttingen, 1976), 366–86 (= *Abhandlungen der Akademie der Wissenschaften in Göttingen, Phil.-Hist. Klasse*, 97/II).

Smith, E. B., *The Dome*, Princeton, 1950.

Swoboda, K. M., "Palazzi antichi e medioevali," *BollCentro*, 11 (1957), 3–32.

———— *Römische und romanische Paläste*, 3rd ed. Vienna, 1969.

Tamm. (Reception halls; the niche and the apse.)

Tosi, G., "Il palazzo principesco dall'arcaismo greco alla Domus Flavia," *Arte antica e moderna*, 7 (1959), 241–60.

Van Aken, A. R. A., *Nieuwe Wegen in de romeinische Woningbouw van Sulla tot Domitians*, Utrecht, 1943.

Ward Perkins, J. B., "Constantine and the Origins of the Christian Basilica," *PBSR*, 22 (1954), 68–69. (Role of the Domus Flavia basilica.)

ARCHITECTS AND BUILDERS

(see also above, Brown, under TEXTS [Vitruvius])

Bianchi Bandinelli, R., "Apollodoros di Damasco," *Enciclopedia dell'arte antica*, 1, 477–80.

Briggs, M. S., *The Architect in History*, Oxford, 1927. (Esp. pp. 28–52; reprinted, New York, 1974.)

Clarke, M. L., "The Architects of Greece and Rome," *Architectural History*, 6 (1963), 9–22.

Cultrera, G., "Apollodoro di Damasco," *EncIt, 3,* 680–81.

Dickinson, H. W., "A Brief History of Draughtsmen's Instruments," *Transactions of the Newcomen Society,* 27 (1949–51), 73–83.

Downey, G., "Byzantine Architects, Their Training and Methods," *Byzantion, 18* (1946–48), 99–118. (Much useful information.)

Frothingham, A. L., "The Architect in History, II, Roman Architects," *The Architectural Record, 25* (1909), 179–92, 281–303.

MacDonald, W. L., "Roman Architects," in *The Architect. Chapters in the History of the Profession,* ed. S. Kostof, New York, 1977, 28–58.

Martin, R., "Apollodorus of Damascus," *Encyclopedia of World Art, I,* cols. 511–14.

Martin, T. H., *Recherches sur la vie et les ouvrages d'Héron d'Alexandrie,* Paris, 1854 (= *Mémoires présentés . . . à l'Académie des inscriptions et belles lettres, 4).*

Paribeni, "Apollodoro di Damasco," *Atti della reale accademia d'Italia, Rendiconti,* 7.4 (1943), 124–30.

Promis, C., "Gli architetti e l'architettura presso i romani," *Reale accademia delle scienze di Torino, Memorie,* 27 (1873), 1–187.

Rivoira, G. T., "Di Adriano architetto e dei monumenti adrianei," *Reale accademia dei Lincei, Rendiconti, 18* (1909), 172–77.

Toynbee, J. M. C., *Some Notes on Artists in the Roman World,* Brussels, 1951 (= *Collection Latomus,* 6). (Architects, pp. 9–15.)

MATERIALS AND TECHNOLOGY

(see also above, Van Deman, under HANDBOOKS; Thatcher, under ITALIAN SITES, OSTIA; Middleton, under ROME; Derand, Goethals, and Rakob, under BUILDING TYPES; and below, Berucci, under DESIGN)

Berriman, A. E., *Historical Metrology,* London and New York, 1953.

Blake, *1* and *2.*

——— Vol. *3: Roman Construction in Italy from Nerva through the Antonines,* ed. D. T. Bishop, Philadelphia, 1973.

Bloch, H., "The Roman Brick Industry and Its Relationship to Roman Architecture," *JSAH, 1* (1941), 3–8.

Choisy, A., *L'art de bâtir chez les romains,* Paris, 1873.

Cohen, M. R., and I. E. Drabkin, *A Source Book in Greek Science,* 2nd ed. Cambridge, Mass., 1958. (See esp. pp. 314–51. There is a valuable review

in *The Journal of the History of Ideas, 13* [1952], where on pp. 579–85 the changing modern evaluation of ancient technology is discussed.)

Corsi, F., *Delle pietre antiche,* Rome, 1845.

Cozzo, G., *Ingegneria romana,* Rome, 1928.

Crema, L., "La volta nell'architettura romana," *L'Ingegnere, 16* (1942), 941–52.

Davey, N., *A History of Building Materials,* London, 1961.

De Angelis d'Ossat, G., "La forma e la costruzione della cupola nell'architettura romana," *Atti, 3,* 223–50.

Drachmann, A. G., *The Mechanical Technology of Greek and Roman Antiquity,* Copenhagen, 1963.

Gest, A. P., *Engineering,* New York, 1930 (in the series *Our Debt to Greece and Rome).*

Giovannoni. (Bibliography up to the 1920s cited in the notes.)

——— "Building and Engineering," in *The Legacy of Ancient Rome,* ed. C. Bailey (Oxford, 1951), pp. 429–74. (A readily accessible version of the book cited immediately above.)

——— "La tecnica costruttiva e l'impero di Roma," *L'Ingegnere, 12* (1938), 299–307.

Gnoli, R., *Marmora romana,* Rome, 1971.

Guerra, G., *Statica e tecnica costruttiva delle cupole antiche e moderne,* Naples, 1958.

Hultsch, F., *Griechische und römische Metrologie,* Berlin, 1882.

Kretzschmer, F., *Bilddokumente römischer Technik,* 3rd ed. Düsseldorf, 1967.

Lugli, *Tecnica.* (Critical bibliography, *1,* 9–23.) Reprinted, New York, 1968.

——— "La terminologia dei sistemi costruttivi usati dai romani," *Accademia dei Lincei, Rendiconti, 5* (1950), 297–306.

MacDonald, W. L., "Some Implications of Later Roman Construction," *JSAH, 17* (1958), 2–8.

Mainstone, R., *Developments in Structural Form,* London, 1975.

I marmi italiani, Rome, 1939.

Merckel, C., *Die Ingenieurtechnik im Alterthum,* Berlin, 1899.

Milani, G. B., *L'ossatura murale: studio statico-costruttivo ed estetico-proporzionale degli organismo architettonici . . . , I,* Turin, 1920.

Neuberger, A., *Die Technik des Altertums,* 4th ed. Leipzig, n.d.

Roccatelli, C., "Brick in Roman Antiquity," in *Brickwork in Italy,* ed. G. C. Mars (Chicago, 1925), pp. 1–46.

Van Deman, E. B., *The Building of the Roman Aqueducts,* Washington, 1934.

Venanzi, C., *Caratteri costruttivi dei monumenti, I, Strutture murarie a Roma e nel Lazio, parte prima,* Rome, 1953.

Ward Perkins, J. B., "Notes on the Structure and Building Methods of Early Byzantine Architecture," in *The Great Palace of the Byzantine Emperors, Second Report,* ed. D. T. Rice (Edinburgh, 1958), pp. 52–102.

ARCHITECTURE AND THE STATE

(see also above, Rodenwaldt, under HANDBOOKS)

Bammer, A., *Architektur und Gesellschaft in der Antike,* Vienna, 1974.

De Ruggiero, E., *Lo stato e le opere pubbliche in Roma antica,* Turin, 1925.

ESAR. (Vol. 5 is titled *Rome and Italy of the Empire;* Vol. 6 is a thorough index to the entire work.)

MacMullen, R., "Roman Imperial Building in the Provinces," *Harvard Studies in Classical Philology,* 64 (1959), 207–35. (Good on architecture and the army.)

Rostovtzeff. (Exhaustive documentation, detailed index.)

DECOR

(see also below, Lehmann, under DESIGN AND MEANING)

Ashby, T., "Drawings of Ancient Paintings in English Collections," *PBSR,* 7 (1914), 1–62.

Becatti, G., *Mosaici e pavimenti marmorei,* 2 vols. Rome, 1961 (= *Scavi di Ostia,* 4).

Blake, M. E., "The Pavements of the Roman Buildings of the Republic and Early Empire," *MAAR,* 8 (1930), 1–159.

——— "Roman Mosaics of the Second Century in Italy," *MAAR,* 13 (1936), 67–214.

Borda, M., *La pittura romana,* Milan, 1958.

Curtius, L., *Die Wandmalerei Pompejis,* Leipzig, 1929.

Dohrn, T., "Crustae," *RM,* 72 (1965), 127–41.

Dorigo, W., *Late Roman Painting,* London, 1971.

Herbig, R., *Nugae Pompeianorum,* Tübingen, 1962.

Lehmann, P. W., *Roman Wall Paintings from Boscoreale in the Metropolitan Museum of Art,* Cambridge, Mass., 1951.

Ling, R., articles on Roman stucco, in *PBSR, 34* (1966) and ff.

Nogara, B., *I mosaici antichi conservati nei palazzi pon-tifici del Vaticano e del Laterano,* Milan, 1910.

Sear, F. B., *Roman Wall and Vault Mosaics,* Heidelberg, 1977 (= *RM, Ergänzungsheft,* 23).

Wadsworth, E. L., "Stucco Reliefs of the First and Second Centuries Still Extant in Rome," *MAAR,* 4 (1924), 9–102.

White, J., *Perspective in Ancient Drawing and Painting,* London, 1956.

Wirth, F., *Römische Wandmalerei vom Untergang Pompejis bis ans Ende des 3. Jh.,* Berlin, 1934.

DESIGN AND MEANING

(see also above, HANDBOOKS AND GENERAL WORKS; Herter, under ITALIAN SITES, TIVOLI; and Milani, under MATERIALS AND TECHNOLOGY)

Berucci, M., "Esperienze costruttive ed estetiche dall' architettura romana," *BollCentro,* 6 (1952), 3–5.

——— "Ragioni statiche ed estetiche delle proporzioni degli ambiente coperti a volta," *BollCentro, 12* (1958), 25–34.

Bettini, S., *Lo spazio architettonico da Roma a Bisanzio,* Bari, 1978.

Drerup, H., "Bildraum und Realraum in der römischen Architektur," *RM,* 66 (1959), 147–74.

Hautecoeur, L., *Mystique et architecture, Symbolisme du cercle et de la coupole,* Paris, 1944.

Lehmann, K., "The Dome of Heaven," *AB,* 27 (1945), 1–27. Reprinted in *Modern Perspectives in Western Art History,* ed. W. E. Kleinbauer, New York, 1971, 227–70.

——— "Piranesi as Interpreter of Roman Architecture," *Piranesi* (an exhibition catalogue with articles), Northampton, Mass., 1961, pp. 88–98.

Riegl, A., *Die spätrömische Kunstindustrie,* Vienna, 1901. (The first chapter, on architecture, is fundamental. There is an Italian ed. entitled *Industria artistica tardoromana,* Florence, 1953.)

Smith, E. B., *Architectural Symbolism of Imperial Rome and the Middle Ages,* Princeton, 1956. (The city gate, the baldachin form, palaces.)

Von Kaschnitz-Weinberg, G., *Die Mittelmeerischen Grundlagen der antiken Kunst,* Frankfurt-am-Main, 1944. (Summarizes the author's pioneering studies of inherent Mediterranean attitudes toward form; see above, Chap. 5, n. 61.)

——— "Vergleichende Studien zur italisch-römischen Struktur, I, Baukunst," *RM, 59* (1944, pub. 1948), 89–128. (Attitudes in Italy toward form and space seen as constant from the earliest times.)

INDEX

(Monuments in Rome are indexed directly)

PLATES

1a. The Porticus Aemilia, "air" view of model at the Museo della civiltà romana

1b. The same, façade toward the Tiber

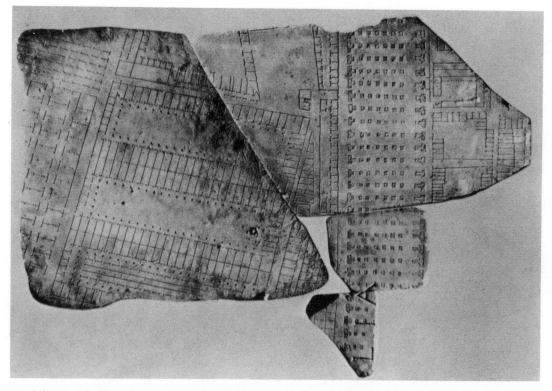

2a.   *The Marble Plan of Rome, fragment showing the Porticus Aemilia and, left, the Horrea Galbae*

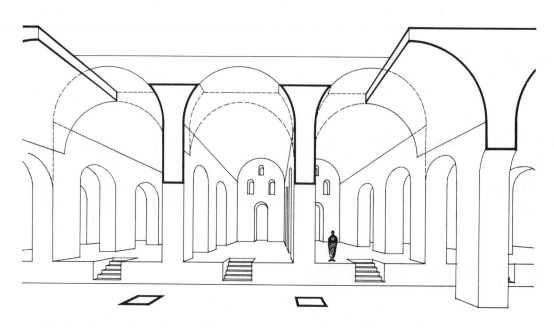

2b.   *Idealized restoration of several units of the Porticus Aemilia*

3. The Market at Ferentino

4. *The Sanctuary of Hercules at Tivoli, detail of construction*

5. *The Sanctuary of Hercules at Tivoli, an arcade*

6. *The Temple of Jupiter at Terracina, an arcade*

7. *The Sanctuary of Fortune at Palestrina*

8. *The Sanctuary of Fortune at Palestrina, model*

9. *The Sanctuary of Fortune at Palestrina, one of the minor hemicycles*

10a. The Sanctuary of Fortune at Palestrina, detail of a minor hemicycle vault

10b. Section of a minor hemicycle

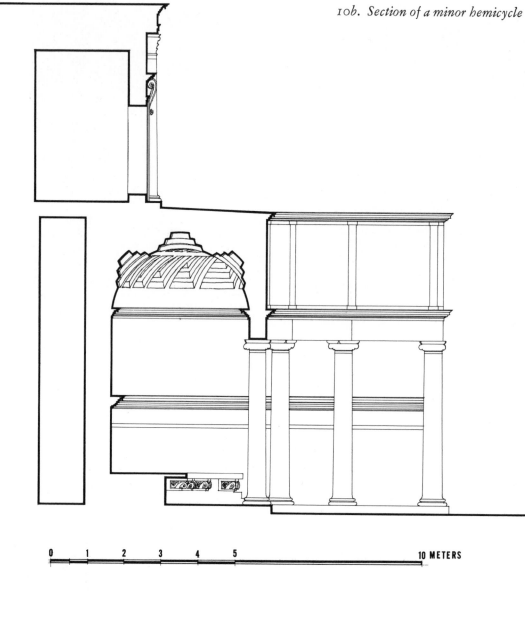

0 1 2 3 4 5   10 METERS

11. *The Tabularium, façade*

12a. The Mausoleum of Augustus,
interior

12b. Exterior

13. The tomb of L. Munatius Plancus at Gaeta, interior

14a. The "Temple of Mercury" at Baia, section of the vault structure

14b. Exterior from above

15. *The Domus Tiberiana with later additions beside the Clivus Victoriae*

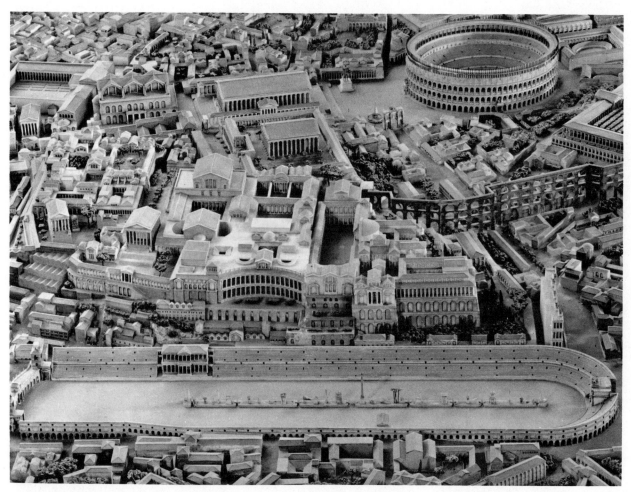

16. *Model of Rome at the Museo della civiltà romana, detail of the Palatine*

17. The Porta Maggiore, exterior

18. The portico of Claudius at Porto, detail of a column

19. *The Claudianum, terrace arcade*

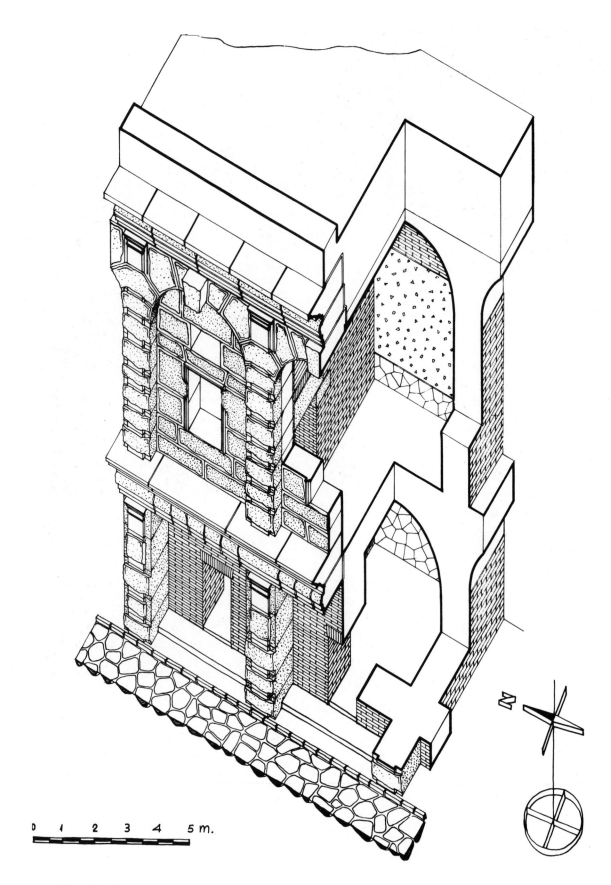

0 1 2 3 4 5 m.

20. *The Claudianum, analytical drawing of two bays of the terrace arcade*

21a. Nymphaeum of the Domus Transitoria under the Domus Flavia, showing foundation wall of the Domus Aurea at the far left

21b. Remains of the Domus Aurea by the Basilica of Maxentius and Constantine

22. *The Baths of Trajan and the site of the Domus Aurea Esquiline wing from the air*

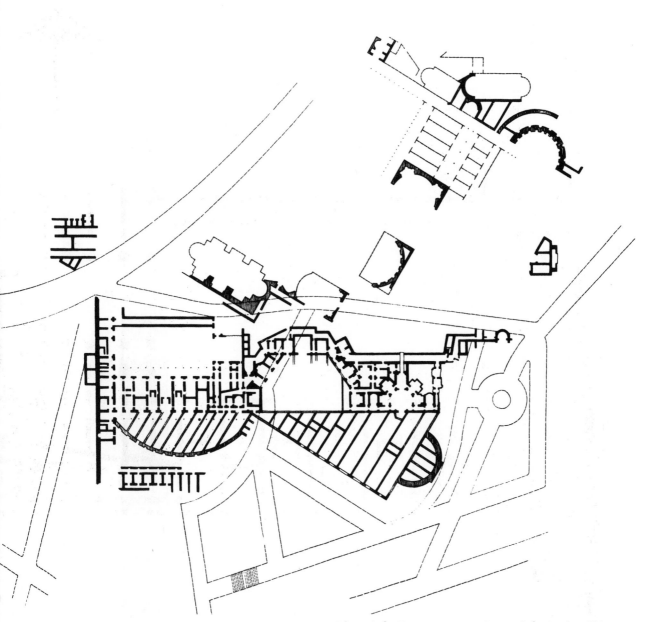

23. *Plan of the Domus Aurea wing and the Baths of Trajan*

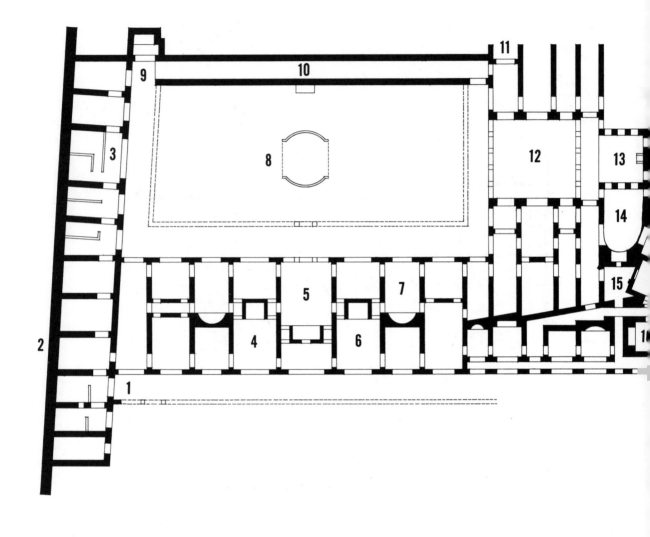

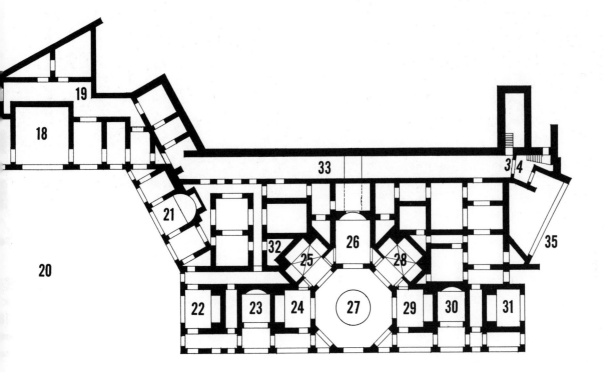

70   80   90   100 METERS

25. *Painting in the house of M. Lucretius Fronto in Pompeii*

26. *The Domus Aurea, room 6 on Plate 24*

27. *The Domus Aurea, room 7 on Plate 24*

28. The Domus Aurea, cryptoporticus, number 33 on Plate 24

29. *The Domus Aurea, interior of the octagon*

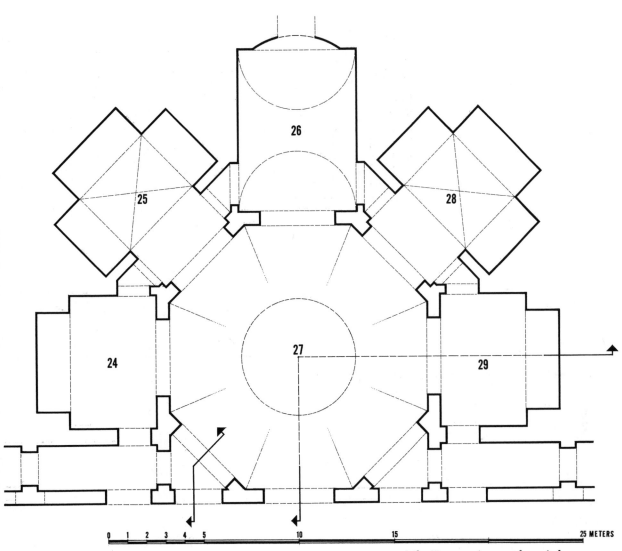

30. *The Domus Aurea, plan of the octagon*

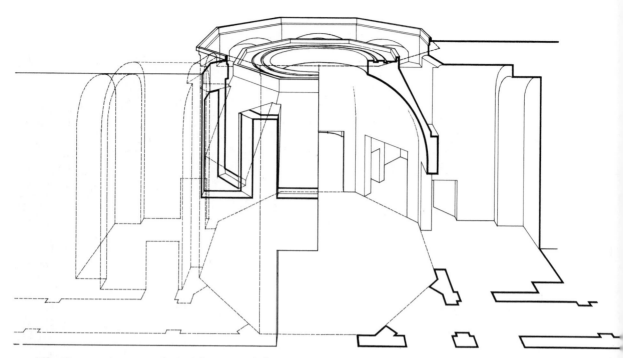

31. *The Domus Aurea, analytical drawing of the octagon*

32. The Domus Aurea, model of the octagon and its dependencies, in the Museo della civiltà romana

33a. *The Domus Aurea, exterior of the octagon superstructure*

33b. *Detail of the superstructure*

34. *The Domus Aurea, detail of the interior of the octagon*

35. *The Suburban Baths at Herculaneum, atrium pavilion*

36. The Suburban Baths at Herculaneum, detail of the atrium pavilion superstructure

37. *Air view of the Palatine and its surroundings*

38. *Domitian's Palace. The ramp between Domitian's vestibule and the Domus Tiberiana*

39. *The Domus Flavia, remains of the libraries*

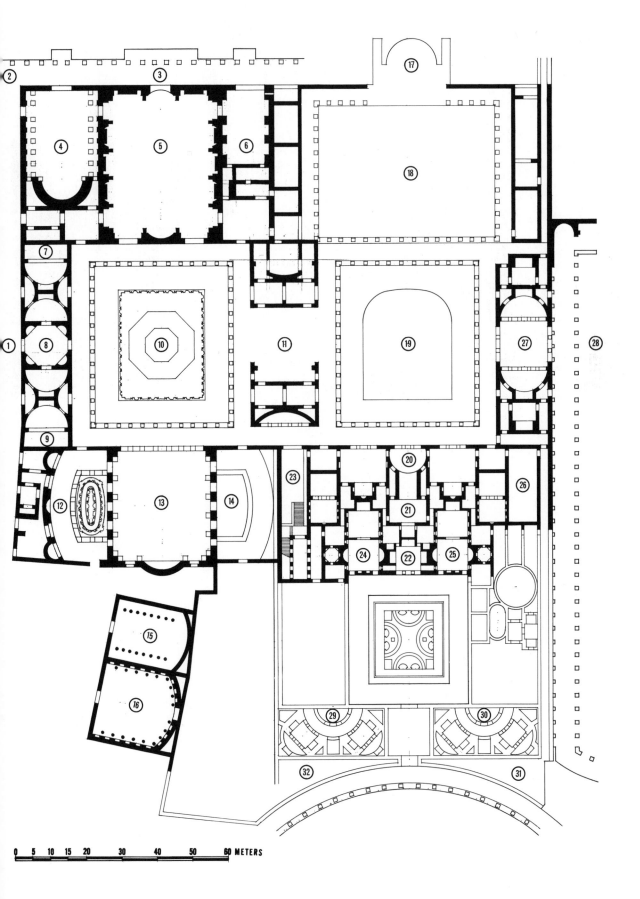

0 5 10 15 20   30   40   50   60 METERS

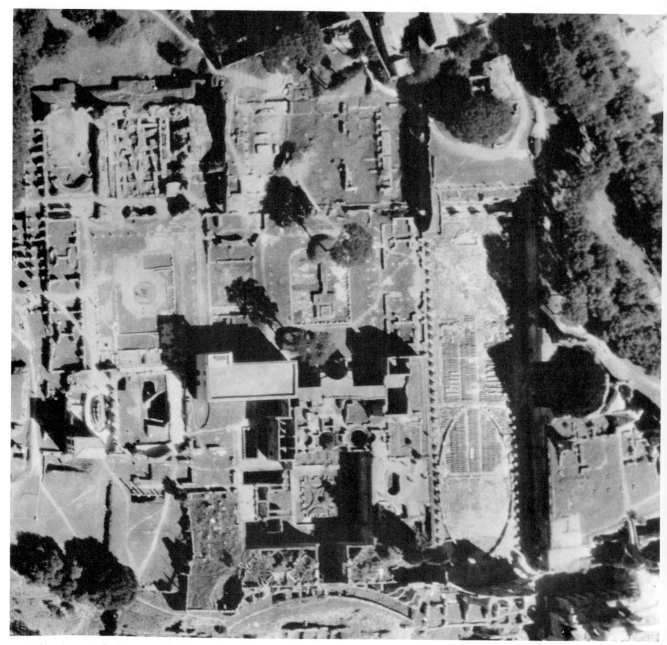

41. *Air view of the Domus Flavia and Domus Augustana*

42. *The Domus Flavia peristyle*

43. *The Domus Flavia basilica, interior and north corner*

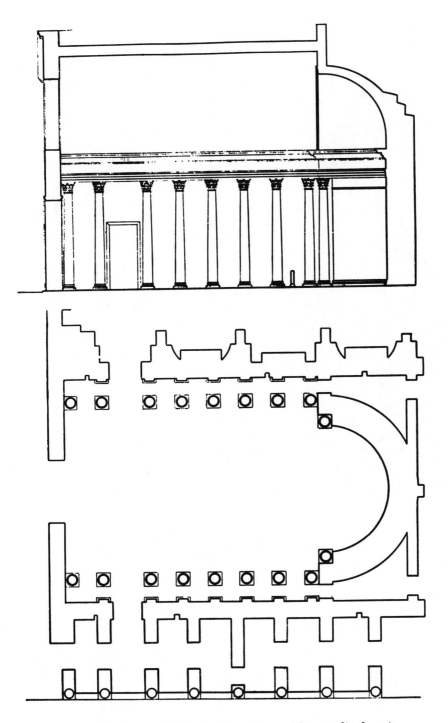

44. *The Domus Flavia basilica, plan and longitudinal section*

45. *The Domus Flavia, restoration of 1900 by G. Tognetti*

46. *The Domus Flavia, rooms northwest of the peristyle*

47. *The Domus Flavia, northwest piers of the triclinium*

48. *The Domus Flavia, entrance to the triclinium and environs*

49. The Domus Flavia, apse of the triclinium

50. The Domus Flavia, nymphaeum by the triclinium

51. *Sestertius of Domitian of 95/96*

52. *Domitian's Palace, the vestibule*

54. *The Domus Flavia, northwest face of the north pier of the aula regia and northeast wall of the basilica, detail*

53. *The Domus Flavia, interior of the north pier of the aula regia*

55. *The Domus Augustana, upper level, peristyle and partially restored southwest rooms*

56. *The Domus Augustana, upper and lower levels, seen from the west*

57. *The Domus Augustana, upper and lower levels, seen from the south*

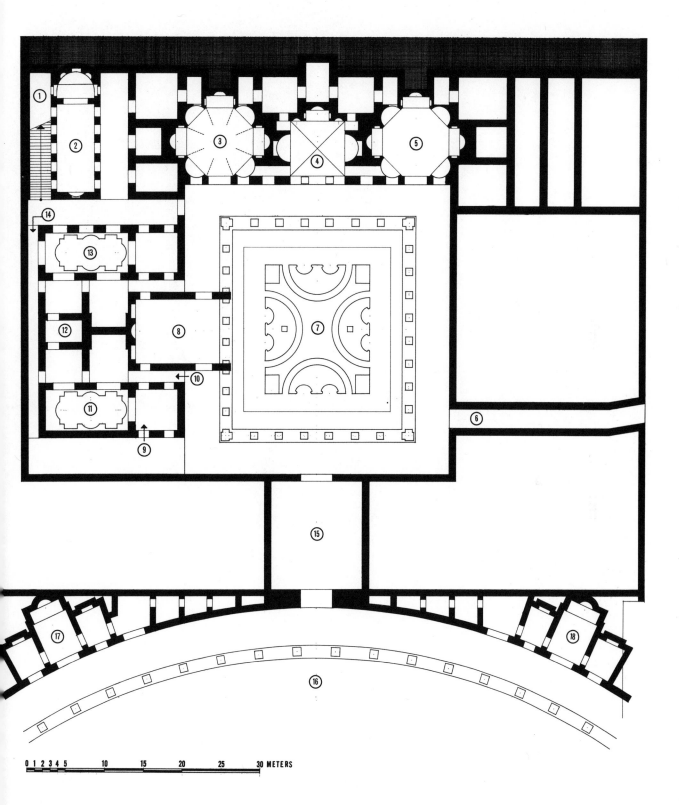

0 1 2 3 4 5   10   15   20   25   30 METERS

59. *The Domus Augustana, looking into one of the octagonal rooms (number 5 on Plate 58) from the east*

60. *The Domus Augustana, the northern niche of room 5 on Plate 58*

61. *The Domus Augustana, detail of Plate 60*

62. *The Domus Augustana, the lower-level imperial suite from the southeast*

63. *The Domus Augustana, the northeast wall of room 8 on Plate 58 and the remains of its pier and doorway arch*

64. *The Domus Augustana, enfilade number 9 on Plate 58, partially restored*

65. *The Domus Augustana, passageway number 10 on Plate 58*

66. *The Domus Augustana, fountain pool number 13 on Plate 58, seen from the southeast*

68. *The Domus Augustana, lower-level court*

67. *The Domus Augustana, corridor number 14 on Plate 58, seen from the northeast*

69. *The Domus Augustana and Hippodromos façades, seen from the northwest*

70. *The Domus Augustana and Hippodromos façades, seen from the southeast*

71. *The Domus Augustana and Hippodromos façades, seen from the Circus Maximus*

72. *The Hippodromos, seen from the southwest*

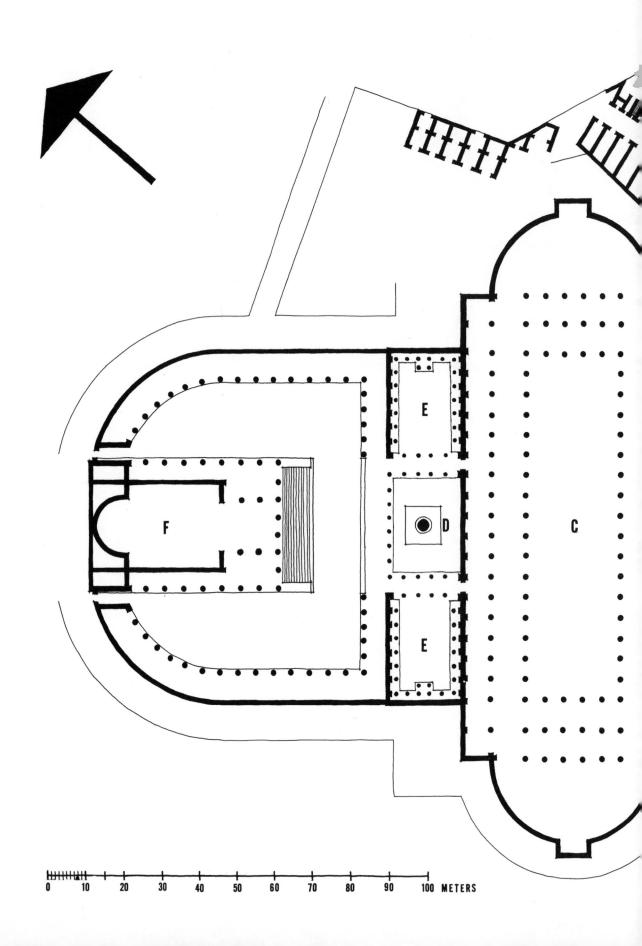

0   10   20   30   40   50   60   70   80   90   100 METERS

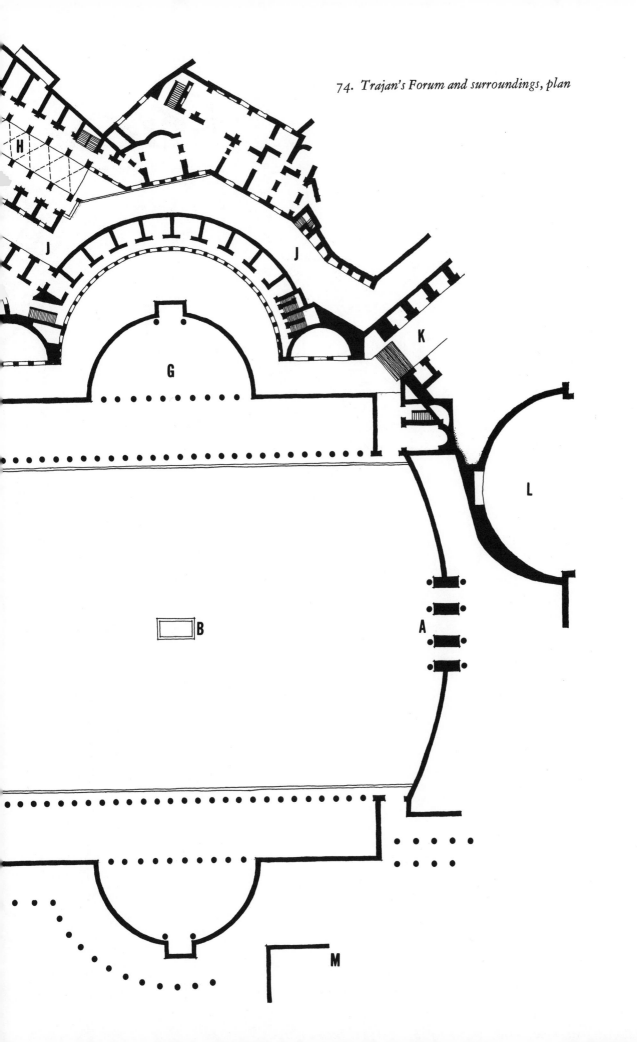

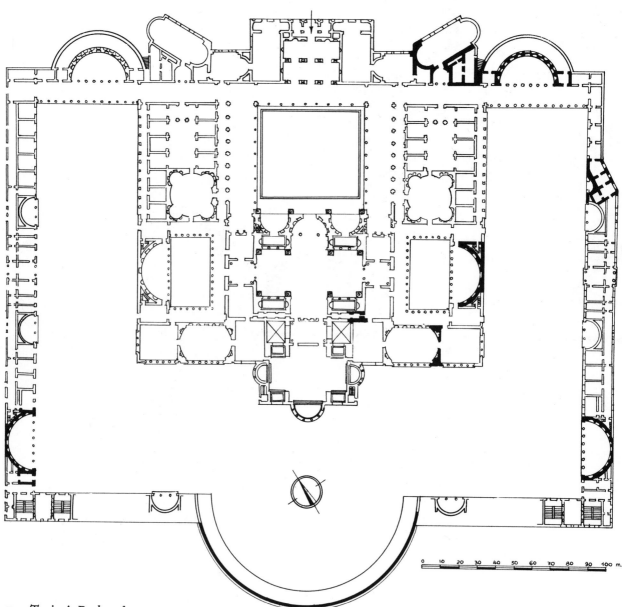

73. *Trajan's Baths, plan*

75. *Trajan's Markets, isometric drawing of the remains*

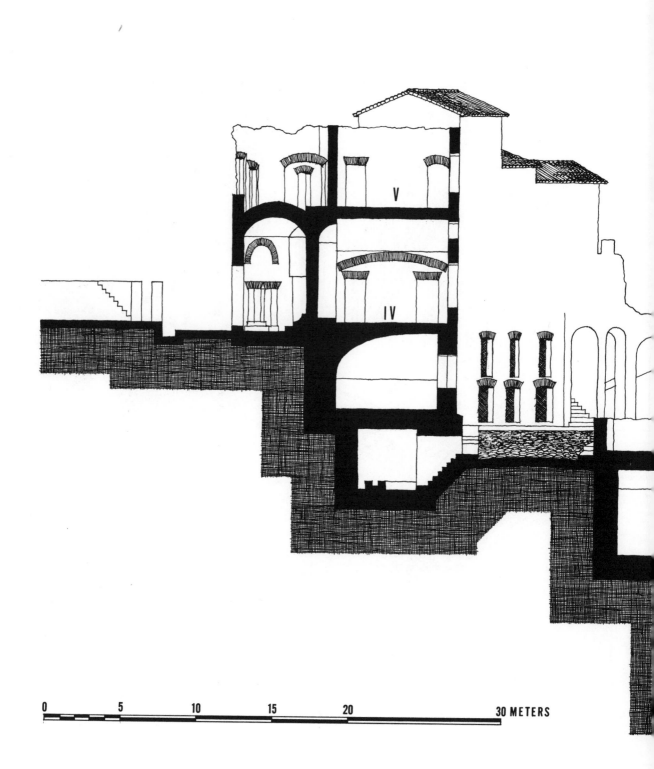

V

IV

0   5   10   15   20   30 METERS

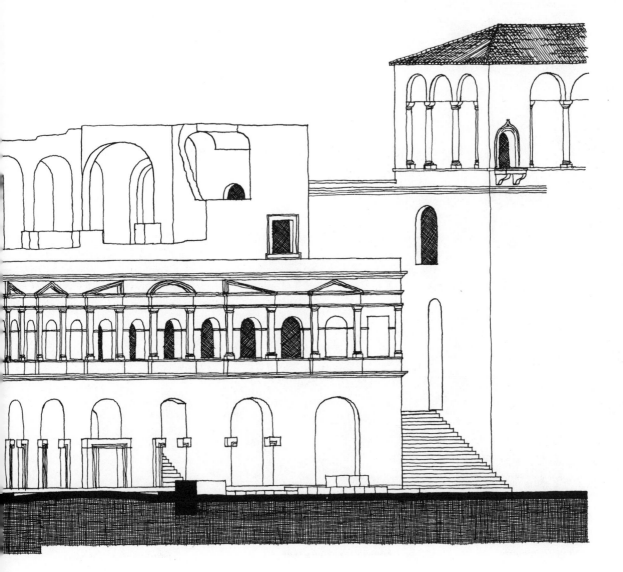

77. *Trajan's Forum, view of the northeast hemicycle from the Markets*

78. *Trajan's Markets, interior of the larger semidomed room of A1*

79. *Trajan's Markets, detail of the lower façade of A1*

80. *Trajan's Markets, extrados of the larger semidomed room of A1*

81. *Trajan's Markets, extrados of the smaller semidomed room of A1*

82. *Trajan's Markets, sections A2, B1, and part of B2, from the south*

83. *Trajan's Markets, sections A2 and B2 seen from the west*

84. *Trajan's Markets, section A2, the Via Biberatica, and section B2 from the northwest*

86. *Trajan's Markets, the restored front of a shop or office of section A2*

85. *Trajan's Markets, the corridor of section A2 at level II*

87. *Trajan's Markets, detail of section A2*

88. *Trajan's Markets, detail of the junction of sections A1 and A2*

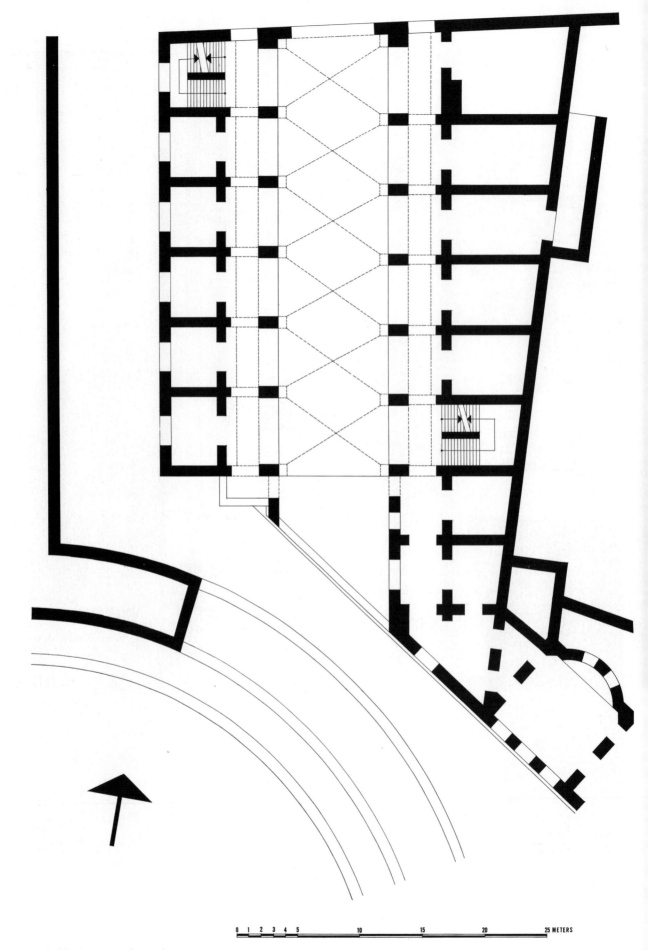

89. *Trajan's Markets, the aula Triana (section B1), plan at gallery level (level IV)*

90. *Trajan's Markets, the Via Biberatica between sections A1 and A2, from the north*

91. *Trajan's Markets, section B1 from the northwest*

92. *Trajan's Markets, interior of the aula of section B1*

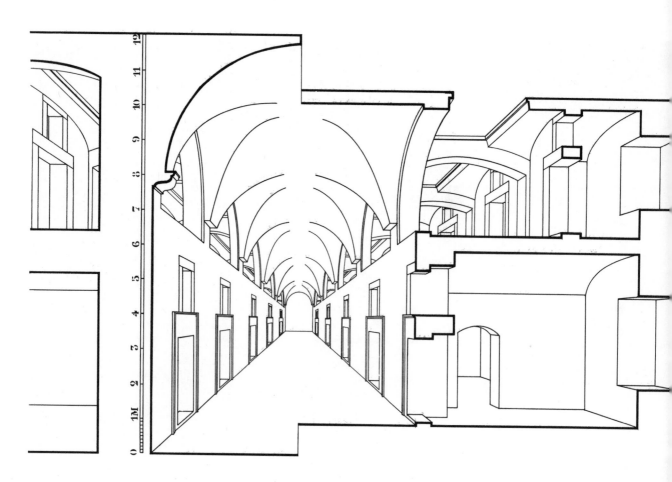

93. *Trajan's Markets, analytical drawing of the aula of section B1*

94. *Trajan's Markets, gallery and piers of the aula of section B1*

95. *Trajan's Markets, rooms in the interior of section B2*

96. *The Pantheon, seen from the north*

97. *The Pantheon, portico column bases and the modern paving over the original steps*

98. *The Pantheon, plan*

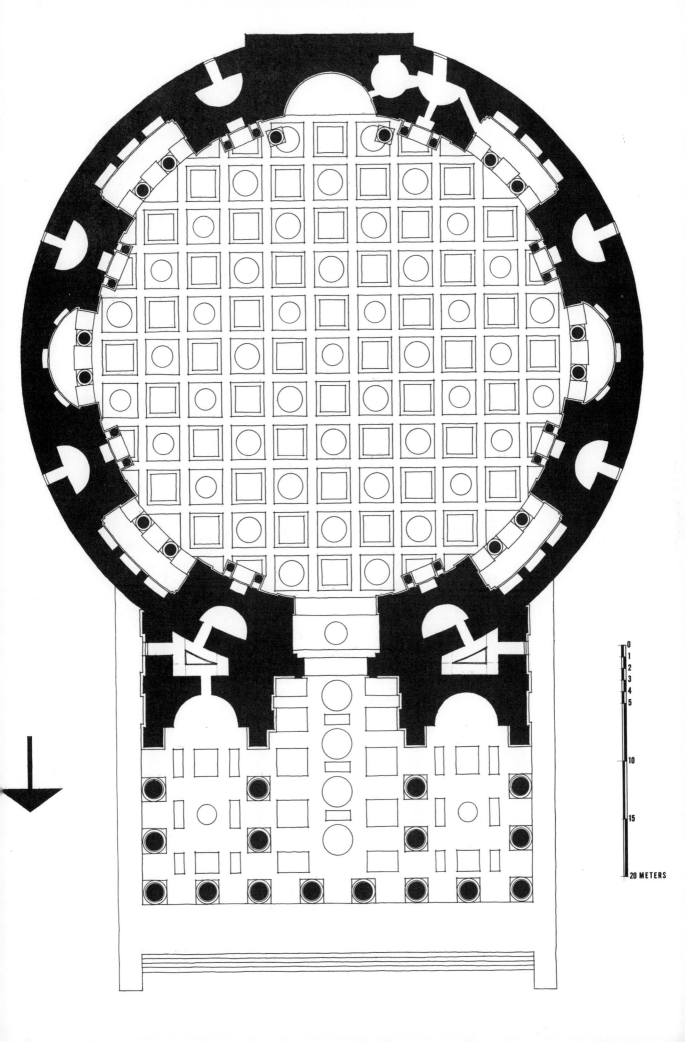

99. *The Pantheon, portico from the west*

100. *The Pantheon, detail of the portico superstructure*

101. *The Pantheon, intermediate block from the northeast*

102. *The Pantheon, detail of the exterior from the north*

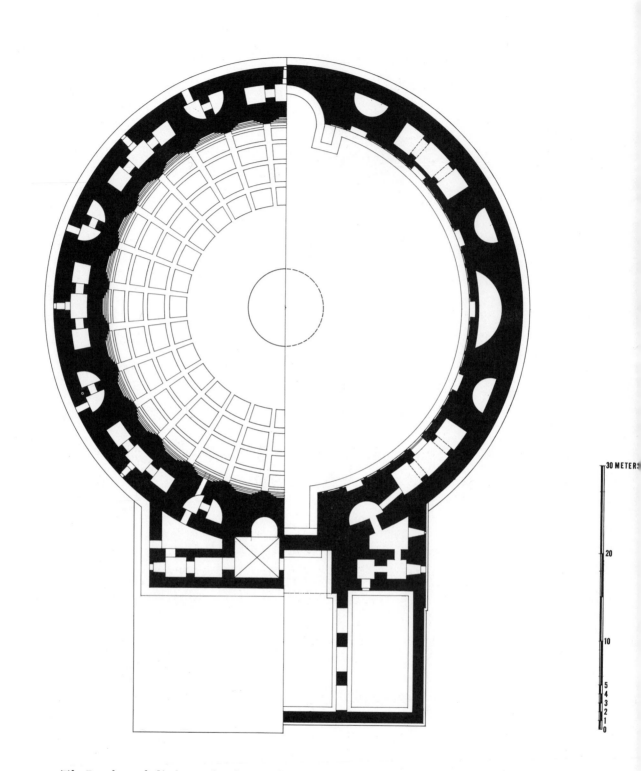

30 METERS

20

10

5
4
3
2
1
0

103. The Pantheon, half plans at level II (right) and level III (left), and half ceiling plan (left)

104. *The Pantheon, entranceway and surroundings from the interior*

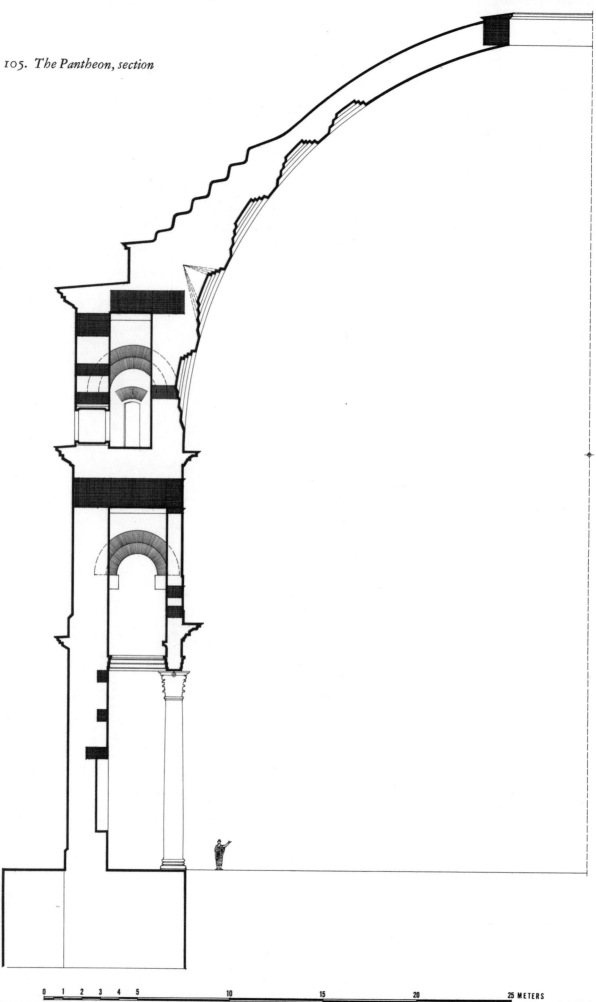

105. *The Pantheon, section*

0 1 2 3 4 5   10   15   20   25 METERS

106. The Pantheon, ana-
lytical drawing of the
structure at positions 3,
7, 11, and 15 (see Figure
9 on p. 101)

108. *The Pantheon, the restored attic at positions 11 and 12, seen from the level III interior cornice*

107. *The Pantheon, apse and environs*

109. *The Pantheon, interior of the dome*

110. *The Pantheon, detail of the coffering*

112a. The Pantheon, detail of the rotunda exterior (the cornice is at level III, the window at position 5)

112b. Part of the exterior end of the great position 5 conical vault (the cornice is at level III)

111. The Pantheon, eastern portion of the rotunda exterior from the northeast

114. *The Pantheon, detail of the interior of the dome, with portions of the vault, arches, and infilling exposed*

113. *The Pantheon, the southeast portion of the rotunda exterior between levels II and IV*

115. *The Pantheon, exterior from the top of the lantern of S. Ivo*

116. The Pantheon, exterior of the dome from the northeast

117. *The Pantheon, detail of the step-rings of the dome*

118. *The Pantheon, oculus*

120a. The Pantheon, detail of the northwest junction of the intermediate block and the rotunda at level I

120b. Another level I exterior base molding block

119. *The Pantheon, flank of the intermediate block and portico from the southeast*

121. The Metropolitan Museum of New York, model of the Pantheon

122. *The Pantheon, drawing of the interior as seen from the niche at position 13*

124. *Raphael, drawing of the interior of the Pantheon*

123. *G. P. Panini, The Interior of the Pantheon, ca. 1750*

125. *The Pantheon, oculus and dome from the apse*

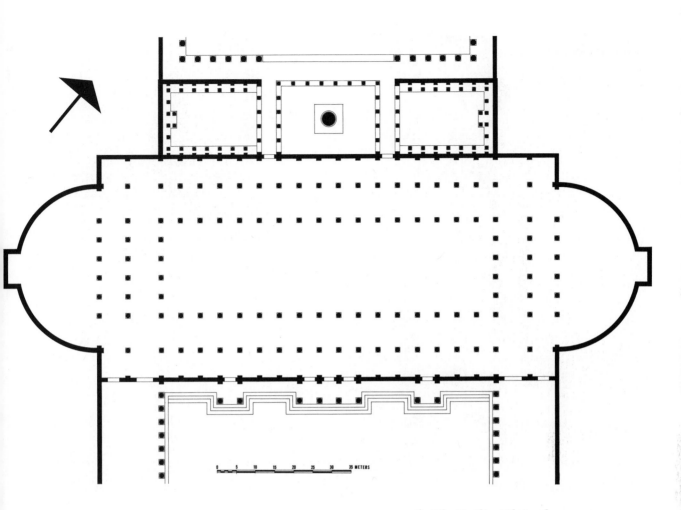

126. The Basilica Ulpia, plan

127. *Mosaic, showing builders and an architect, in the Bardo Museum, Tunis*

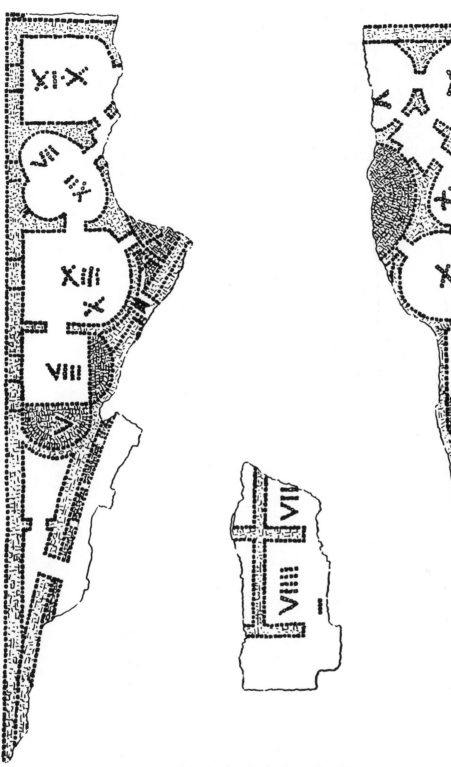

128. Mosaic plan in the Capitoline Museum

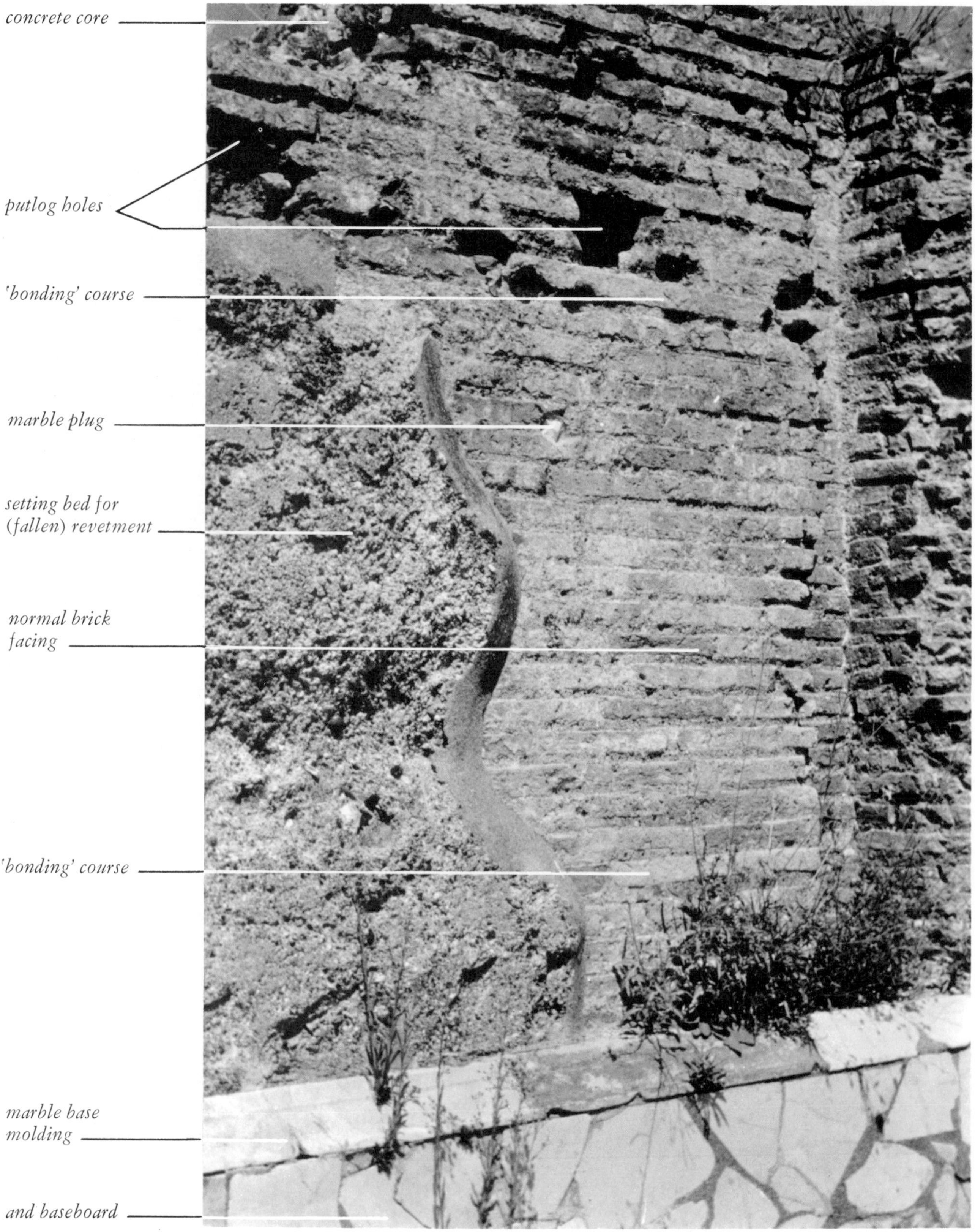

concrete core

putlog holes

'bonding' course

marble plug

setting bed for
(fallen) revetment

normal brick
facing

'bonding' course

marble base
molding

and baseboard

129. *The Domus Flavia, detail of the peristyle wall*

130a. The Domus Augustana, detail of an upper-level wall

130b. Tomb of Trebius Justus, wall painting

131a. The Domus Flavia, detail of the northwest inner wall of the Basilica

131b. Ostia, the Piccolo Mercato, detail of a pier

632

132. *Shrine in the barracks of the seventh urban cohort*

134. The Amphitheatre at Pozzuoli, substructure vaults

133. The Hippodromos of Domitian's Palace, detail of an engaged column

135. *The Amphitheatre at Pozzuoli, view of a basement corridor*